CASE CLOSED

V O L U M E   49

Gosho Aoyama

Case Briefing:

Subject: Jimmy Kudo, a.k.a. Conan Edogawa
Occupation: High School Student/Detective
Special Skills: Analytical thinking and deductive reasoning, Soccer
Equipment: Bow Tie Voice Transmitter, Super Sneakers,
Homing Glasses, Stretchy Suspenders

The subject is hot on the trail of a pair of suspicious men in black when he is attacked from behind and administered a strange substance which physically transforms him into a first grader. When the subject confides in the eccentric inventor Dr. Agasa, they decide to keep the subject's true identity a secret for the safety of everyone around him. Assuming the new identity of first-grader Conan Edogawa, the subject continues to assist the police force on their most baffling cases. The only problem is that most crime-solving professionals won't take a little kid's advice!

Table of Contents

CONFIDEN

CASE CLOSED

Volume 49
Shonen Sunday Edition

Story and Art by GOSHO AOYAMA

MEITANTEI CONAN Vol. 49
by Gosho AOYAMA
© 1994 Gosho AOYAMA
All rights reserved.
Original Japanese edition published by SHOGAKUKAN.
English translation rights in the United States of America, Canada,
the United Kingdom and Ireland arranged with SHOGAKUKAN.

Translation
Tetsuichiro Miyaki

Touch-up & Lettering
Freeman Wong

Cover & Graphic Design
Andrea Rice

Editor
Shaenon K. Garrity

Printed in Canada

Published by VIZ Media, LLC
P.O. Box 77010
San Francisco, CA 94107

10 9 8 7 6 5 4 3 2 1
First printing, January 2014

www.viz.com

FILE 1: PURSUE THE TARGET!

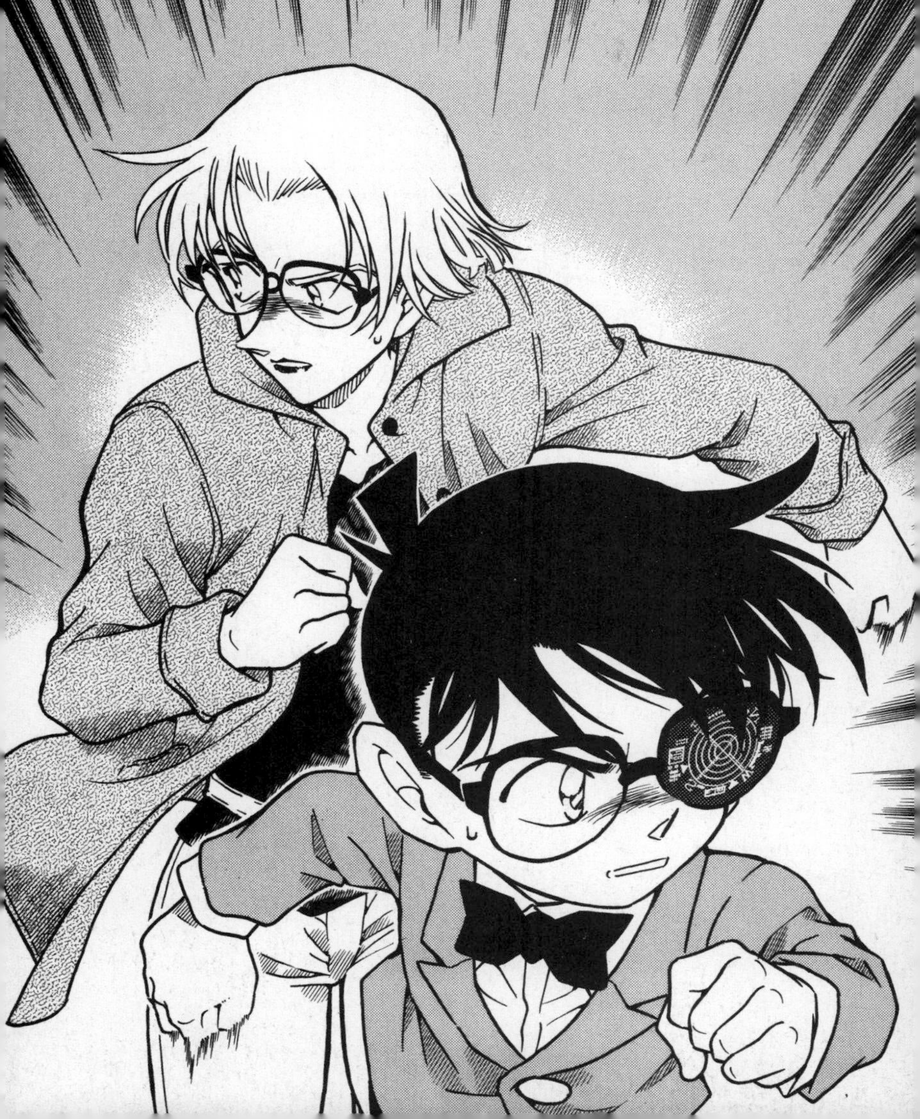

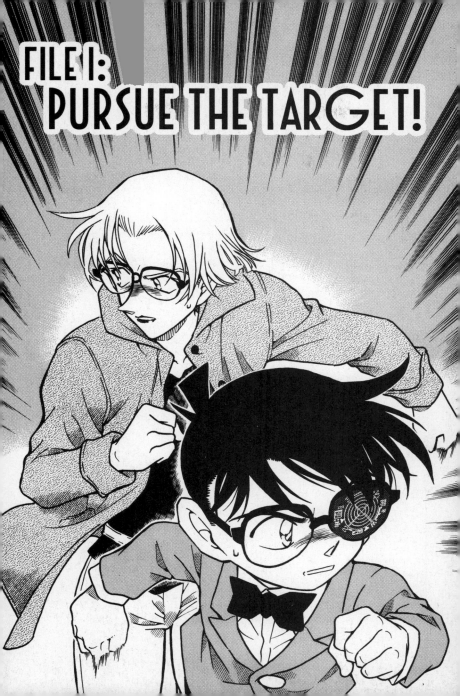

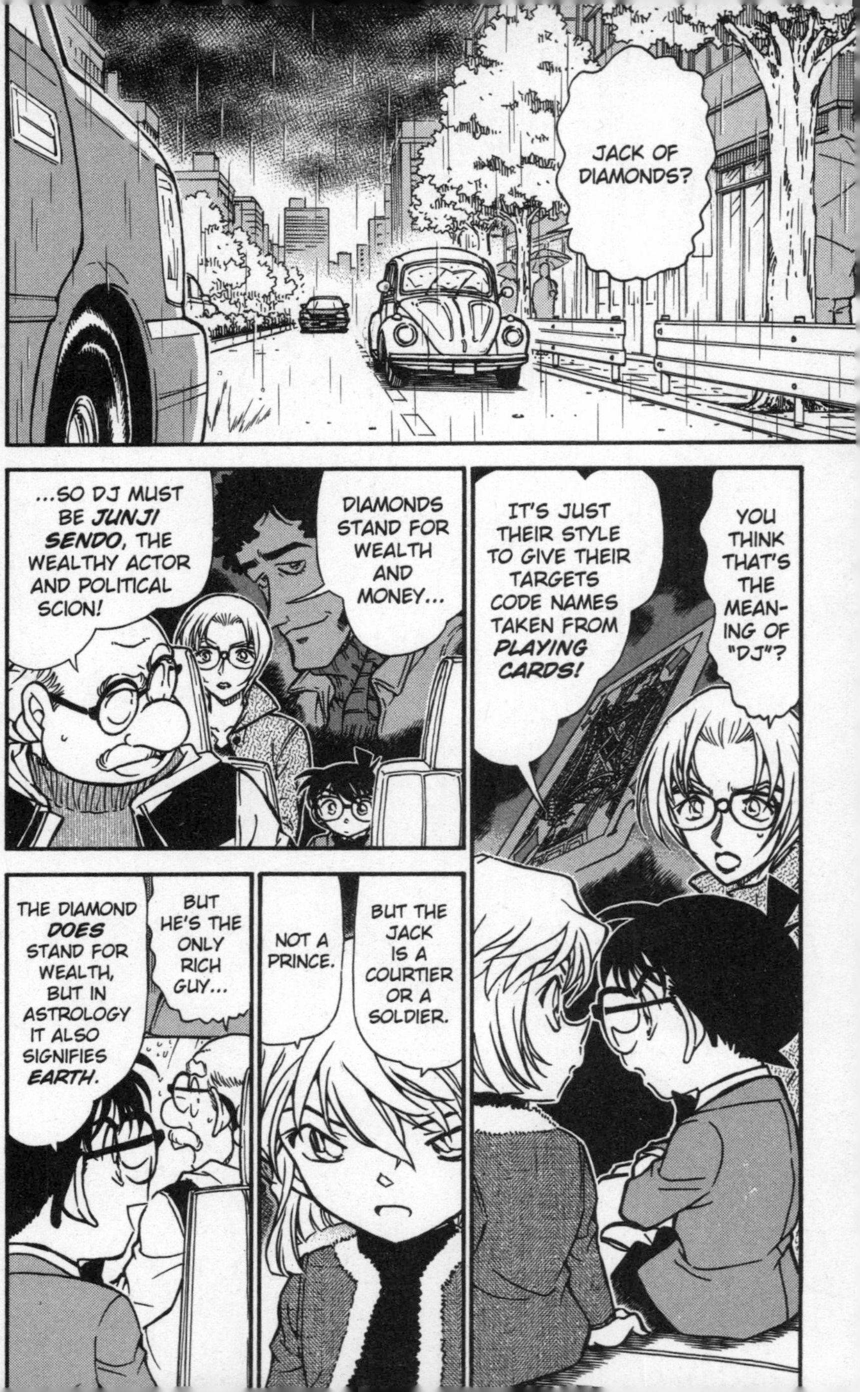

JACK OF DIAMONDS?
YOU THINK THAT'S THE MEANING OF "DJ"?
IT'S JUST THEIR STYLE TO GIVE THEIR TARGETS CODE NAMES TAKEN FROM *PLAYING CARDS!*
DIAMONDS STAND FOR WEALTH AND MONEY...
...SO DJ MUST BE *JUNJI SENDO*, THE WEALTHY ACTOR AND POLITICAL SCION!
BUT THE JACK IS A COURTIER OR A SOLDIER.
NOT A PRINCE.
BUT HE'S THE ONLY RICH GUY...
THE DIAMOND *DOES* STAND FOR WEALTH, BUT IN ASTROLOGY IT ALSO SIGNIFIES *EARTH*.

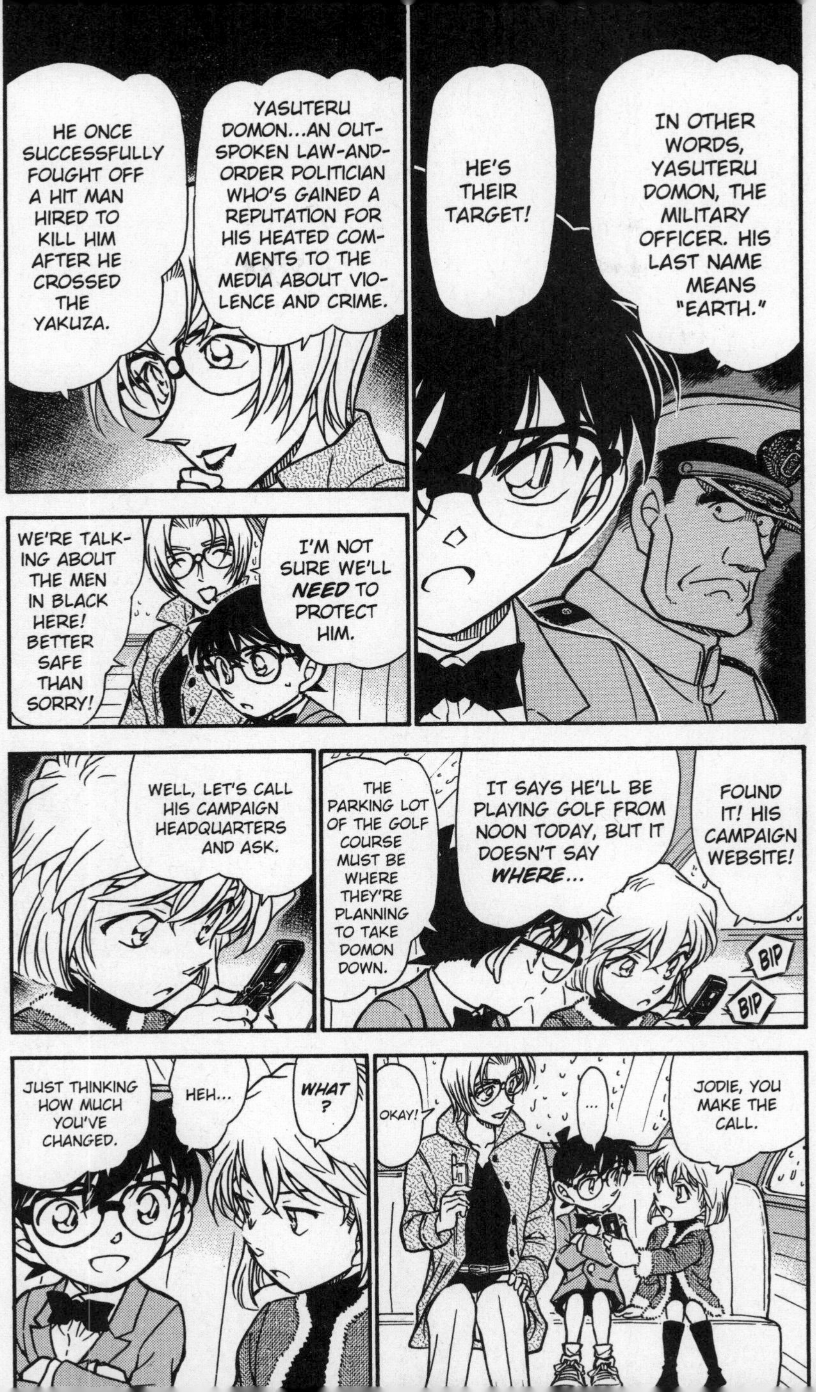
IN OTHER WORDS, YASUTERU DOMON, THE MILITARY OFFICER. HIS LAST NAME MEANS "EARTH."
HE'S THEIR TARGET!
YASUTERU DOMON...AN OUT-SPOKEN LAW-AND-ORDER POLITICIAN WHO'S GAINED A REPUTATION FOR HIS HEATED COM-MENTS TO THE MEDIA ABOUT VIO-LENCE AND CRIME.
HE ONCE SUCCESSFULLY FOUGHT OFF A HIT MAN HIRED TO KILL HIM AFTER HE CROSSED THE YAKUZA.
I'M NOT SURE WE'LL *NEED* TO PROTECT HIM.
WE'RE TALK-ING ABOUT THE MEN IN BLACK HERE! BETTER SAFE THAN SORRY!
FOUND IT! HIS CAMPAIGN WEBSITE!
BIP
BIP
IT SAYS HE'LL BE PLAYING GOLF FROM NOON TODAY, BUT IT DOESN'T SAY *WHERE*...
THE PARKING LOT OF THE GOLF COURSE MUST BE WHERE THEY'RE PLANNING TO TAKE DOMON DOWN.
WELL, LET'S CALL HIS CAMPAIGN HEADQUARTERS AND ASK.
JODIE, YOU MAKE THE CALL.
...
OKAY!
WHAT?
HEH...
JUST THINKING HOW MUCH YOU'VE CHANGED.

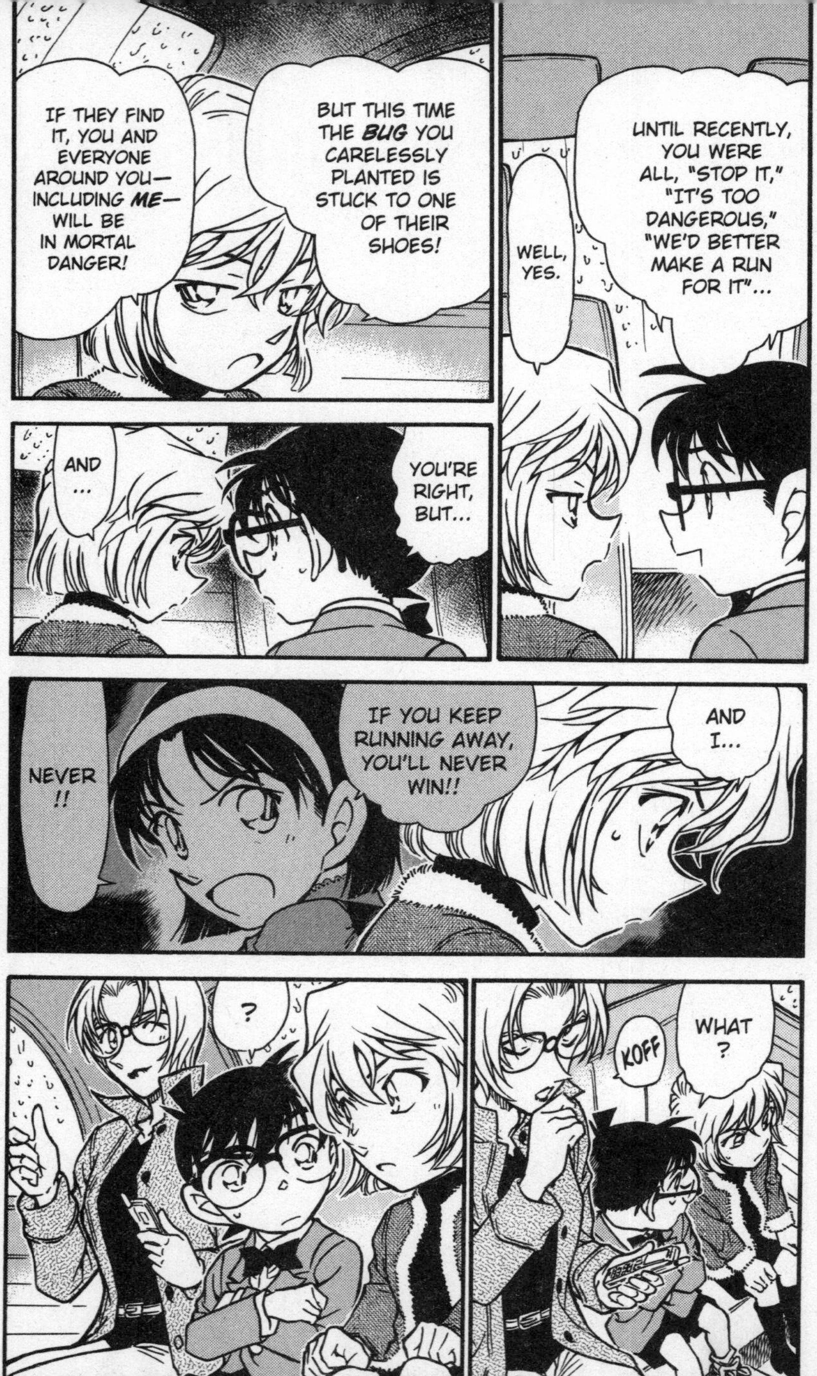
UNTIL RECENTLY, YOU WERE ALL, "STOP IT," "IT'S TOO DANGEROUS," "WE'D BETTER MAKE A RUN FOR IT"...
WELL, YES.
BUT THIS TIME THE *BUG* YOU CARELESSLY PLANTED IS STUCK TO ONE OF THEIR SHOES!
IF THEY FIND IT, YOU AND EVERYONE AROUND YOU—INCLUDING *ME*—WILL BE IN MORTAL DANGER!
YOU'RE RIGHT, BUT...
AND ...
AND I...
IF YOU KEEP RUNNING AWAY, YOU'LL NEVER WIN!!
NEVER !!
WHAT ?
KOFF
?

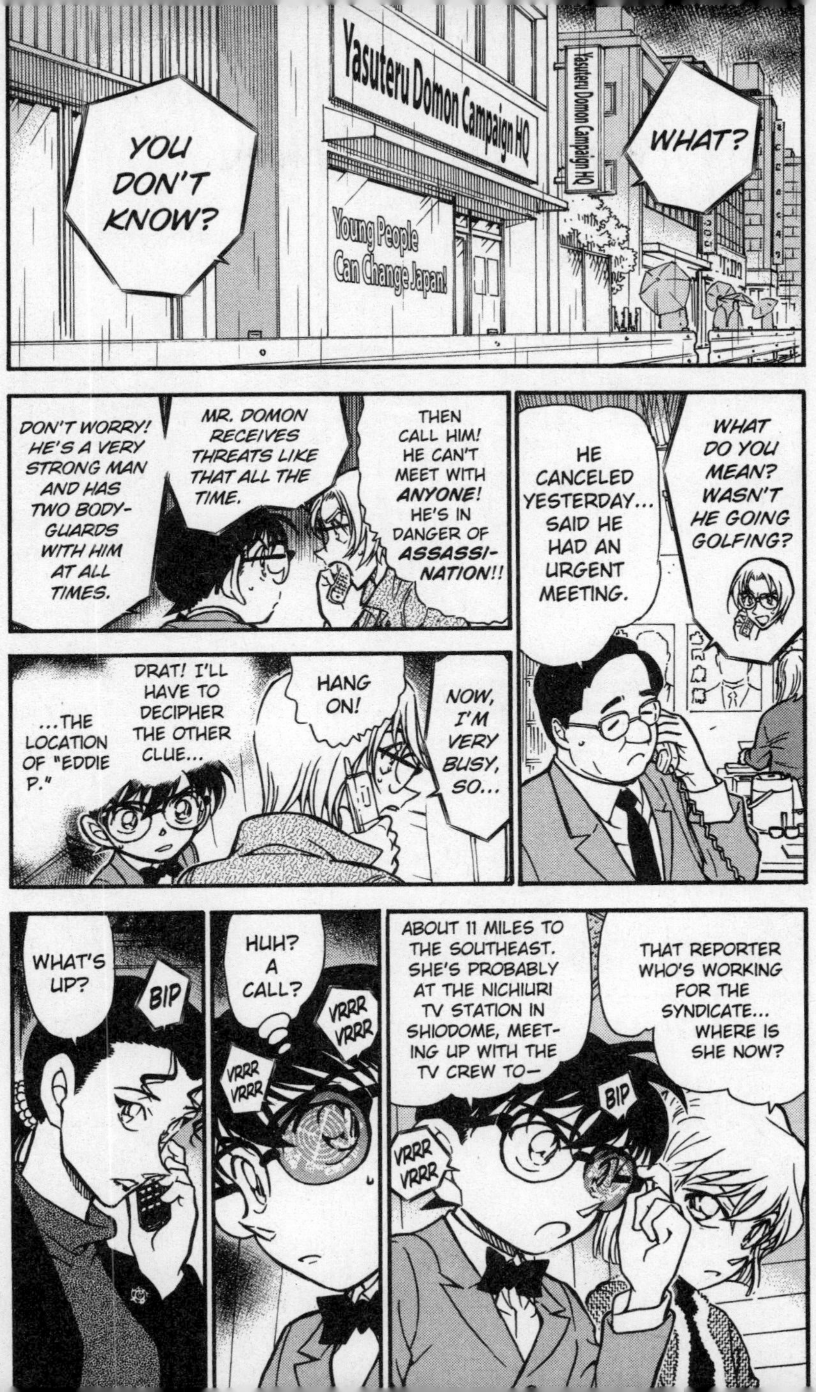
Yasuteru Domon Campaign HQ
Yasuteru Domon Campaign HQ
Young People Can Change Japan!
WHAT?
YOU DON'T KNOW?
WHAT DO YOU MEAN? WASN'T HE GOING GOLFING?
HE CANCELED YESTERDAY... SAID HE HAD AN URGENT MEETING.
THEN CALL HIM! HE CAN'T MEET WITH ANYONE! HE'S IN DANGER OF ASSASSINATION!!
MR. DOMON RECEIVES THREATS LIKE THAT ALL THE TIME.
DON'T WORRY! HE'S A VERY STRONG MAN AND HAS TWO BODYGUARDS WITH HIM AT ALL TIMES.
NOW, I'M VERY BUSY, SO...
HANG ON!
DRAT! I'LL HAVE TO DECIPHER THE OTHER CLUE...
...THE LOCATION OF "EDDIE P."
THAT REPORTER WHO'S WORKING FOR THE SYNDICATE... WHERE IS SHE NOW?
BIP
VRRR VRRR
ABOUT 11 MILES TO THE SOUTHEAST. SHE'S PROBABLY AT THE NICHIURI TV STATION IN SHIODOME, MEETING UP WITH THE TV CREW TO—
VRRR VRRR
HUH? A CALL?
VRRR VRRR
BIP
WHAT'S UP?

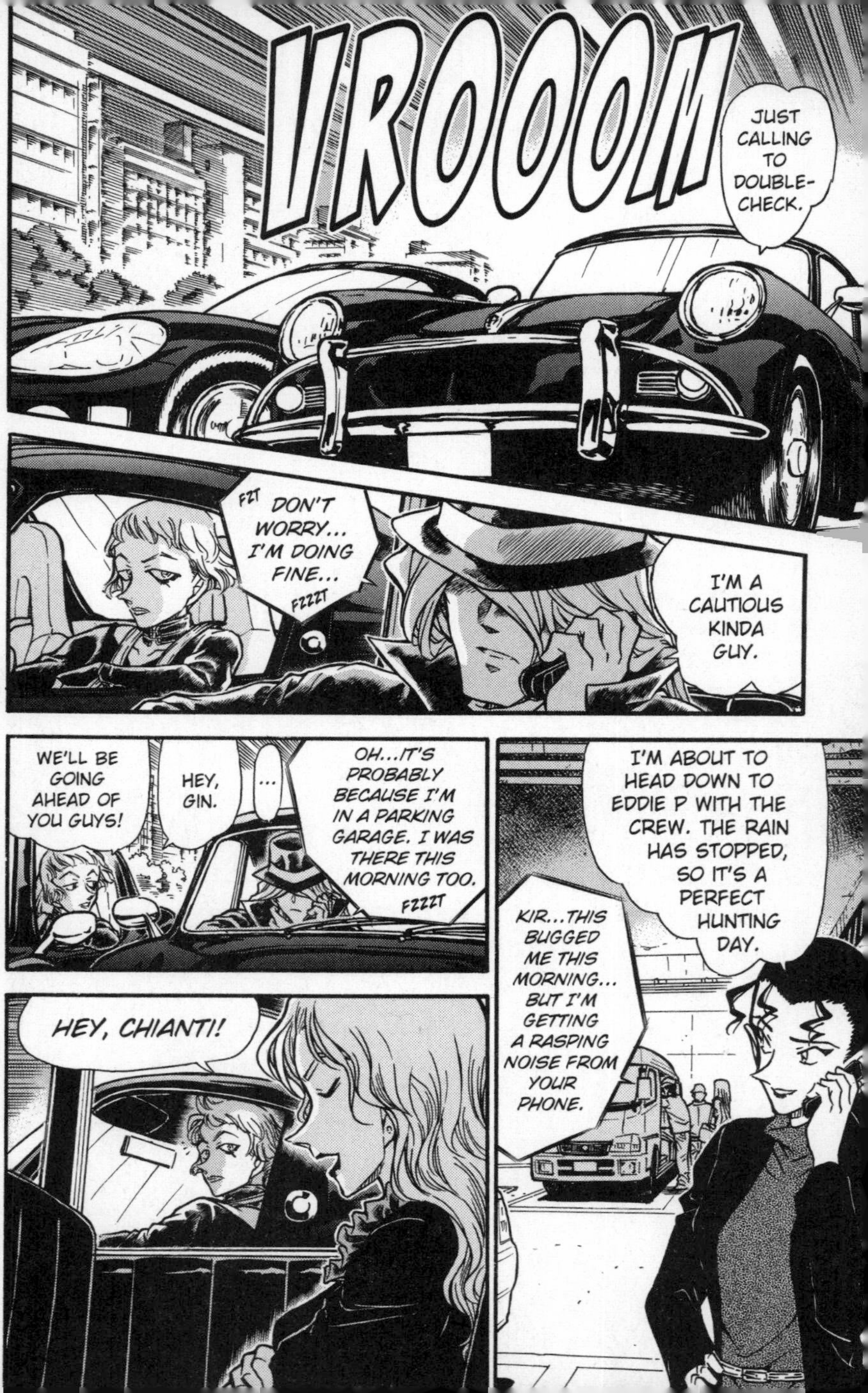
VROOOM
JUST CALLING TO DOUBLE-CHECK.
I'M A CAUTIOUS KINDA GUY.
FZT
DON'T WORRY... I'M DOING FINE...
FZZZT
I'M ABOUT TO HEAD DOWN TO EDDIE P WITH THE CREW. THE RAIN HAS STOPPED, SO IT'S A PERFECT HUNTING DAY.
KIR...THIS BUGGED ME THIS MORNING... BUT I'M GETTING A RASPING NOISE FROM YOUR PHONE.
OH...IT'S PROBABLY BECAUSE I'M IN A PARKING GARAGE. I WAS THERE THIS MORNING TOO.
FZZZT
...
HEY, GIN.
WE'LL BE GOING AHEAD OF YOU GUYS!
HEY, CHIANTI!

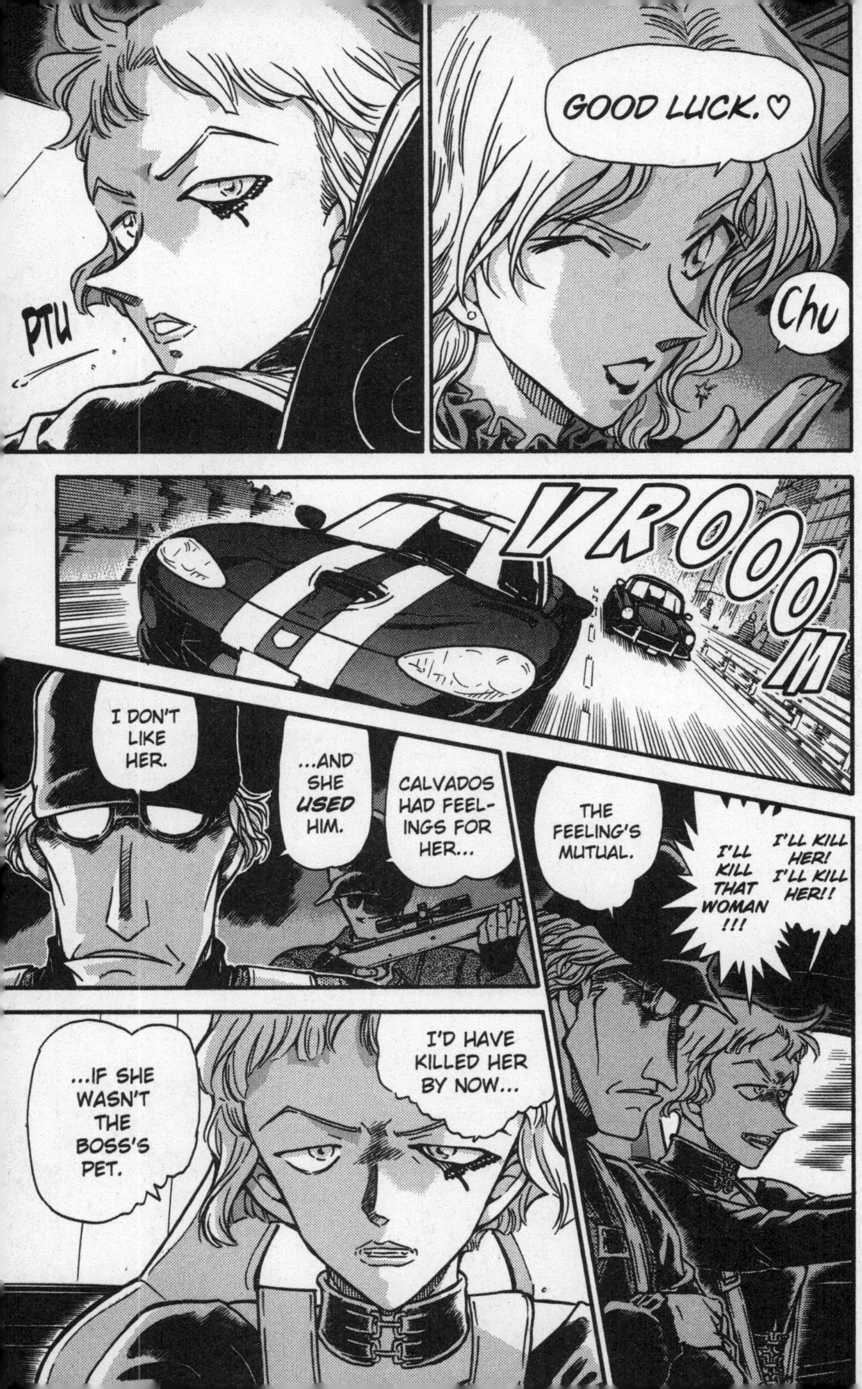
GOOD LUCK. ♡
Chu
PTU
VROOOM
I'LL KILL HER! I'LL KILL HER!!
I'LL KILL THAT WOMAN!!!
THE FEELING'S MUTUAL.
CALVADOS HAD FEEL-INGS FOR HER...
...AND SHE *USED* HIM.
I DON'T LIKE HER.
I'D HAVE KILLED HER BY NOW...
...IF SHE WASN'T THE BOSS'S PET.

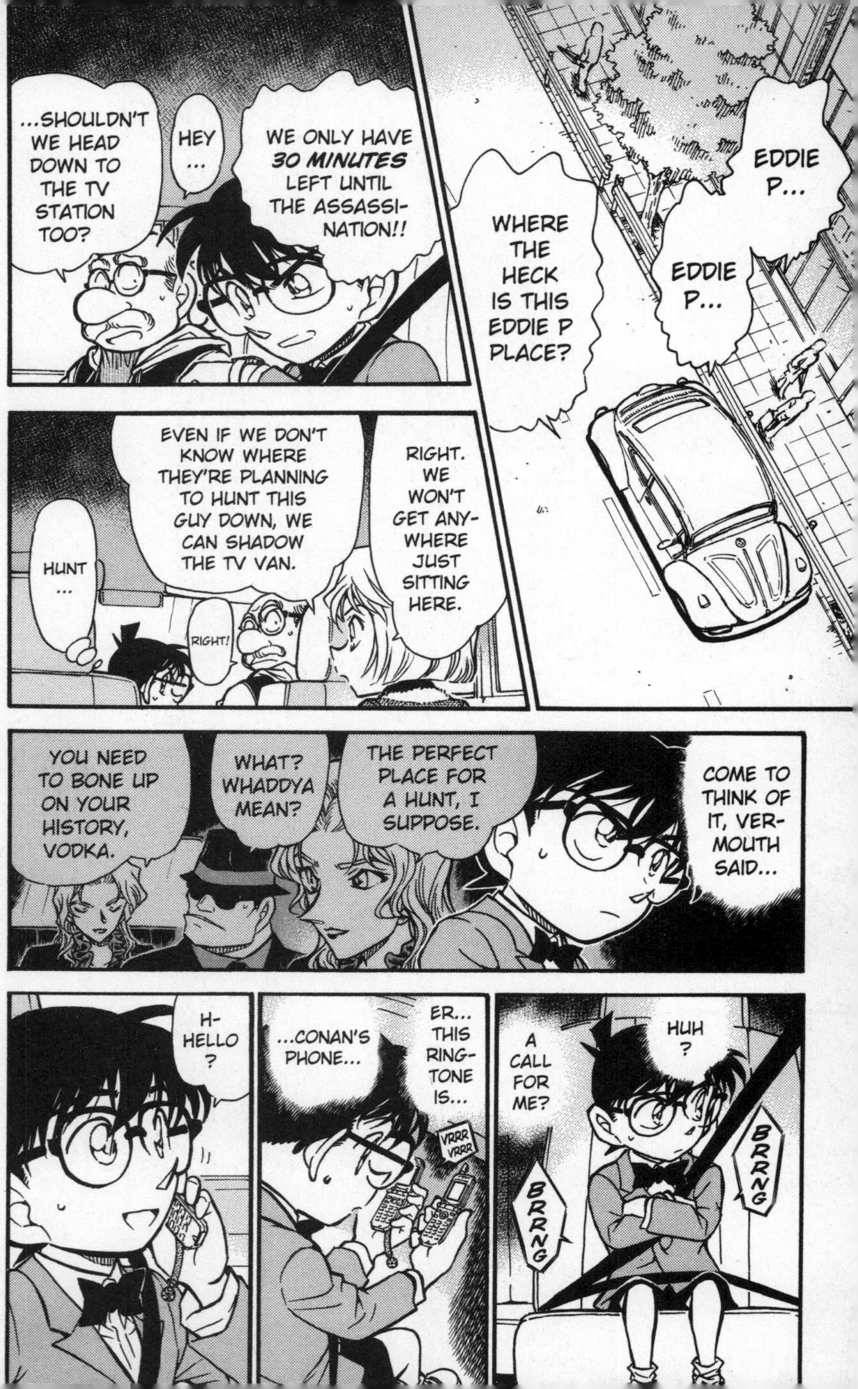
EDDIE P...
EDDIE P...
WHERE THE HECK IS THIS EDDIE P PLACE?
WE ONLY HAVE *30 MINUTES* LEFT UNTIL THE ASSASSINATION!!
HEY...
...SHOULDN'T WE HEAD DOWN TO THE TV STATION TOO?
RIGHT. WE WON'T GET ANYWHERE JUST SITTING HERE.
EVEN IF WE DON'T KNOW WHERE THEY'RE PLANNING TO HUNT THIS GUY DOWN, WE CAN SHADOW THE TV VAN.
RIGHT!
HUNT...
COME TO THINK OF IT, VERMOUTH SAID...
THE PERFECT PLACE FOR A HUNT, I SUPPOSE.
WHAT? WHADDYA MEAN?
YOU NEED TO BONE UP ON YOUR HISTORY, VODKA.
HUH?
A CALL FOR ME?
BRRNG
BRRNG
ER... THIS RINGTONE IS...
VRRR VRRR
...CONAN'S PHONE...
H-HELLO?

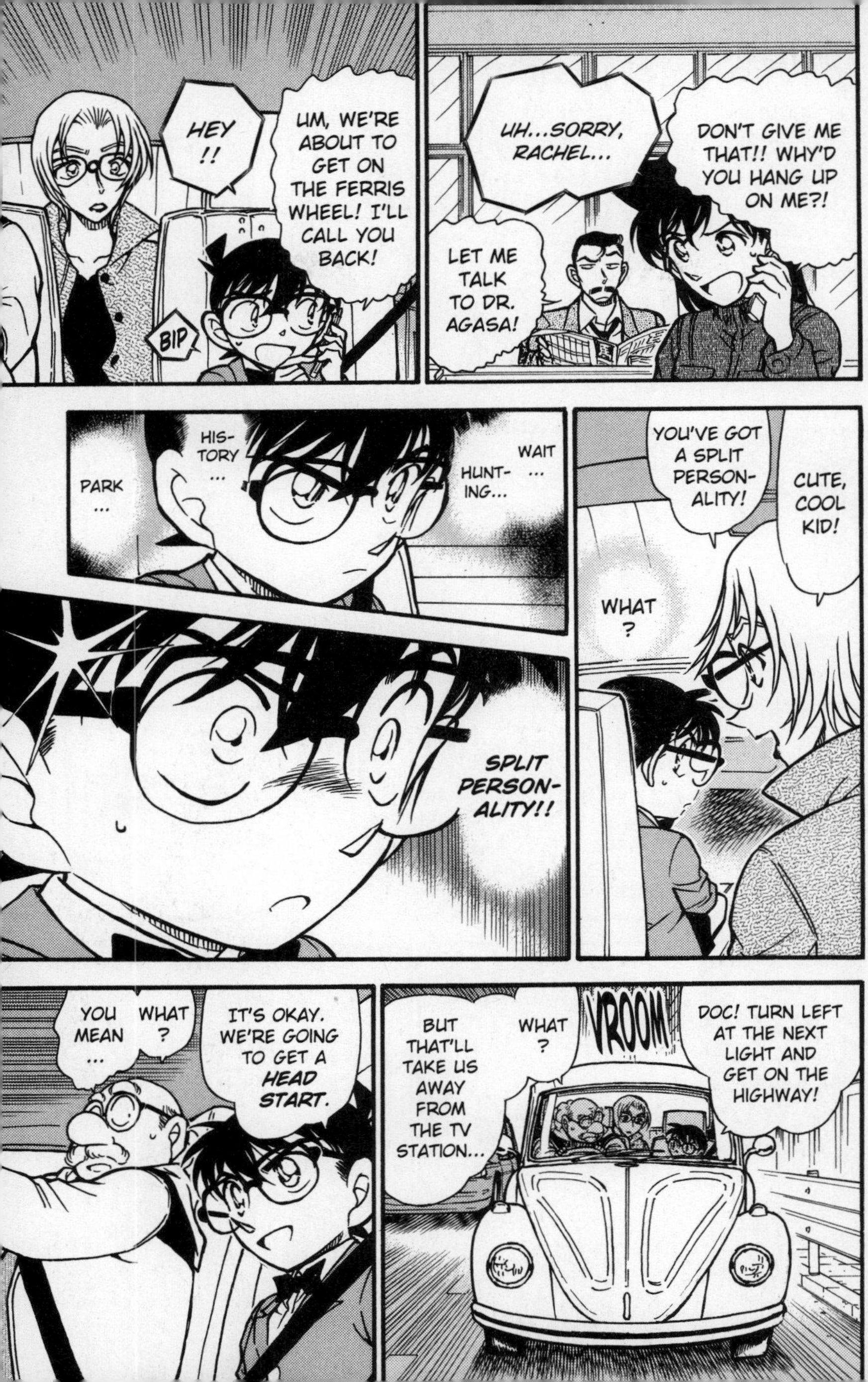
DON'T GIVE ME THAT!! WHY'D YOU HANG UP ON ME?!
UH...SORRY, RACHEL...
LET ME TALK TO DR. AGASA!
UM, WE'RE ABOUT TO GET ON THE FERRIS WHEEL! I'LL CALL YOU BACK!
HEY !!
BIP
CUTE, COOL KID!
YOU'VE GOT A SPLIT PERSONALITY!
WHAT ?
WAIT ...
HUNTING...
HISTORY ...
PARK ...
SPLIT PERSONALITY!!
DOC! TURN LEFT AT THE NEXT LIGHT AND GET ON THE HIGHWAY!
VROOM
WHAT ?
BUT THAT'LL TAKE US AWAY FROM THE TV STATION...
IT'S OKAY. WE'RE GOING TO GET A HEAD START.
WHAT ?
YOU MEAN ...

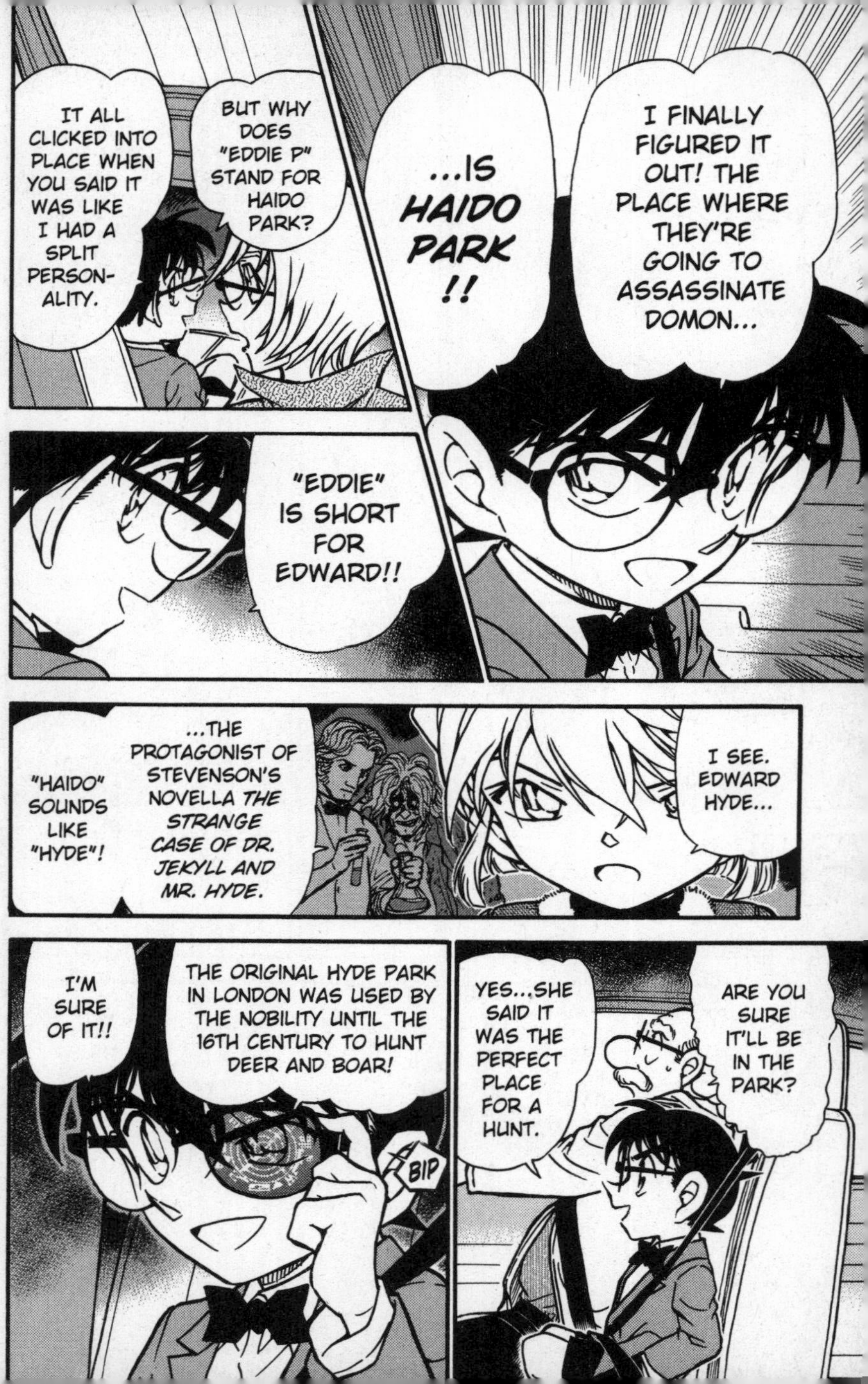
I FINALLY FIGURED IT OUT! THE PLACE WHERE THEY'RE GOING TO ASSASSINATE DOMON...
...IS HAIDO PARK!!
BUT WHY DOES "EDDIE P" STAND FOR HAIDO PARK?
IT ALL CLICKED INTO PLACE WHEN YOU SAID IT WAS LIKE I HAD A SPLIT PERSON-ALITY.
"EDDIE" IS SHORT FOR EDWARD!!
I SEE. EDWARD HYDE...
...THE PROTAGONIST OF STEVENSON'S NOVELLA THE STRANGE CASE OF DR. JEKYLL AND MR. HYDE.
"HAIDO" SOUNDS LIKE "HYDE"!
ARE YOU SURE IT'LL BE IN THE PARK?
YES...SHE SAID IT WAS THE PERFECT PLACE FOR A HUNT.
THE ORIGINAL HYDE PARK IN LONDON WAS USED BY THE NOBILITY UNTIL THE 16TH CENTURY TO HUNT DEER AND BOAR!
I'M SURE OF IT!!
BIP

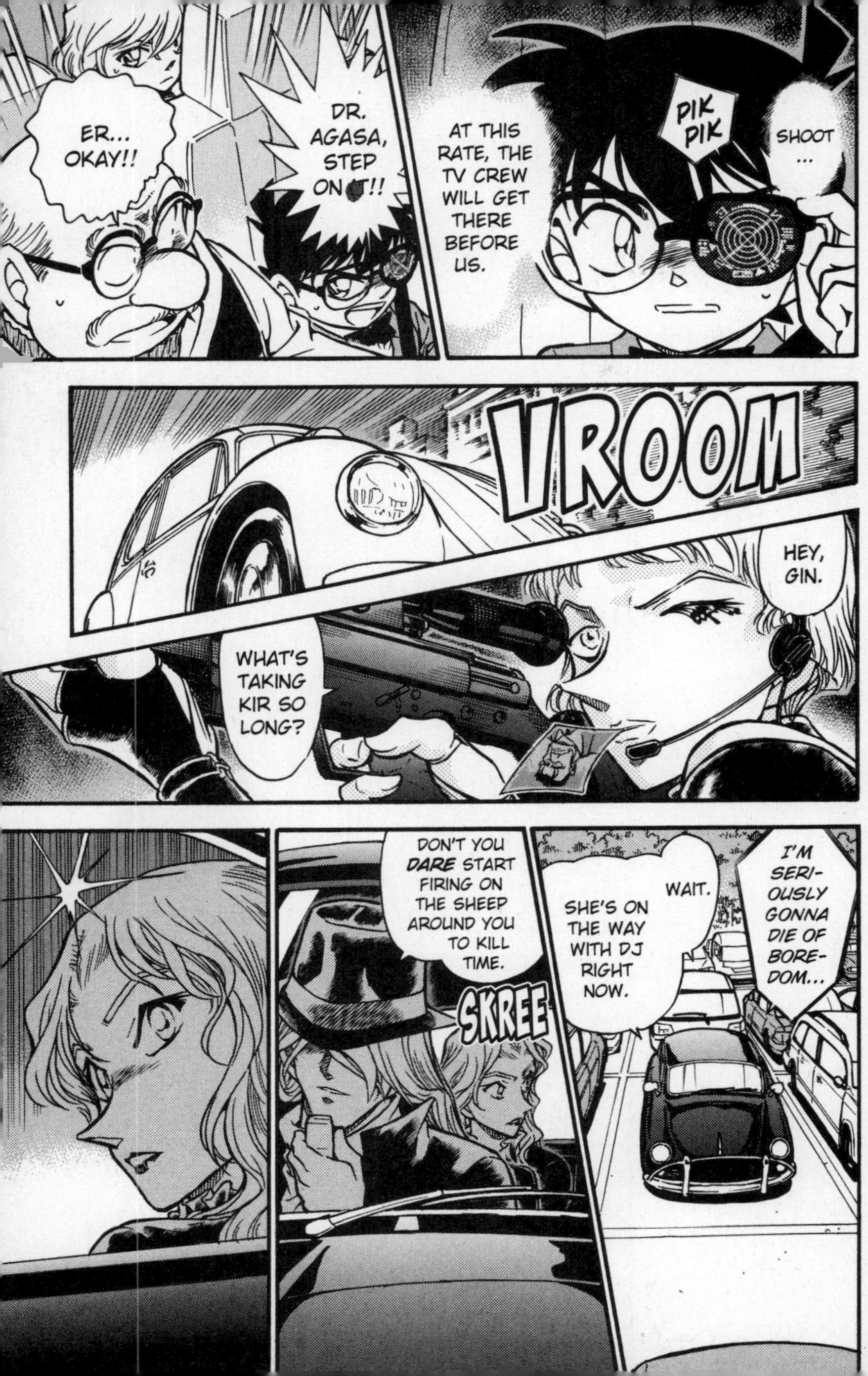
PIK PIK
SHOOT...
AT THIS RATE, THE TV CREW WILL GET THERE BEFORE US.
DR. AGASA, STEP ON IT!!
ER... OKAY!!
VROOM
HEY, GIN.
WHAT'S TAKING KIR SO LONG?
I'M SERIOUSLY GONNA DIE OF BOREDOM...
WAIT.
SHE'S ON THE WAY WITH DJ RIGHT NOW.
DON'T YOU DARE START FIRING ON THE SHEEP AROUND YOU TO KILL TIME.
SKREE

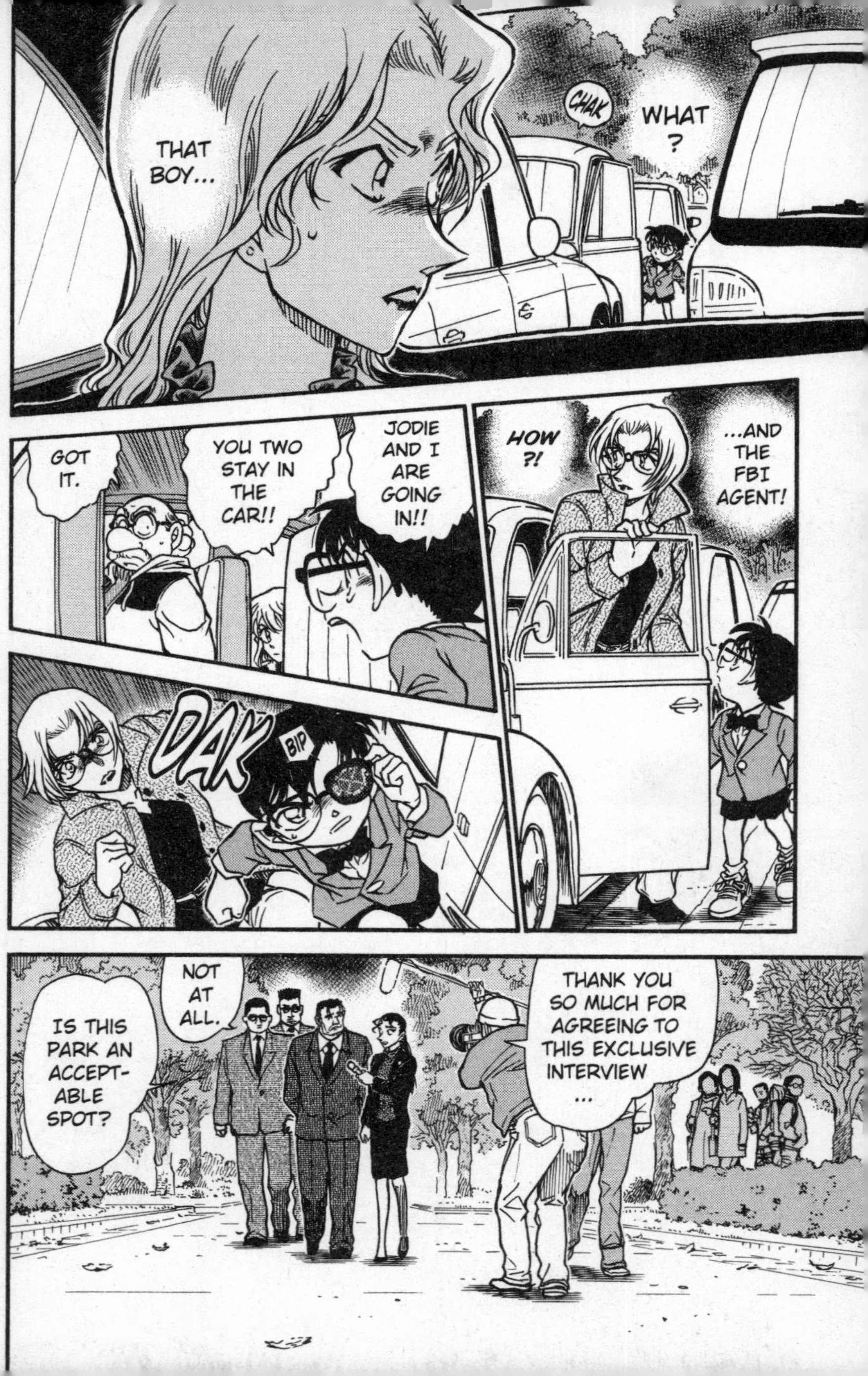
WHAT ?
CHAK
THAT BOY...
...AND THE FBI AGENT!
HOW ?!
JODIE AND I ARE GOING IN!!
YOU TWO STAY IN THE CAR!!
GOT IT.
BIP
DAK
THANK YOU SO MUCH FOR AGREEING TO THIS EXCLUSIVE INTERVIEW ...
NOT AT ALL.
IS THIS PARK AN ACCEPTABLE SPOT?

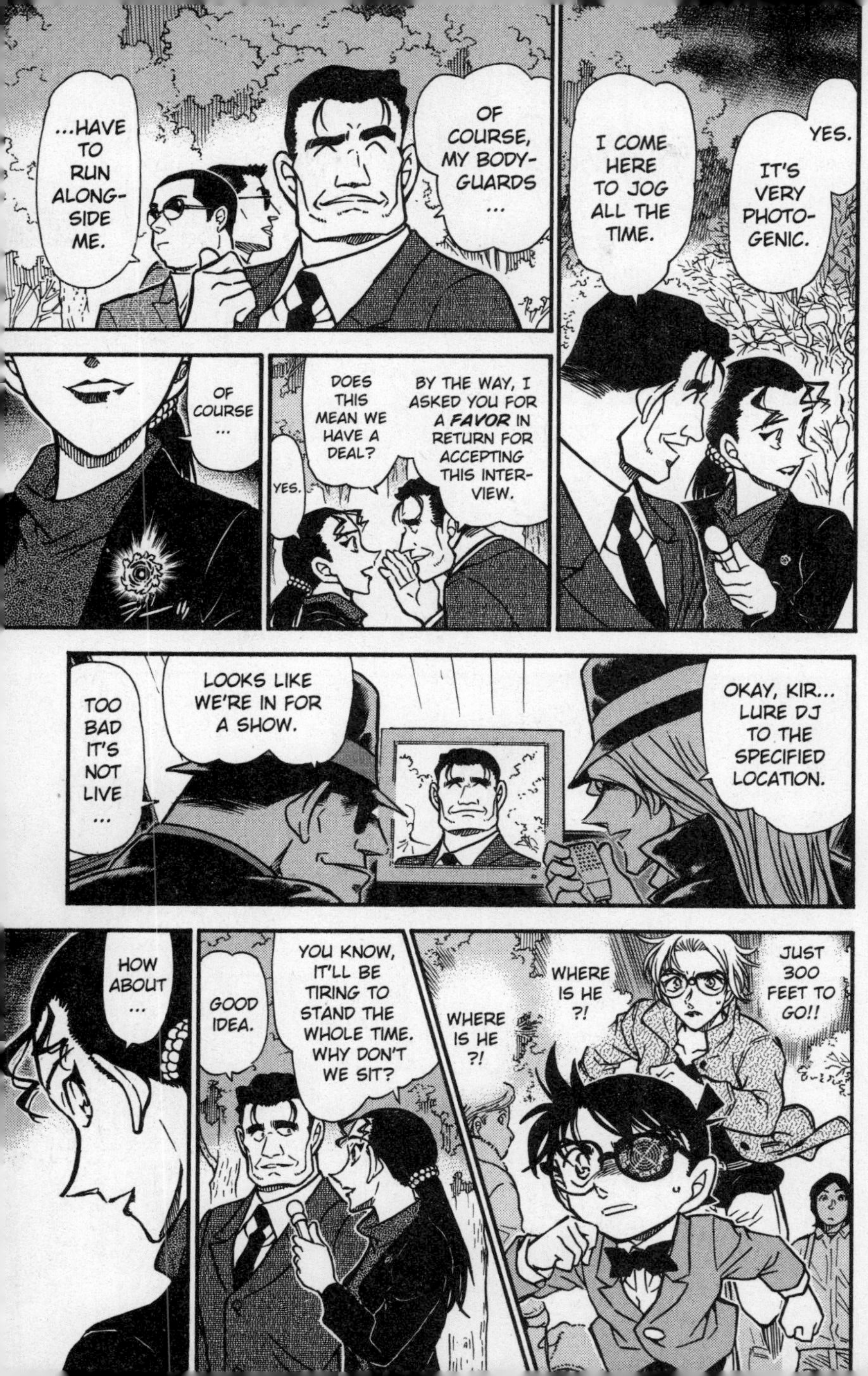
YES.
IT'S VERY PHOTOGENIC.
I COME HERE TO JOG ALL THE TIME.
OF COURSE, MY BODYGUARDS...
...HAVE TO RUN ALONGSIDE ME.
BY THE WAY, I ASKED YOU FOR A *FAVOR* IN RETURN FOR ACCEPTING THIS INTERVIEW.
DOES THIS MEAN WE HAVE A DEAL?
YES.
OF COURSE...
OKAY, KIR... LURE DJ TO THE SPECIFIED LOCATION.
LOOKS LIKE WE'RE IN FOR A SHOW.
TOO BAD IT'S NOT LIVE...
JUST 300 FEET TO GO!!
WHERE IS HE ?!
WHERE IS HE ?!
YOU KNOW, IT'LL BE TIRING TO STAND THE WHOLE TIME. WHY DON'T WE SIT?
GOOD IDEA.
HOW ABOUT...

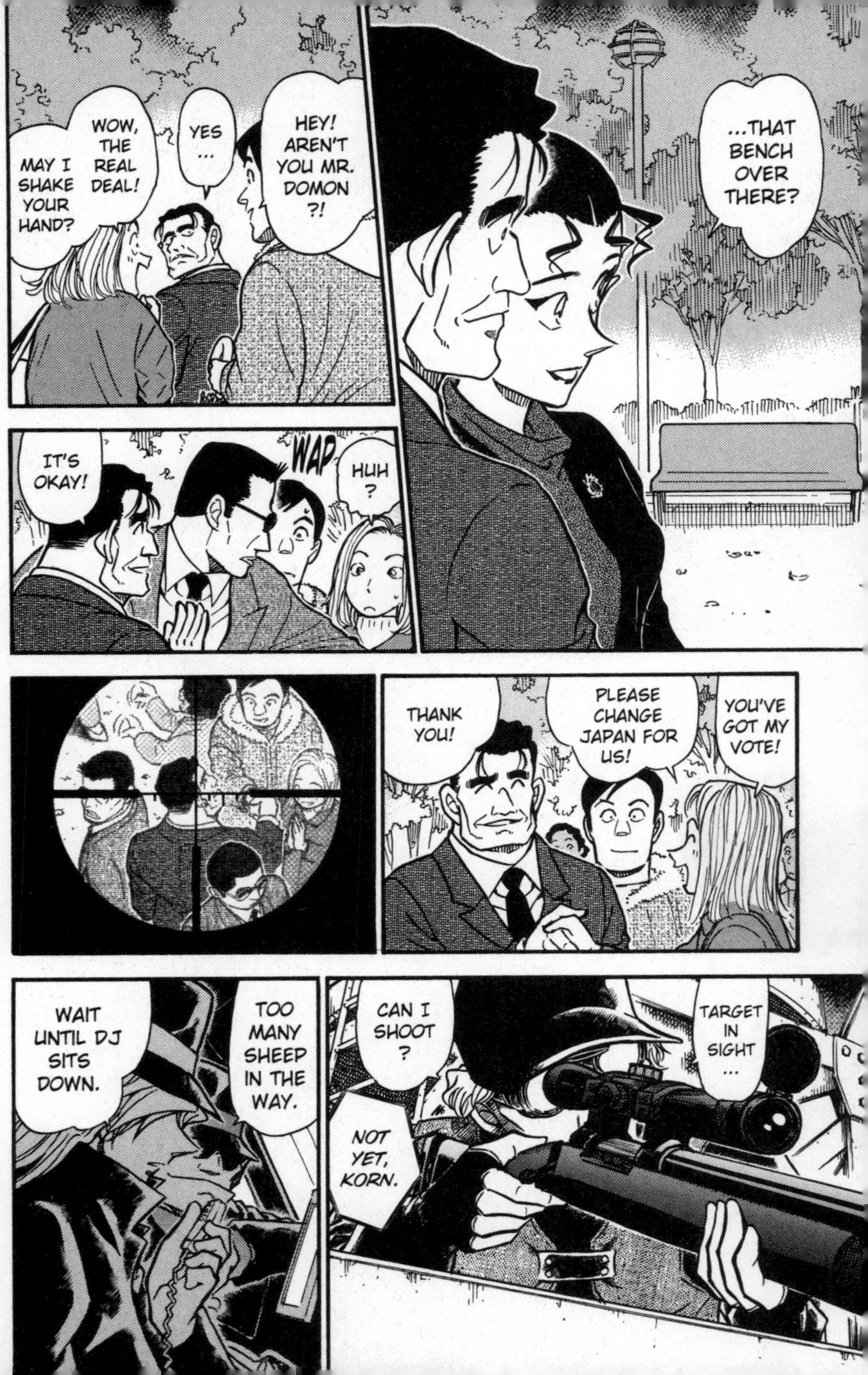
...THAT BENCH OVER THERE?
HEY! AREN'T YOU MR. DOMON?!
YES ...
WOW, THE REAL DEAL!
MAY I SHAKE YOUR HAND?
WAP
HUH?
IT'S OKAY!
YOU'VE GOT MY VOTE!
PLEASE CHANGE JAPAN FOR US!
THANK YOU!
TARGET IN SIGHT ...
CAN I SHOOT?
NOT YET, KORN.
TOO MANY SHEEP IN THE WAY.
WAIT UNTIL DJ SITS DOWN.

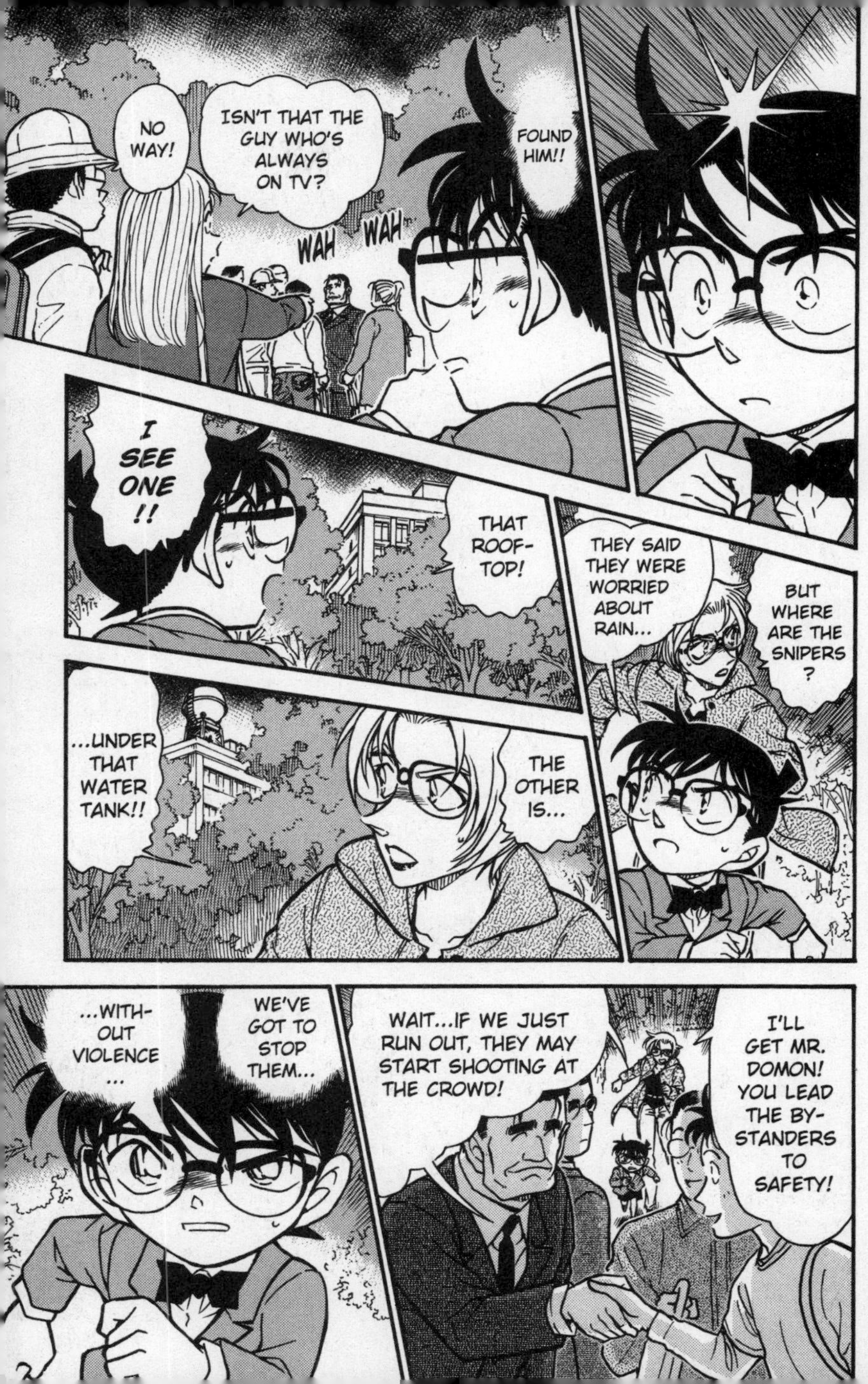
FOUND HIM!!
ISN'T THAT THE GUY WHO'S ALWAYS ON TV?
NO WAY!
WAH WAH
THEY SAID THEY WERE WORRIED ABOUT RAIN...
BUT WHERE ARE THE SNIPERS?
I SEE ONE!!
THAT ROOF-TOP!
THE OTHER IS...
...UNDER THAT WATER TANK!!
I'LL GET MR. DOMON! YOU LEAD THE BY-STANDERS TO SAFETY!
WAIT...IF WE JUST RUN OUT, THEY MAY START SHOOTING AT THE CROWD!
WE'VE GOT TO STOP THEM...
...WITH-OUT VIOLENCE ...

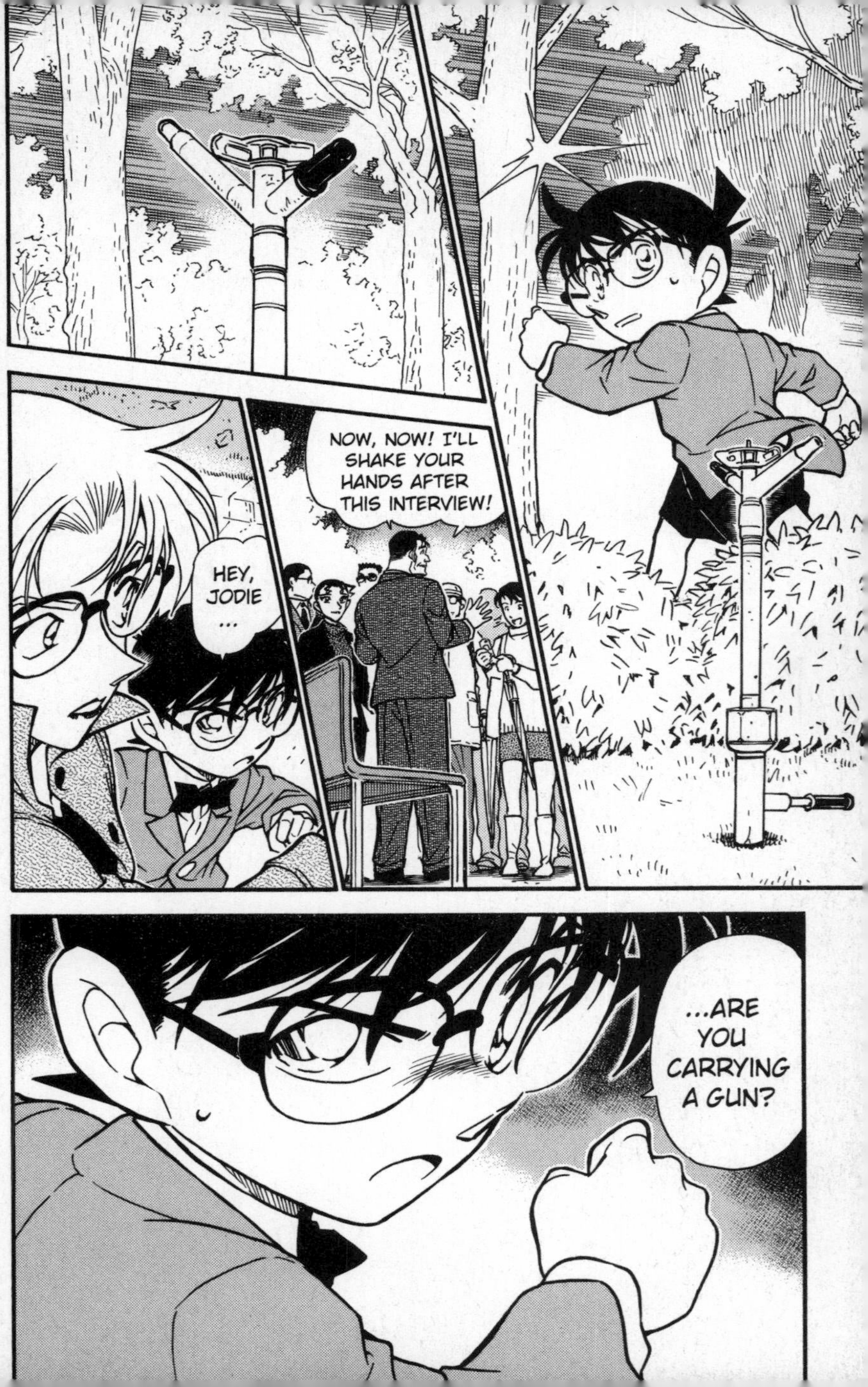
NOW, NOW! I'LL SHAKE YOUR HANDS AFTER THIS INTERVIEW!
HEY, JODIE ...
...ARE YOU CARRYING A GUN?

FILE 2: A NEW MISSION

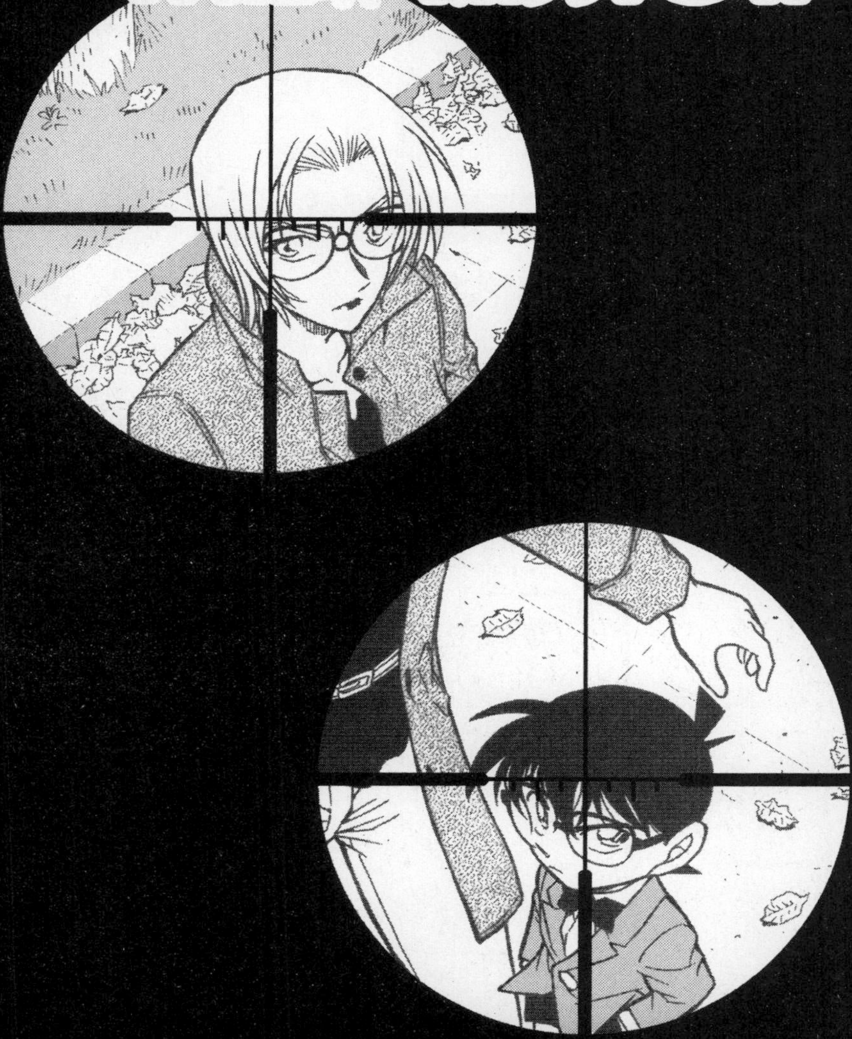

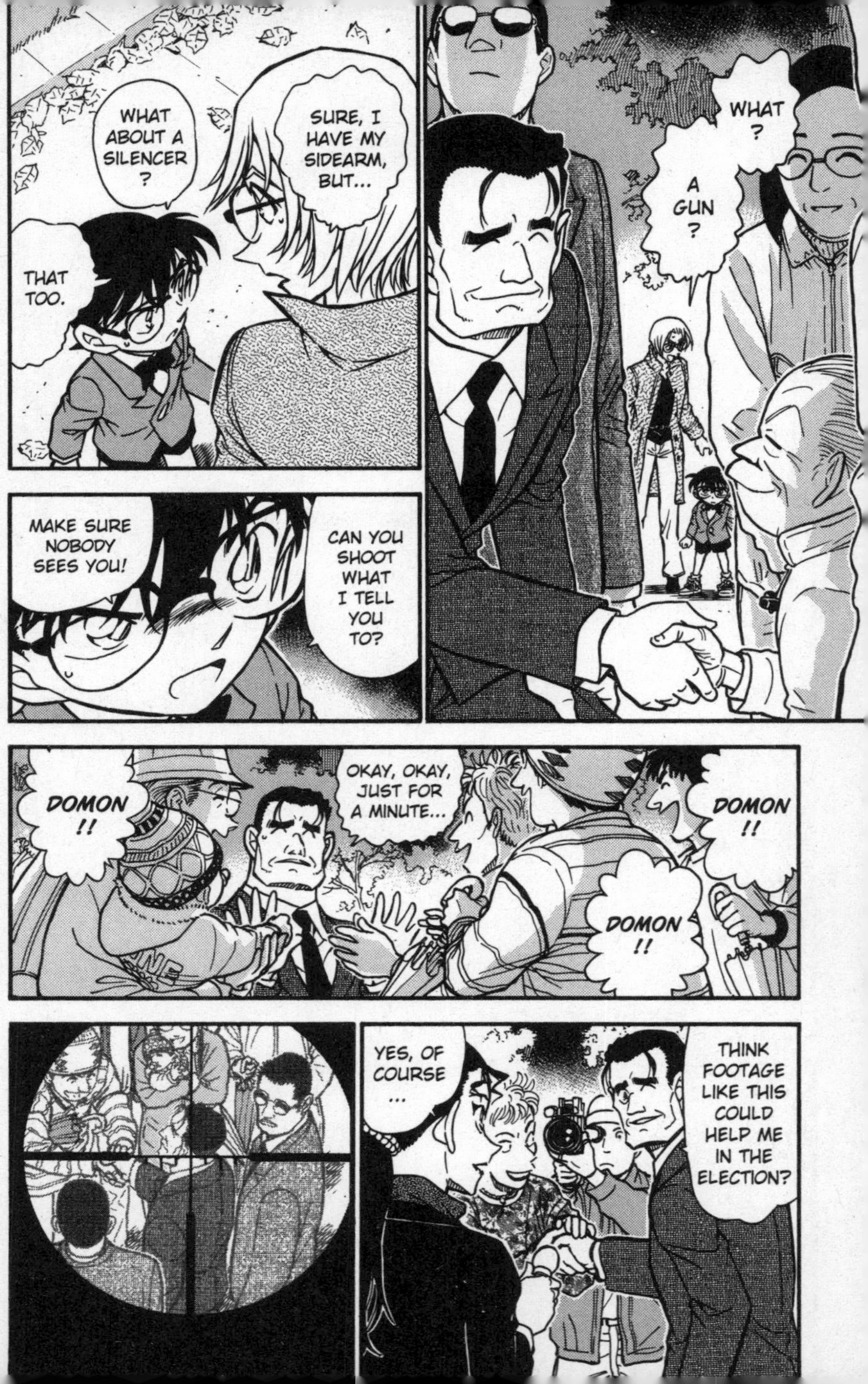
WHAT?
A GUN?
SURE, I HAVE MY SIDEARM, BUT...
WHAT ABOUT A SILENCER?
THAT TOO.
CAN YOU SHOOT WHAT I TELL YOU TO?
MAKE SURE NOBODY SEES YOU!
DOMON!!
DOMON!!
OKAY, OKAY, JUST FOR A MINUTE...
DOMON!!
THINK FOOTAGE LIKE THIS COULD HELP ME IN THE ELECTION?
YES, OF COURSE...

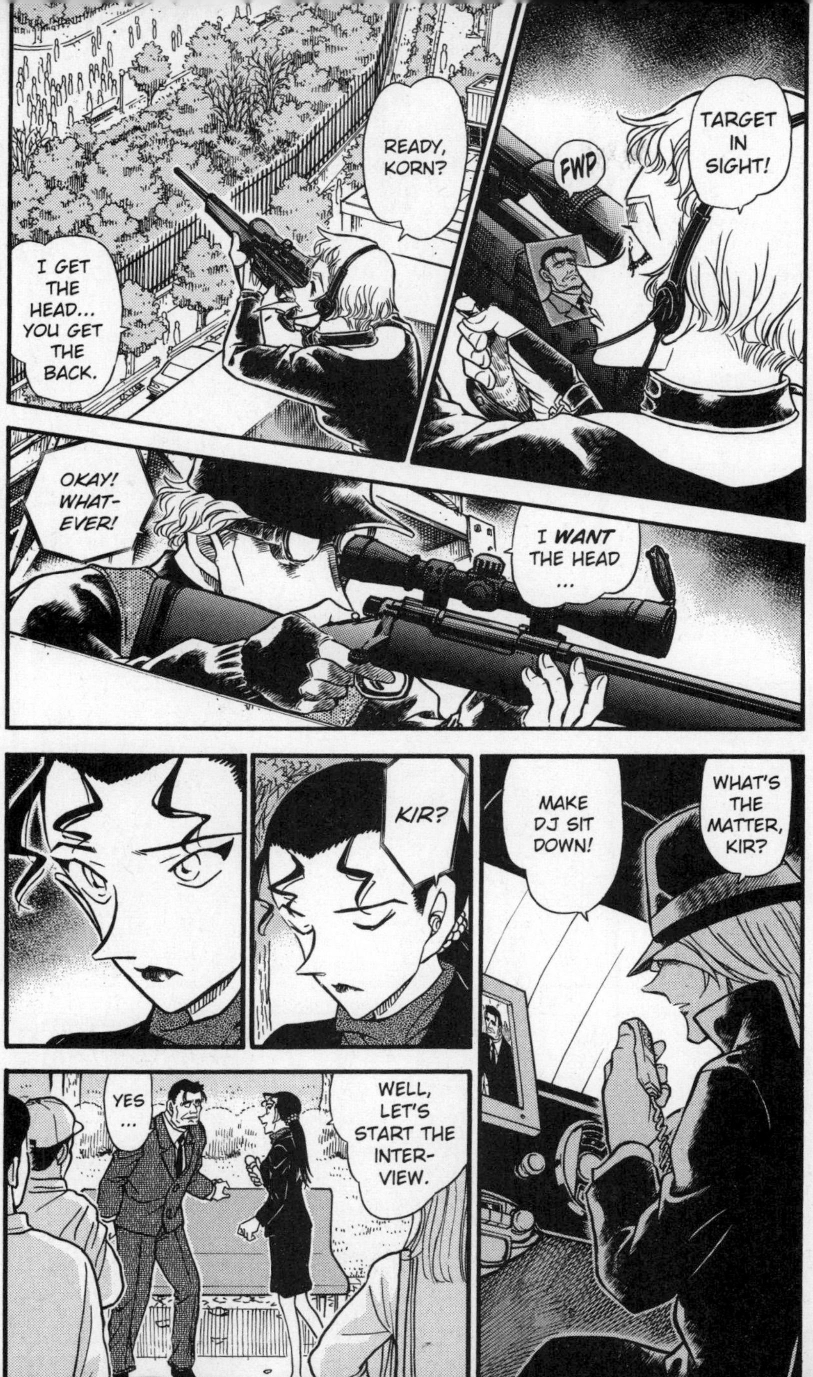
TARGET IN SIGHT!
FWP
READY, KORN?
I GET THE HEAD... YOU GET THE BACK.
I *WANT* THE HEAD ...
OKAY! WHATEVER!
WHAT'S THE MATTER, KIR?
MAKE DJ SIT DOWN!
KIR?
WELL, LET'S START THE INTER-VIEW.
YES ...

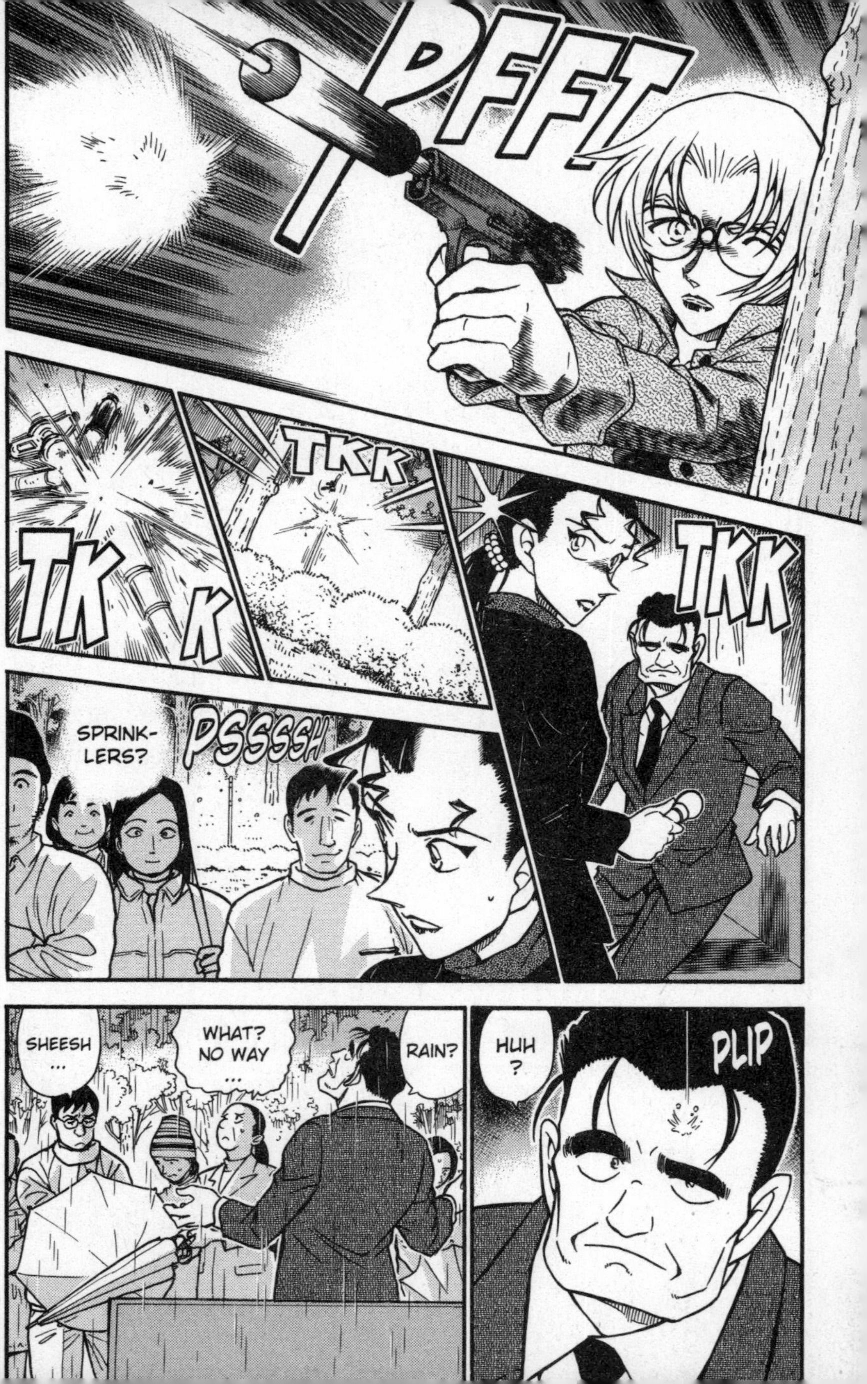
PFFT
TKK
TKK
TK K
PSSSSH
SPRINKLERS?
PLIP
HUH?
RAIN?
WHAT? NO WAY ...
SHEESH ...

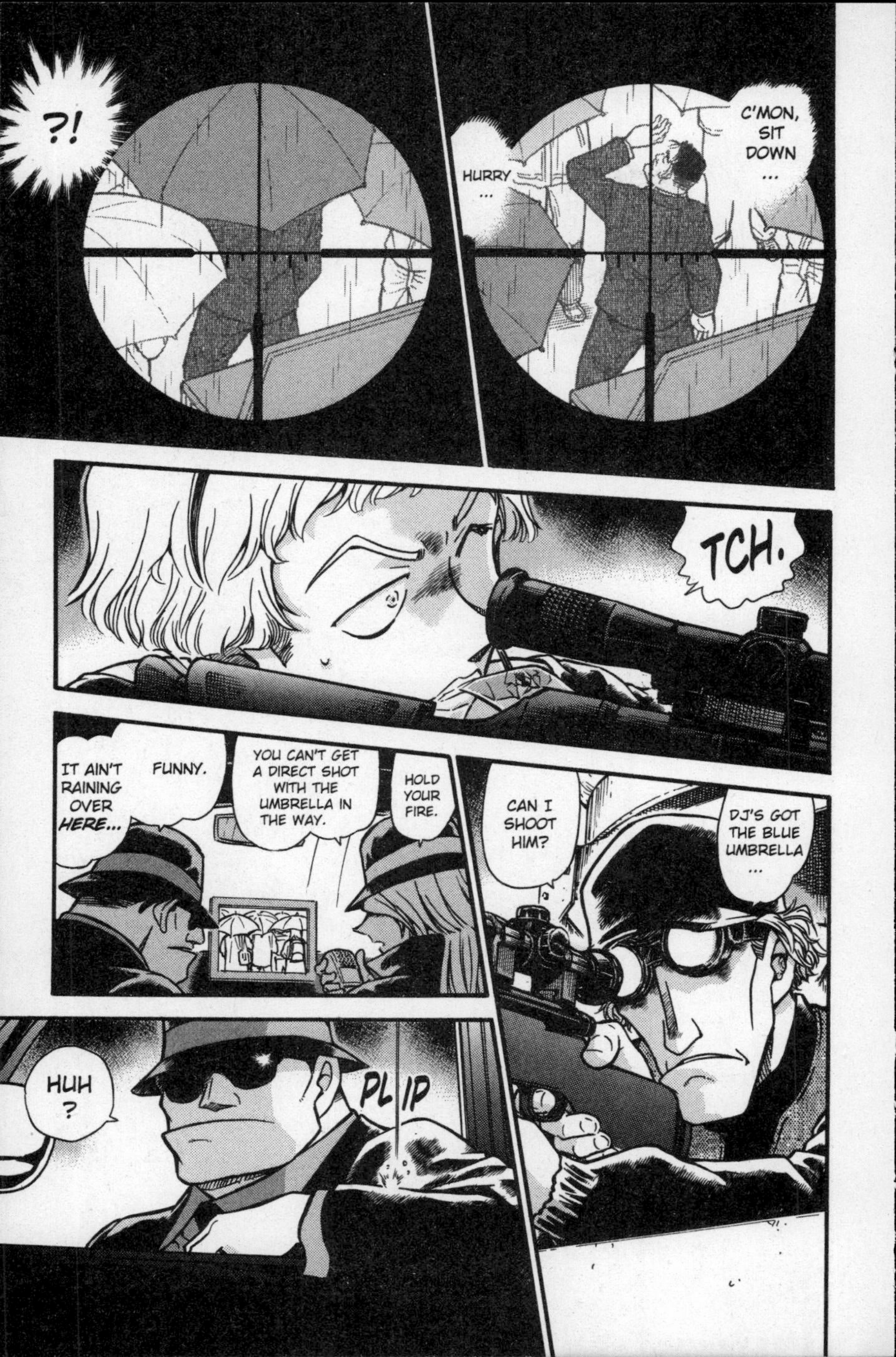
C'MON, SIT DOWN ...
HURRY ...
?!
TCH.
DJ'S GOT THE BLUE UMBRELLA ...
CAN I SHOOT HIM?
HOLD YOUR FIRE.
YOU CAN'T GET A DIRECT SHOT WITH THE UMBRELLA IN THE WAY.
FUNNY.
IT AIN'T RAINING OVER *HERE...*
PLIP
HUH ?

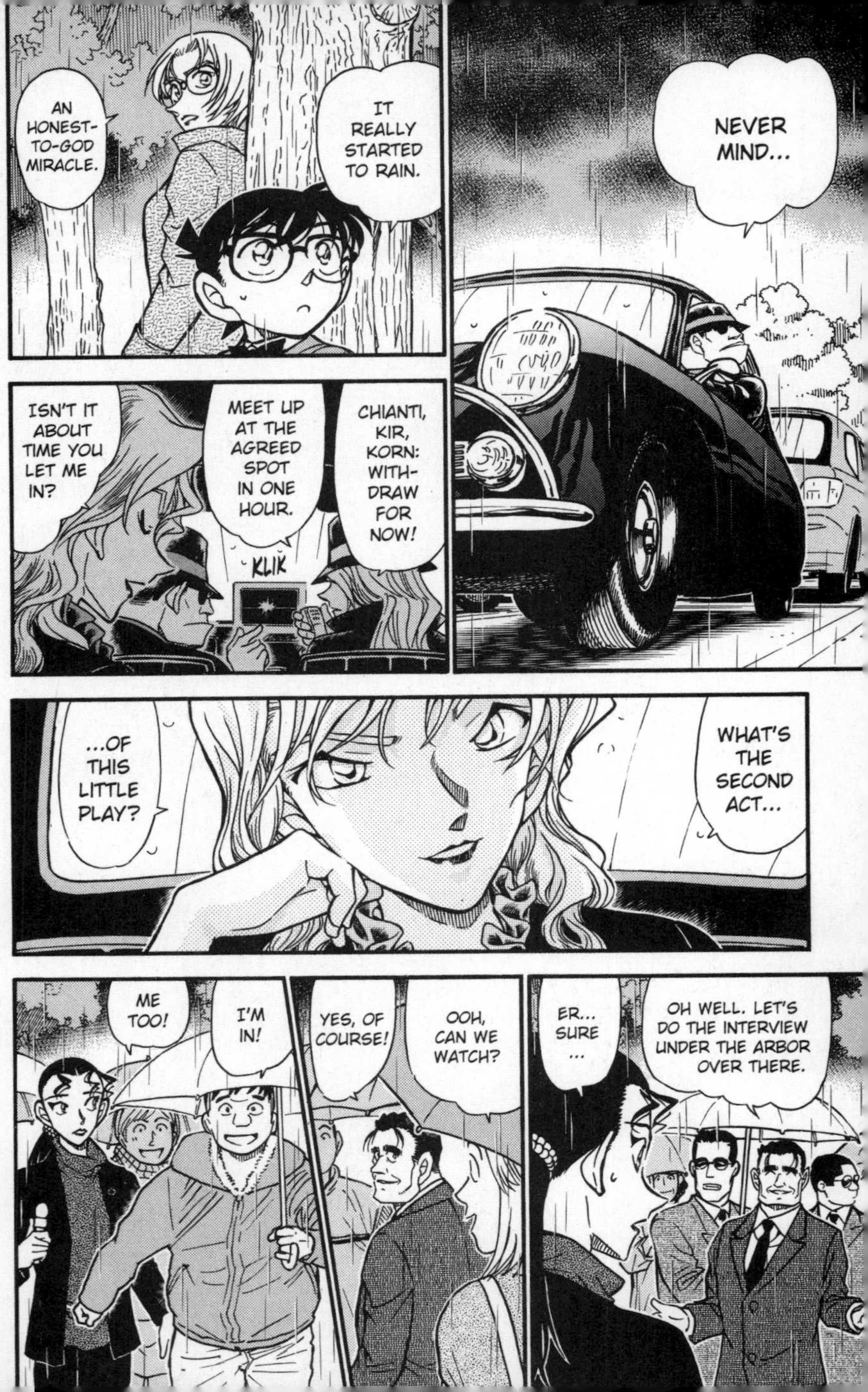
NEVER MIND...
IT REALLY STARTED TO RAIN.
AN HONEST-TO-GOD MIRACLE.
CHIANTI, KIR, KORN: WITH-DRAW FOR NOW!
MEET UP AT THE AGREED SPOT IN ONE HOUR.
KLIK
ISN'T IT ABOUT TIME YOU LET ME IN?
WHAT'S THE SECOND ACT...
...OF THIS LITTLE PLAY?
OH WELL. LET'S DO THE INTERVIEW UNDER THE ARBOR OVER THERE.
ER... SURE ...
OOH, CAN WE WATCH?
YES, OF COURSE!
I'M IN!
ME TOO!

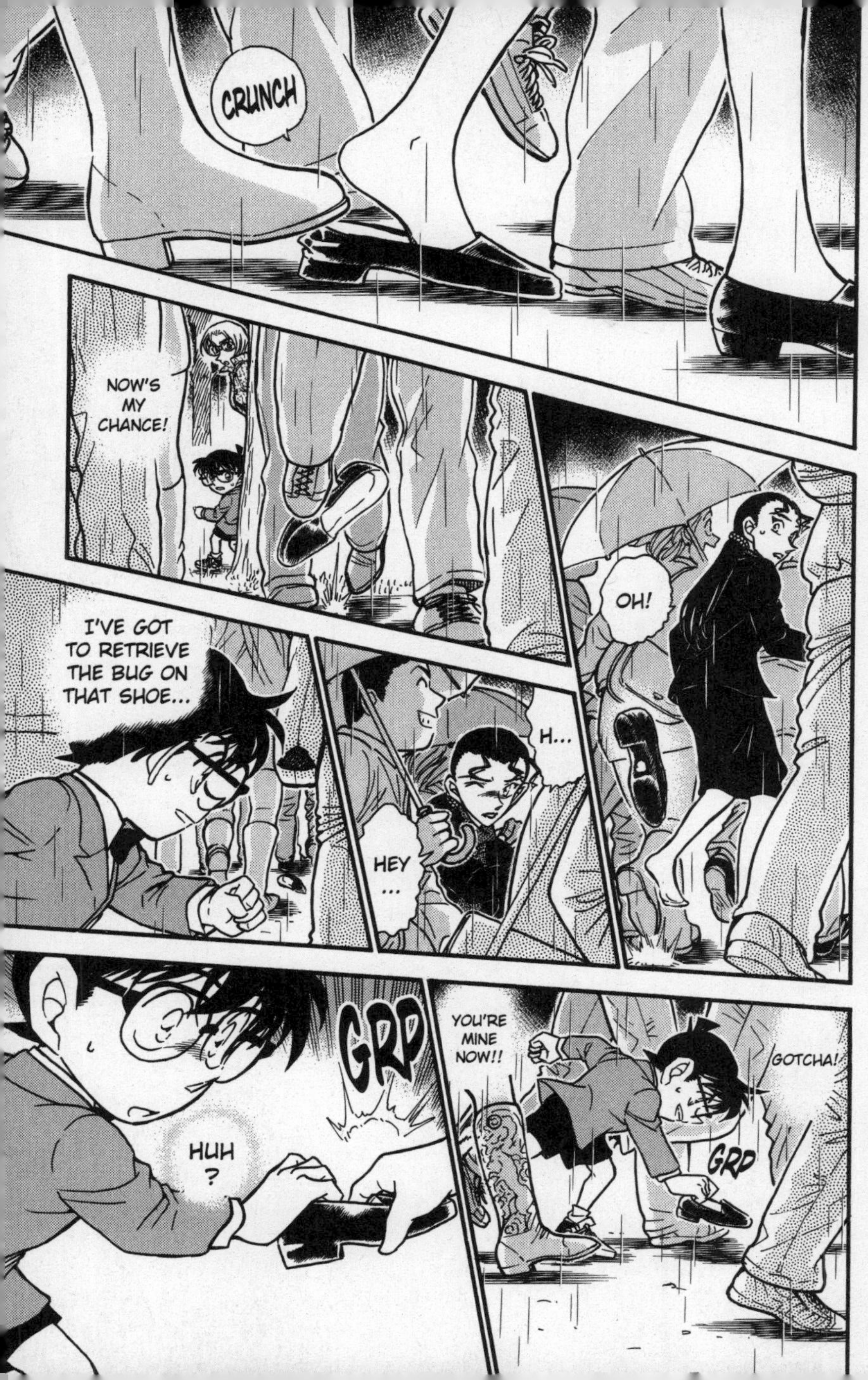
CRUNCH
OH!
NOW'S MY CHANCE!
H...
HEY ...
I'VE GOT TO RETRIEVE THE BUG ON THAT SHOE...
GOTCHA!
YOU'RE MINE NOW!!
GRP
GRP
HUH ?

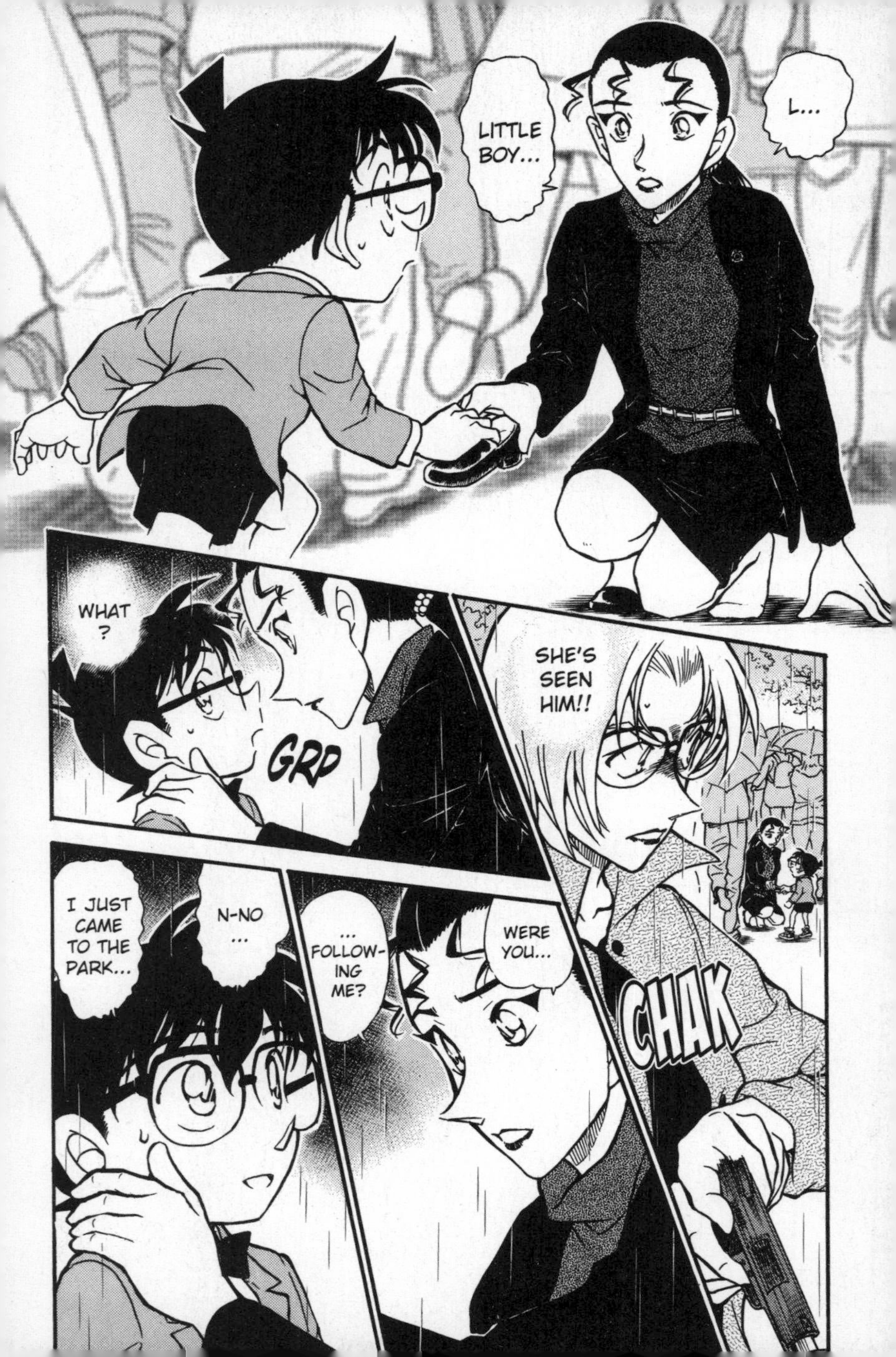
L...
LITTLE BOY...
SHE'S SEEN HIM!!
CHAK
WHAT?
GRP
WERE YOU...
... FOLLOWING ME?
N-NO ...
I JUST CAME TO THE PARK...

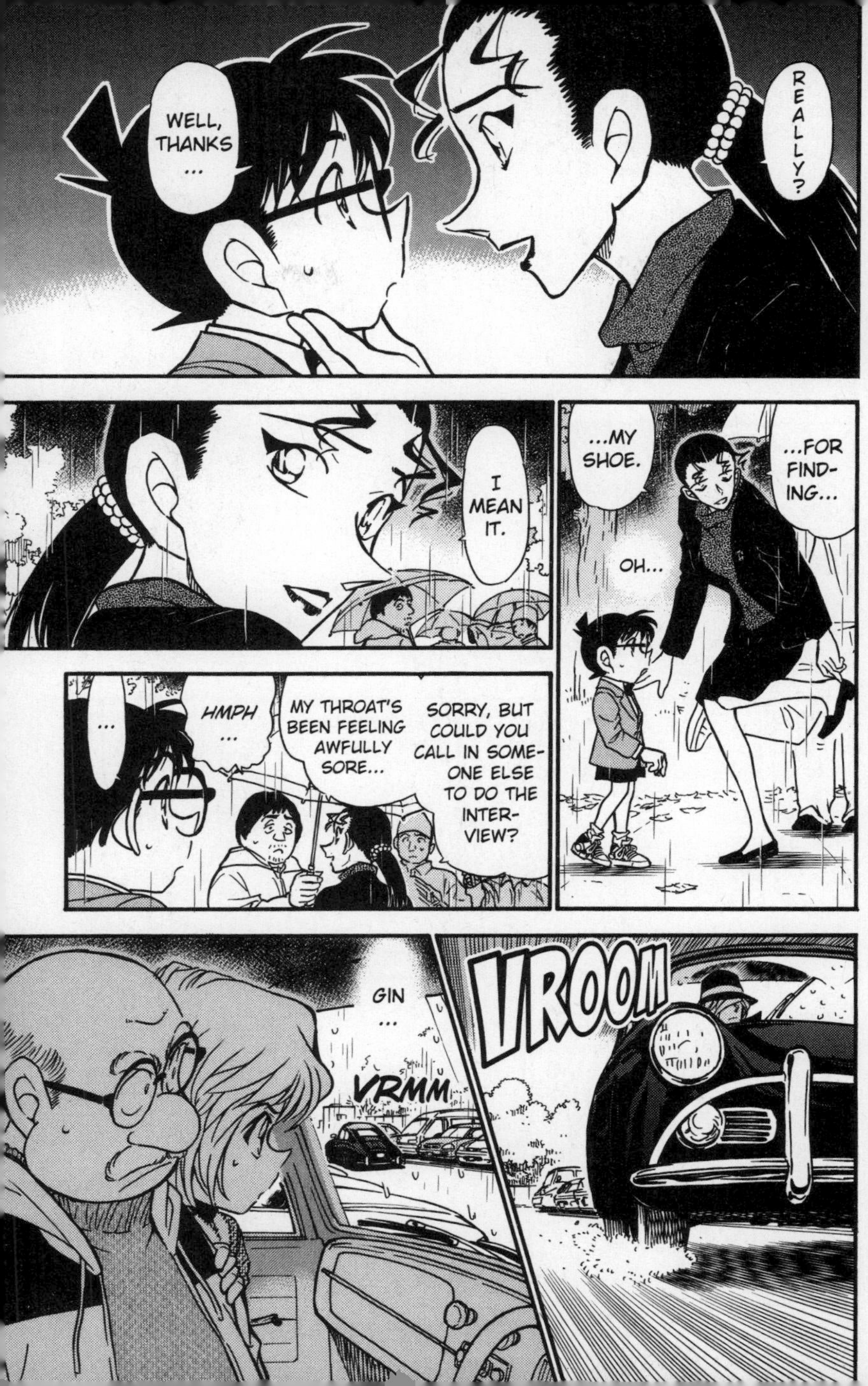
REALLY?
WELL, THANKS ...
...FOR FINDING...
...MY SHOE.
OH...
I MEAN IT.
SORRY, BUT COULD YOU CALL IN SOMEONE ELSE TO DO THE INTERVIEW?
MY THROAT'S BEEN FEELING AWFULLY SORE...
HMPH ...
...
VROOM
GIN ...
VRMM

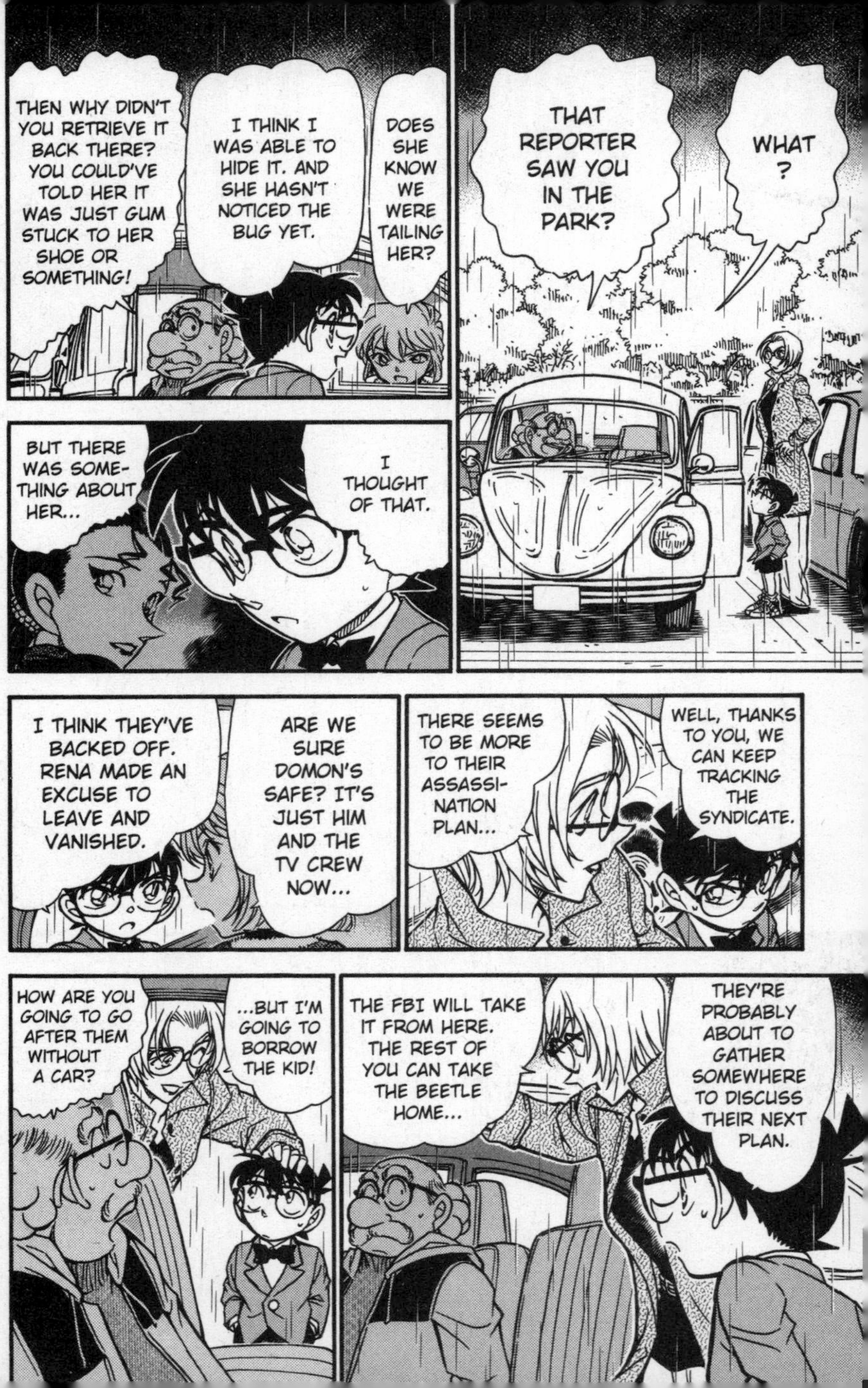
WHAT?
THAT REPORTER SAW YOU IN THE PARK?
DOES SHE KNOW WE WERE TAILING HER?
I THINK I WAS ABLE TO HIDE IT. AND SHE HASN'T NOTICED THE BUG YET.
THEN WHY DIDN'T YOU RETRIEVE IT BACK THERE? YOU COULD'VE TOLD HER IT WAS JUST GUM STUCK TO HER SHOE OR SOMETHING!
I THOUGHT OF THAT.
BUT THERE WAS SOME-THING ABOUT HER...
WELL, THANKS TO YOU, WE CAN KEEP TRACKING THE SYNDICATE.
THERE SEEMS TO BE MORE TO THEIR ASSASSI-NATION PLAN...
ARE WE SURE DOMON'S SAFE? IT'S JUST HIM AND THE TV CREW NOW...
I THINK THEY'VE BACKED OFF. RENA MADE AN EXCUSE TO LEAVE AND VANISHED.
THEY'RE PROBABLY ABOUT TO GATHER SOMEWHERE TO DISCUSS THEIR NEXT PLAN.
THE FBI WILL TAKE IT FROM HERE. THE REST OF YOU CAN TAKE THE BEETLE HOME...
...BUT I'M GOING TO BORROW THE KID!
HOW ARE YOU GOING TO GO AFTER THEM WITHOUT A CAR?

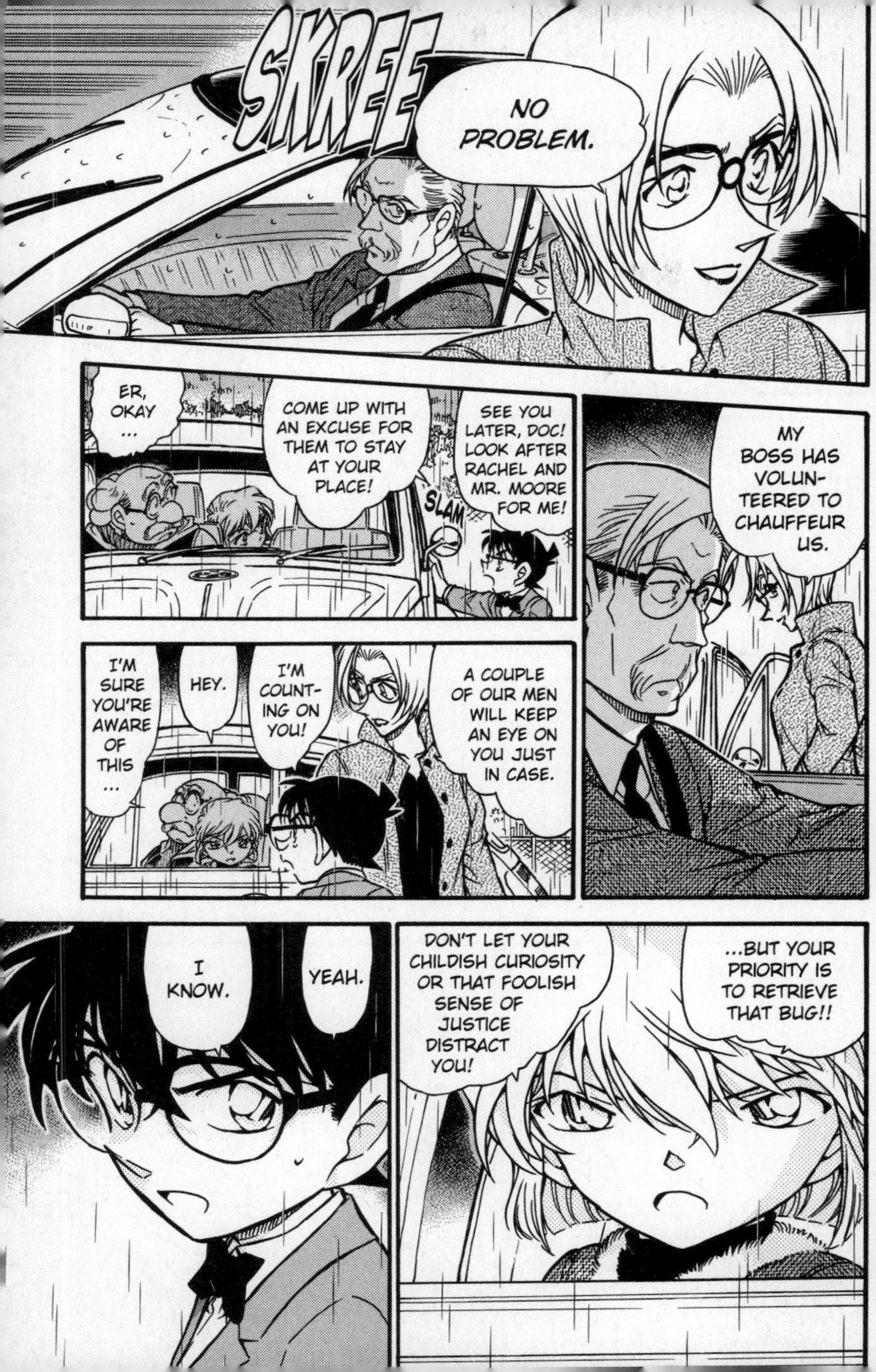
SKREE
NO PROBLEM.
MY BOSS HAS VOLUNTEERED TO CHAUFFEUR US.
SEE YOU LATER, DOC! LOOK AFTER RACHEL AND MR. MOORE FOR ME!
SLAM
COME UP WITH AN EXCUSE FOR THEM TO STAY AT YOUR PLACE!
ER, OKAY ...
A COUPLE OF OUR MEN WILL KEEP AN EYE ON YOU JUST IN CASE.
I'M COUNTING ON YOU!
HEY.
I'M SURE YOU'RE AWARE OF THIS ...
...BUT YOUR PRIORITY IS TO RETRIEVE THAT BUG!!
DON'T LET YOUR CHILDISH CURIOSITY OR THAT FOOLISH SENSE OF JUSTICE DISTRACT YOU!
YEAH.
I KNOW.

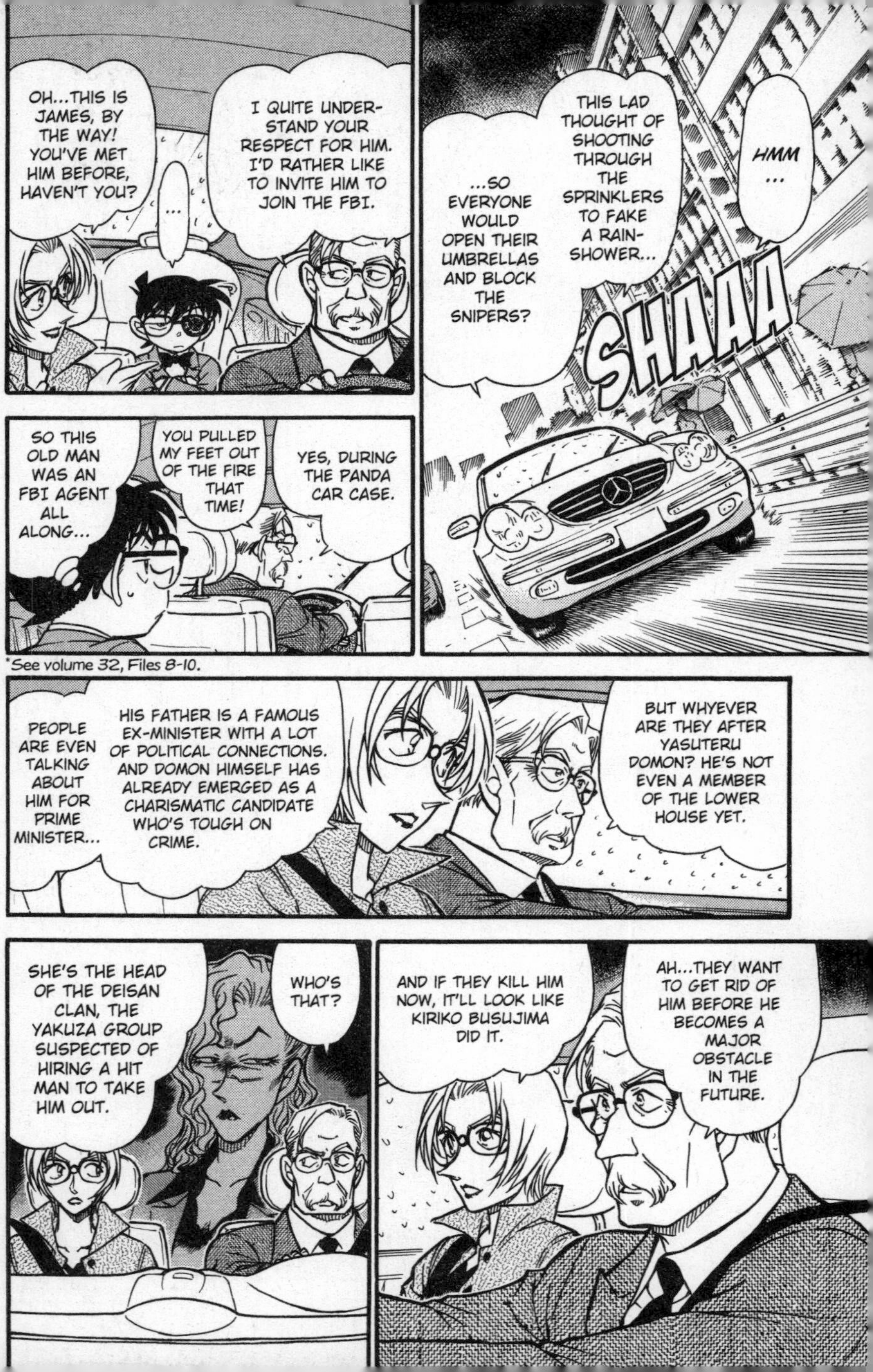
HMM...
THIS LAD THOUGHT OF SHOOTING THROUGH THE SPRINKLERS TO FAKE A RAIN-SHOWER...
...SO EVERYONE WOULD OPEN THEIR UMBRELLAS AND BLOCK THE SNIPERS?
SHAAA
I QUITE UNDER-STAND YOUR RESPECT FOR HIM. I'D RATHER LIKE TO INVITE HIM TO JOIN THE FBI.
...
OH...THIS IS JAMES, BY THE WAY! YOU'VE MET HIM BEFORE, HAVEN'T YOU?
YES, DURING THE PANDA CAR CASE.
YOU PULLED MY FEET OUT OF THE FIRE THAT TIME!
SO THIS OLD MAN WAS AN FBI AGENT ALL ALONG...
BUT WHYEVER ARE THEY AFTER YASUTERU DOMON? HE'S NOT EVEN A MEMBER OF THE LOWER HOUSE YET.
HIS FATHER IS A FAMOUS EX-MINISTER WITH A LOT OF POLITICAL CONNECTIONS. AND DOMON HIMSELF HAS ALREADY EMERGED AS A CHARISMATIC CANDIDATE WHO'S TOUGH ON CRIME.
PEOPLE ARE EVEN TALKING ABOUT HIM FOR PRIME MINISTER...
AH...THEY WANT TO GET RID OF HIM BEFORE HE BECOMES A MAJOR OBSTACLE IN THE FUTURE.
AND IF THEY KILL HIM NOW, IT'LL LOOK LIKE KIRIKO BUSUJIMA DID IT.
WHO'S THAT?
SHE'S THE HEAD OF THE DEISAN CLAN, THE YAKUZA GROUP SUSPECTED OF HIRING A HIT MAN TO TAKE HIM OUT.
*See volume 32, Files 8-10.

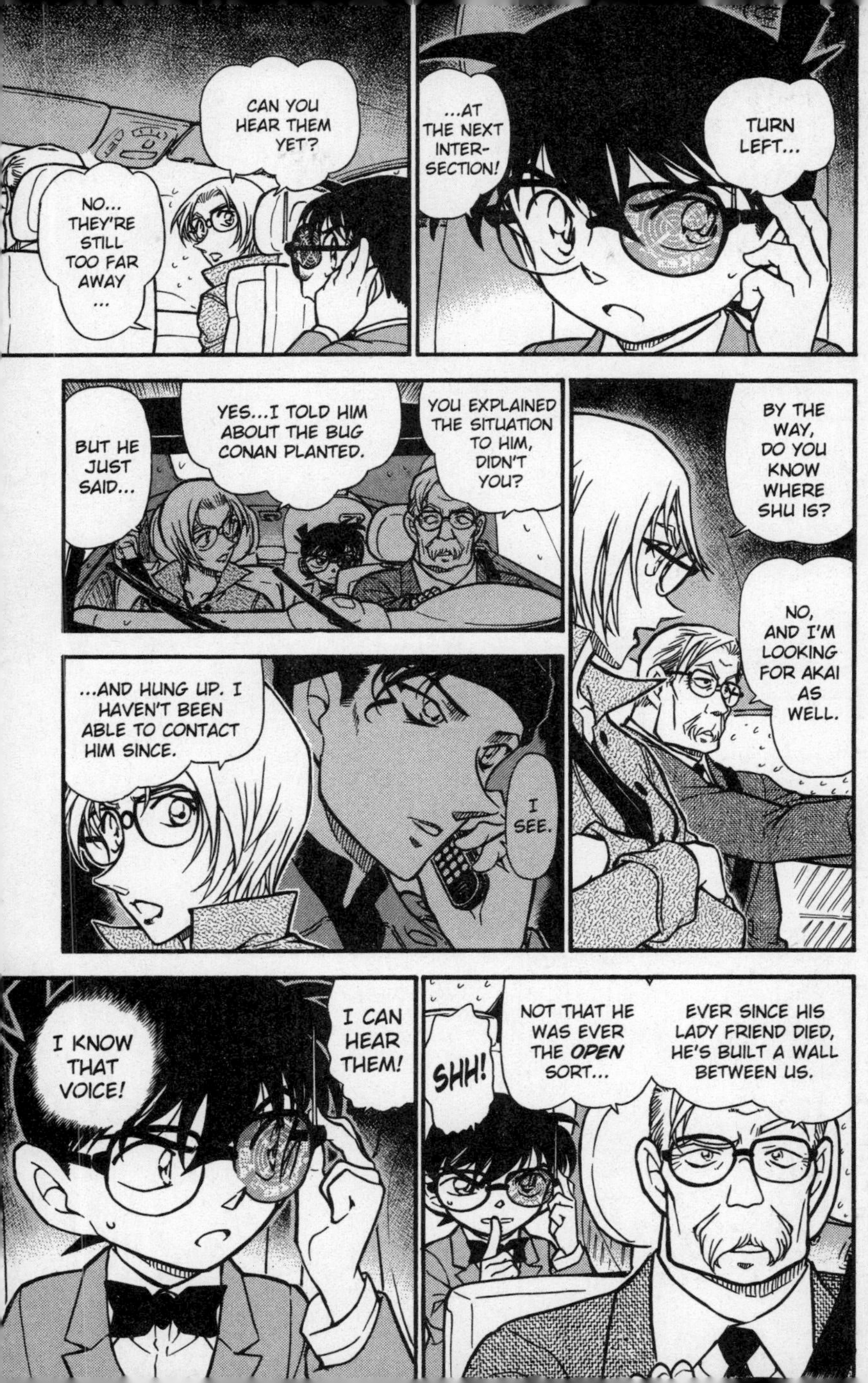
TURN LEFT...
...AT THE NEXT INTER-SECTION!
CAN YOU HEAR THEM YET?
NO... THEY'RE STILL TOO FAR AWAY ...
BY THE WAY, DO YOU KNOW WHERE SHU IS?
NO, AND I'M LOOKING FOR AKAI AS WELL.
YOU EXPLAINED THE SITUATION TO HIM, DIDN'T YOU?
YES...I TOLD HIM ABOUT THE BUG CONAN PLANTED.
BUT HE JUST SAID...
I SEE.
...AND HUNG UP. I HAVEN'T BEEN ABLE TO CONTACT HIM SINCE.
EVER SINCE HIS LADY FRIEND DIED, HE'S BUILT A WALL BETWEEN US.
NOT THAT HE WAS EVER THE *OPEN* SORT...
SHH!
I CAN HEAR THEM!
I KNOW THAT VOICE!

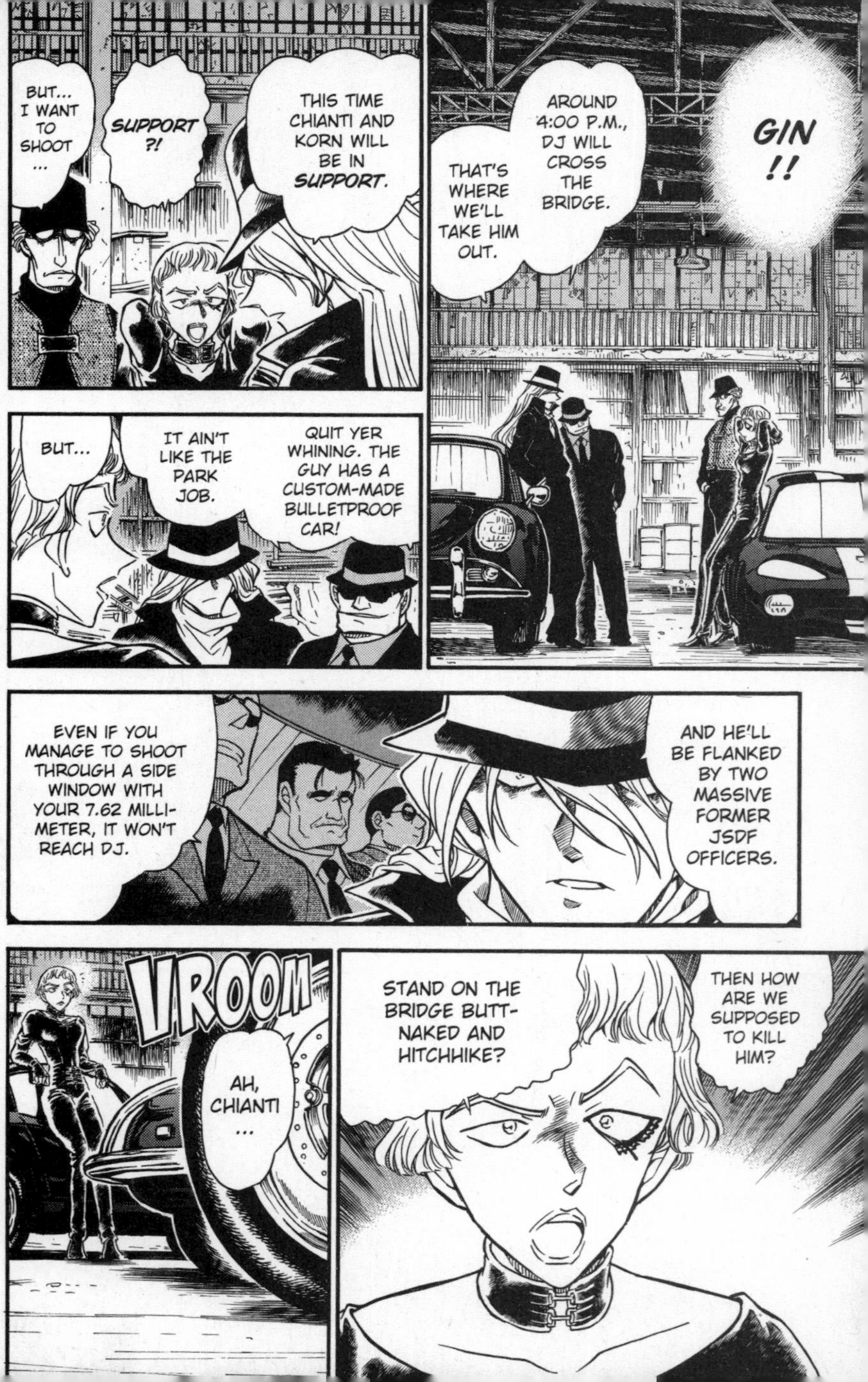
GIN !!
AROUND 4:00 P.M., DJ WILL CROSS THE BRIDGE.
THAT'S WHERE WE'LL TAKE HIM OUT.
THIS TIME CHIANTI AND KORN WILL BE IN SUPPORT.
SUPPORT?!
BUT... I WANT TO SHOOT ...
QUIT YER WHINING. THE GUY HAS A CUSTOM-MADE BULLETPROOF CAR!
IT AIN'T LIKE THE PARK JOB.
BUT...
AND HE'LL BE FLANKED BY TWO MASSIVE FORMER JSDF OFFICERS.
EVEN IF YOU MANAGE TO SHOOT THROUGH A SIDE WINDOW WITH YOUR 7.62 MILLI-METER, IT WON'T REACH DJ.
THEN HOW ARE WE SUPPOSED TO KILL HIM?
STAND ON THE BRIDGE BUTT-NAKED AND HITCHHIKE?
VROOM
AH, CHIANTI ...

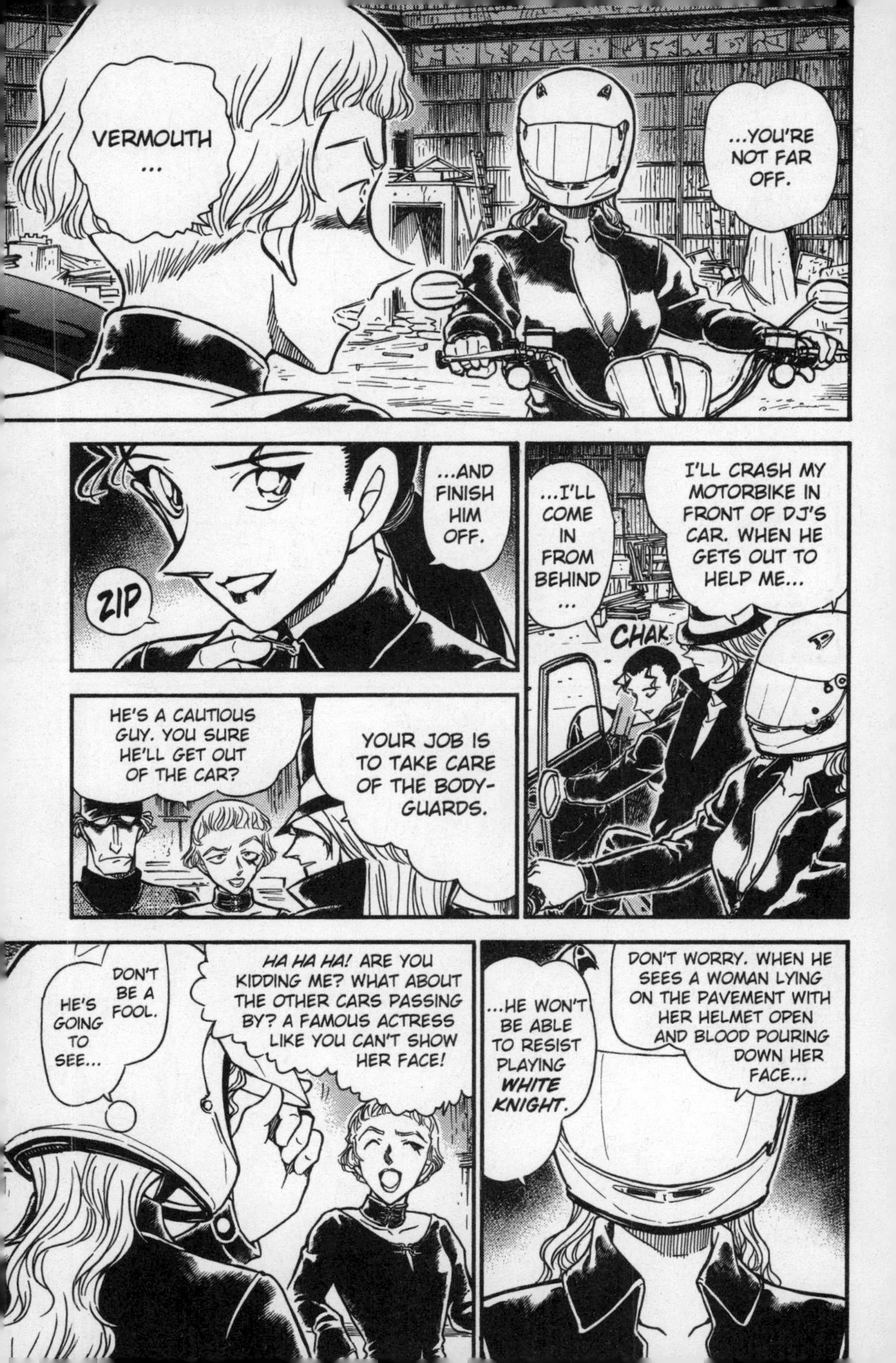
...YOU'RE NOT FAR OFF.
VERMOUTH ...
I'LL CRASH MY MOTORBIKE IN FRONT OF DJ'S CAR. WHEN HE GETS OUT TO HELP ME...
...I'LL COME IN FROM BEHIND ...
CHAK
...AND FINISH HIM OFF.
ZIP
YOUR JOB IS TO TAKE CARE OF THE BODY-GUARDS.
HE'S A CAUTIOUS GUY. YOU SURE HE'LL GET OUT OF THE CAR?
DON'T WORRY. WHEN HE SEES A WOMAN LYING ON THE PAVEMENT WITH HER HELMET OPEN AND BLOOD POURING DOWN HER FACE...
...HE WON'T BE ABLE TO RESIST PLAYING *WHITE KNIGHT*.
HA HA HA! ARE YOU KIDDING ME? WHAT ABOUT THE OTHER CARS PASSING BY? A FAMOUS ACTRESS LIKE YOU CAN'T SHOW HER FACE!
DON'T BE A FOOL.
HE'S GOING TO SEE...

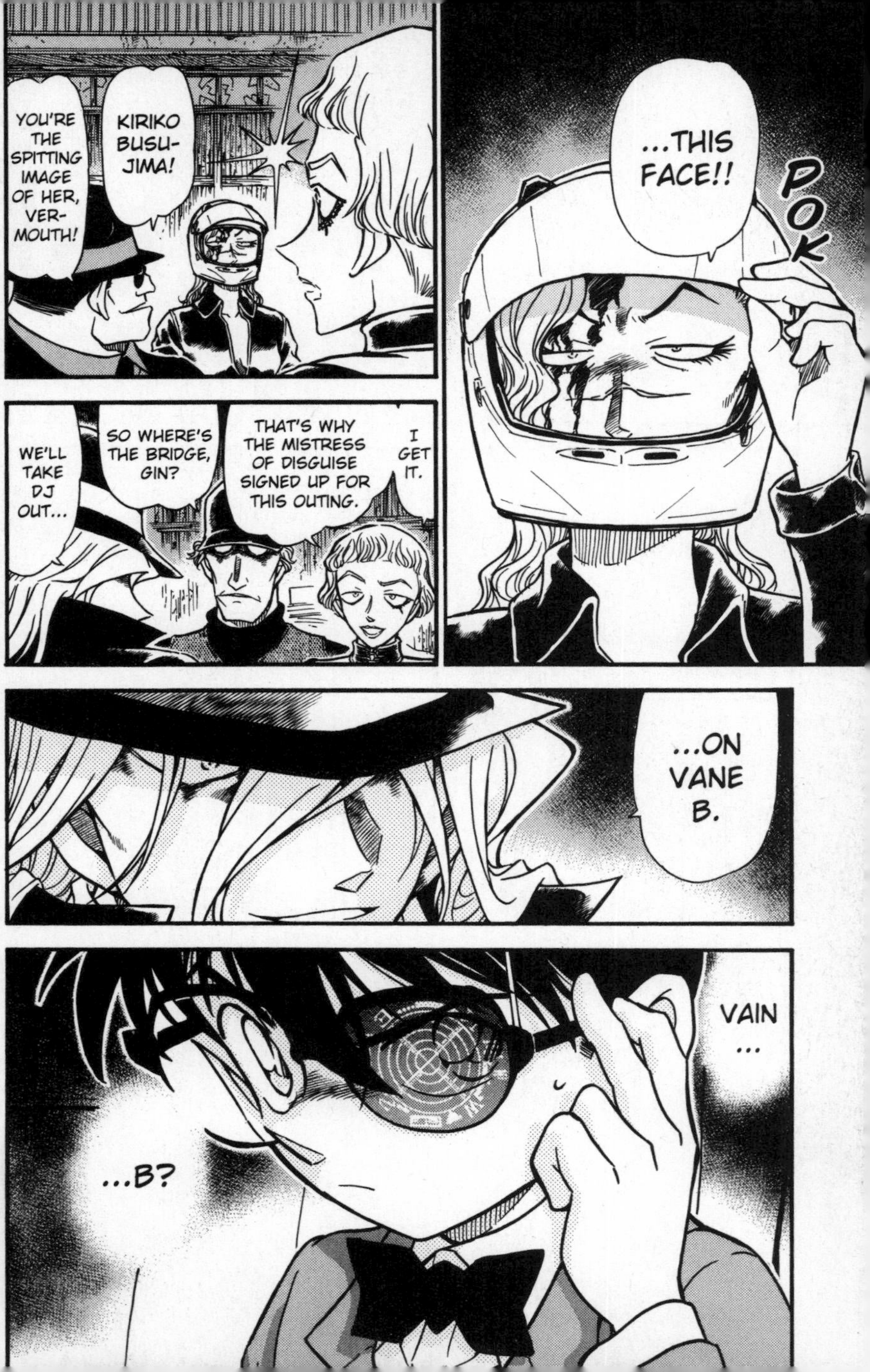
...THIS FACE!!
POK
KIRIKO BUSU-JIMA!
YOU'RE THE SPITTING IMAGE OF HER, VER-MOUTH!
I GET IT.
THAT'S WHY THE MISTRESS OF DISGUISE SIGNED UP FOR THIS OUTING.
SO WHERE'S THE BRIDGE, GIN?
WE'LL TAKE DJ OUT...
...ON VANE B.
VAIN ...
...B?

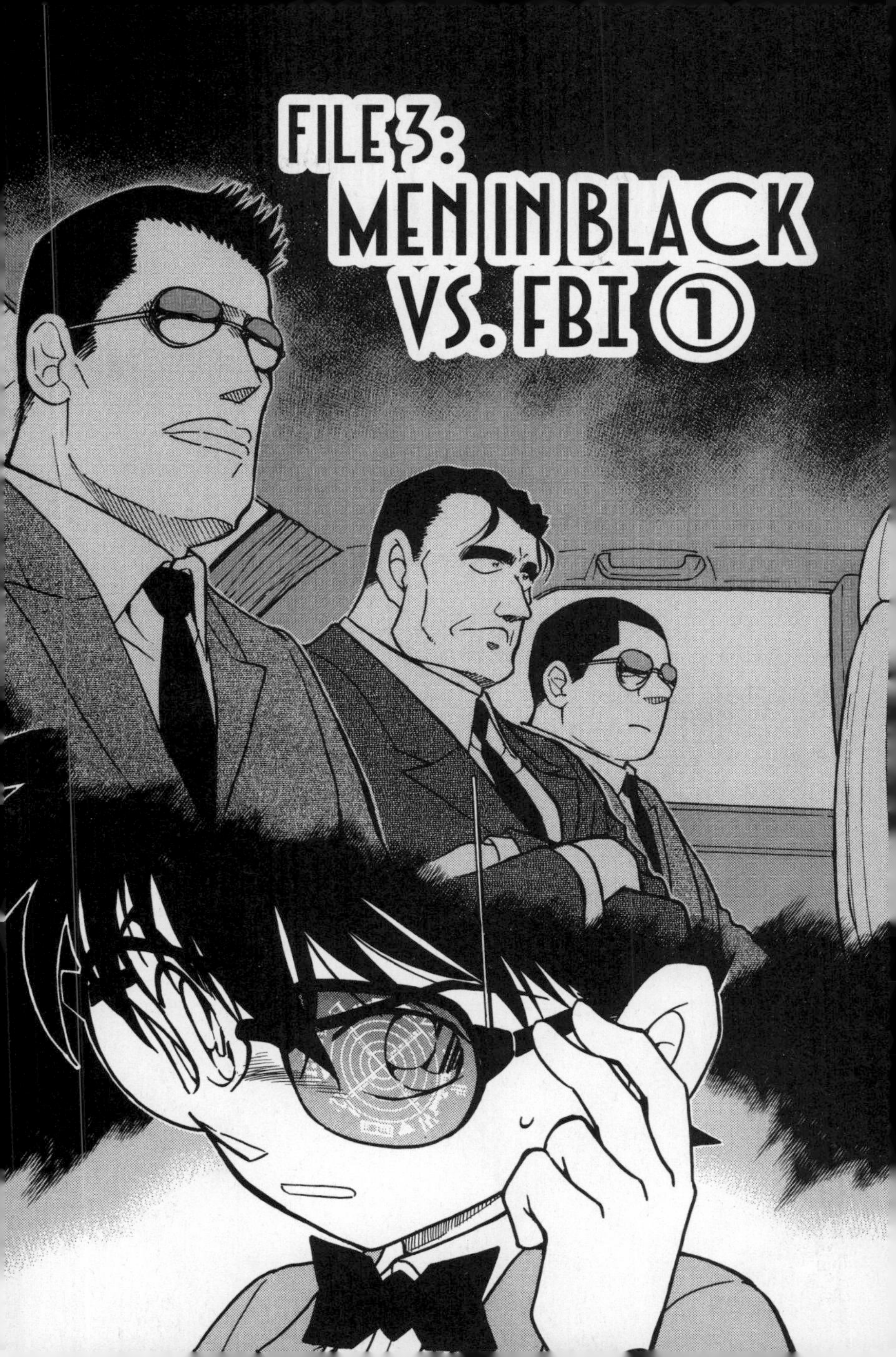
FILE 3:
MEN IN BLACK VS. FBI ①

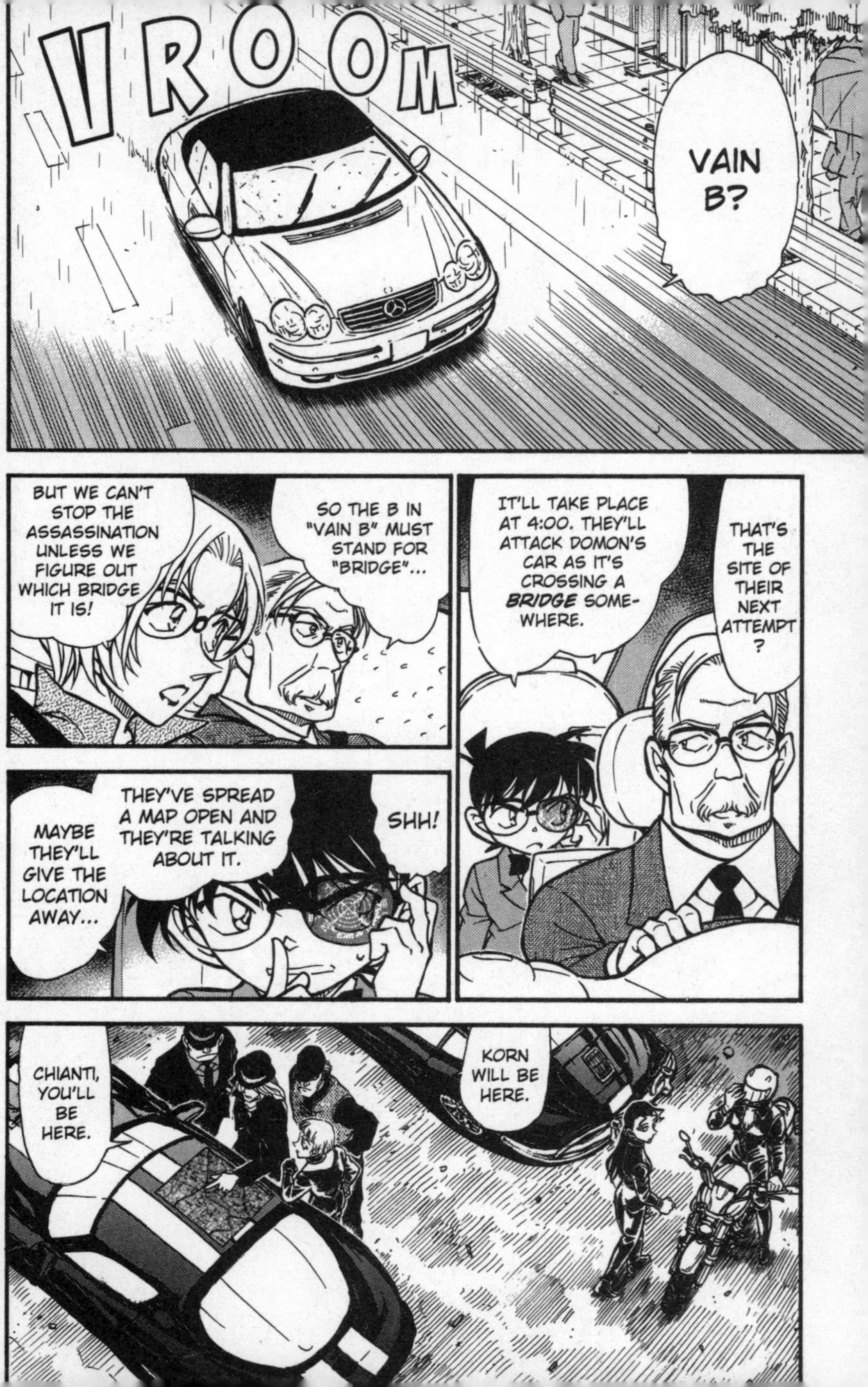
VROOM
VAIN B?
THAT'S THE SITE OF THEIR NEXT ATTEMPT?
IT'LL TAKE PLACE AT 4:00. THEY'LL ATTACK DOMON'S CAR AS IT'S CROSSING A *BRIDGE* SOMEWHERE.
SO THE B IN "VAIN B" MUST STAND FOR "BRIDGE"...
BUT WE CAN'T STOP THE ASSASSINATION UNLESS WE FIGURE OUT WHICH BRIDGE IT IS!
SHH!
THEY'VE SPREAD A MAP OPEN AND THEY'RE TALKING ABOUT IT.
MAYBE THEY'LL GIVE THE LOCATION AWAY...
KORN WILL BE HERE.
CHIANTI, YOU'LL BE HERE.

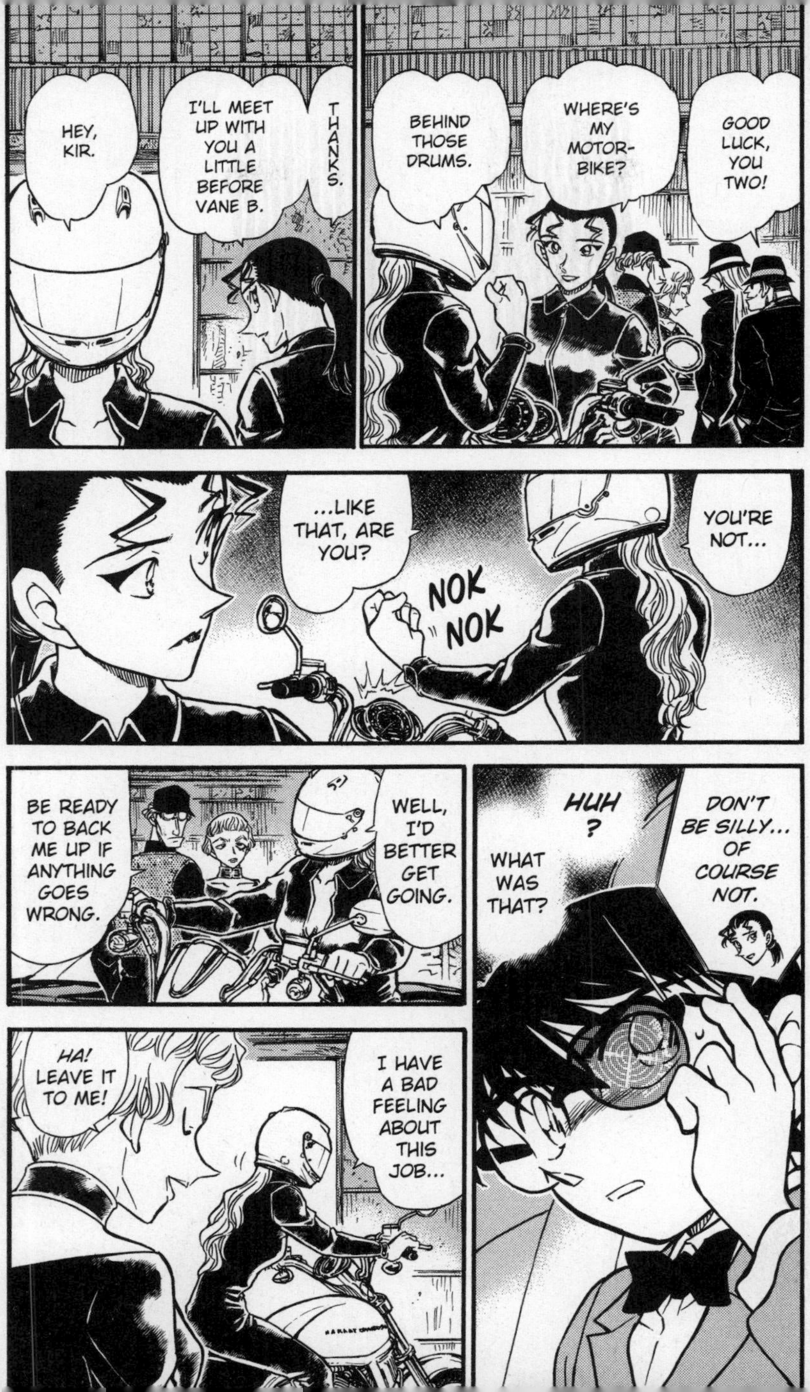
GOOD LUCK, YOU TWO!
WHERE'S MY MOTOR-BIKE?
BEHIND THOSE DRUMS.
THANKS.
I'LL MEET UP WITH YOU A LITTLE BEFORE VANE B.
HEY, KIR.
YOU'RE NOT...
NOK NOK
...LIKE THAT, ARE YOU?
DON'T BE SILLY... OF COURSE NOT.
HUH?
WHAT WAS THAT?
WELL, I'D BETTER GET GOING.
BE READY TO BACK ME UP IF ANYTHING GOES WRONG.
I HAVE A BAD FEELING ABOUT THIS JOB...
HA! LEAVE IT TO ME!

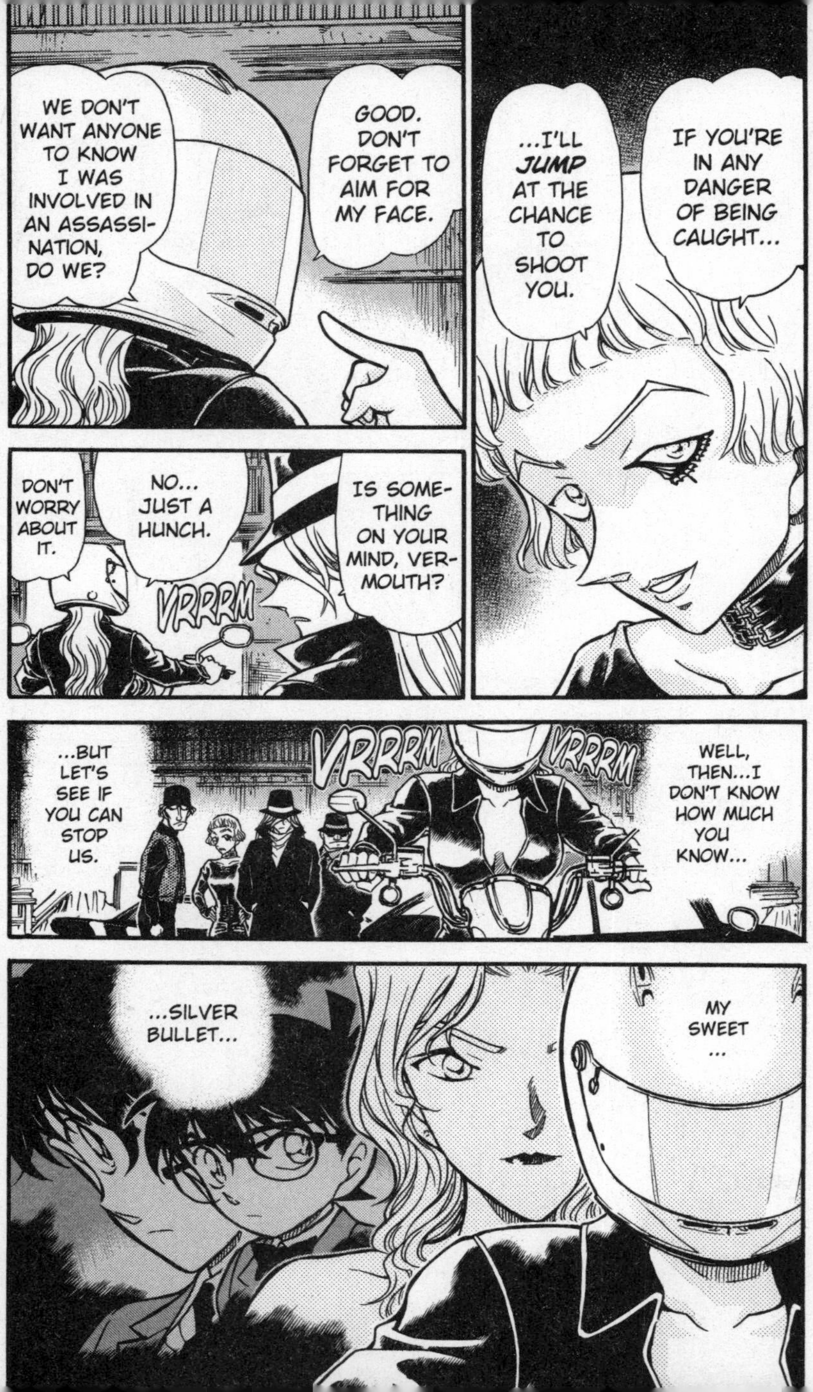
IF YOU'RE IN ANY DANGER OF BEING CAUGHT...
...I'LL JUMP AT THE CHANCE TO SHOOT YOU.
GOOD. DON'T FORGET TO AIM FOR MY FACE.
WE DON'T WANT ANYONE TO KNOW I WAS INVOLVED IN AN ASSASSI-NATION, DO WE?
IS SOME-THING ON YOUR MIND, VER-MOUTH?
VRRRM
NO... JUST A HUNCH.
DON'T WORRY ABOUT IT.
WELL, THEN...I DON'T KNOW HOW MUCH YOU KNOW...
VRRRM
VRRRM
...BUT LET'S SEE IF YOU CAN STOP US.
MY SWEET ...
...SILVER BULLET...

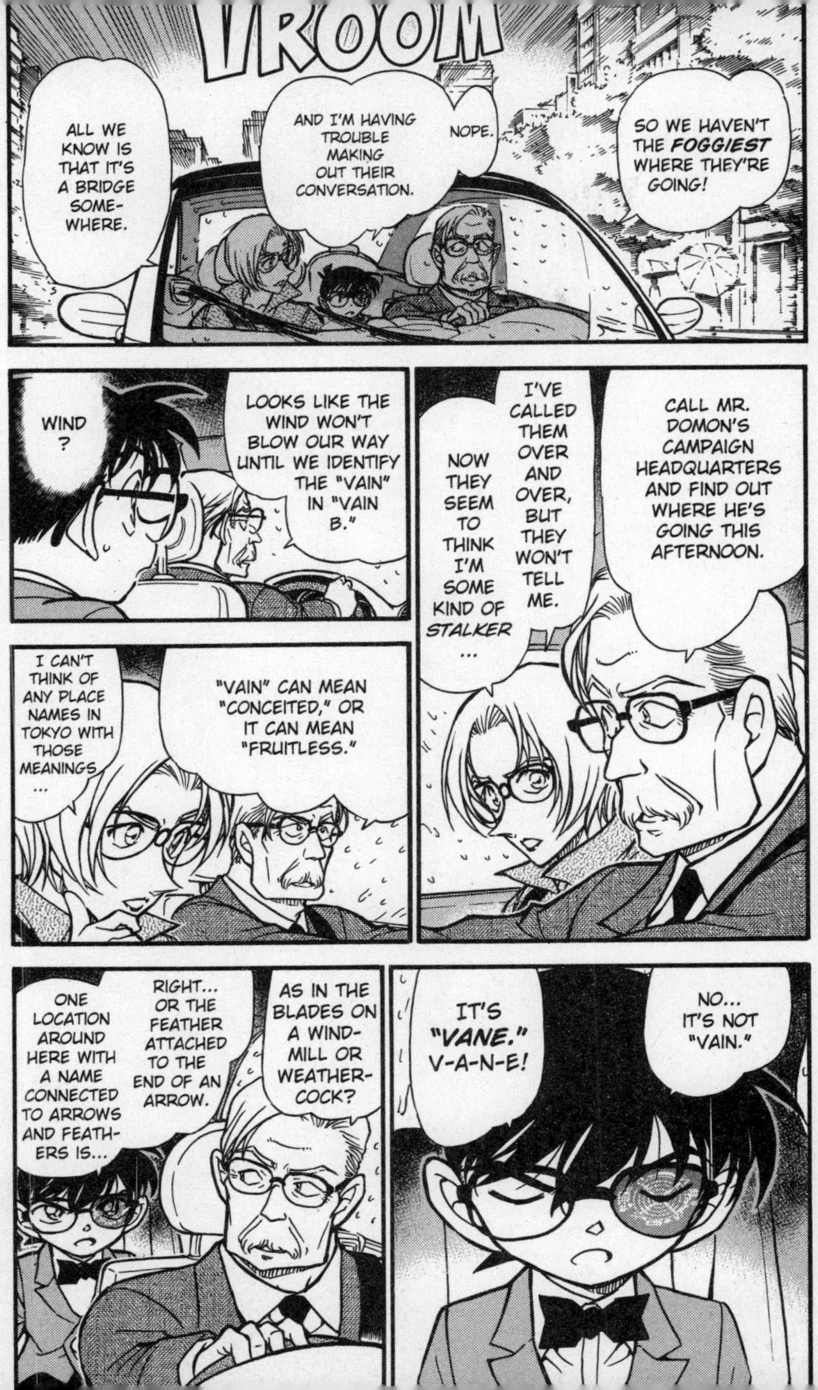
VROOM
SO WE HAVEN'T THE *FOGGIEST* WHERE THEY'RE GOING!
NOPE.
AND I'M HAVING TROUBLE MAKING OUT THEIR CONVERSATION.
ALL WE KNOW IS THAT IT'S A BRIDGE SOME-WHERE.
CALL MR. DOMON'S CAMPAIGN HEADQUARTERS AND FIND OUT WHERE HE'S GOING THIS AFTERNOON.
I'VE CALLED THEM OVER AND OVER, BUT THEY WON'T TELL ME.
NOW THEY SEEM TO THINK I'M SOME KIND OF *STALKER*...
LOOKS LIKE THE WIND WON'T BLOW OUR WAY UNTIL WE IDENTIFY THE "VAIN" IN "VAIN B."
WIND?
"VAIN" CAN MEAN "CONCEITED," OR IT CAN MEAN "FRUITLESS."
I CAN'T THINK OF ANY PLACE NAMES IN TOKYO WITH THOSE MEANINGS...
NO... IT'S NOT "VAIN."
IT'S *"VANE."* V-A-N-E!
AS IN THE BLADES ON A WIND-MILL OR WEATHER-COCK?
RIGHT... OR THE FEATHER ATTACHED TO THE END OF AN ARROW.
ONE LOCATION AROUND HERE WITH A NAME CONNECTED TO ARROWS AND FEATH-ERS IS...

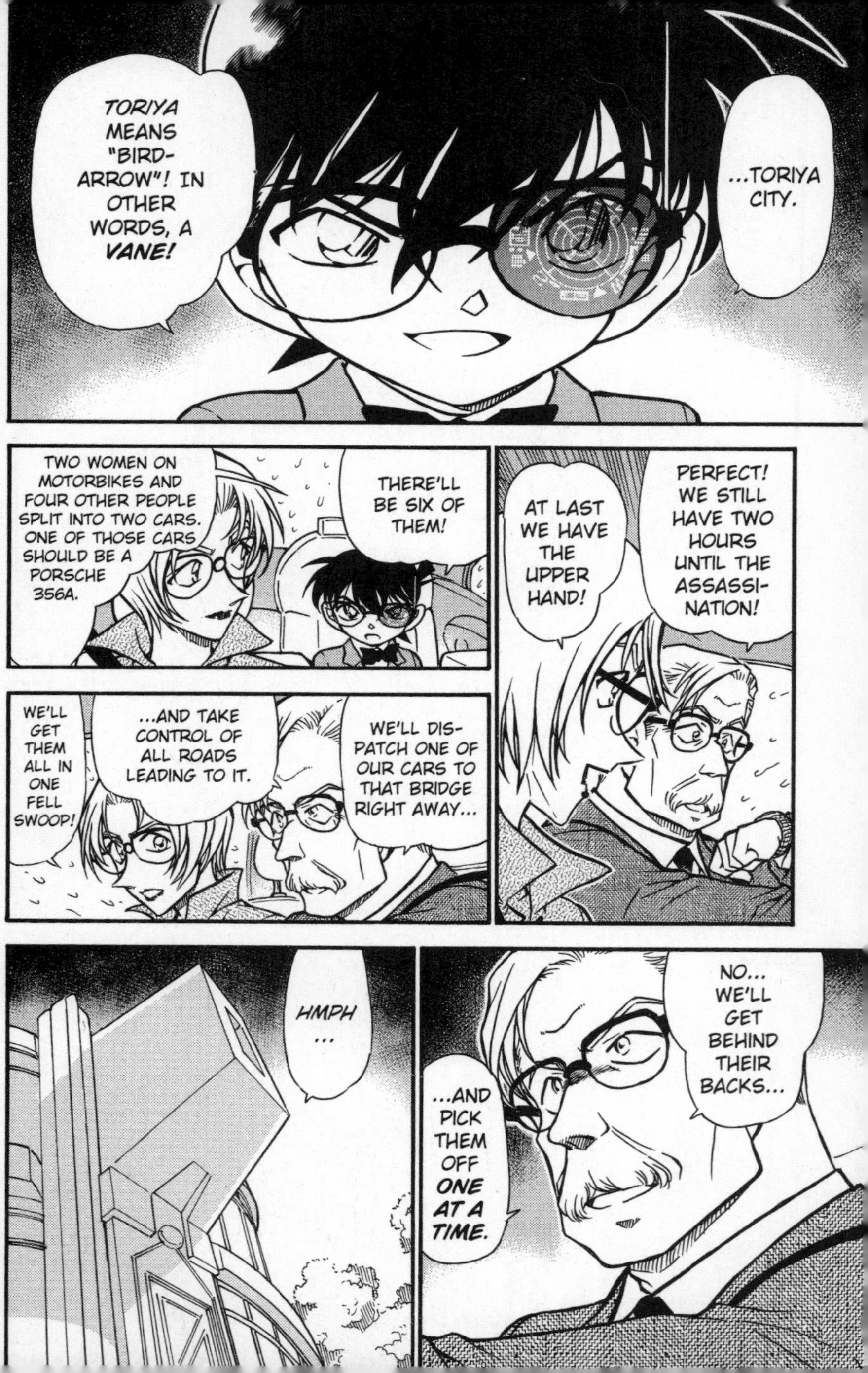
...TORIYA CITY.
TORIYA MEANS "BIRD-ARROW"! IN OTHER WORDS, A VANE!
PERFECT! WE STILL HAVE TWO HOURS UNTIL THE ASSASSINATION!
AT LAST WE HAVE THE UPPER HAND!
THERE'LL BE SIX OF THEM!
TWO WOMEN ON MOTORBIKES AND FOUR OTHER PEOPLE SPLIT INTO TWO CARS. ONE OF THOSE CARS SHOULD BE A PORSCHE 356A.
WE'LL DISPATCH ONE OF OUR CARS TO THAT BRIDGE RIGHT AWAY...
...AND TAKE CONTROL OF ALL ROADS LEADING TO IT.
WE'LL GET THEM ALL IN ONE FELL SWOOP!
NO... WE'LL GET BEHIND THEIR BACKS...
...AND PICK THEM OFF ONE AT A TIME.
HMPH ...

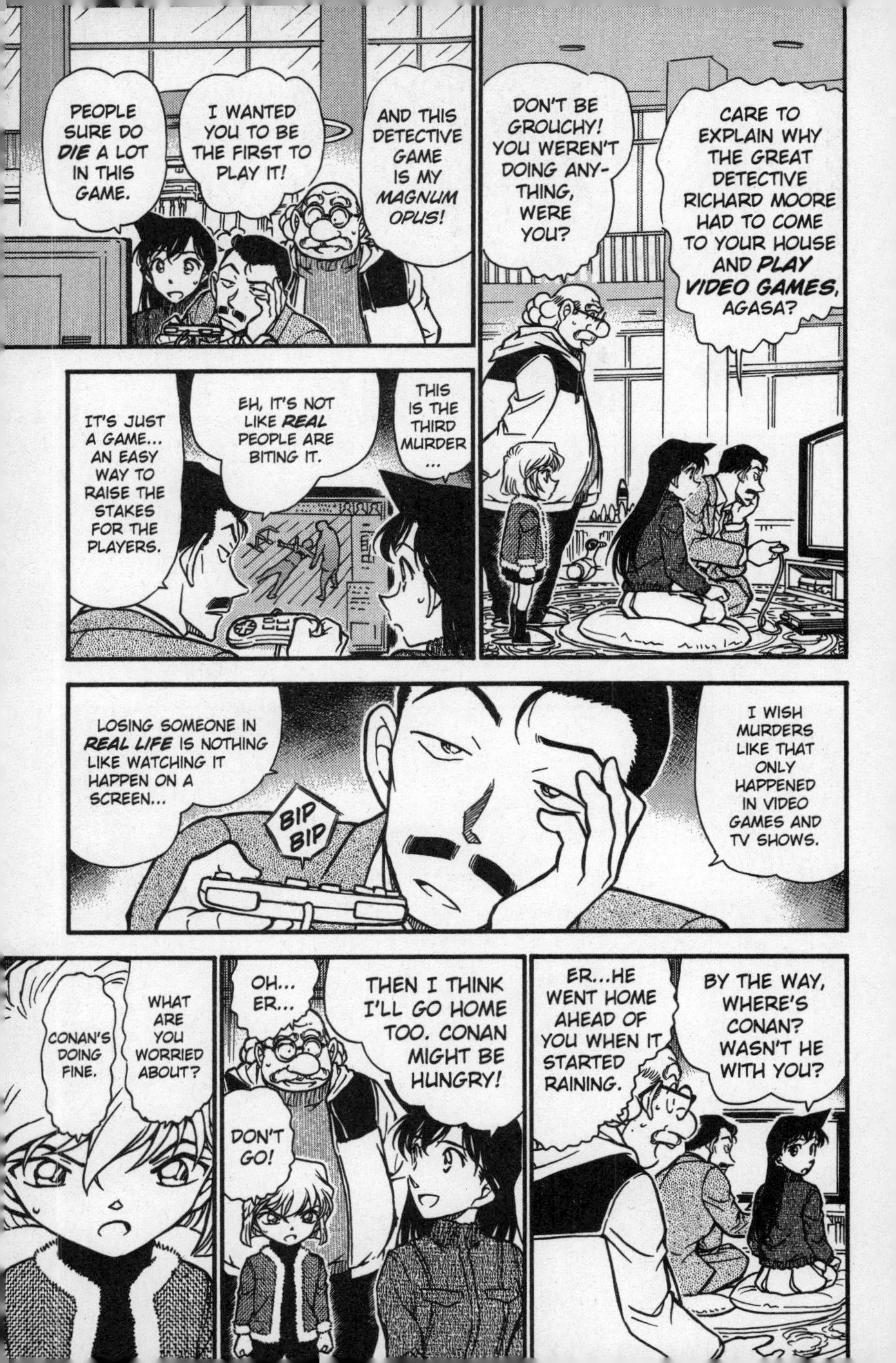
CARE TO EXPLAIN WHY THE GREAT DETECTIVE RICHARD MOORE HAD TO COME TO YOUR HOUSE AND PLAY VIDEO GAMES, AGASA?
DON'T BE GROUCHY! YOU WEREN'T DOING ANY-THING, WERE YOU?
AND THIS DETECTIVE GAME IS MY MAGNUM OPUS!
I WANTED YOU TO BE THE FIRST TO PLAY IT!
PEOPLE SURE DO DIE A LOT IN THIS GAME.
THIS IS THE THIRD MURDER...
EH, IT'S NOT LIKE REAL PEOPLE ARE BITING IT.
IT'S JUST A GAME... AN EASY WAY TO RAISE THE STAKES FOR THE PLAYERS.
I WISH MURDERS LIKE THAT ONLY HAPPENED IN VIDEO GAMES AND TV SHOWS.
BIP BIP
LOSING SOMEONE IN REAL LIFE IS NOTHING LIKE WATCHING IT HAPPEN ON A SCREEN...
BY THE WAY, WHERE'S CONAN? WASN'T HE WITH YOU?
ER...HE WENT HOME AHEAD OF YOU WHEN IT STARTED RAINING.
THEN I THINK I'LL GO HOME TOO. CONAN MIGHT BE HUNGRY!
OH... ER...
DON'T GO!
WHAT ARE YOU WORRIED ABOUT?
CONAN'S DOING FINE.

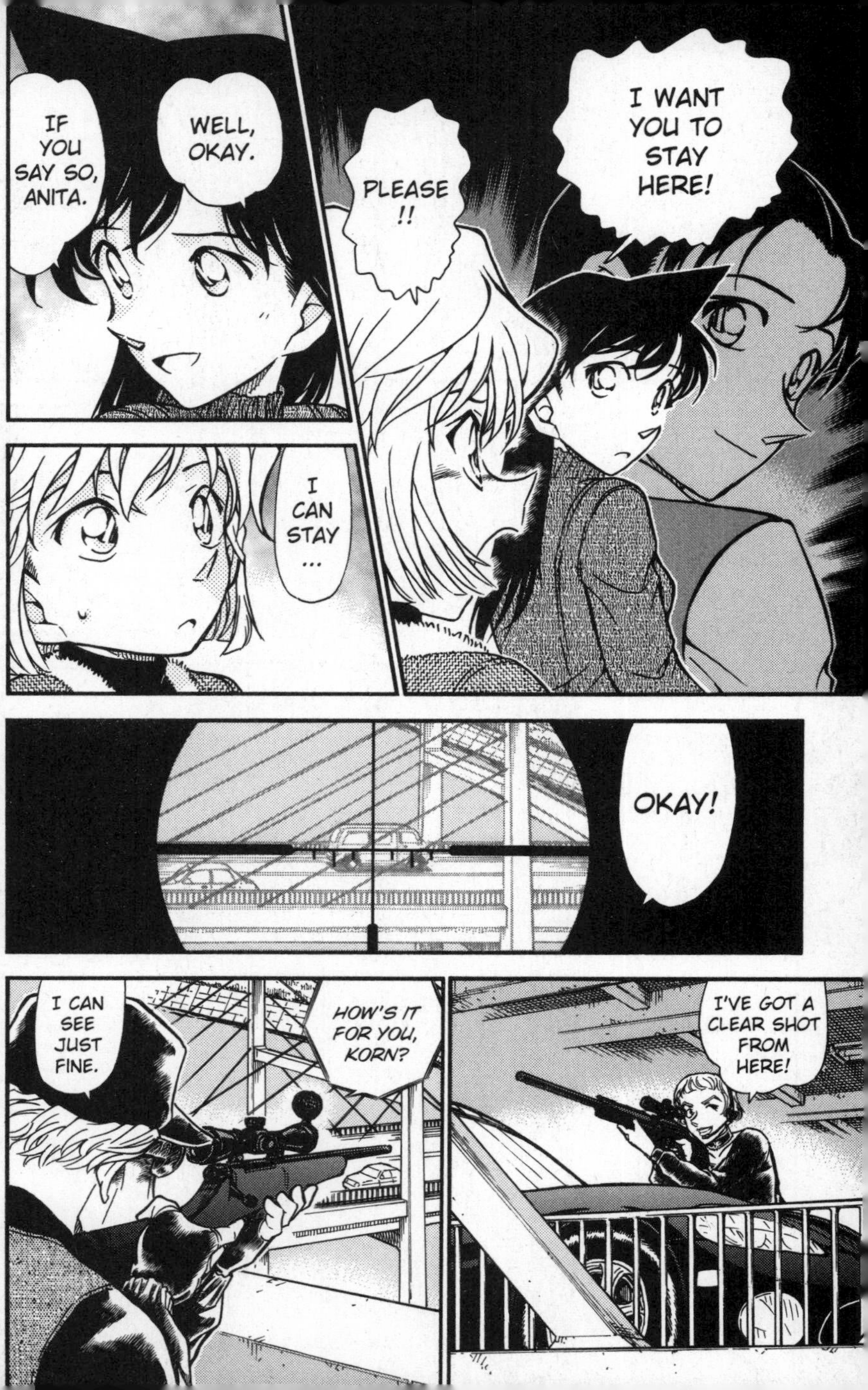
I WANT YOU TO STAY HERE!
PLEASE!!
WELL, OKAY.
IF YOU SAY SO, ANITA.
I CAN STAY...
OKAY!
I'VE GOT A CLEAR SHOT FROM HERE!
HOW'S IT FOR YOU, KORN?
I CAN SEE JUST FINE.

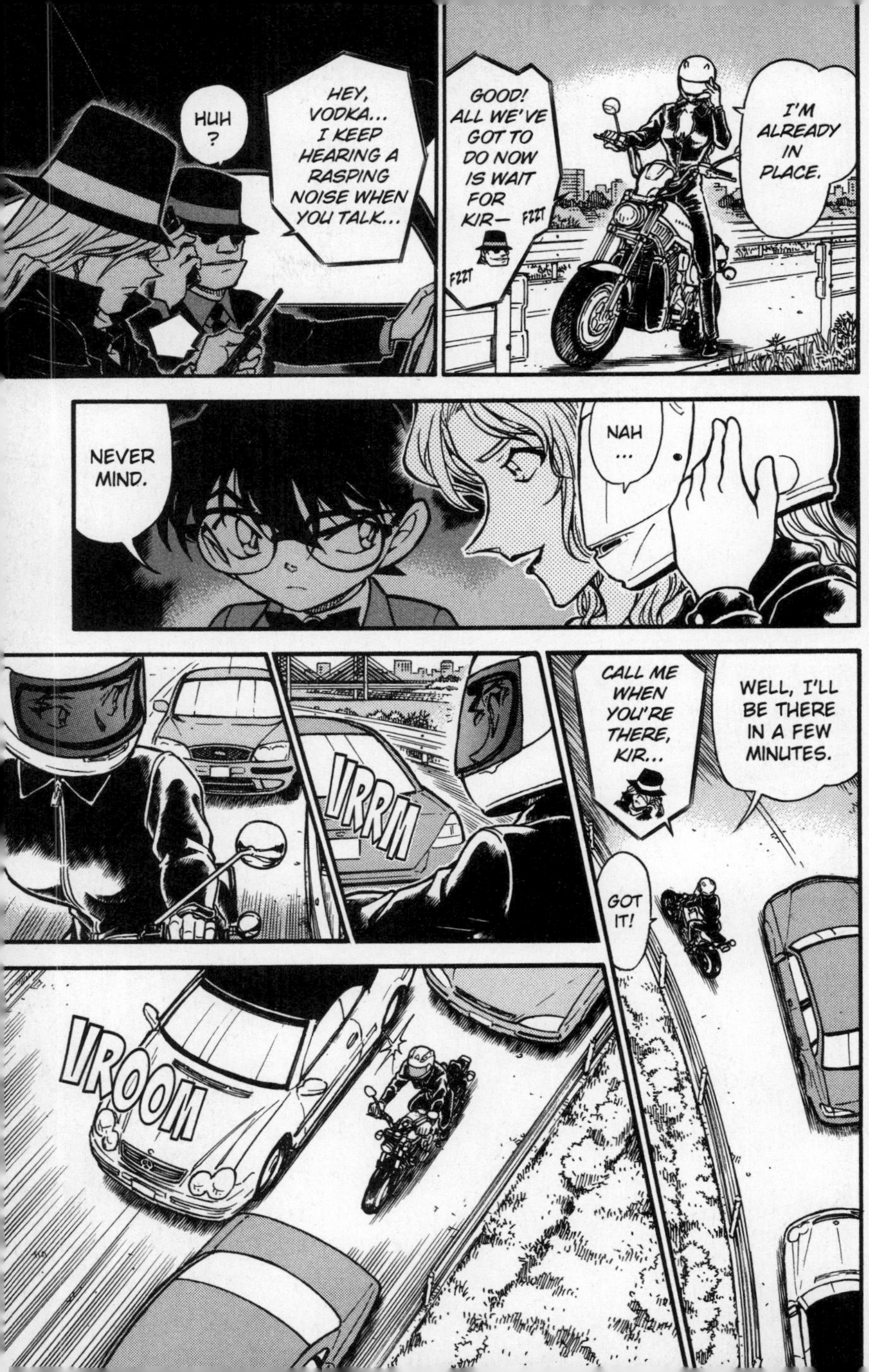
I'M ALREADY IN PLACE.
GOOD! ALL WE'VE GOT TO DO NOW IS WAIT FOR KIR—
FZZT
FZZT
HEY, VODKA... I KEEP HEARING A RASPING NOISE WHEN YOU TALK...
HUH ?
NAH ...
NEVER MIND.
WELL, I'LL BE THERE IN A FEW MINUTES.
CALL ME WHEN YOU'RE THERE, KIR...
GOT IT!
VRRM
VROOM

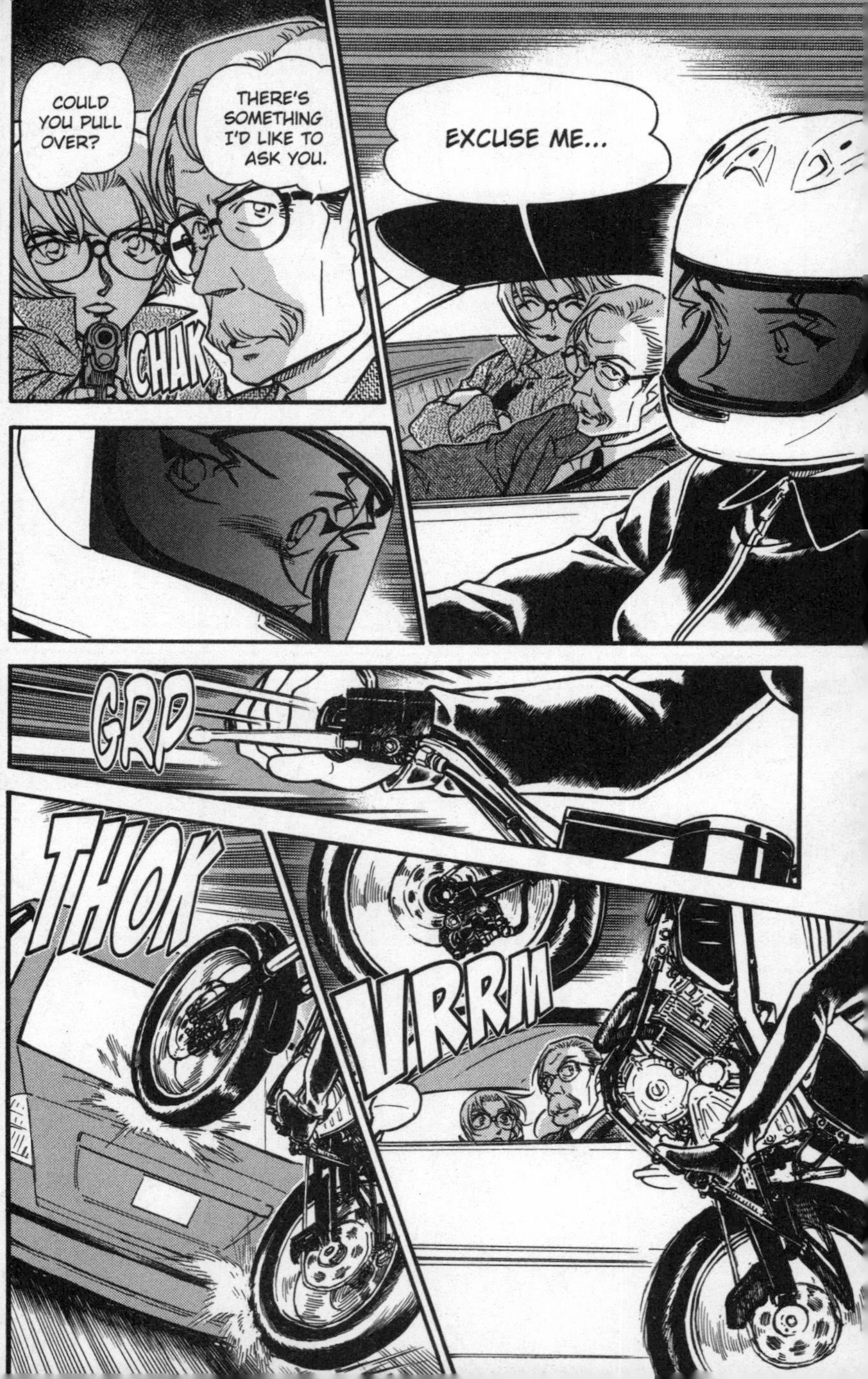
EXCUSE ME...
THERE'S SOMETHING I'D LIKE TO ASK YOU.
COULD YOU PULL OVER?
CHAK
GRP
VRRM
THOK

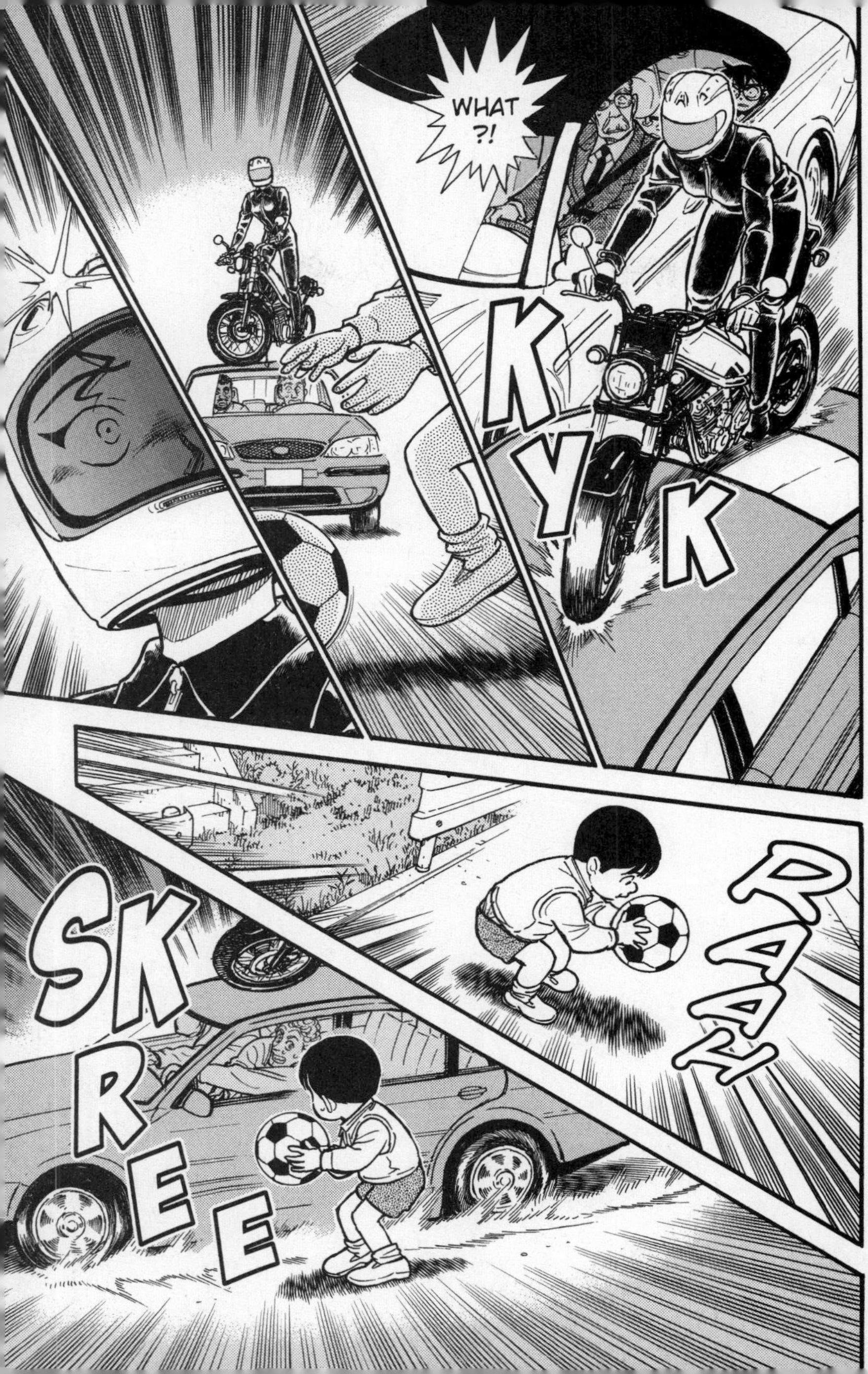
WHAT ?!
KYK
RAAH
SKREEE

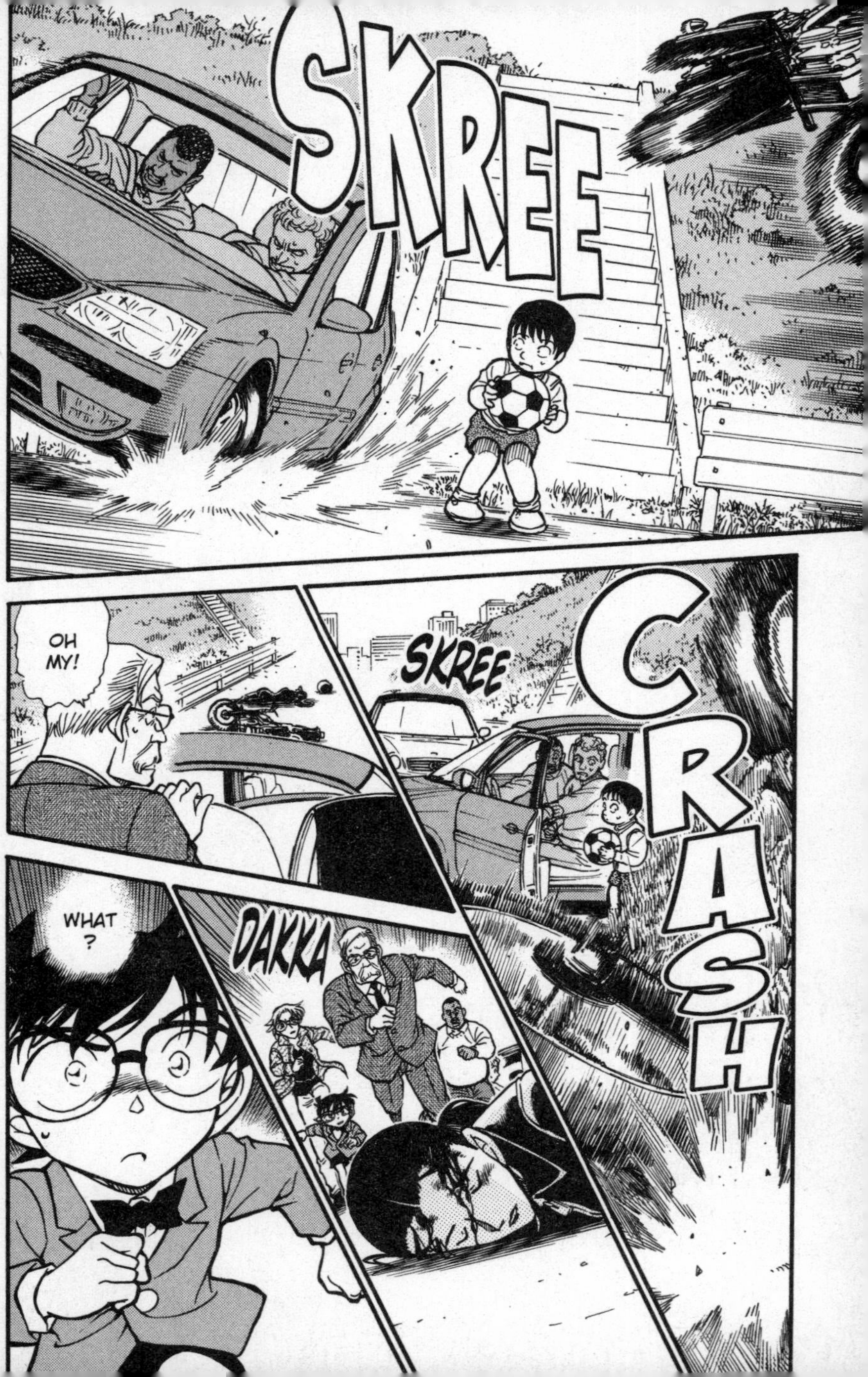
SKREE
SKREE
CRASH
OH MY!
DAKKA
WHAT ?

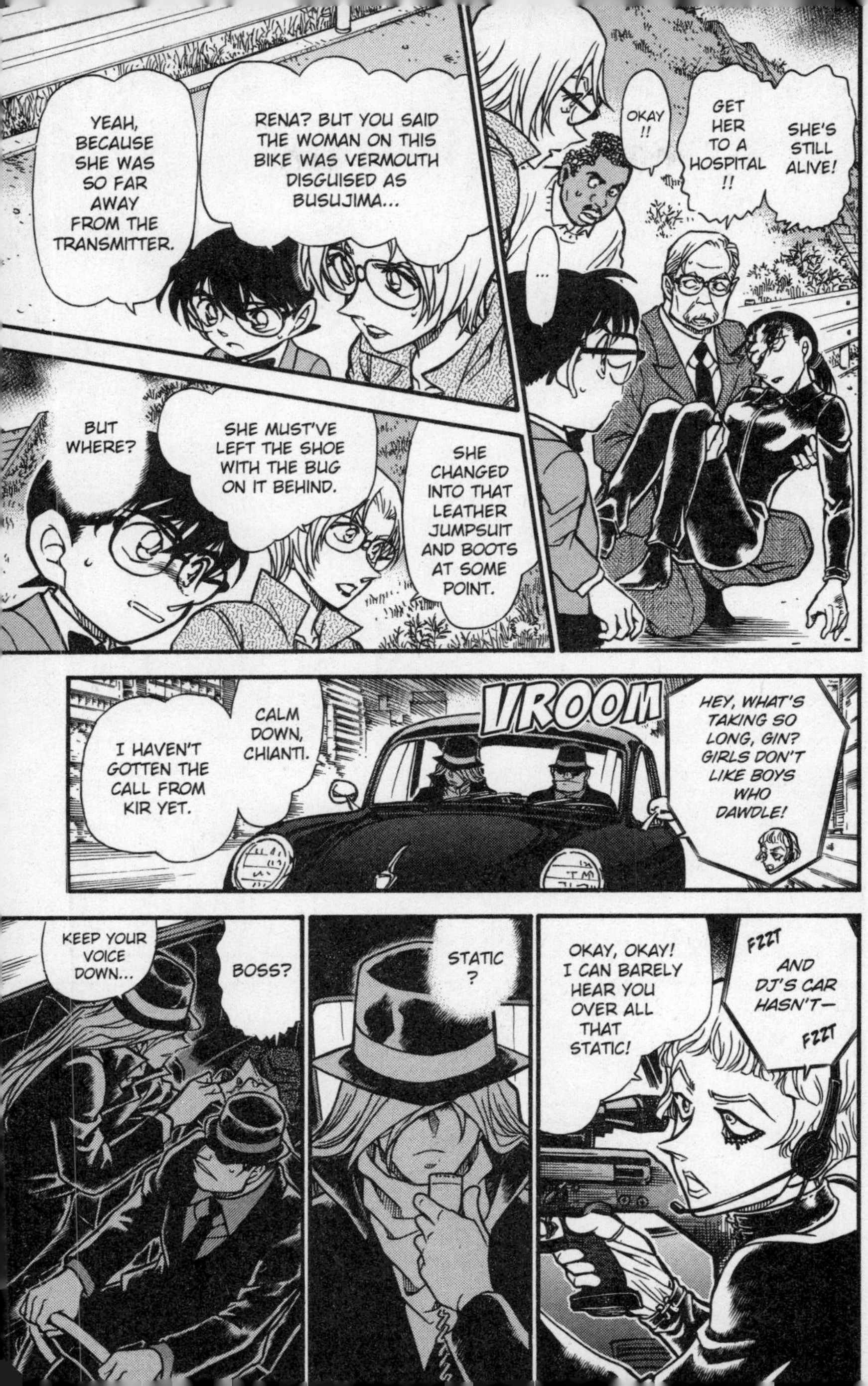
SHE'S STILL ALIVE!
GET HER TO A HOSPITAL !!
OKAY !!
...
RENA? BUT YOU SAID THE WOMAN ON THIS BIKE WAS VERMOUTH DISGUISED AS BUSUJIMA...
YEAH, BECAUSE SHE WAS SO FAR AWAY FROM THE TRANSMITTER.
SHE CHANGED INTO THAT LEATHER JUMPSUIT AND BOOTS AT SOME POINT.
SHE MUST'VE LEFT THE SHOE WITH THE BUG ON IT BEHIND.
BUT WHERE?
HEY, WHAT'S TAKING SO LONG, GIN? GIRLS DON'T LIKE BOYS WHO DAWDLE!
VROOM
CALM DOWN, CHIANTI.
I HAVEN'T GOTTEN THE CALL FROM KIR YET.
FZZT
AND DJ'S CAR HASN'T—
FZZT
OKAY, OKAY! I CAN BARELY HEAR YOU OVER ALL THAT STATIC!
STATIC ?
BOSS?
KEEP YOUR VOICE DOWN...

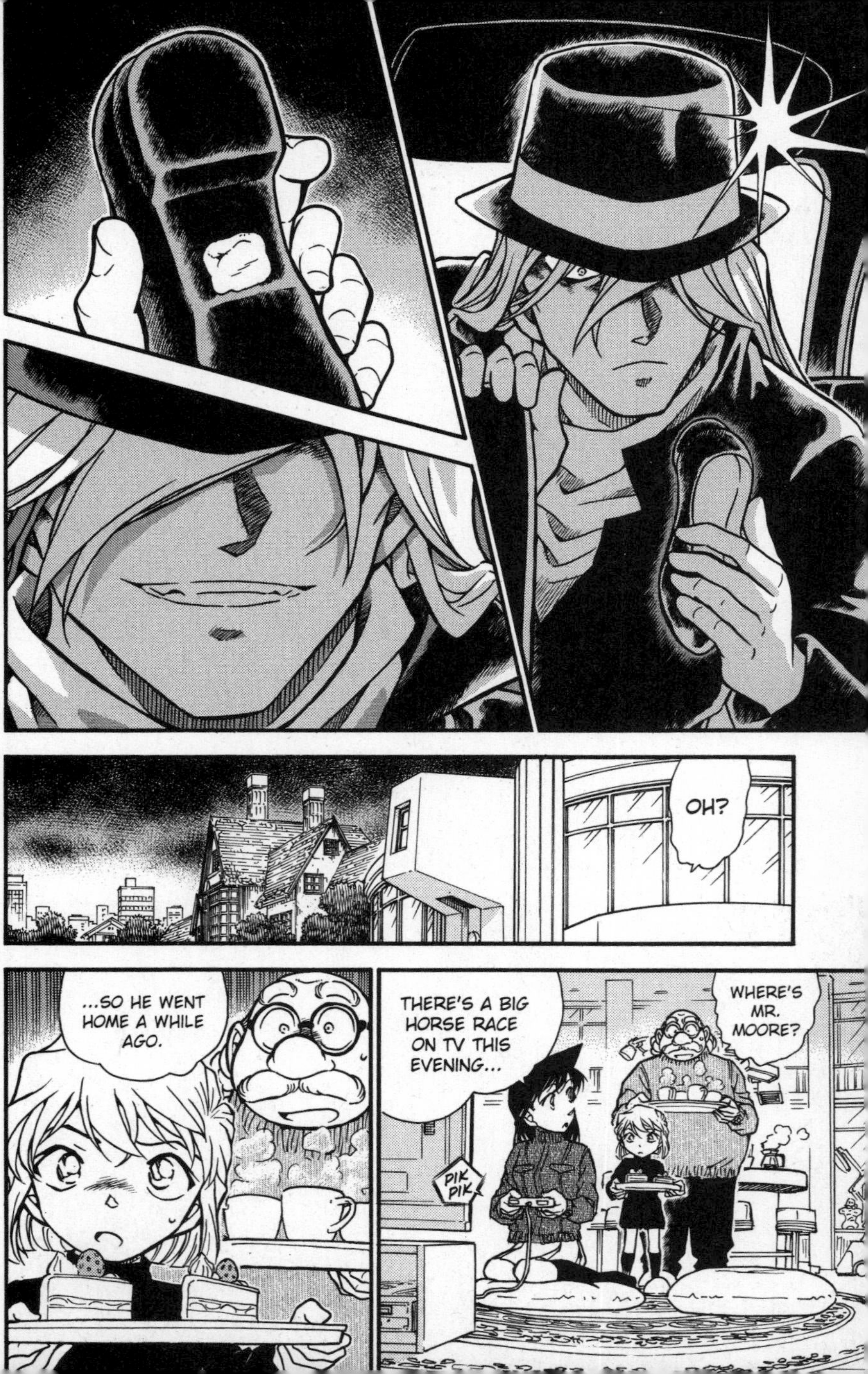
OH?
WHERE'S MR. MOORE?
THERE'S A BIG HORSE RACE ON TV THIS EVENING...
PIK PIK
...SO HE WENT HOME A WHILE AGO.

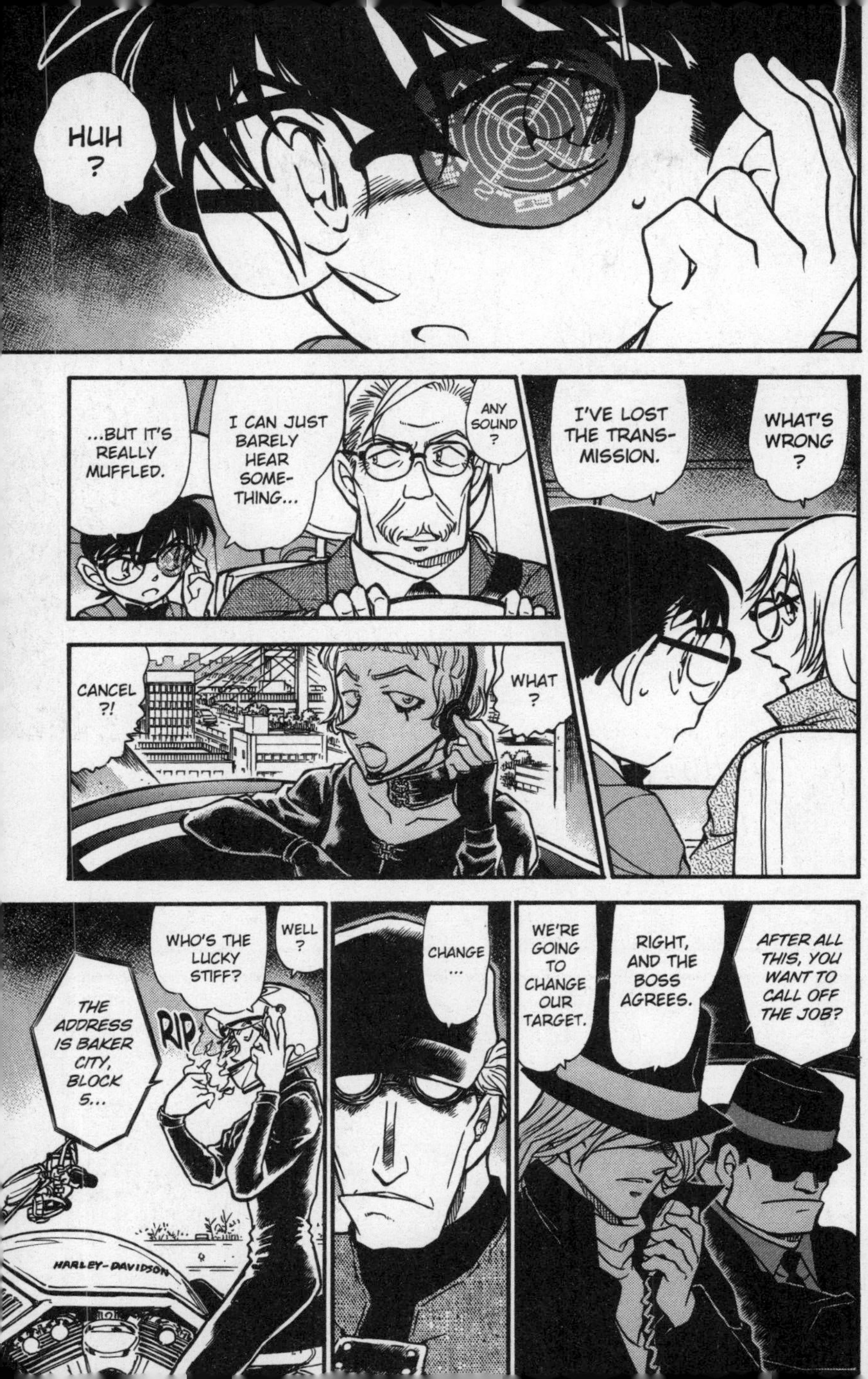
HUH ?
WHAT'S WRONG ?
I'VE LOST THE TRANS- MISSION.
ANY SOUND ?
I CAN JUST BARELY HEAR SOME- THING...
...BUT IT'S REALLY MUFFLED.
WHAT ?
CANCEL ?!
AFTER ALL THIS, YOU WANT TO CALL OFF THE JOB?
RIGHT, AND THE BOSS AGREES.
WE'RE GOING TO CHANGE OUR TARGET.
CHANGE ...
WELL ?
WHO'S THE LUCKY STIFF?
RIP
THE ADDRESS IS BAKER CITY, BLOCK 5...
HARLEY-DAVIDSON

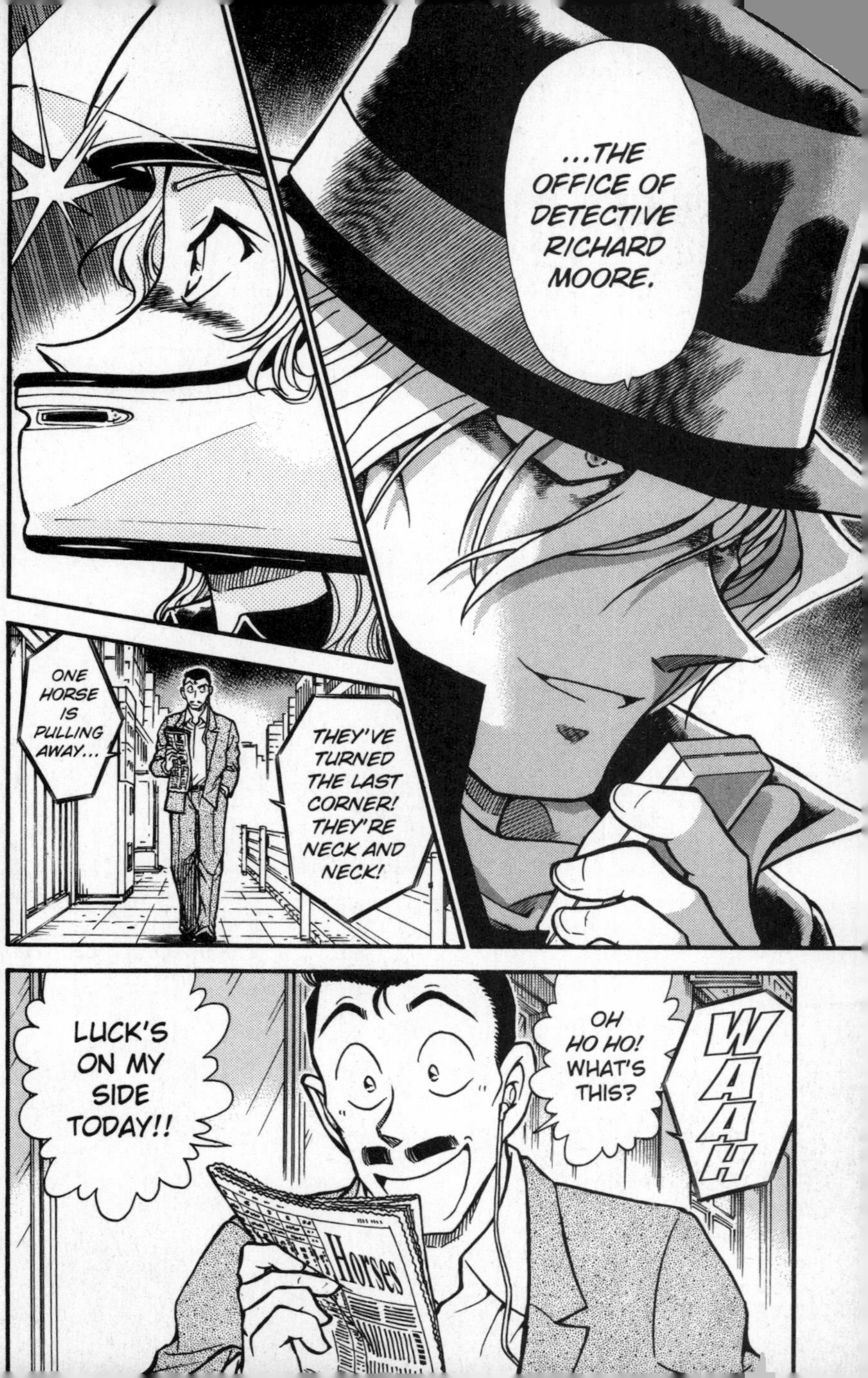
...THE OFFICE OF DETECTIVE RICHARD MOORE.
THEY'VE TURNED THE LAST CORNER! THEY'RE NECK AND NECK!
ONE HORSE IS PULLING AWAY...
WAAAH
OH HO HO! WHAT'S THIS?
LUCK'S ON MY SIDE TODAY!!
Horses

FILE 4: MEN IN BLACK VS. FBI ②

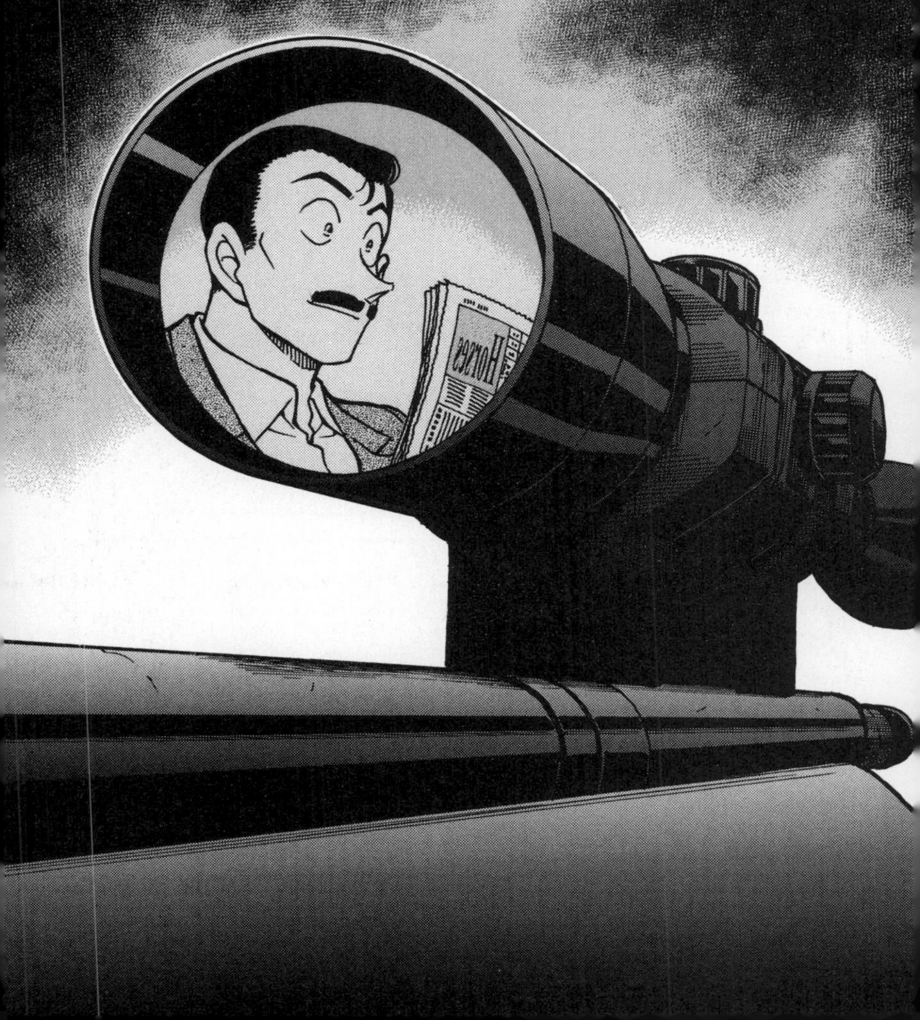

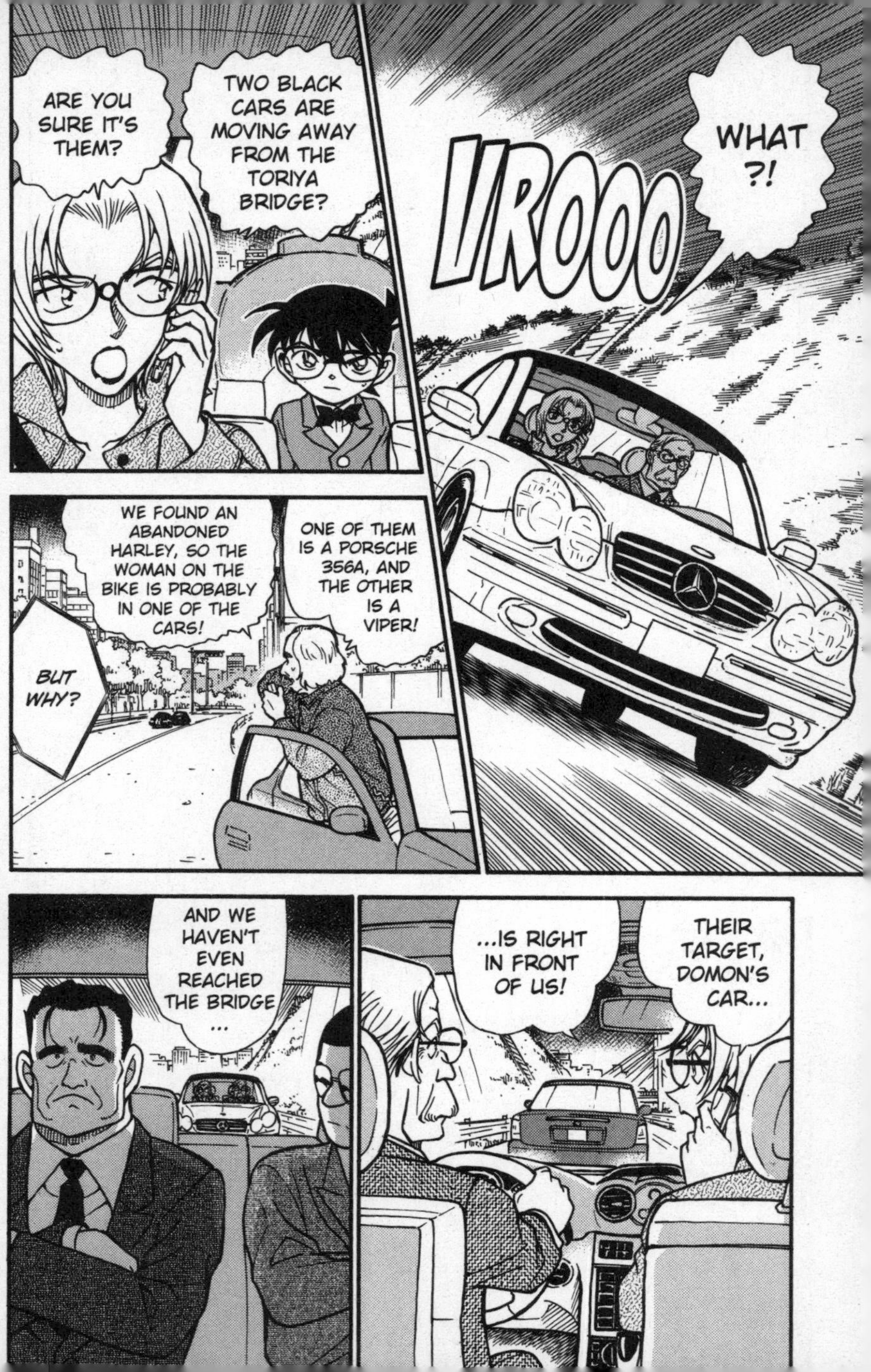
VROOO
WHAT ?!
TWO BLACK CARS ARE MOVING AWAY FROM THE TORIYA BRIDGE?
ARE YOU SURE IT'S THEM?
ONE OF THEM IS A PORSCHE 356A, AND THE OTHER IS A VIPER!
WE FOUND AN ABANDONED HARLEY, SO THE WOMAN ON THE BIKE IS PROBABLY IN ONE OF THE CARS!
BUT WHY?
THEIR TARGET, DOMON'S CAR...
...IS RIGHT IN FRONT OF US!
AND WE HAVEN'T EVEN REACHED THE BRIDGE ...

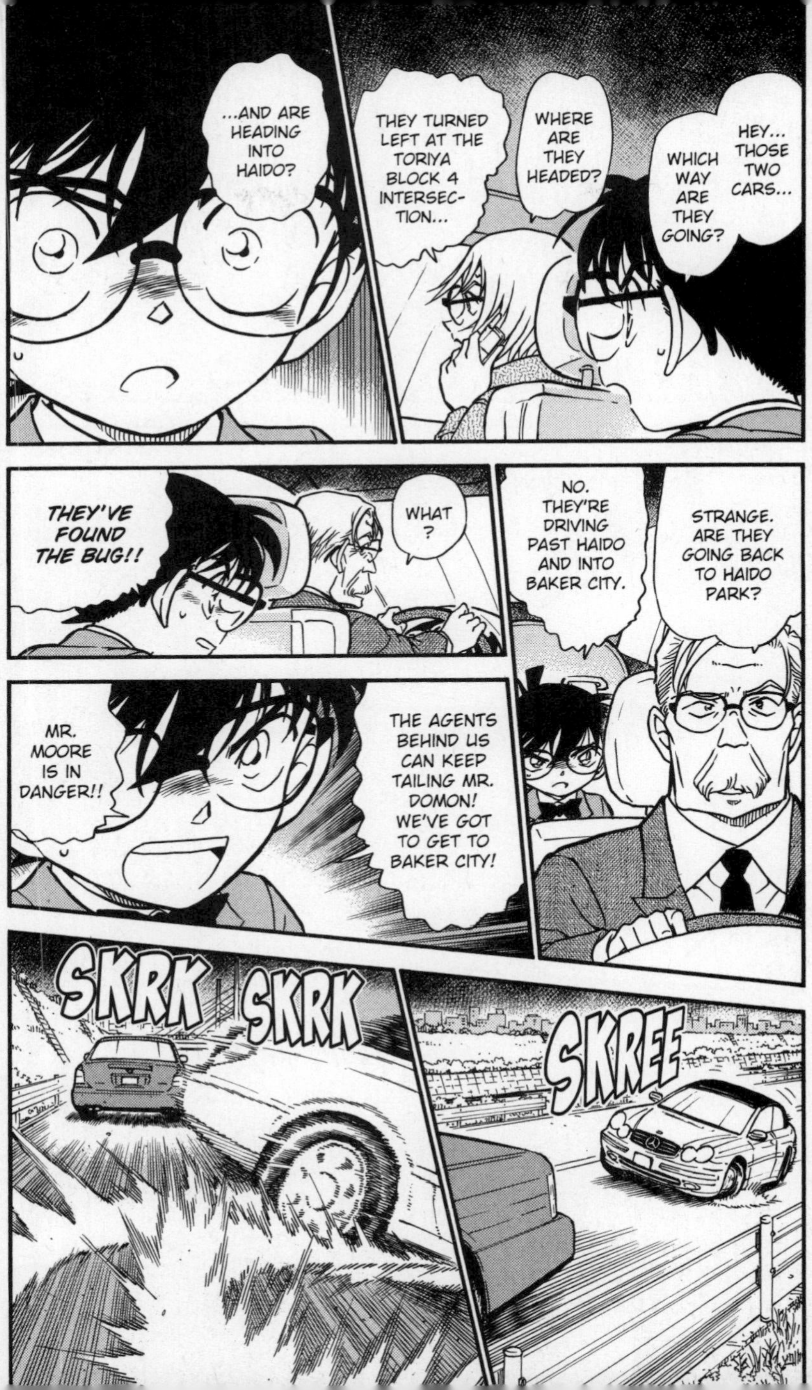
HEY... THOSE TWO CARS...
WHICH WAY ARE THEY GOING?
WHERE ARE THEY HEADED?
THEY TURNED LEFT AT THE TORIYA BLOCK 4 INTERSEC-TION...
...AND ARE HEADING INTO HAIDO?
STRANGE. ARE THEY GOING BACK TO HAIDO PARK?
NO. THEY'RE DRIVING PAST HAIDO AND INTO BAKER CITY.
WHAT?
THEY'VE FOUND THE BUG!!
THE AGENTS BEHIND US CAN KEEP TAILING MR. DOMON! WE'VE GOT TO GET TO BAKER CITY!
MR. MOORE IS IN DANGER!!
SKREE
SKRK SKRK

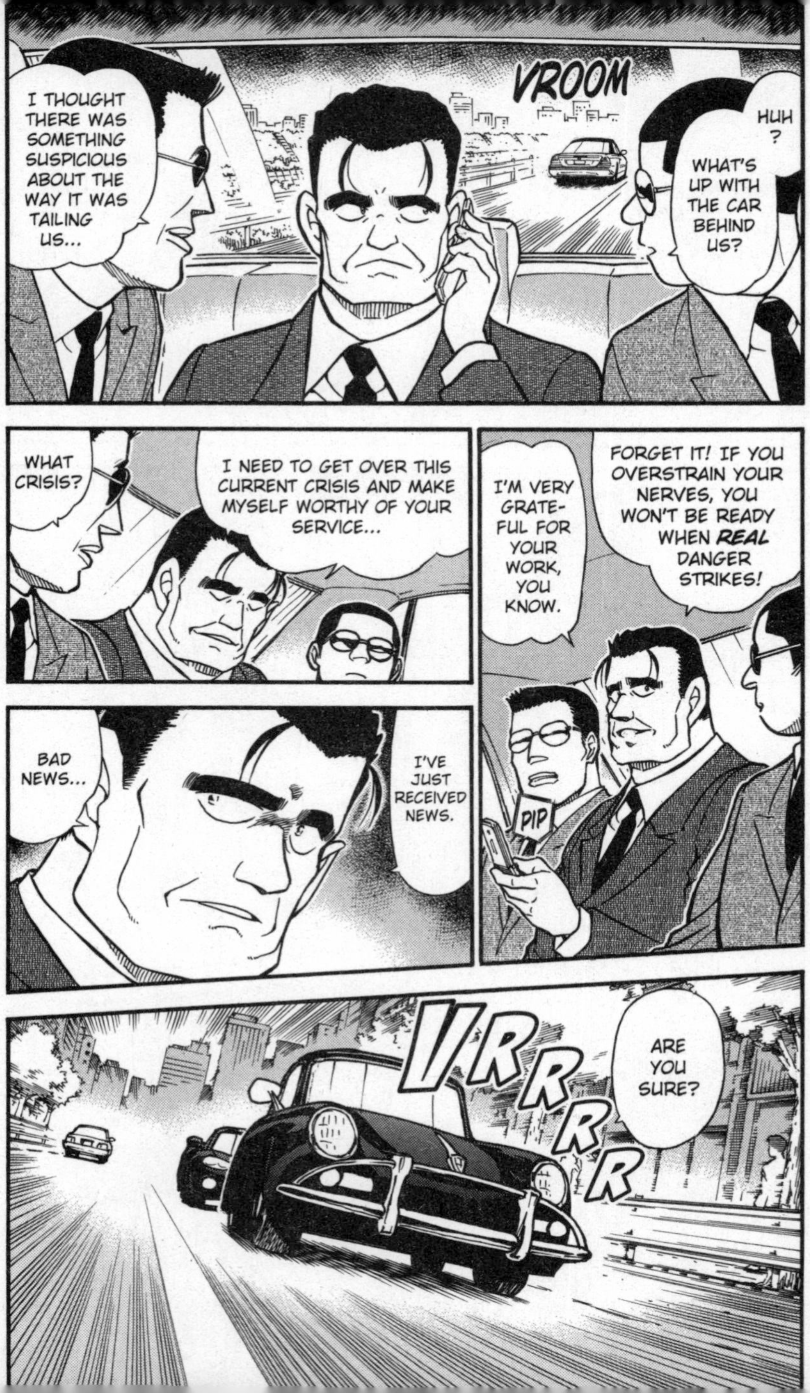

HUH ?
WHAT'S UP WITH THE CAR BEHIND US?
VROOM
I THOUGHT THERE WAS SOMETHING SUSPICIOUS ABOUT THE WAY IT WAS TAILING US...
FORGET IT! IF YOU OVERSTRAIN YOUR NERVES, YOU WON'T BE READY WHEN *REAL* DANGER STRIKES!
I'M VERY GRATEFUL FOR YOUR WORK, YOU KNOW.
PIP
I NEED TO GET OVER THIS CURRENT CRISIS AND MAKE MYSELF WORTHY OF YOUR SERVICE...
WHAT CRISIS?
I'VE JUST RECEIVED NEWS.
BAD NEWS...
ARE YOU SURE?
VRRRRR

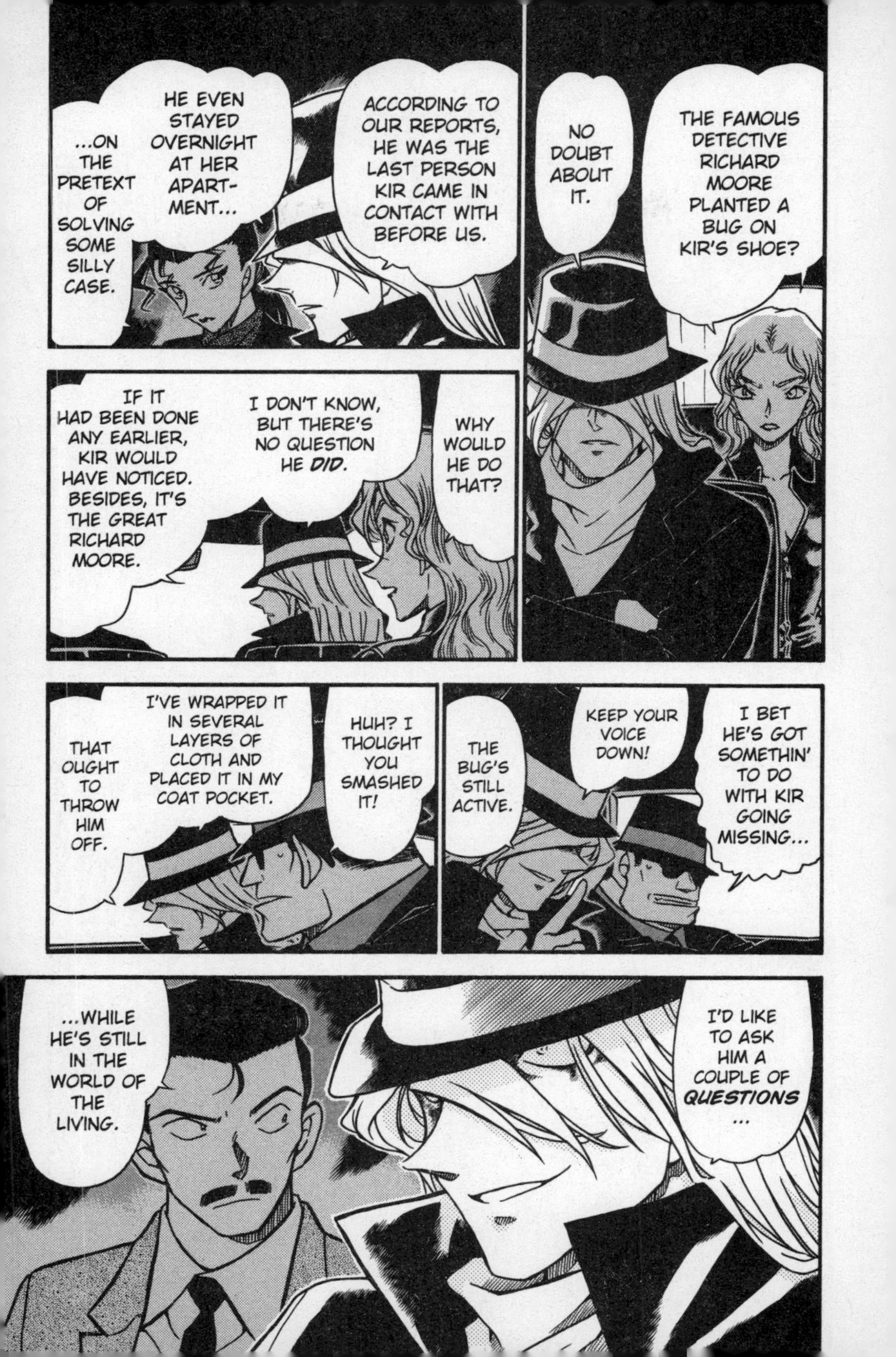
THE FAMOUS DETECTIVE RICHARD MOORE PLANTED A BUG ON KIR'S SHOE?
NO DOUBT ABOUT IT.
ACCORDING TO OUR REPORTS, HE WAS THE LAST PERSON KIR CAME IN CONTACT WITH BEFORE US.
HE EVEN STAYED OVERNIGHT AT HER APARTMENT...
...ON THE PRETEXT OF SOLVING SOME SILLY CASE.
WHY WOULD HE DO THAT?
I DON'T KNOW, BUT THERE'S NO QUESTION HE *DID*.
IF IT HAD BEEN DONE ANY EARLIER, KIR WOULD HAVE NOTICED. BESIDES, IT'S THE GREAT RICHARD MOORE.
I BET HE'S GOT SOMETHIN' TO DO WITH KIR GOING MISSING...
KEEP YOUR VOICE DOWN!
THE BUG'S STILL ACTIVE.
HUH? I THOUGHT YOU SMASHED IT!
I'VE WRAPPED IT IN SEVERAL LAYERS OF CLOTH AND PLACED IT IN MY COAT POCKET.
THAT OUGHT TO THROW HIM OFF.
I'D LIKE TO ASK HIM A COUPLE OF **QUESTIONS** ...
...WHILE HE'S STILL IN THE WORLD OF THE LIVING.

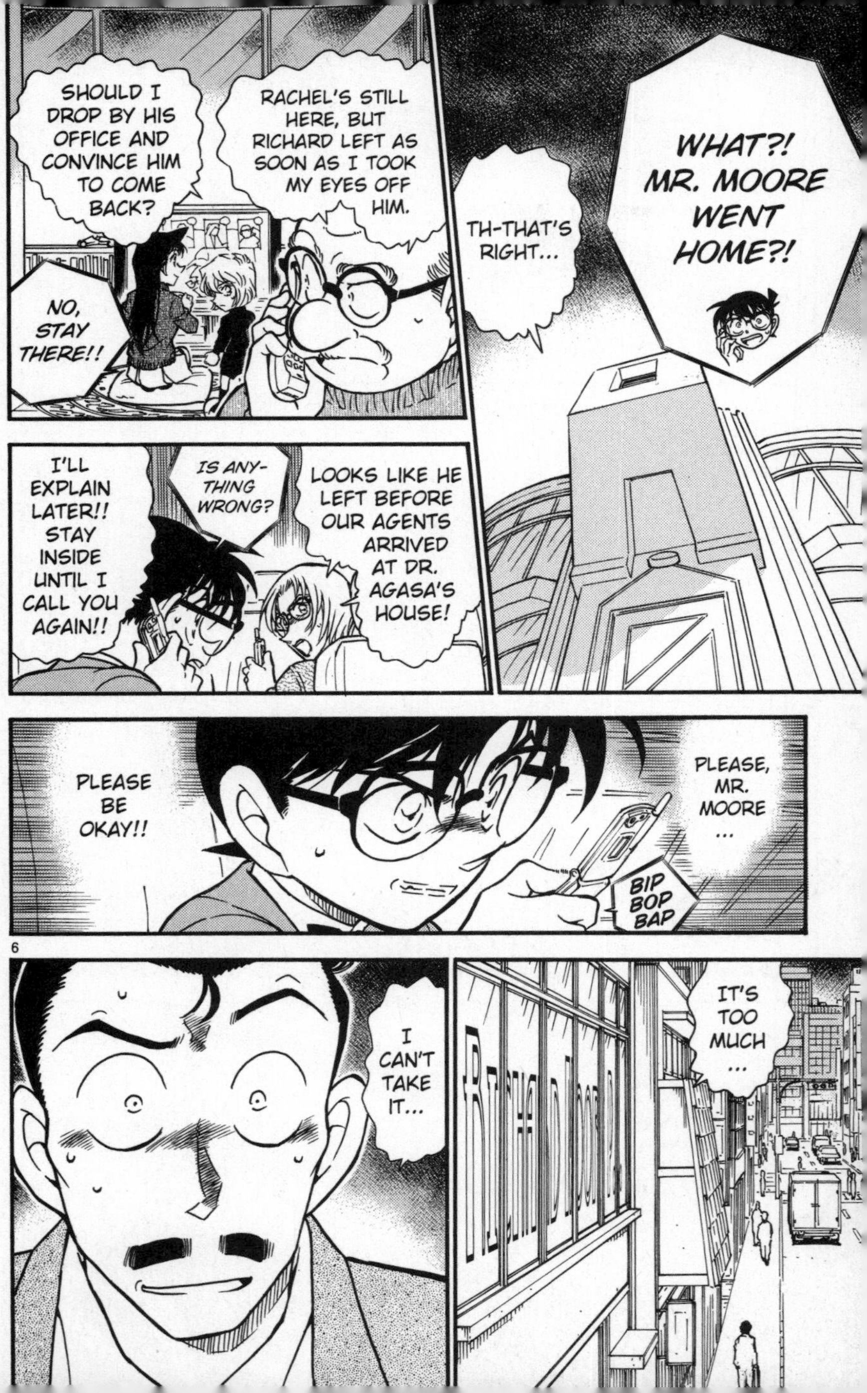
WHAT?! MR. MOORE WENT HOME?!
TH-THAT'S RIGHT...
RACHEL'S STILL HERE, BUT RICHARD LEFT AS SOON AS I TOOK MY EYES OFF HIM.
SHOULD I DROP BY HIS OFFICE AND CONVINCE HIM TO COME BACK?
NO, STAY THERE!!
LOOKS LIKE HE LEFT BEFORE OUR AGENTS ARRIVED AT DR. AGASA'S HOUSE!
IS ANYTHING WRONG?
I'LL EXPLAIN LATER!! STAY INSIDE UNTIL I CALL YOU AGAIN!!
PLEASE, MR. MOORE ...
BIP BOP BAP
PLEASE BE OKAY!!
IT'S TOO MUCH ...
I CAN'T TAKE IT...

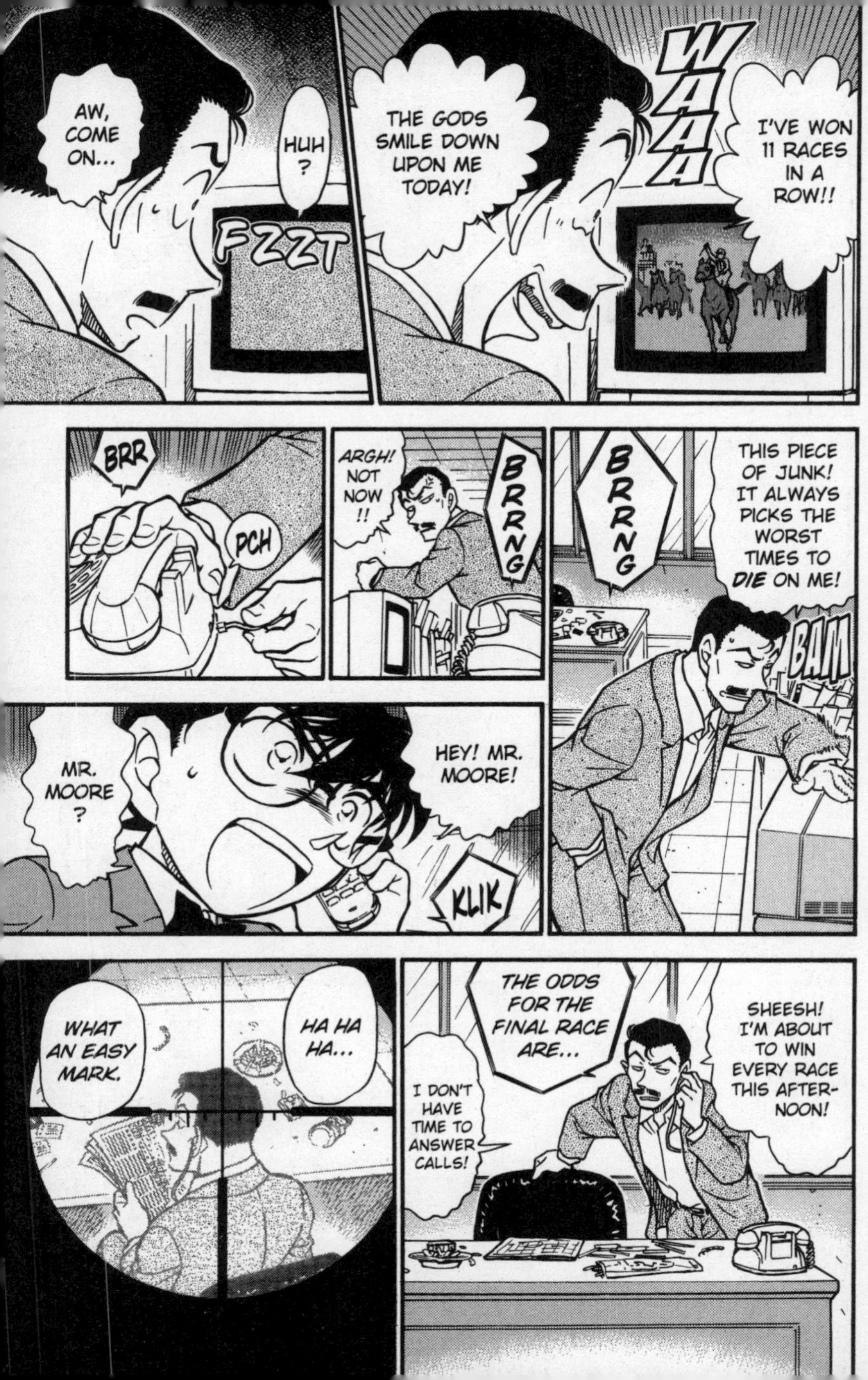
WAAA
I'VE WON 11 RACES IN A ROW!!
THE GODS SMILE DOWN UPON ME TODAY!
HUH?
FZZT
AW, COME ON...
THIS PIECE OF JUNK! IT ALWAYS PICKS THE WORST TIMES TO *DIE* ON ME!
BRRNG
BAM
BRRNG
ARGH! NOT NOW!!
BRR
PCH
HEY! MR. MOORE!
KLIK
MR. MOORE?
SHEESH! I'M ABOUT TO WIN EVERY RACE THIS AFTERNOON!
THE ODDS FOR THE FINAL RACE ARE...
I DON'T HAVE TIME TO ANSWER CALLS!
HA HA HA...
WHAT AN EASY MARK.

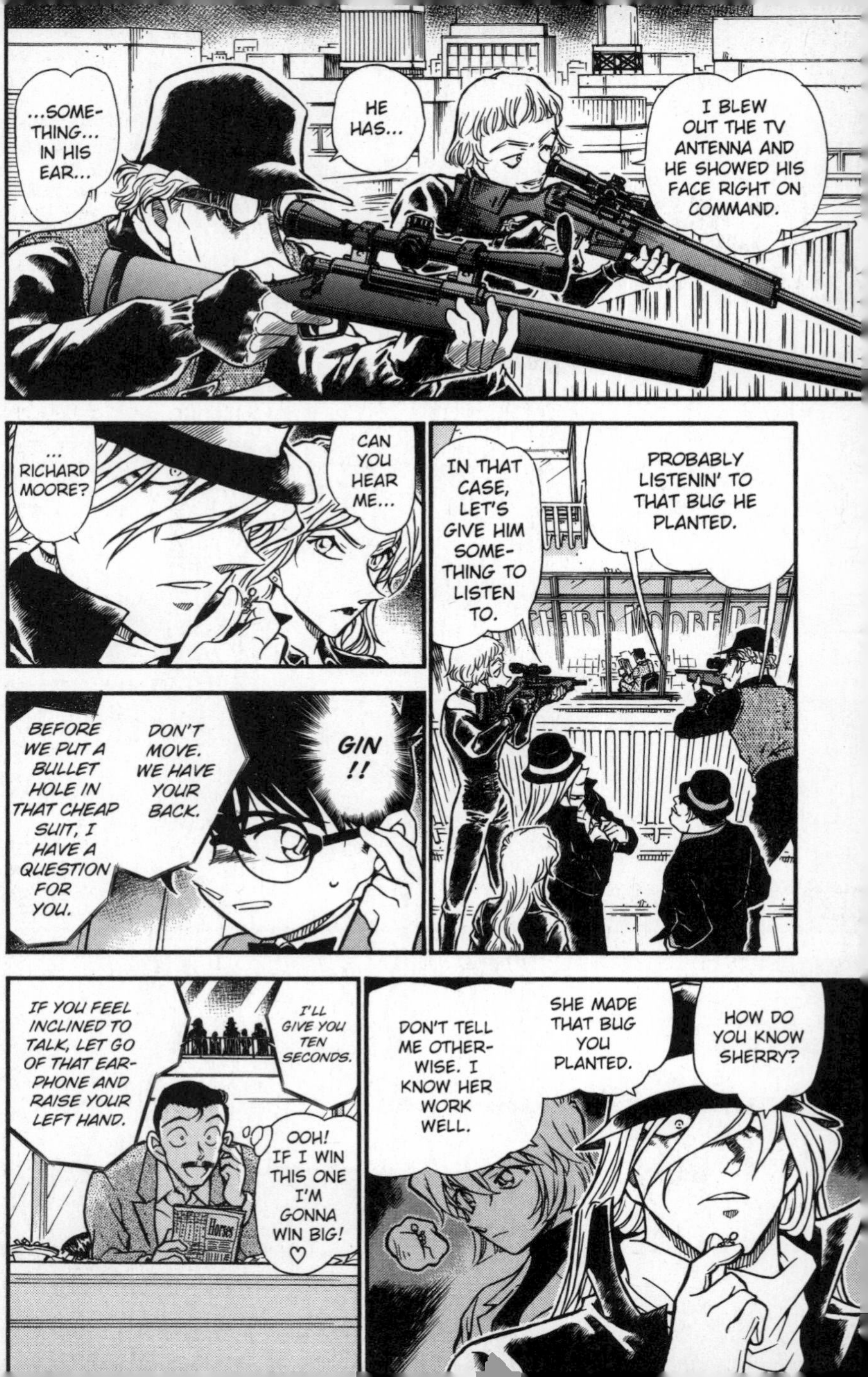
I BLEW OUT THE TV ANTENNA AND HE SHOWED HIS FACE RIGHT ON COMMAND.
HE HAS...
...SOME-THING... IN HIS EAR...
PROBABLY LISTENIN' TO THAT BUG HE PLANTED.
IN THAT CASE, LET'S GIVE HIM SOME-THING TO LISTEN TO.
CAN YOU HEAR ME...
... RICHARD MOORE?
GIN!!
DON'T MOVE. WE HAVE YOUR BACK.
BEFORE WE PUT A BULLET HOLE IN THAT CHEAP SUIT, I HAVE A QUESTION FOR YOU.
HOW DO YOU KNOW SHERRY?
SHE MADE THAT BUG YOU PLANTED.
DON'T TELL ME OTHER-WISE. I KNOW HER WORK WELL.
I'LL GIVE YOU TEN SECONDS.
IF YOU FEEL INCLINED TO TALK, LET GO OF THAT EAR-PHONE AND RAISE YOUR LEFT HAND.
OOH! IF I WIN THIS ONE I'M GONNA WIN BIG! ♡
Horses

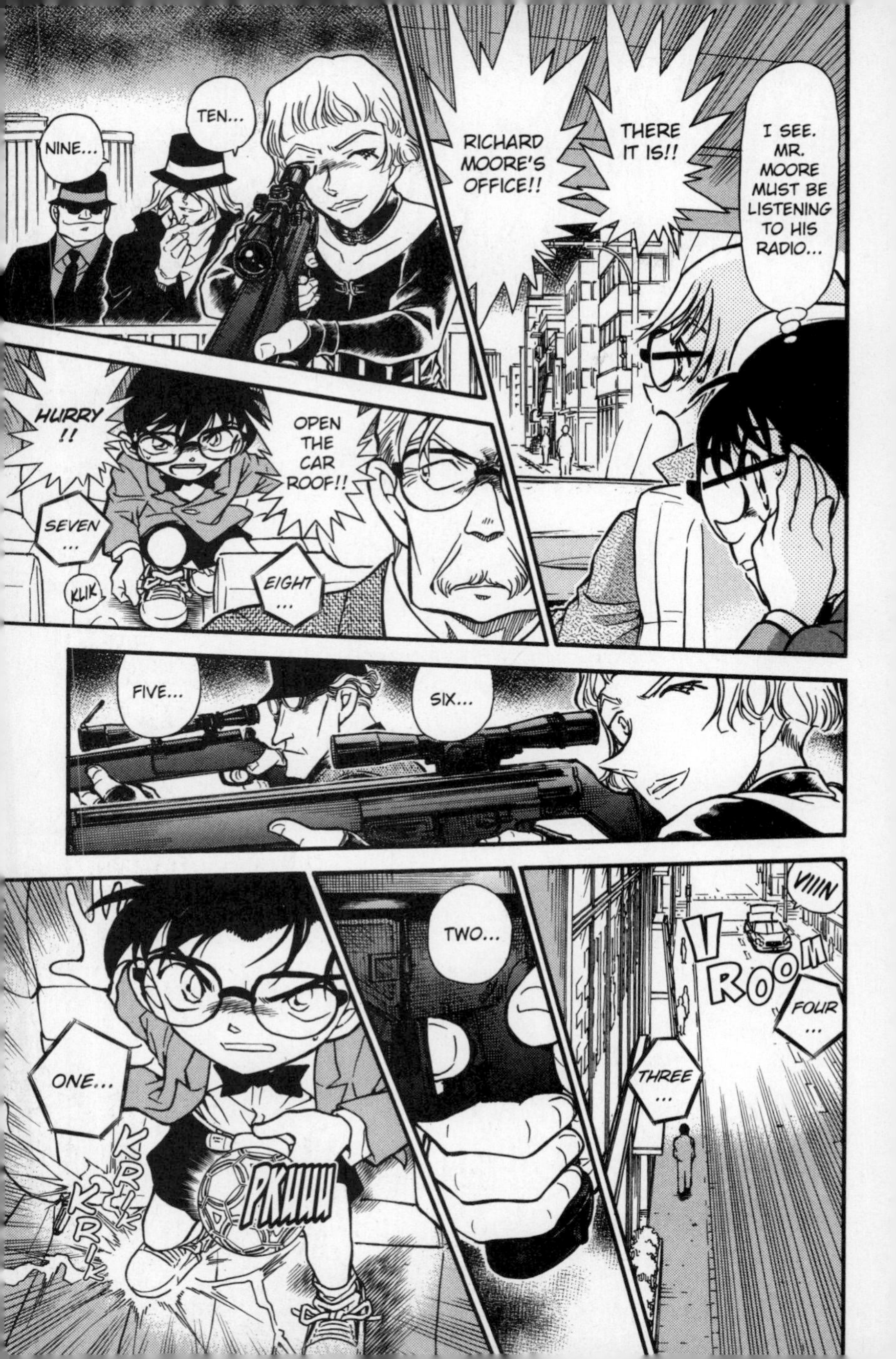
I SEE. MR. MOORE MUST BE LISTENING TO HIS RADIO...
THERE IT IS!!
RICHARD MOORE'S OFFICE!!
TEN...
NINE...
OPEN THE CAR ROOF!!
EIGHT...
HURRY!!
SEVEN...
KLIK
SIX...
FIVE...
VIIIN
VROOM
FOUR...
THREE...
TWO...
ONE...
KRIK
KRIK
PKUUU

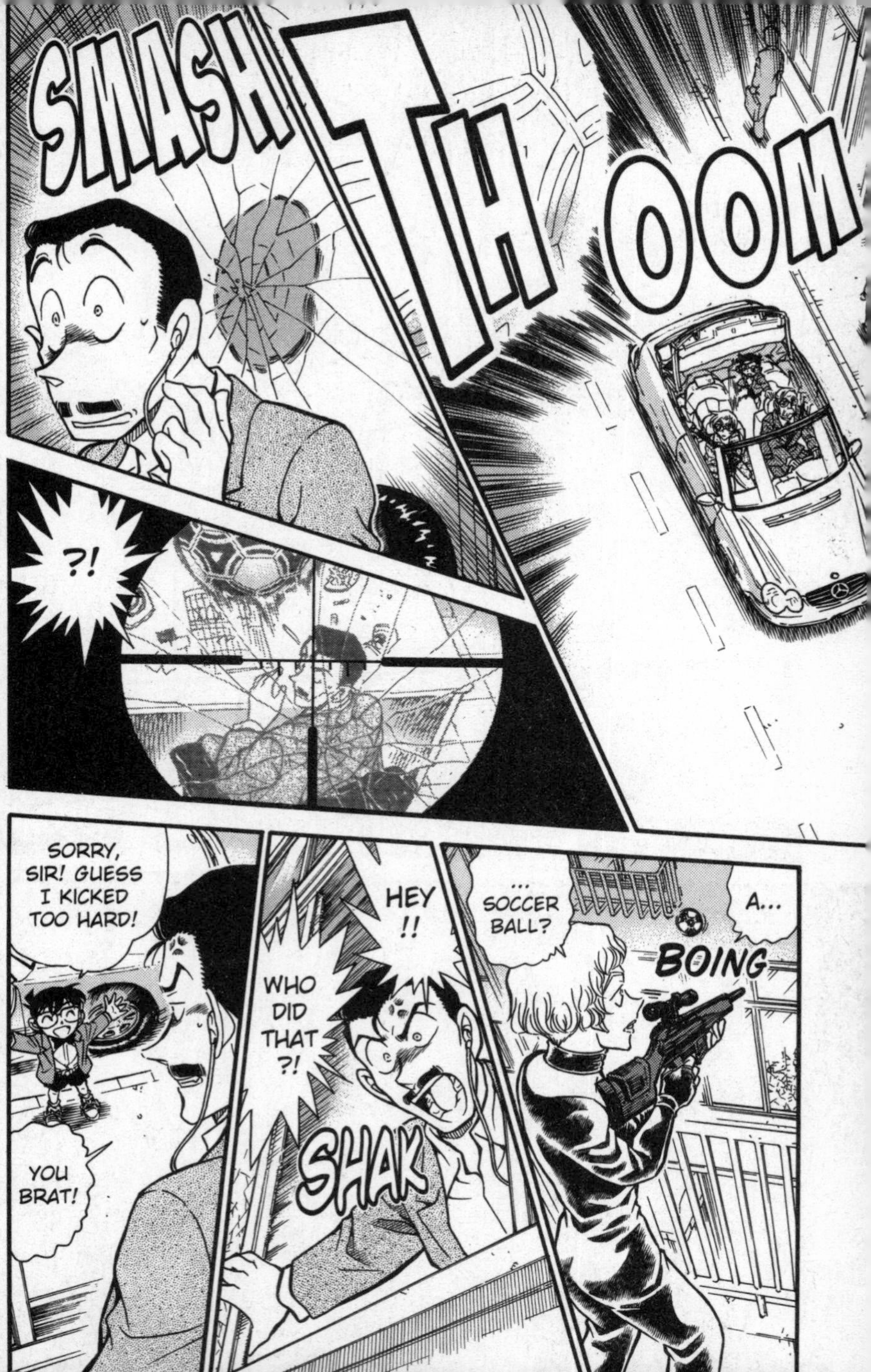
THOOM
SMASH
?!
A...
... SOCCER BALL?
BOING
HEY !!
WHO DID THAT ?!
SHAK
SORRY, SIR! GUESS I KICKED TOO HARD!
YOU BRAT!

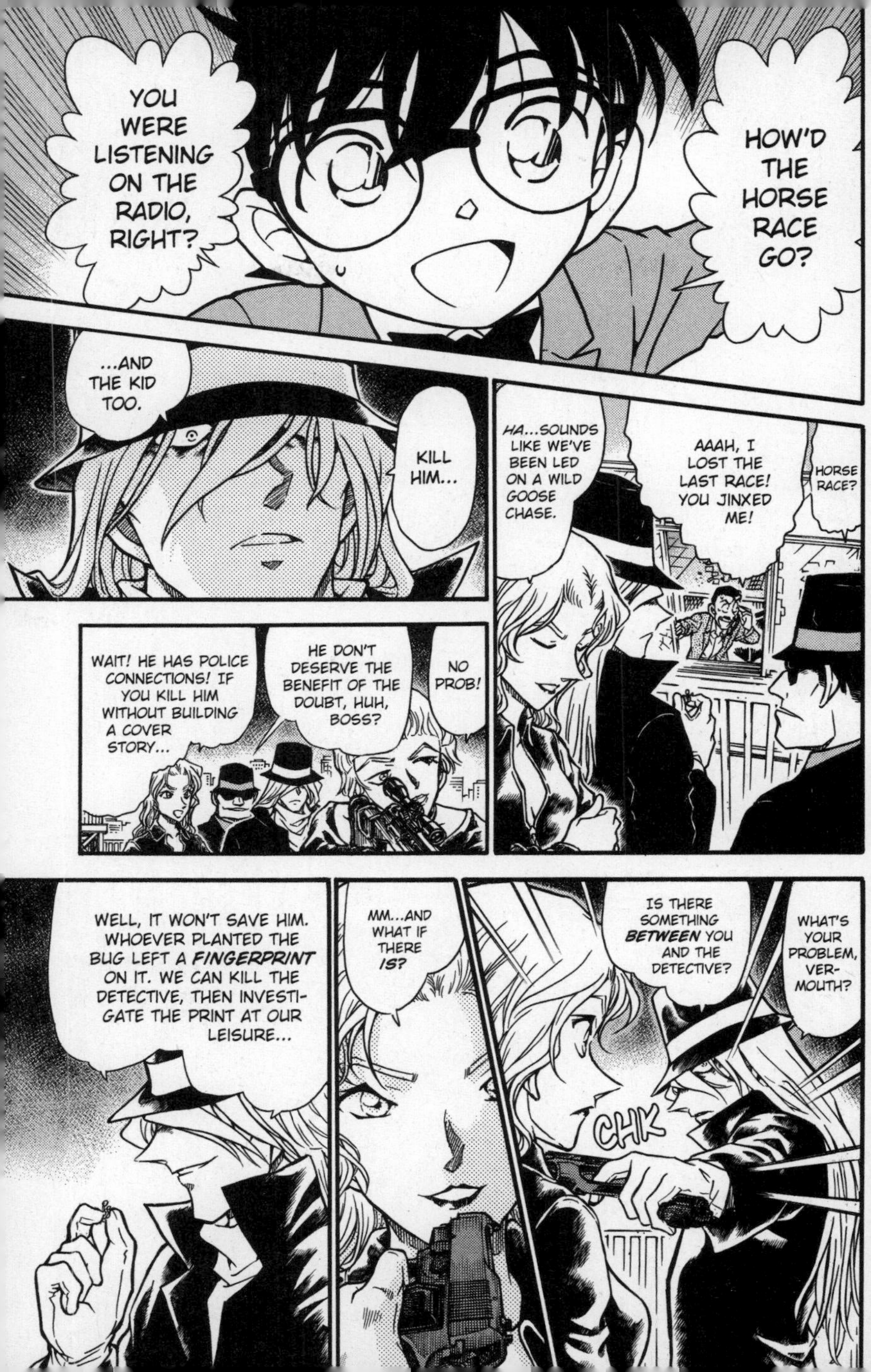
HOW'D THE HORSE RACE GO?
YOU WERE LISTENING ON THE RADIO, RIGHT?
HORSE RACE?
AAAH, I LOST THE LAST RACE! YOU JINXED ME!
HA...SOUNDS LIKE WE'VE BEEN LED ON A WILD GOOSE CHASE.
KILL HIM...
...AND THE KID TOO.
NO PROB!
HE DON'T DESERVE THE BENEFIT OF THE DOUBT, HUH, BOSS?
WAIT! HE HAS POLICE CONNECTIONS! IF YOU KILL HIM WITHOUT BUILDING A COVER STORY...
WHAT'S YOUR PROBLEM, VER-MOUTH?
IS THERE SOMETHING *BETWEEN* YOU AND THE DETECTIVE?
CHK
MM...AND WHAT IF THERE *IS?*
WELL, IT WON'T SAVE HIM. WHOEVER PLANTED THE BUG LEFT A *FINGERPRINT* ON IT. WE CAN KILL THE DETECTIVE, THEN INVESTI-GATE THE PRINT AT OUR LEISURE...

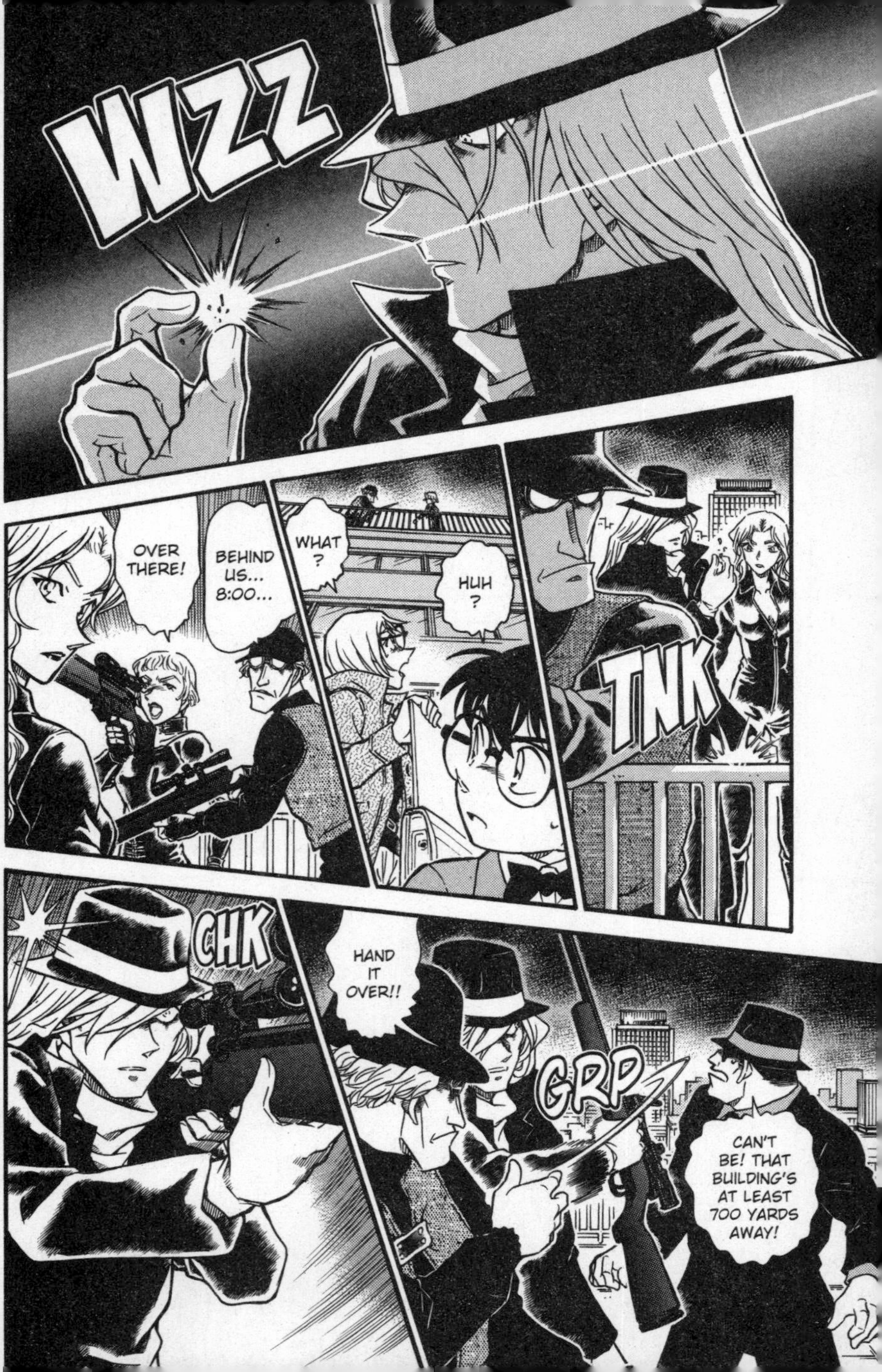
WZZ
TNK
WHAT ?
HUH ?
BEHIND US... 8:00...
OVER THERE!
HAND IT OVER!!
GRP
CAN'T BE! THAT BUILDING'S AT LEAST 700 YARDS AWAY!
CHK

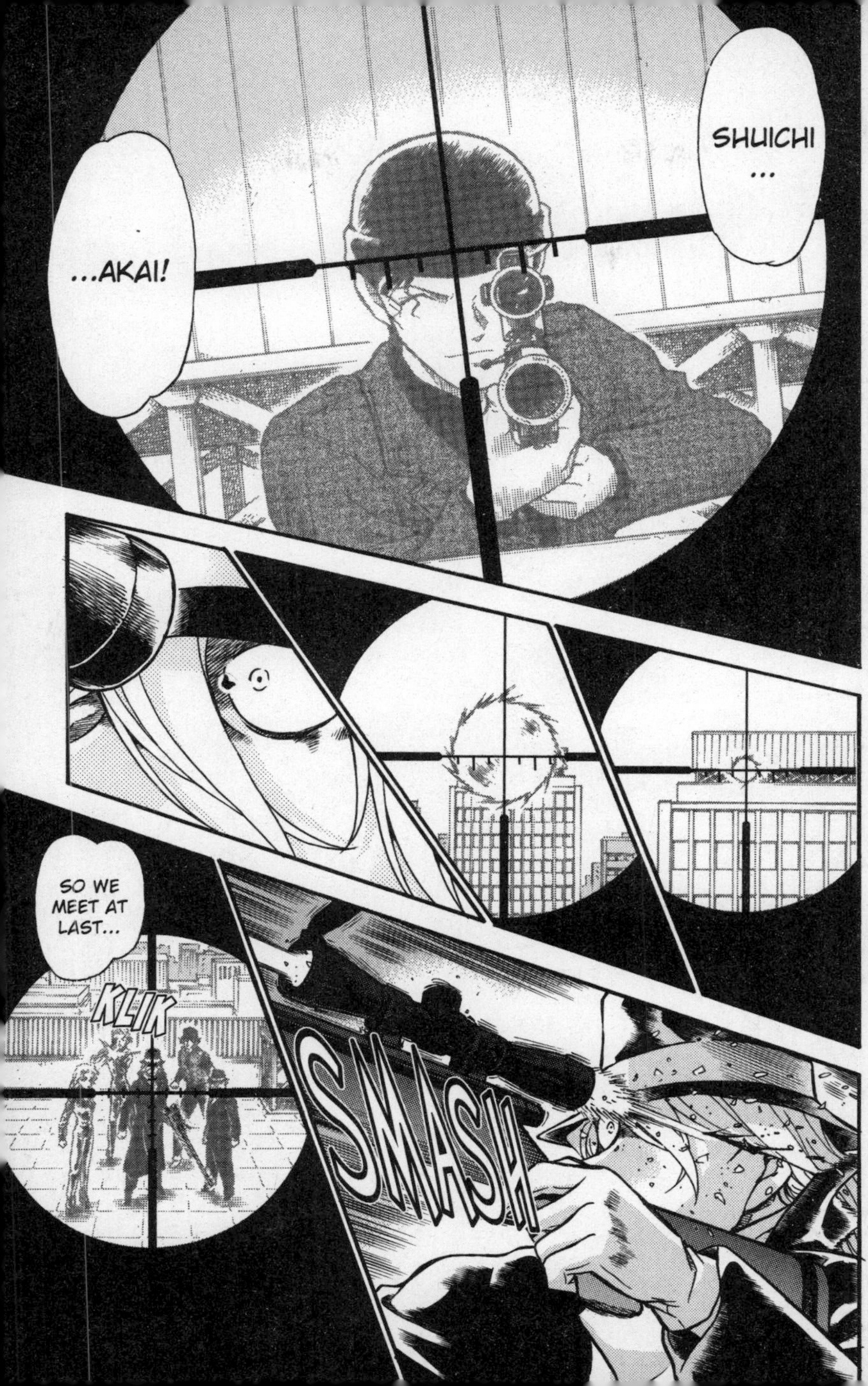
SHUICHI ...
...AKAI!
SMASH
SO WE MEET AT LAST...
KLIK

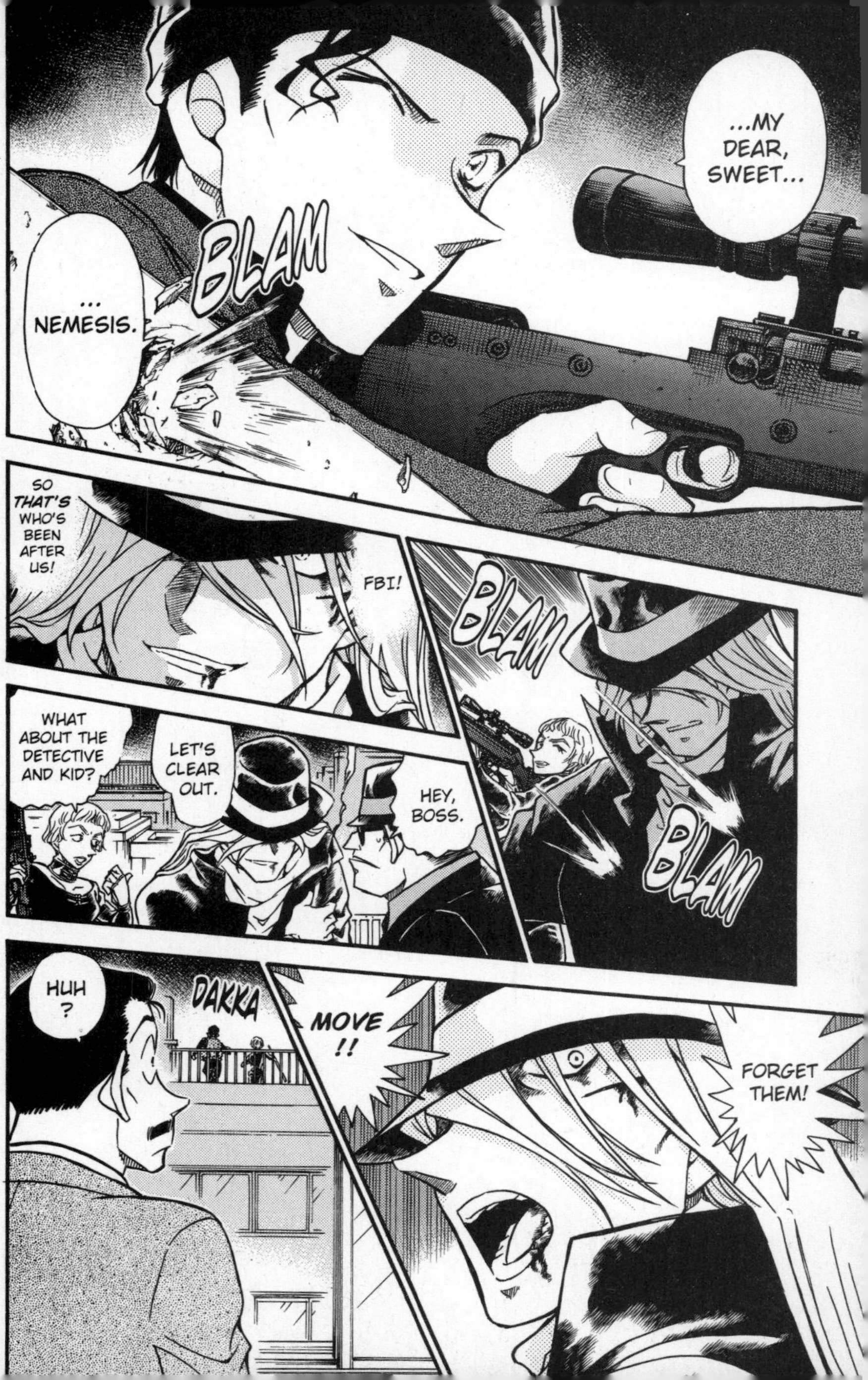
...MY DEAR, SWEET...
BLAM
... NEMESIS.
BLAM
BLAM
BLAM
SO THAT'S WHO'S BEEN AFTER US!
FBI!
HEY, BOSS.
LET'S CLEAR OUT.
WHAT ABOUT THE DETECTIVE AND KID?
MOVE !!
FORGET THEM!
DAKKA
HUH ?

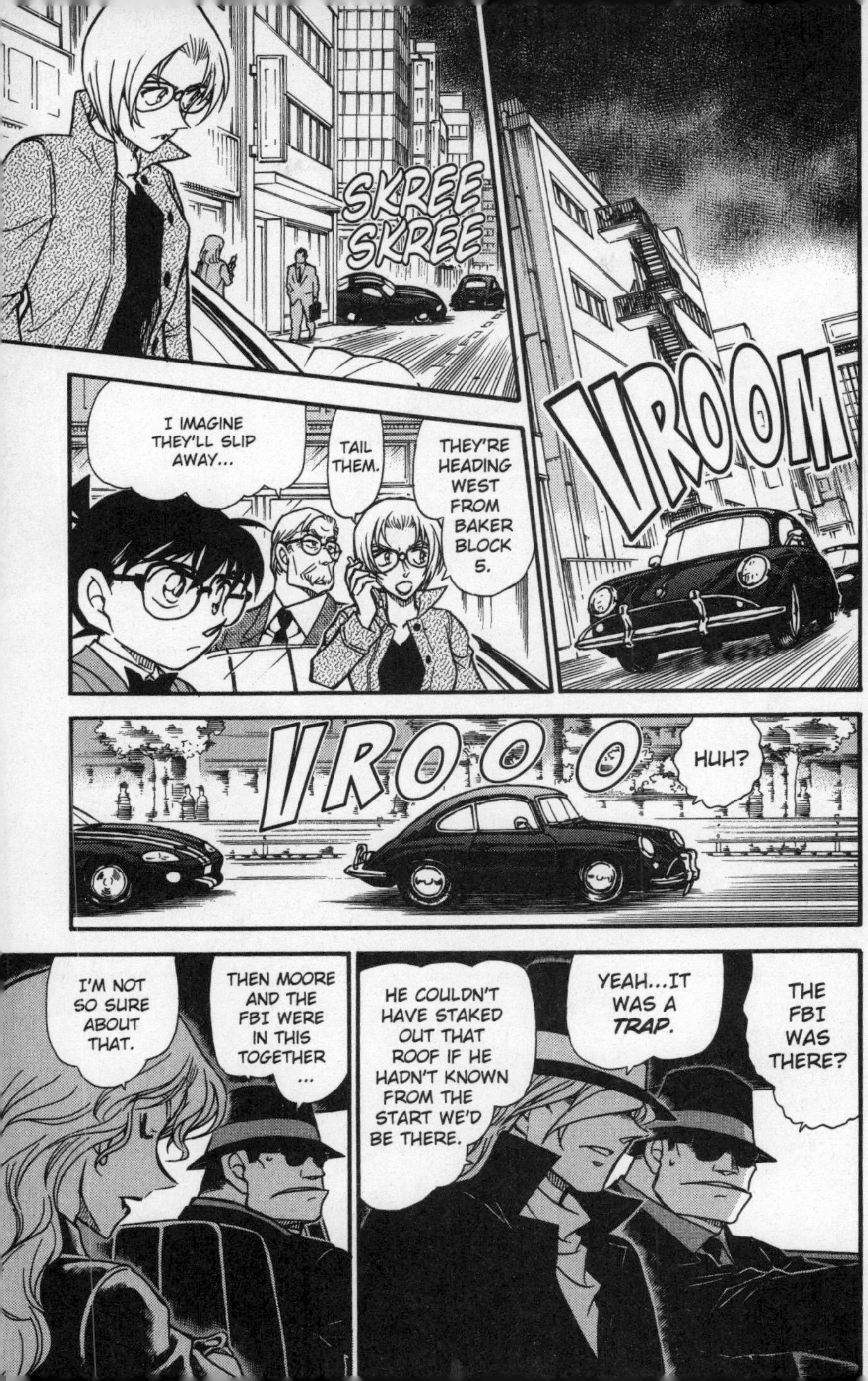
VROOM
SKREE SKREE
THEY'RE HEADING WEST FROM BAKER BLOCK 5.
TAIL THEM.
I IMAGINE THEY'LL SLIP AWAY...
HUH?
VROOO
THE FBI WAS THERE?
YEAH...IT WAS A *TRAP*.
HE COULDN'T HAVE STAKED OUT THAT ROOF IF HE HADN'T KNOWN FROM THE START WE'D BE THERE.
THEN MOORE AND THE FBI WERE IN THIS TOGETHER...
I'M NOT SO SURE ABOUT THAT.

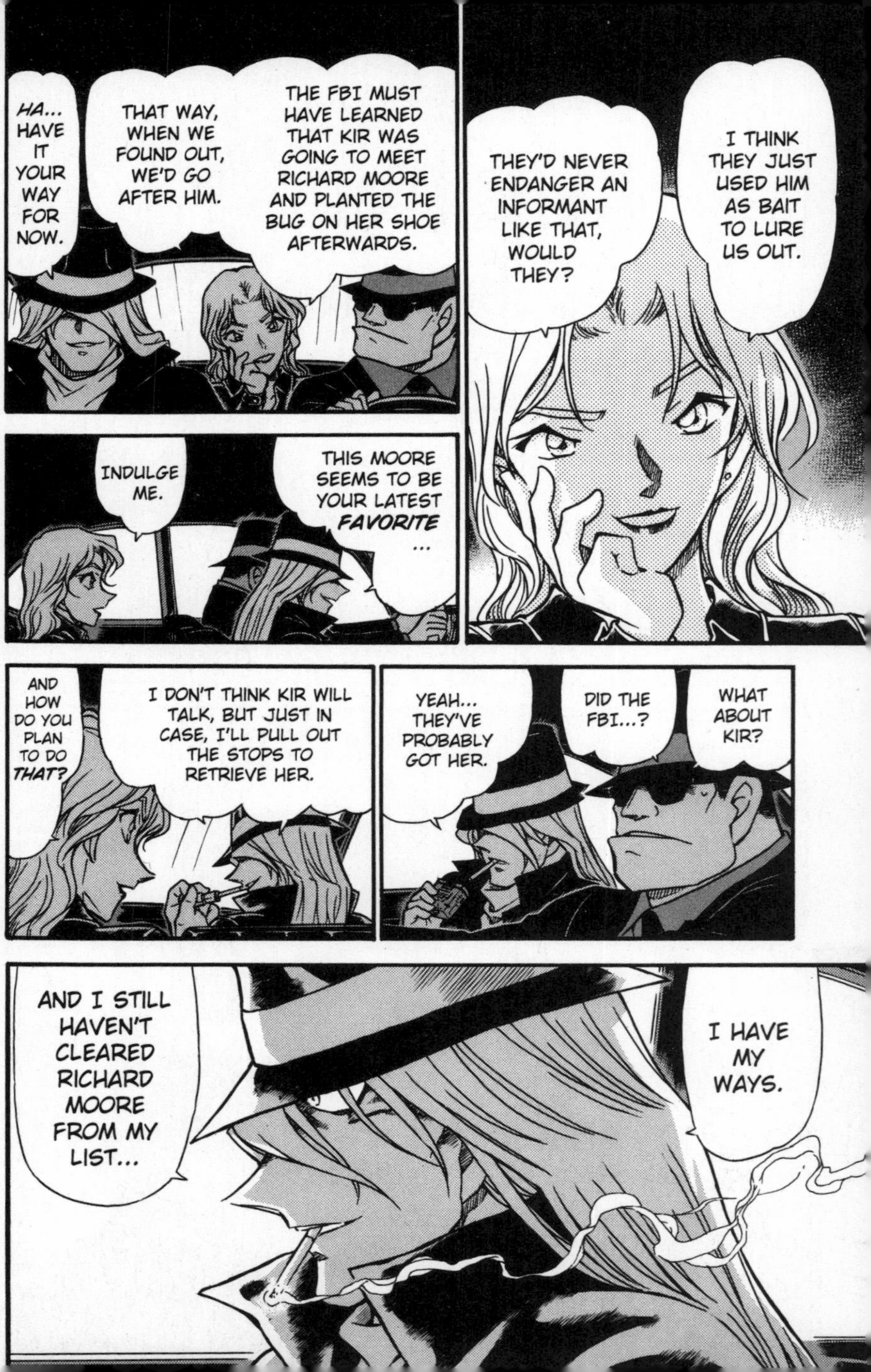
I THINK THEY JUST USED HIM AS BAIT TO LURE US OUT.
THEY'D NEVER ENDANGER AN INFORMANT LIKE THAT, WOULD THEY?
THE FBI MUST HAVE LEARNED THAT KIR WAS GOING TO MEET RICHARD MOORE AND PLANTED THE BUG ON HER SHOE AFTERWARDS.
THAT WAY, WHEN WE FOUND OUT, WE'D GO AFTER HIM.
HA... HAVE IT YOUR WAY FOR NOW.
THIS MOORE SEEMS TO BE YOUR LATEST ***FAVORITE*** ...
INDULGE ME.
WHAT ABOUT KIR?
DID THE FBI...?
YEAH... THEY'VE PROBABLY GOT HER.
I DON'T THINK KIR WILL TALK, BUT JUST IN CASE, I'LL PULL OUT THE STOPS TO RETRIEVE HER.
AND HOW DO YOU PLAN TO DO ***THAT***?
I HAVE MY WAYS.
AND I STILL HAVEN'T CLEARED RICHARD MOORE FROM MY LIST...

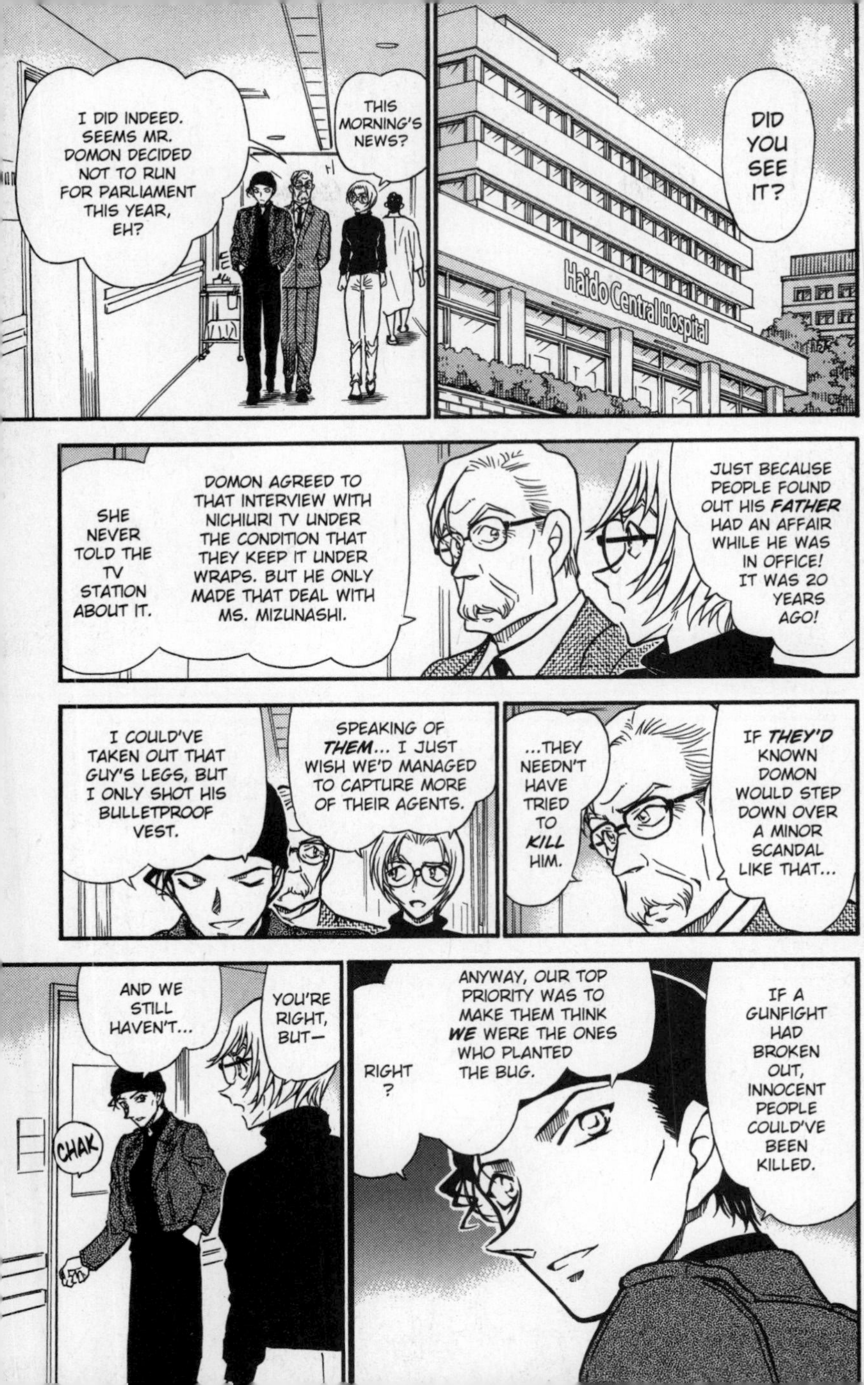
DID YOU SEE IT?
Haido Central Hospital
THIS MORNING'S NEWS?
I DID INDEED. SEEMS MR. DOMON DECIDED NOT TO RUN FOR PARLIAMENT THIS YEAR, EH?
JUST BECAUSE PEOPLE FOUND OUT HIS FATHER HAD AN AFFAIR WHILE HE WAS IN OFFICE! IT WAS 20 YEARS AGO!
DOMON AGREED TO THAT INTERVIEW WITH NICHIURI TV UNDER THE CONDITION THAT THEY KEEP IT UNDER WRAPS. BUT HE ONLY MADE THAT DEAL WITH MS. MIZUNASHI.
SHE NEVER TOLD THE TV STATION ABOUT IT.
IF THEY'D KNOWN DOMON WOULD STEP DOWN OVER A MINOR SCANDAL LIKE THAT...
...THEY NEEDN'T HAVE TRIED TO KILL HIM.
SPEAKING OF THEM... I JUST WISH WE'D MANAGED TO CAPTURE MORE OF THEIR AGENTS.
I COULD'VE TAKEN OUT THAT GUY'S LEGS, BUT I ONLY SHOT HIS BULLETPROOF VEST.
IF A GUNFIGHT HAD BROKEN OUT, INNOCENT PEOPLE COULD'VE BEEN KILLED.
ANYWAY, OUR TOP PRIORITY WAS TO MAKE THEM THINK WE WERE THE ONES WHO PLANTED THE BUG.
RIGHT?
YOU'RE RIGHT, BUT—
AND WE STILL HAVEN'T...
CHAK

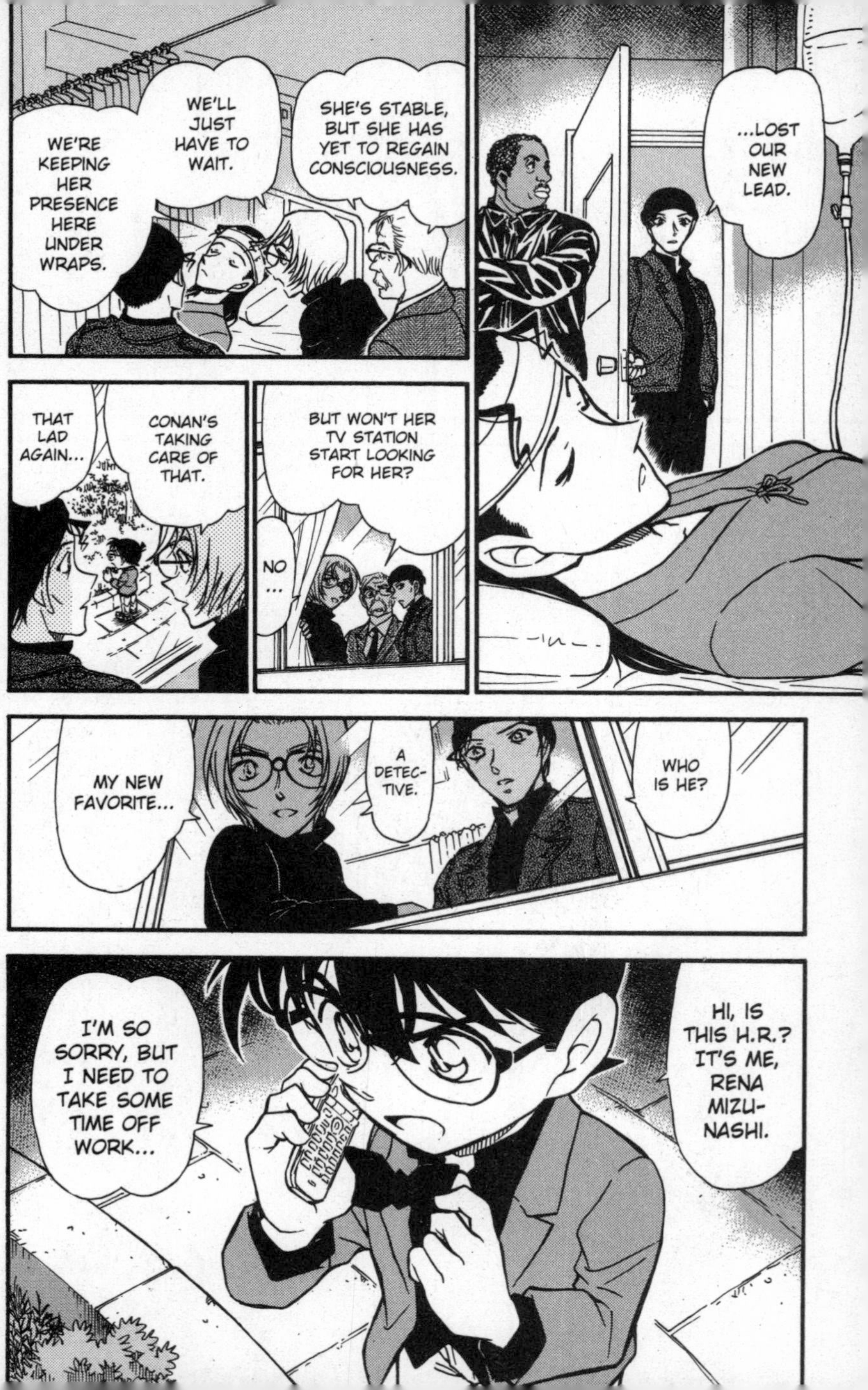
...LOST OUR NEW LEAD.
SHE'S STABLE, BUT SHE HAS YET TO REGAIN CONSCIOUSNESS.
WE'LL JUST HAVE TO WAIT.
WE'RE KEEPING HER PRESENCE HERE UNDER WRAPS.
BUT WON'T HER TV STATION START LOOKING FOR HER?
NO ...
CONAN'S TAKING CARE OF THAT.
THAT LAD AGAIN...
WHO IS HE?
A DETEC-TIVE.
MY NEW FAVORITE...
HI, IS THIS H.R.? IT'S ME, RENA MIZU-NASHI.
I'M SO SORRY, BUT I NEED TO TAKE SOME TIME OFF WORK...

FILE 5: THE NEW TEACHER

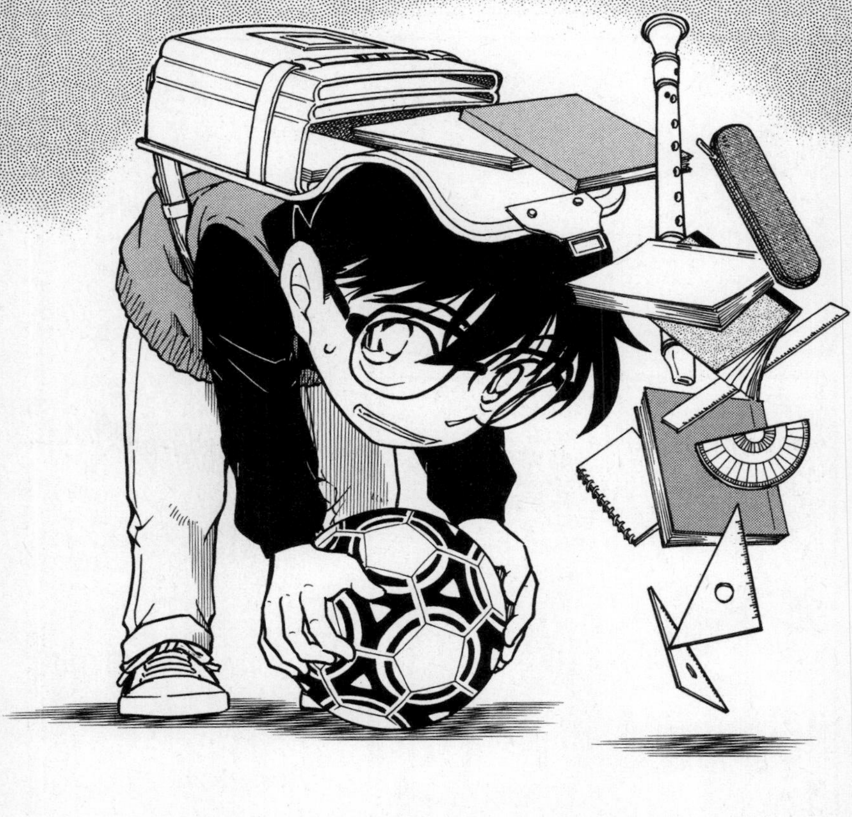

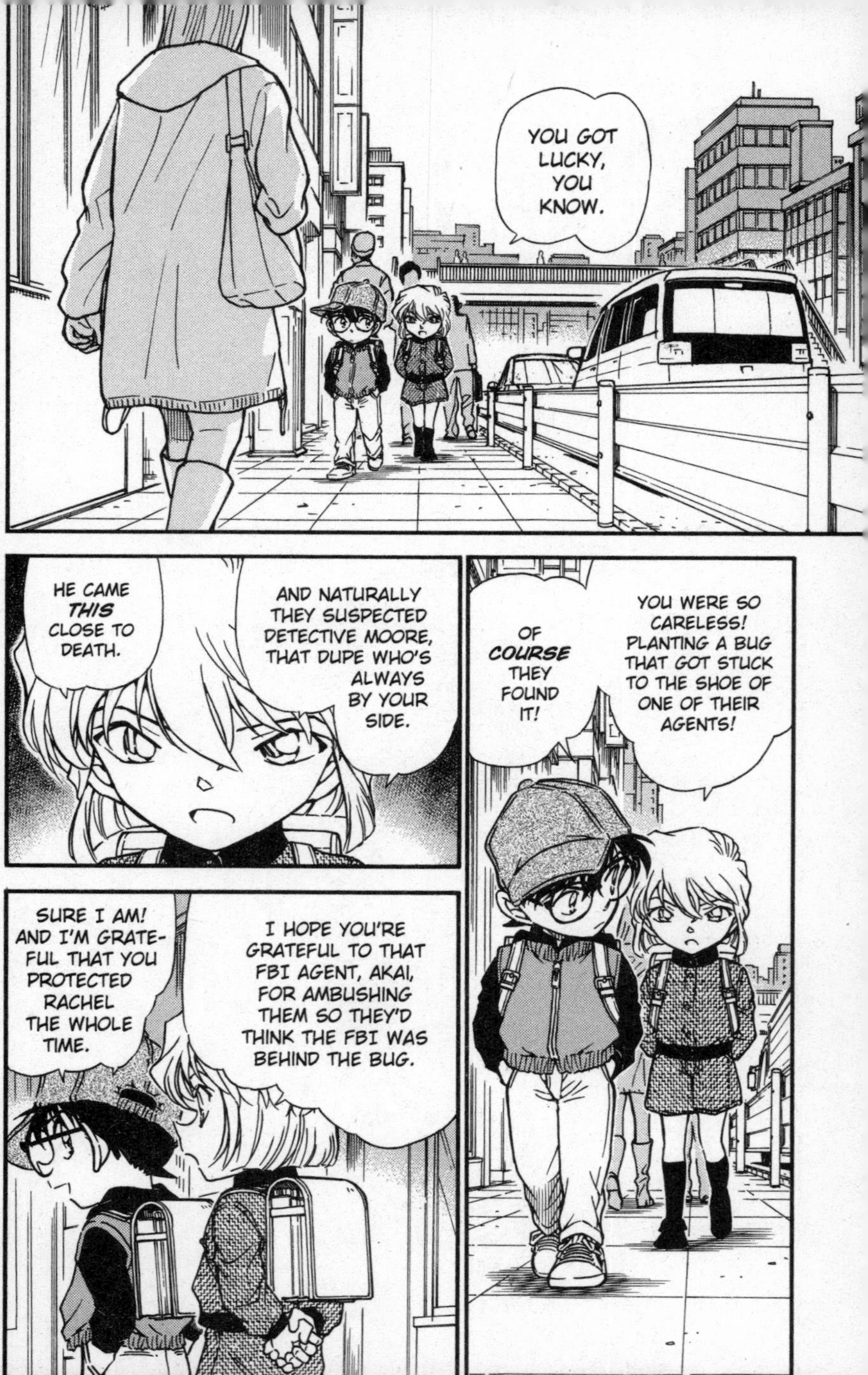
YOU GOT LUCKY, YOU KNOW.
YOU WERE SO CARELESS! PLANTING A BUG THAT GOT STUCK TO THE SHOE OF ONE OF THEIR AGENTS!
OF *COURSE* THEY FOUND IT!
AND NATURALLY THEY SUSPECTED DETECTIVE MOORE, THAT DUPE WHO'S ALWAYS BY YOUR SIDE.
HE CAME *THIS* CLOSE TO DEATH.
I HOPE YOU'RE GRATEFUL TO THAT FBI AGENT, AKAI, FOR AMBUSHING THEM SO THEY'D THINK THE FBI WAS BEHIND THE BUG.
SURE I AM! AND I'M GRATE-FUL THAT YOU PROTECTED RACHEL THE WHOLE TIME.

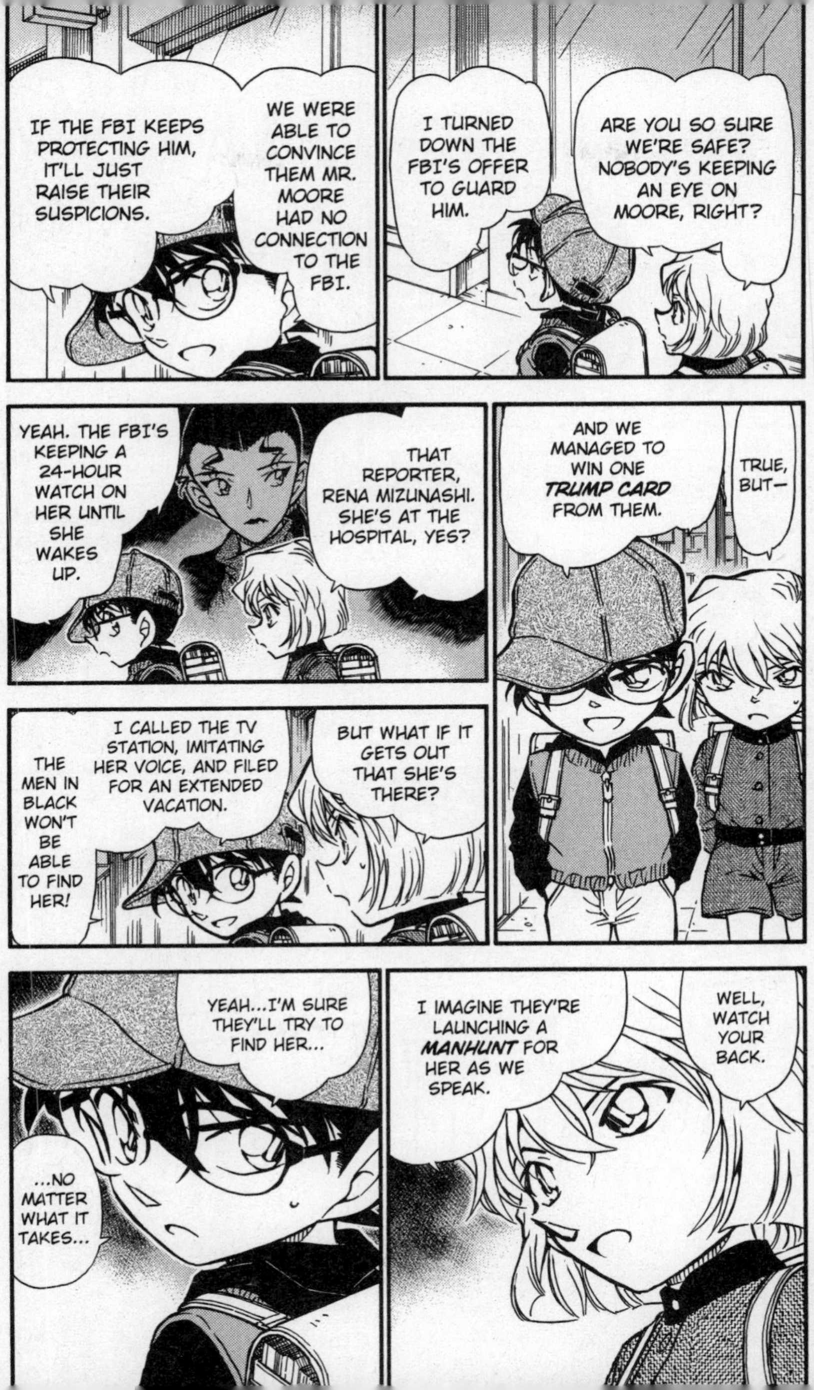
ARE YOU SO SURE WE'RE SAFE? NOBODY'S KEEPING AN EYE ON MOORE, RIGHT?
I TURNED DOWN THE FBI'S OFFER TO GUARD HIM.
WE WERE ABLE TO CONVINCE THEM MR. MOORE HAD NO CONNECTION TO THE FBI.
IF THE FBI KEEPS PROTECTING HIM, IT'LL JUST RAISE THEIR SUSPICIONS.
TRUE, BUT—
AND WE MANAGED TO WIN ONE *TRUMP CARD* FROM THEM.
THAT REPORTER, RENA MIZUNASHI. SHE'S AT THE HOSPITAL, YES?
YEAH. THE FBI'S KEEPING A 24-HOUR WATCH ON HER UNTIL SHE WAKES UP.
BUT WHAT IF IT GETS OUT THAT SHE'S THERE?
I CALLED THE TV STATION, IMITATING HER VOICE, AND FILED FOR AN EXTENDED VACATION.
THE MEN IN BLACK WON'T BE ABLE TO FIND HER!
WELL, WATCH YOUR BACK.
I IMAGINE THEY'RE LAUNCHING A *MANHUNT* FOR HER AS WE SPEAK.
YEAH...I'M SURE THEY'LL TRY TO FIND HER...
...NO MATTER WHAT IT TAKES...

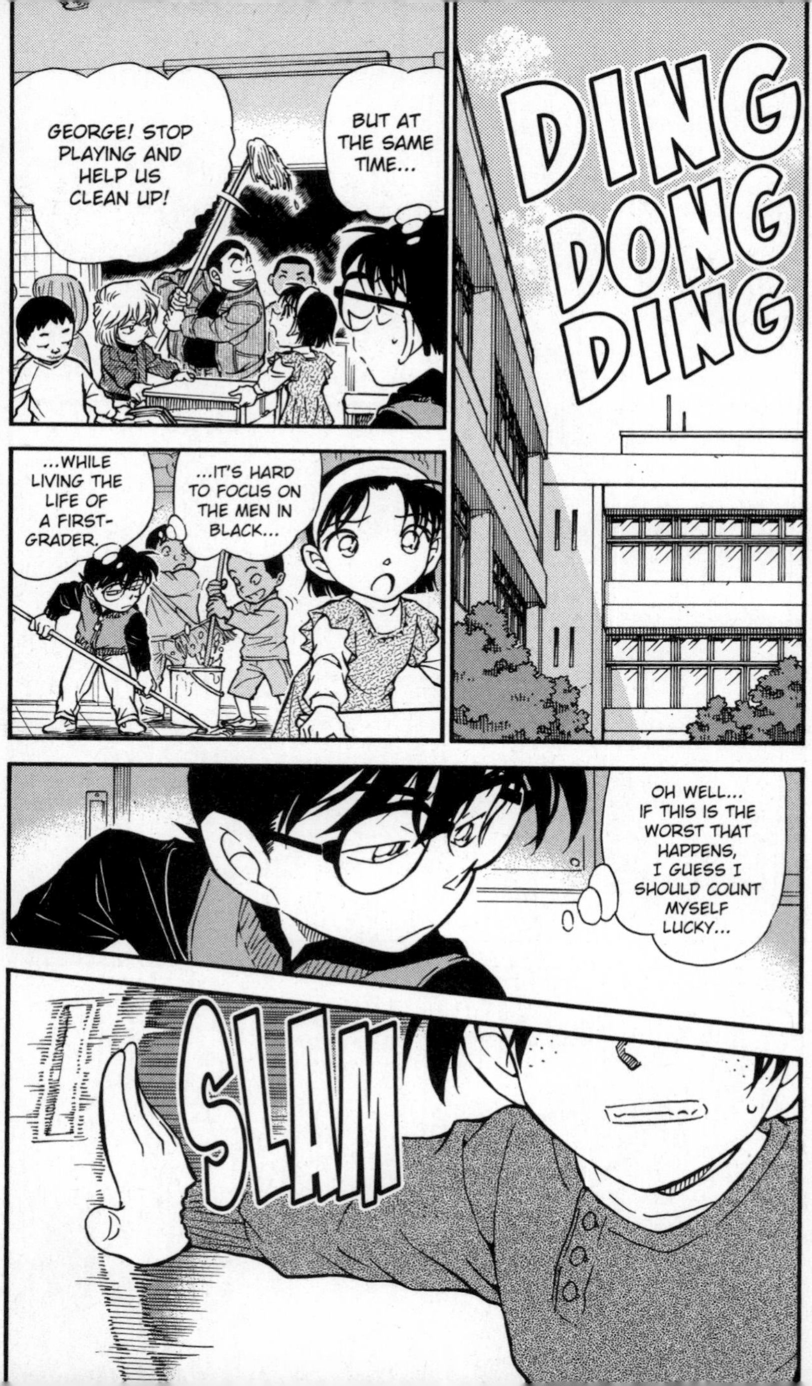
DING DONG DING
BUT AT THE SAME TIME...
GEORGE! STOP PLAYING AND HELP US CLEAN UP!
...IT'S HARD TO FOCUS ON THE MEN IN BLACK...
...WHILE LIVING THE LIFE OF A FIRST-GRADER.
OH WELL... IF THIS IS THE WORST THAT HAPPENS, I GUESS I SHOULD COUNT MYSELF LUCKY...
SLAM

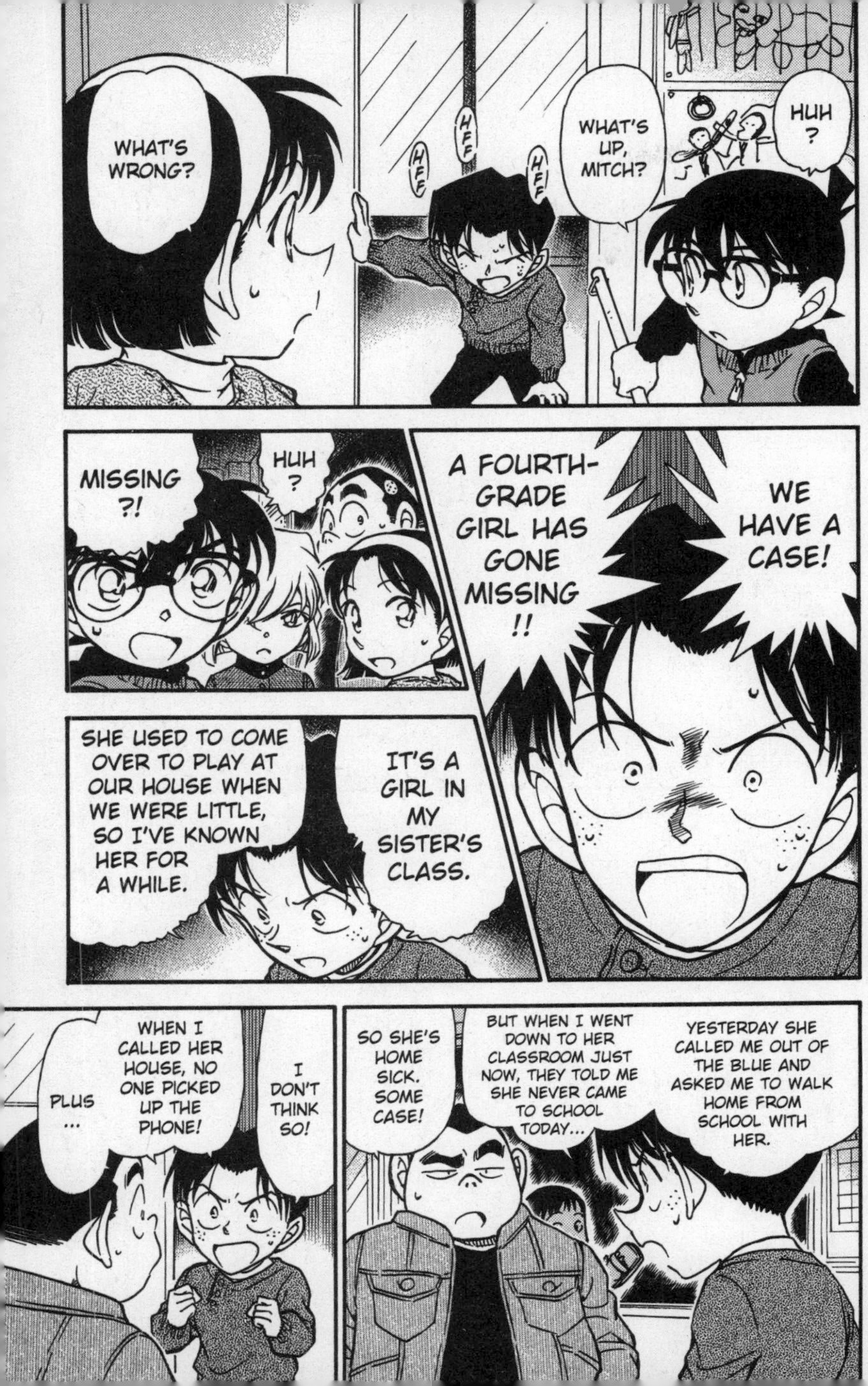
HUH ?
WHAT'S UP, MITCH?
HFF
HFF
HFF
WHAT'S WRONG?
WE HAVE A CASE!
A FOURTH-GRADE GIRL HAS GONE MISSING!!
HUH ?
MISSING ?!
IT'S A GIRL IN MY SISTER'S CLASS.
SHE USED TO COME OVER TO PLAY AT OUR HOUSE WHEN WE WERE LITTLE, SO I'VE KNOWN HER FOR A WHILE.
YESTERDAY SHE CALLED ME OUT OF THE BLUE AND ASKED ME TO WALK HOME FROM SCHOOL WITH HER.
BUT WHEN I WENT DOWN TO HER CLASSROOM JUST NOW, THEY TOLD ME SHE NEVER CAME TO SCHOOL TODAY...
SO SHE'S HOME SICK. SOME CASE!
I DON'T THINK SO!
WHEN I CALLED HER HOUSE, NO ONE PICKED UP THE PHONE!
PLUS ...

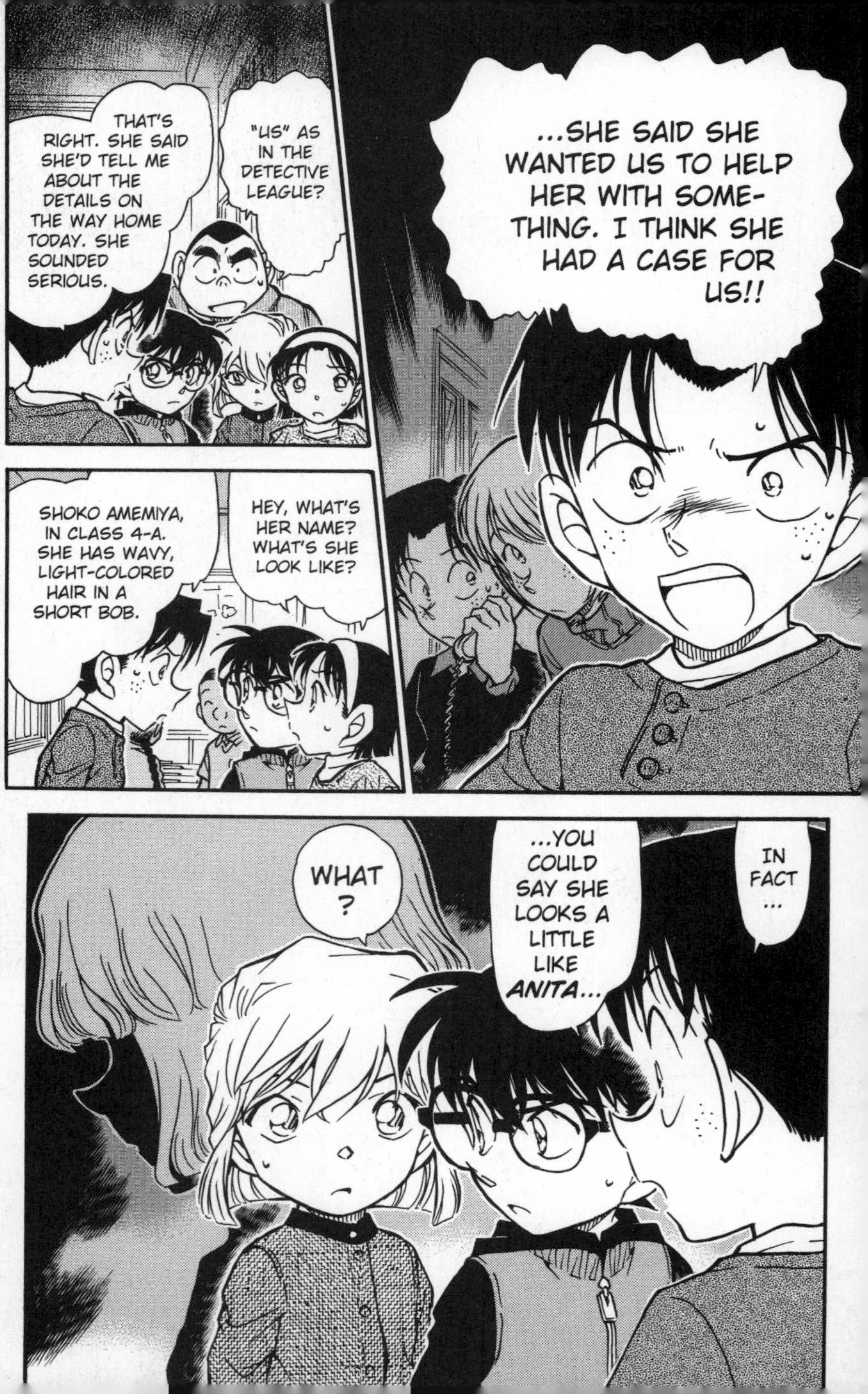
...SHE SAID SHE WANTED US TO HELP HER WITH SOME-THING. I THINK SHE HAD A CASE FOR US!!
"US" AS IN THE DETECTIVE LEAGUE?
THAT'S RIGHT. SHE SAID SHE'D TELL ME ABOUT THE DETAILS ON THE WAY HOME TODAY. SHE SOUNDED SERIOUS.
HEY, WHAT'S HER NAME? WHAT'S SHE LOOK LIKE?
SHOKO AMEMIYA, IN CLASS 4-A. SHE HAS WAVY, LIGHT-COLORED HAIR IN A SHORT BOB.
IN FACT...
...YOU COULD SAY SHE LOOKS A LITTLE LIKE ANITA...
WHAT?

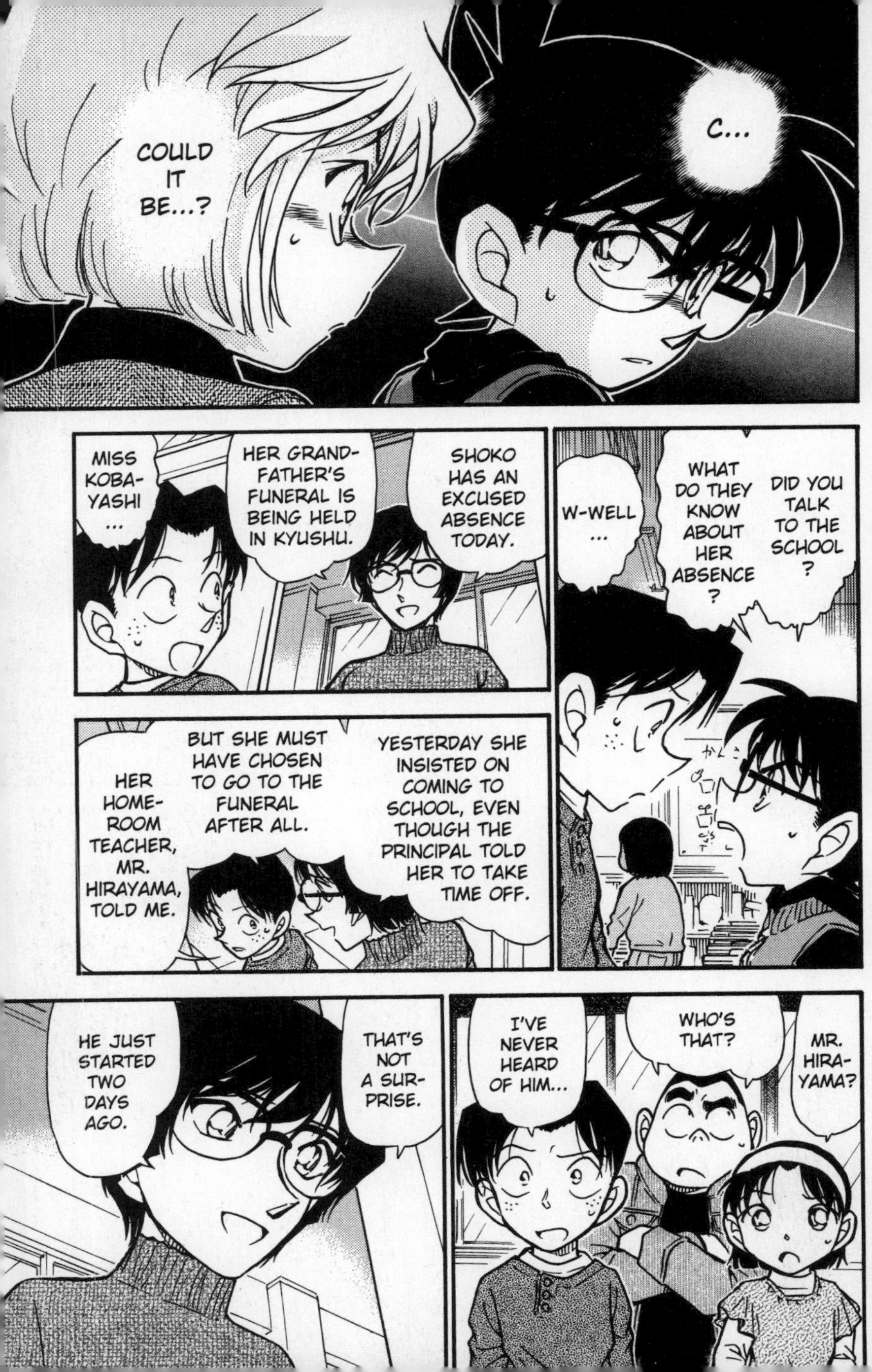
C...
COULD IT BE...?
DID YOU TALK TO THE SCHOOL?
WHAT DO THEY KNOW ABOUT HER ABSENCE?
W-WELL...
SHOKO HAS AN EXCUSED ABSENCE TODAY.
HER GRAND-FATHER'S FUNERAL IS BEING HELD IN KYUSHU.
MISS KOBAYASHI...
YESTERDAY SHE INSISTED ON COMING TO SCHOOL, EVEN THOUGH THE PRINCIPAL TOLD HER TO TAKE TIME OFF.
BUT SHE MUST HAVE CHOSEN TO GO TO THE FUNERAL AFTER ALL.
HER HOME-ROOM TEACHER, MR. HIRAYAMA, TOLD ME.
MR. HIRA-YAMA?
WHO'S THAT?
I'VE NEVER HEARD OF HIM...
THAT'S NOT A SUR-PRISE.
HE JUST STARTED TWO DAYS AGO.

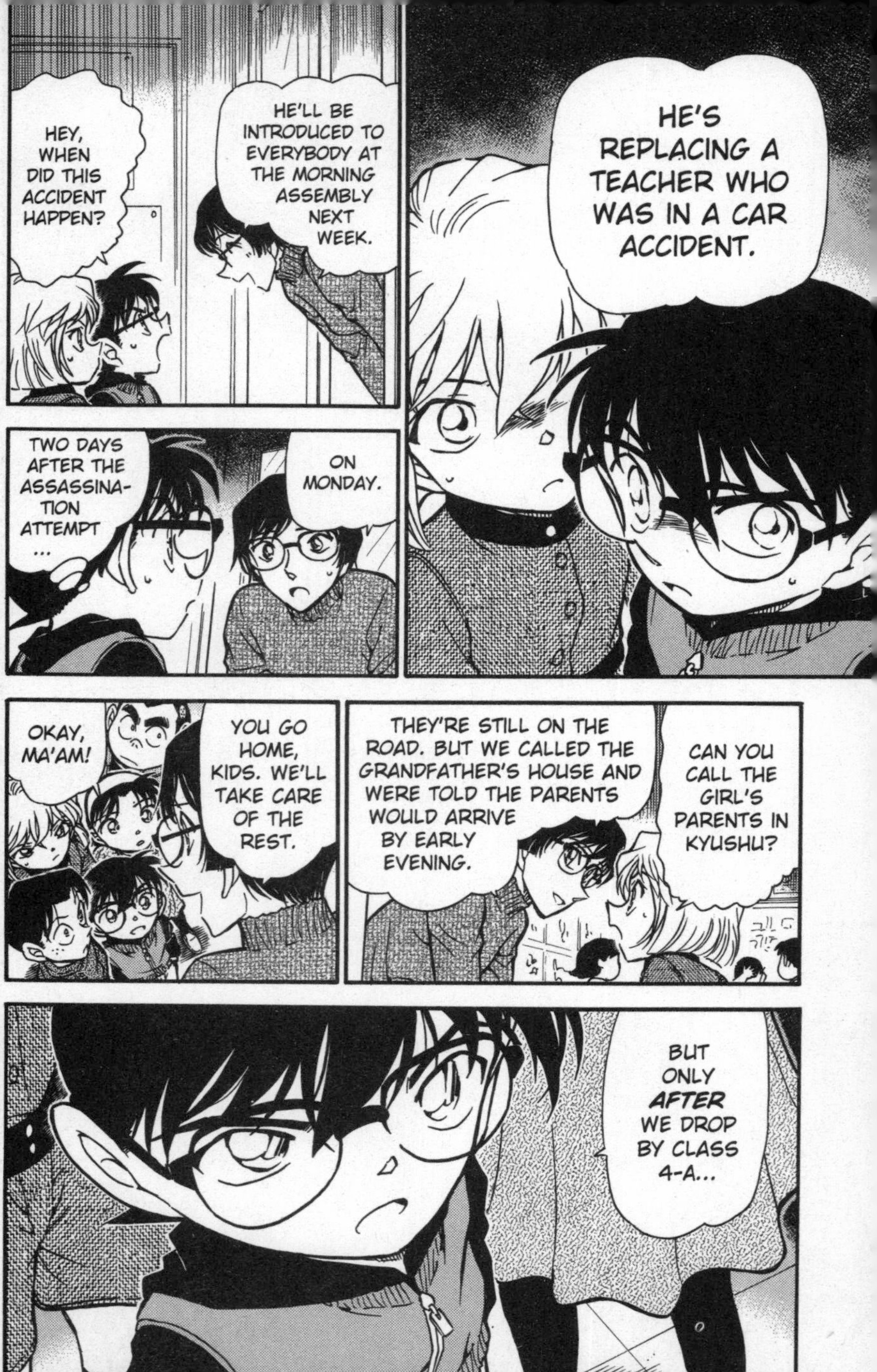
HE'S REPLACING A TEACHER WHO WAS IN A CAR ACCIDENT.
HE'LL BE INTRODUCED TO EVERYBODY AT THE MORNING ASSEMBLY NEXT WEEK.
HEY, WHEN DID THIS ACCIDENT HAPPEN?
ON MONDAY.
TWO DAYS AFTER THE ASSASSINATION ATTEMPT ...
CAN YOU CALL THE GIRL'S PARENTS IN KYUSHU?
THEY'RE STILL ON THE ROAD. BUT WE CALLED THE GRANDFATHER'S HOUSE AND WERE TOLD THE PARENTS WOULD ARRIVE BY EARLY EVENING.
YOU GO HOME, KIDS. WE'LL TAKE CARE OF THE REST.
OKAY, MA'AM!
BUT ONLY *AFTER* WE DROP BY CLASS 4-A...

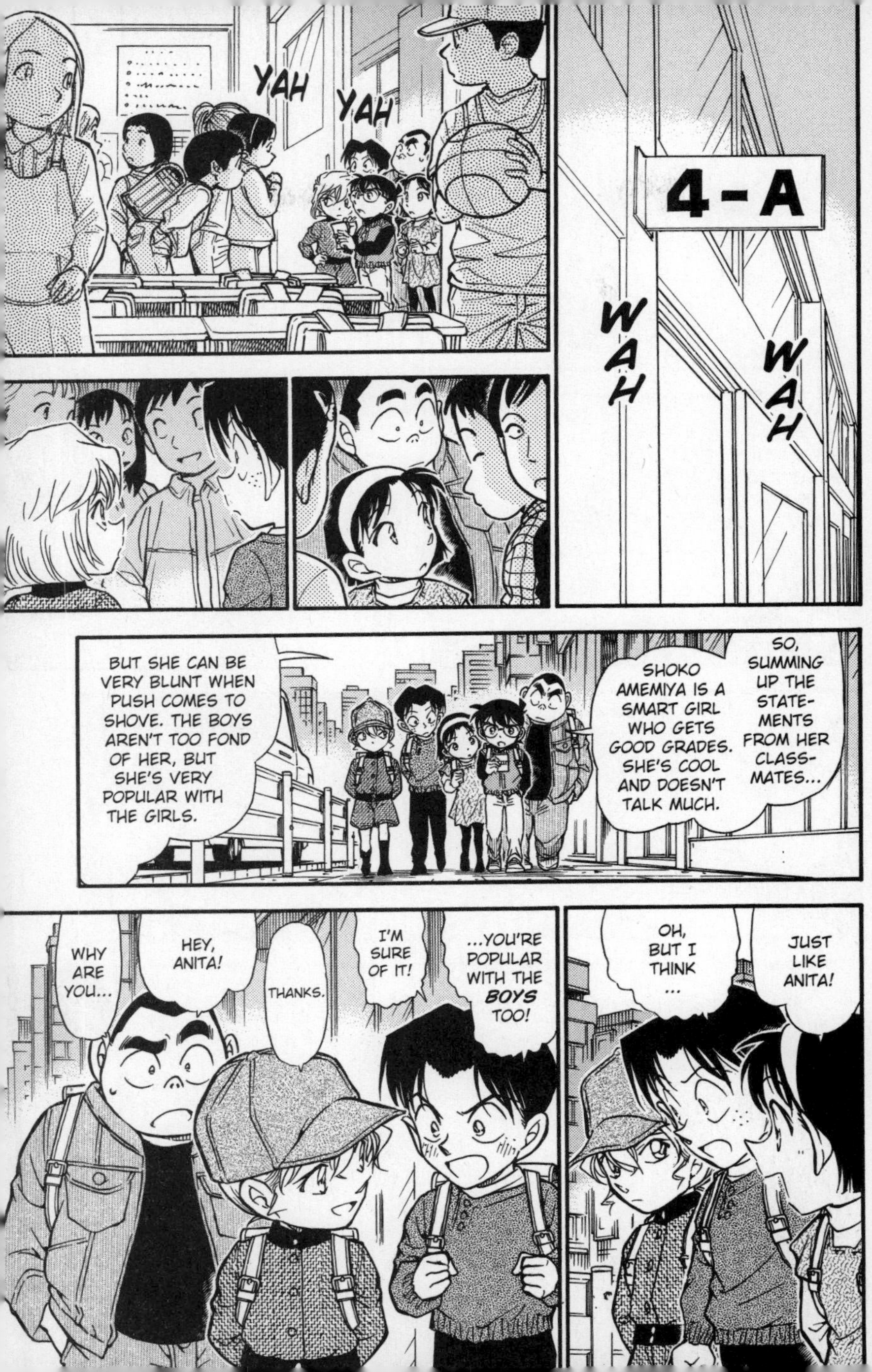
4-A
WAH
WAH
YAH
YAH
SO, SUMMING UP THE STATE-MENTS FROM HER CLASS-MATES...
SHOKO AMEMIYA IS A SMART GIRL WHO GETS GOOD GRADES. SHE'S COOL AND DOESN'T TALK MUCH.
BUT SHE CAN BE VERY BLUNT WHEN PUSH COMES TO SHOVE. THE BOYS AREN'T TOO FOND OF HER, BUT SHE'S VERY POPULAR WITH THE GIRLS.
JUST LIKE ANITA!
OH, BUT I THINK ...
...YOU'RE POPULAR WITH THE *BOYS* TOO!
I'M SURE OF IT!
THANKS.
HEY, ANITA!
WHY ARE YOU...

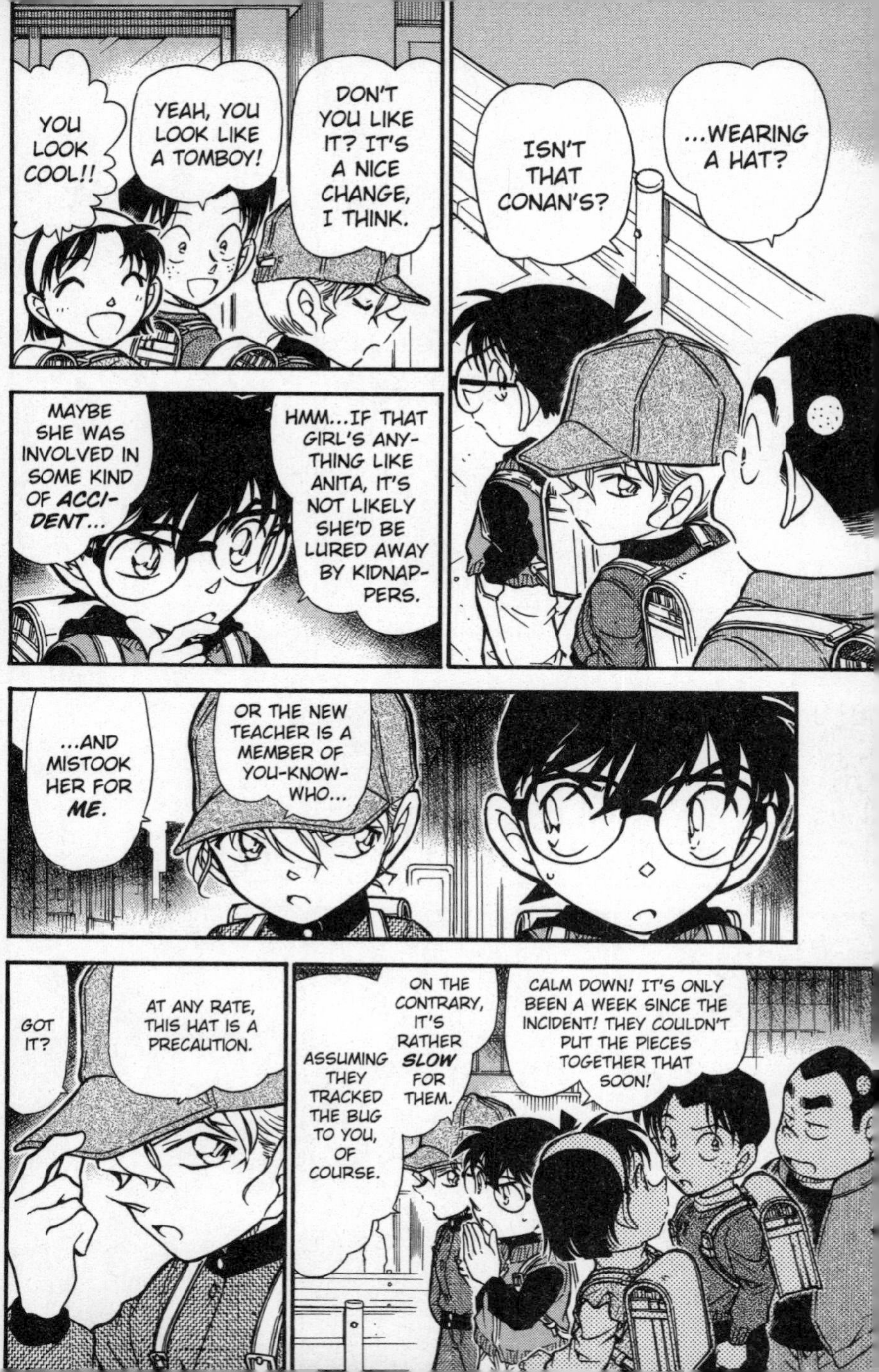
...WEARING A HAT?
ISN'T THAT CONAN'S?
DON'T YOU LIKE IT? IT'S A NICE CHANGE, I THINK.
YEAH, YOU LOOK LIKE A TOMBOY!
YOU LOOK COOL!!
HMM...IF THAT GIRL'S ANYTHING LIKE ANITA, IT'S NOT LIKELY SHE'D BE LURED AWAY BY KIDNAPPERS.
MAYBE SHE WAS INVOLVED IN SOME KIND OF ACCIDENT...
OR THE NEW TEACHER IS A MEMBER OF YOU-KNOW-WHO...
...AND MISTOOK HER FOR ME.
CALM DOWN! IT'S ONLY BEEN A WEEK SINCE THE INCIDENT! THEY COULDN'T PUT THE PIECES TOGETHER THAT SOON!
ON THE CONTRARY, IT'S RATHER SLOW FOR THEM.
ASSUMING THEY TRACKED THE BUG TO YOU, OF COURSE.
AT ANY RATE, THIS HAT IS A PRECAUTION.
GOT IT?

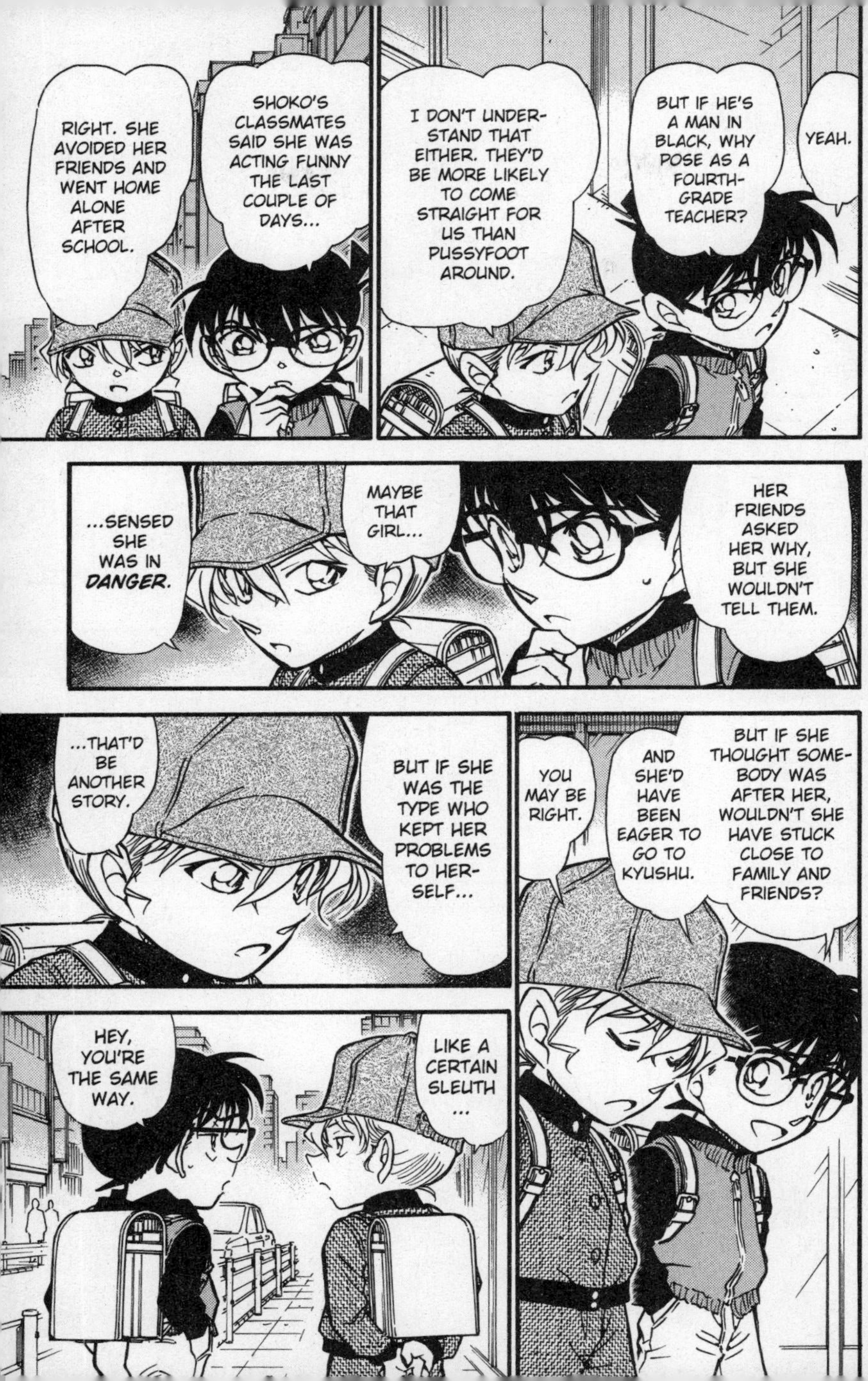
YEAH.
BUT IF HE'S A MAN IN BLACK, WHY POSE AS A FOURTH-GRADE TEACHER?
I DON'T UNDERSTAND THAT EITHER. THEY'D BE MORE LIKELY TO COME STRAIGHT FOR US THAN PUSSYFOOT AROUND.
SHOKO'S CLASSMATES SAID SHE WAS ACTING FUNNY THE LAST COUPLE OF DAYS...
RIGHT. SHE AVOIDED HER FRIENDS AND WENT HOME ALONE AFTER SCHOOL.
HER FRIENDS ASKED HER WHY, BUT SHE WOULDN'T TELL THEM.
MAYBE THAT GIRL...
...SENSED SHE WAS IN **DANGER**.
BUT IF SHE THOUGHT SOMEBODY WAS AFTER HER, WOULDN'T SHE HAVE STUCK CLOSE TO FAMILY AND FRIENDS?
AND SHE'D HAVE BEEN EAGER TO GO TO KYUSHU.
YOU MAY BE RIGHT.
BUT IF SHE WAS THE TYPE WHO KEPT HER PROBLEMS TO HERSELF...
...THAT'D BE ANOTHER STORY.
LIKE A CERTAIN SLEUTH ...
HEY, YOU'RE THE SAME WAY.

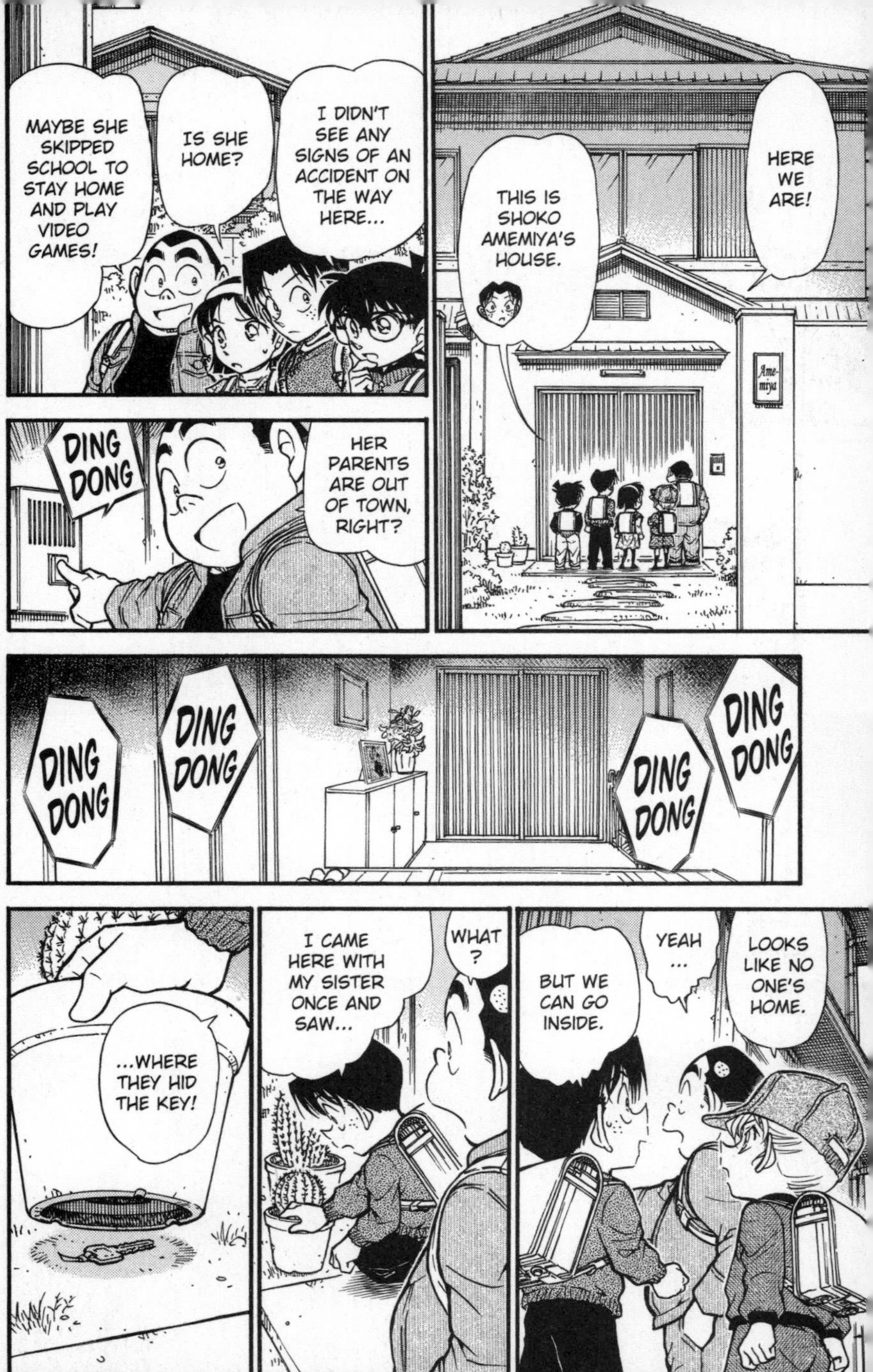
HERE WE ARE!
THIS IS SHOKO AMEMIYA'S HOUSE.
Ame-miya
I DIDN'T SEE ANY SIGNS OF AN ACCIDENT ON THE WAY HERE...
IS SHE HOME?
MAYBE SHE SKIPPED SCHOOL TO STAY HOME AND PLAY VIDEO GAMES!
HER PARENTS ARE OUT OF TOWN, RIGHT?
DING DONG
DING DONG
DING DONG
DING DONG
DING DONG
LOOKS LIKE NO ONE'S HOME.
YEAH...
BUT WE CAN GO INSIDE.
WHAT?
I CAME HERE WITH MY SISTER ONCE AND SAW...
...WHERE THEY HID THE KEY!

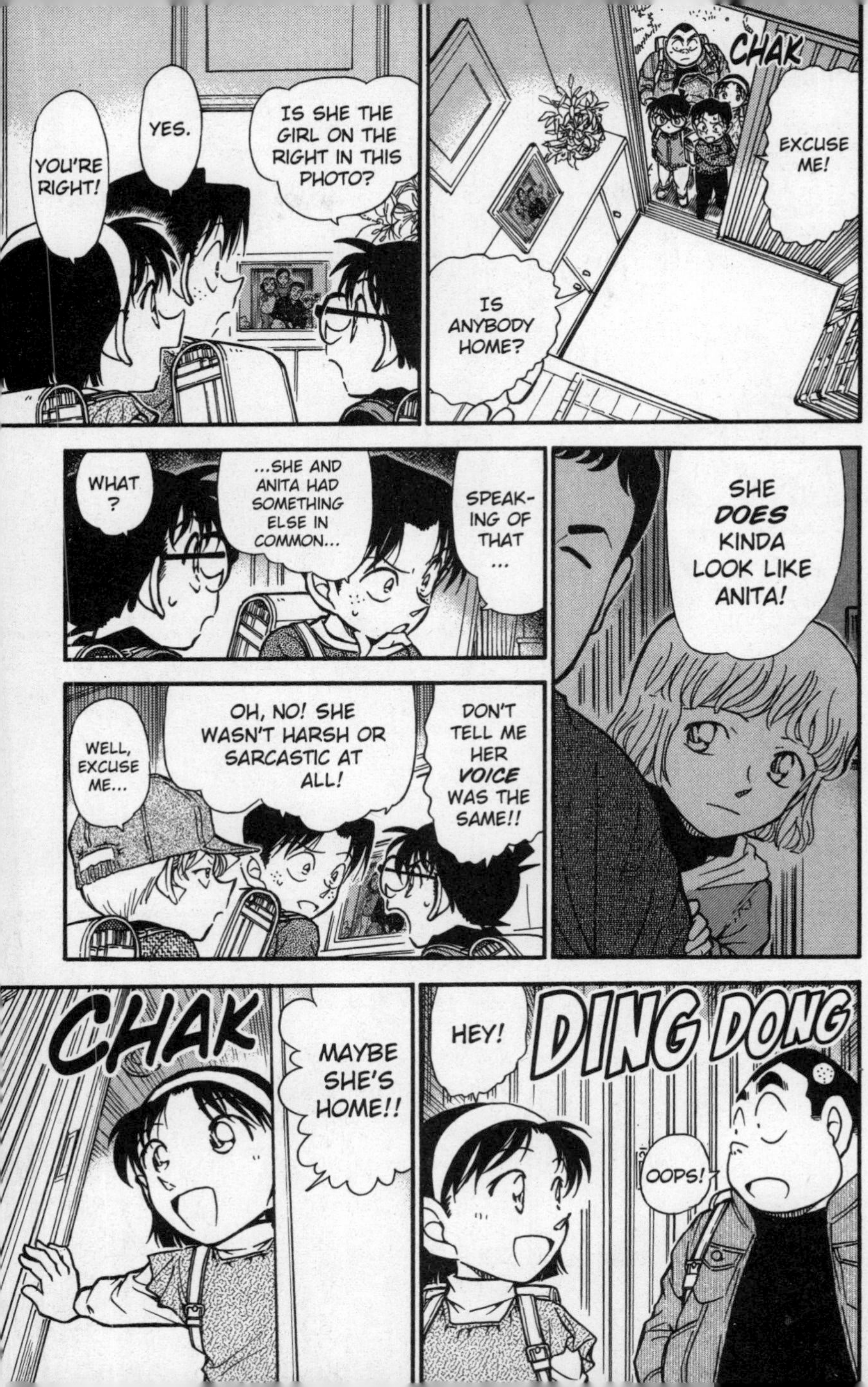
CHAK
EXCUSE ME!
IS ANYBODY HOME?
IS SHE THE GIRL ON THE RIGHT IN THIS PHOTO?
YES.
YOU'RE RIGHT!
SHE **DOES** KINDA LOOK LIKE ANITA!
SPEAK-ING OF THAT...
...SHE AND ANITA HAD SOMETHING ELSE IN COMMON...
WHAT?
DON'T TELL ME HER **VOICE** WAS THE SAME!!
OH, NO! SHE WASN'T HARSH OR SARCASTIC AT ALL!
WELL, EXCUSE ME...
DING DONG
HEY!
OOPS!
MAYBE SHE'S HOME!!
CHAK

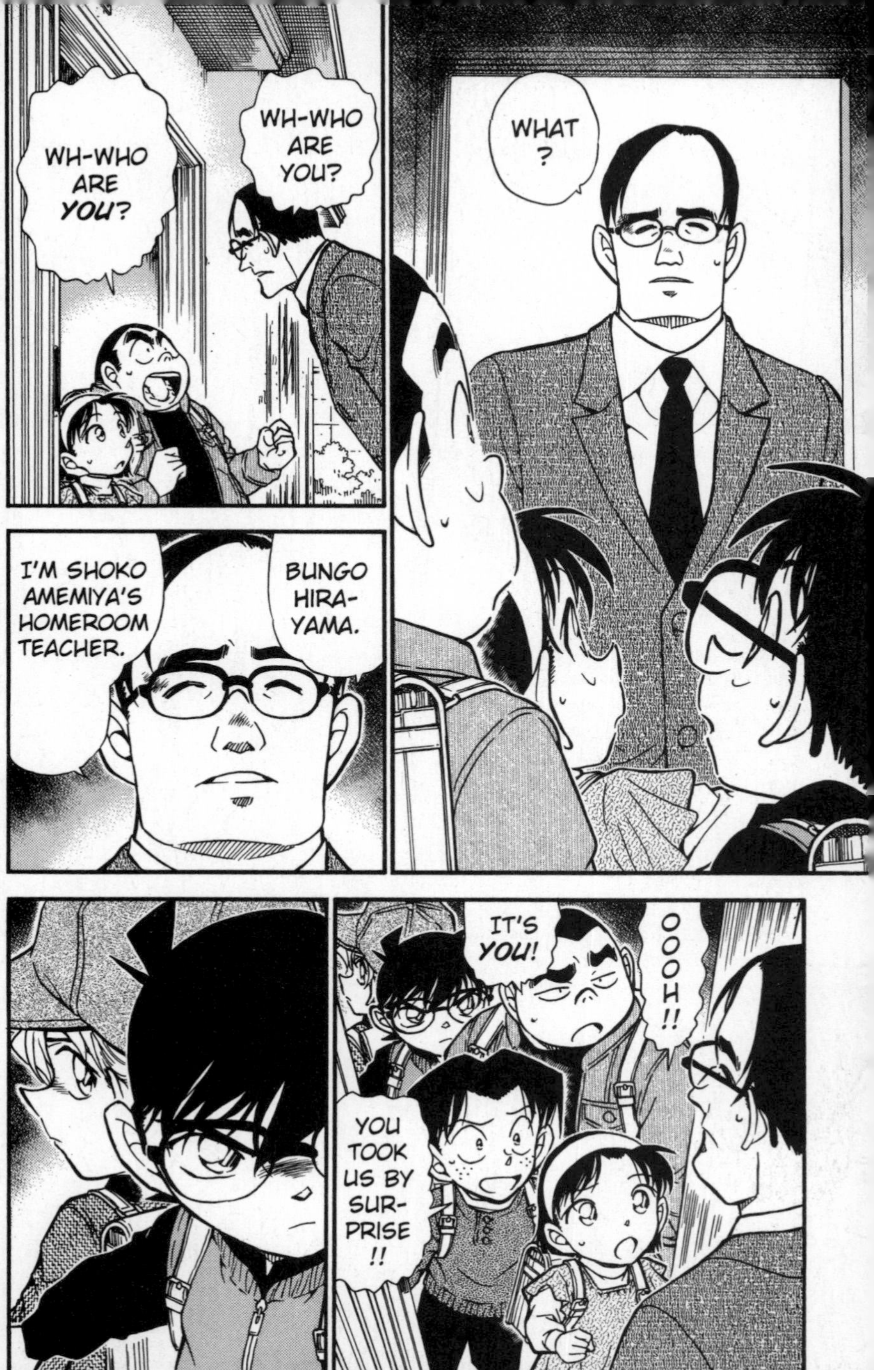
WHAT ?
WH-WHO ARE YOU?
WH-WHO ARE *YOU*?
BUNGO HIRA-YAMA.
I'M SHOKO AMEMIYA'S HOMEROOM TEACHER.
OOOOH!!
IT'S *YOU*!
YOU TOOK US BY SUR-PRISE!!

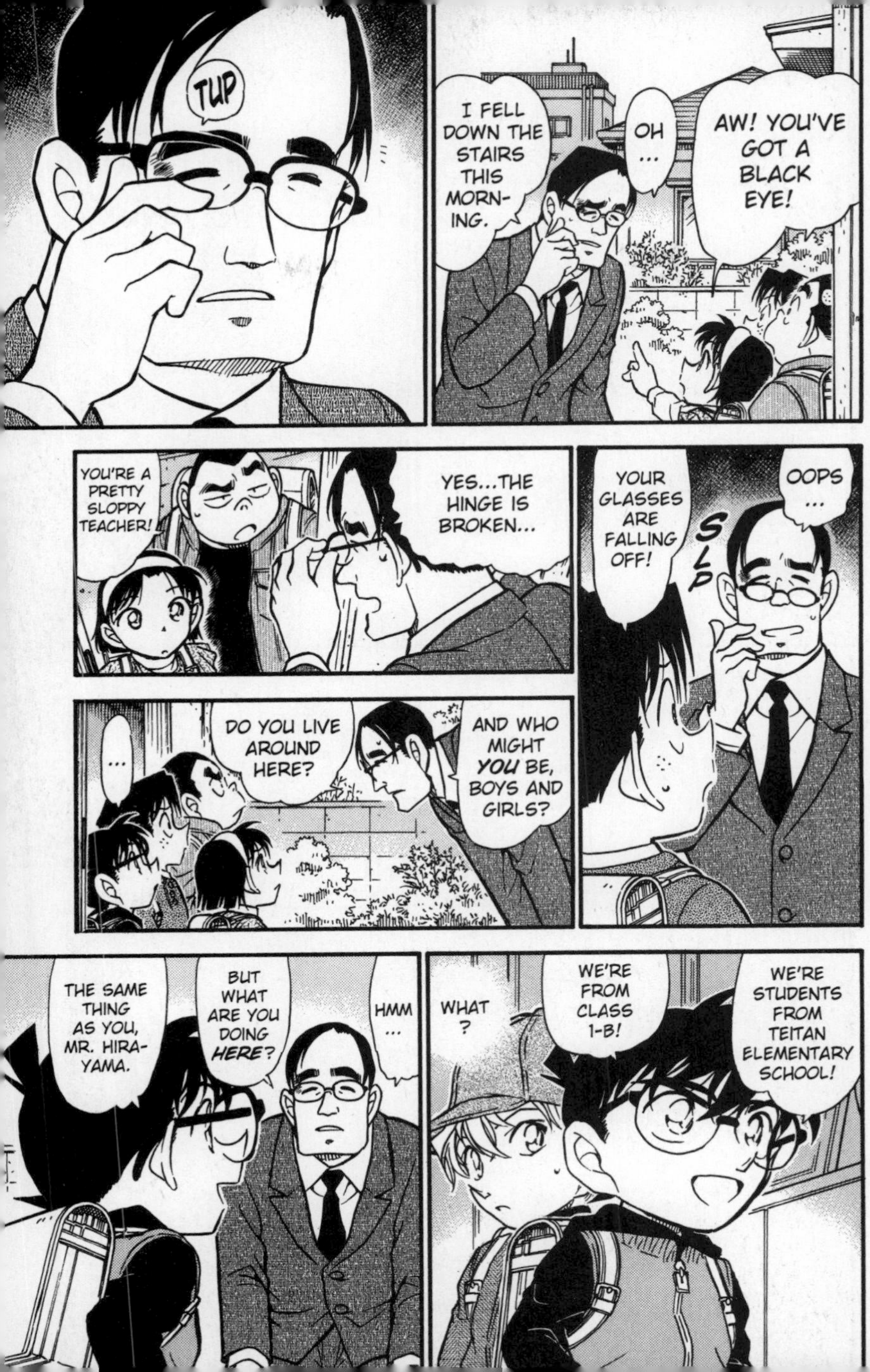
AW! YOU'VE GOT A BLACK EYE!
OH ...
I FELL DOWN THE STAIRS THIS MORN-ING.
TUP
OOPS ...
SLP
YOUR GLASSES ARE FALLING OFF!
YES...THE HINGE IS BROKEN...
YOU'RE A PRETTY SLOPPY TEACHER!
AND WHO MIGHT *YOU* BE, BOYS AND GIRLS?
DO YOU LIVE AROUND HERE?
...
WE'RE STUDENTS FROM TEITAN ELEMENTARY SCHOOL!
WE'RE FROM CLASS 1-B!
WHAT ?
HMM ...
BUT WHAT ARE YOU DOING *HERE*?
THE SAME THING AS YOU, MR. HIRA-YAMA.

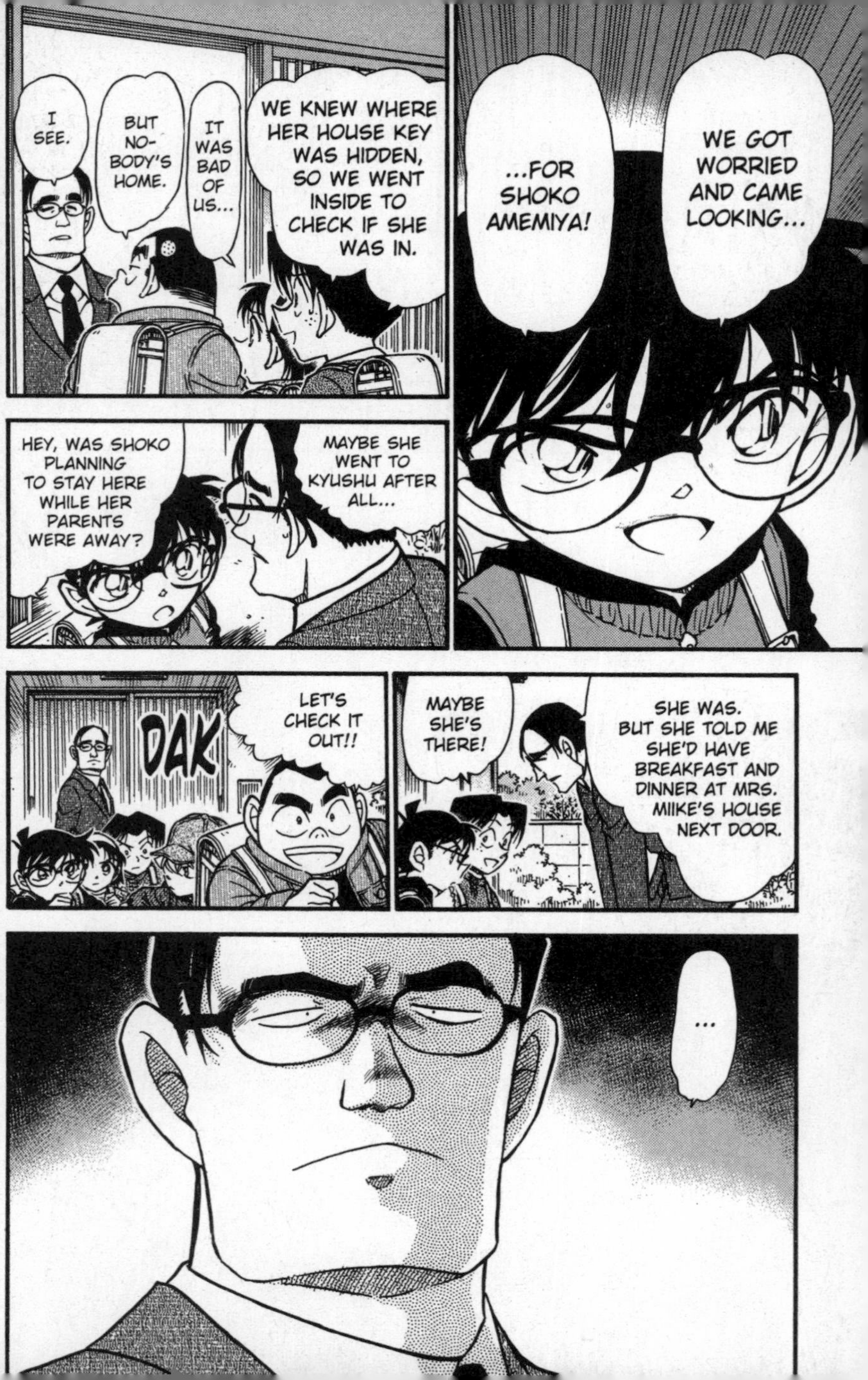
WE GOT WORRIED AND CAME LOOKING...
...FOR SHOKO AMEMIYA!
WE KNEW WHERE HER HOUSE KEY WAS HIDDEN, SO WE WENT INSIDE TO CHECK IF SHE WAS IN.
IT WAS BAD OF US...
BUT NO-BODY'S HOME.
I SEE.
MAYBE SHE WENT TO KYUSHU AFTER ALL...
HEY, WAS SHOKO PLANNING TO STAY HERE WHILE HER PARENTS WERE AWAY?
SHE WAS. BUT SHE TOLD ME SHE'D HAVE BREAKFAST AND DINNER AT MRS. MIIKE'S HOUSE NEXT DOOR.
MAYBE SHE'S THERE!
LET'S CHECK IT OUT!!
DAK
...

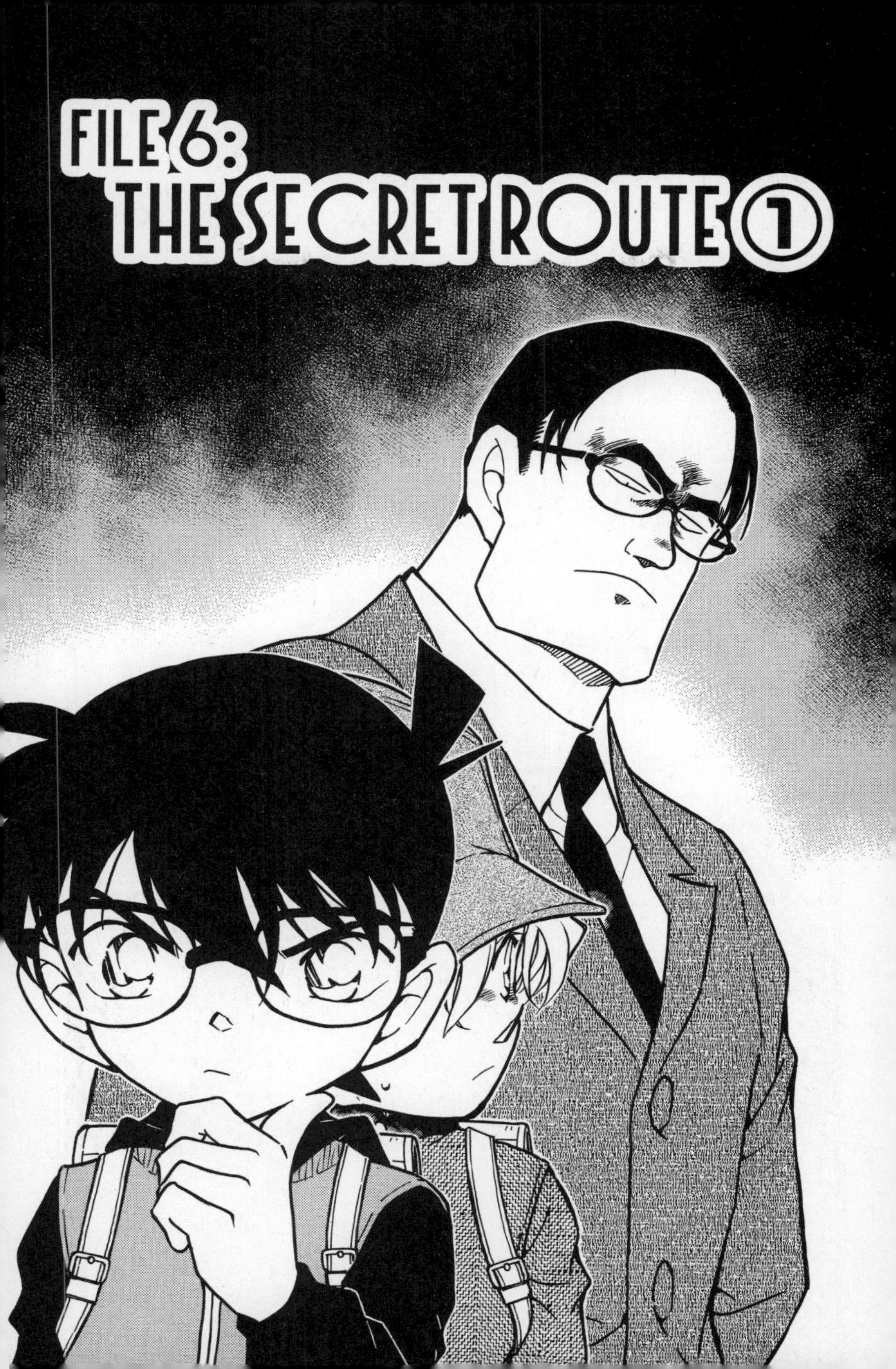
FILE 6:
THE SECRET ROUTE ①

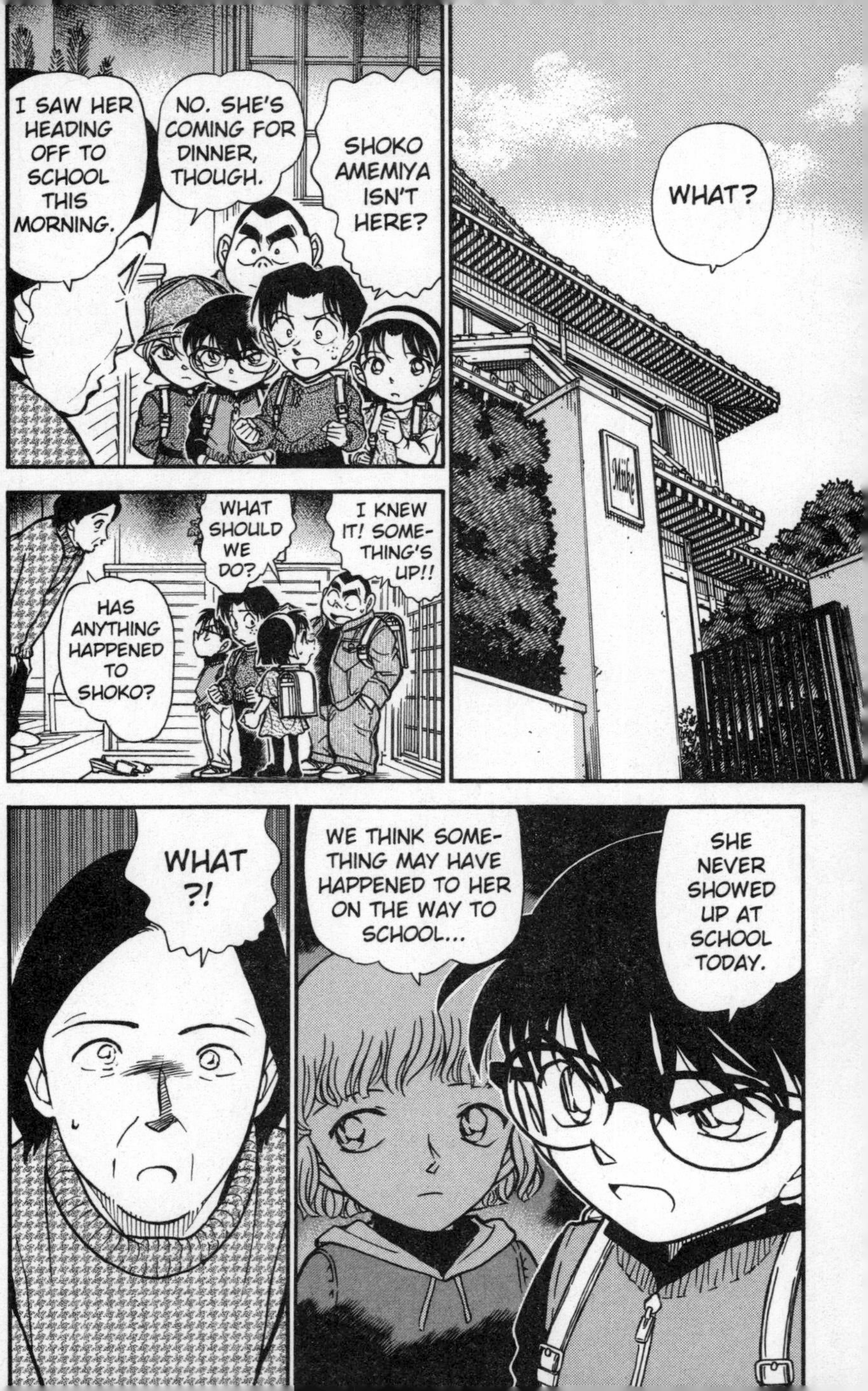
WHAT?
SHOKO AMEMIYA ISN'T HERE?
NO. SHE'S COMING FOR DINNER, THOUGH.
I SAW HER HEADING OFF TO SCHOOL THIS MORNING.
I KNEW IT! SOME-THING'S UP!!
WHAT SHOULD WE DO?
HAS ANYTHING HAPPENED TO SHOKO?
SHE NEVER SHOWED UP AT SCHOOL TODAY.
WE THINK SOME-THING MAY HAVE HAPPENED TO HER ON THE WAY TO SCHOOL...
WHAT ?!

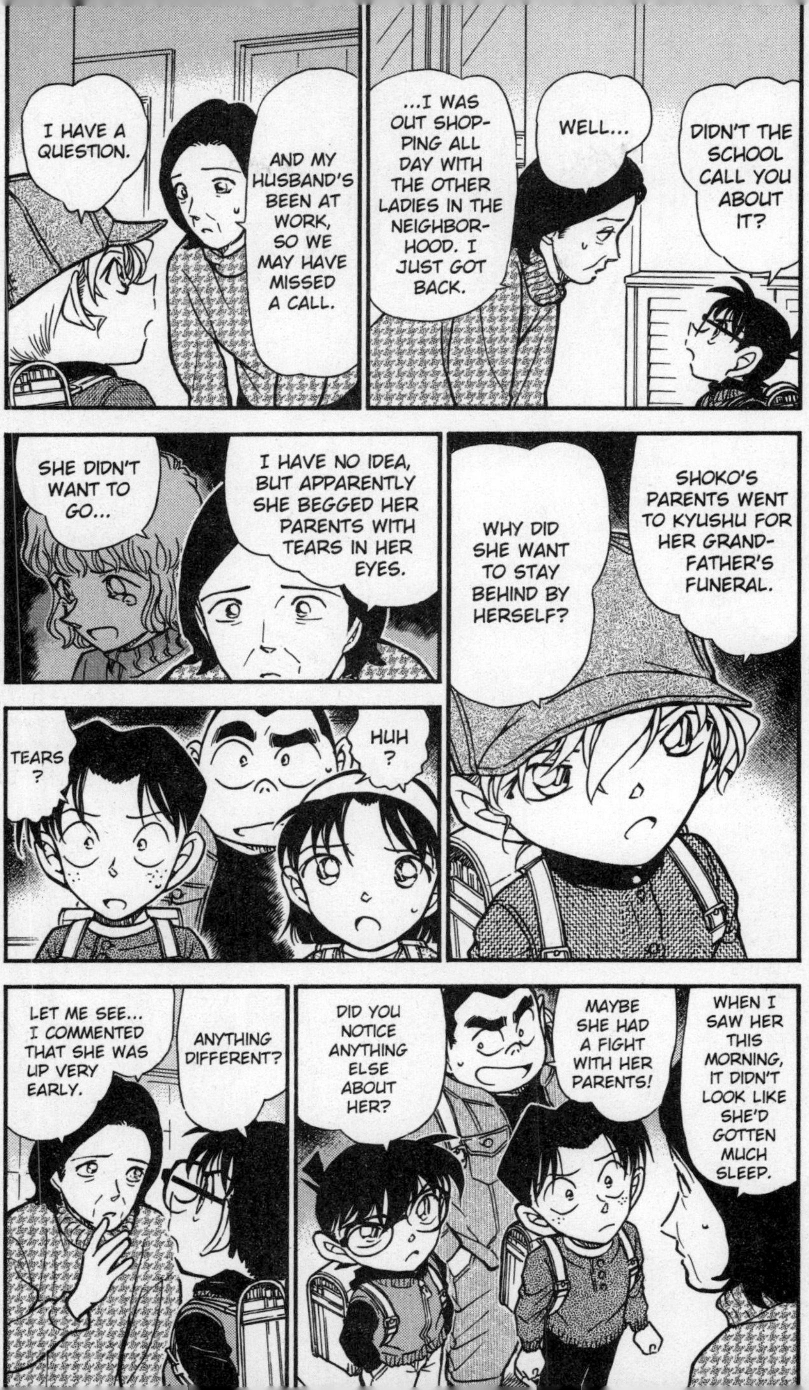
DIDN'T THE SCHOOL CALL YOU ABOUT IT?
WELL...
...I WAS OUT SHOPPING ALL DAY WITH THE OTHER LADIES IN THE NEIGHBORHOOD. I JUST GOT BACK.
AND MY HUSBAND'S BEEN AT WORK, SO WE MAY HAVE MISSED A CALL.
I HAVE A QUESTION.
SHOKO'S PARENTS WENT TO KYUSHU FOR HER GRANDFATHER'S FUNERAL.
WHY DID SHE WANT TO STAY BEHIND BY HERSELF?
I HAVE NO IDEA, BUT APPARENTLY SHE BEGGED HER PARENTS WITH TEARS IN HER EYES.
SHE DIDN'T WANT TO GO...
HUH?
TEARS?
WHEN I SAW HER THIS MORNING, IT DIDN'T LOOK LIKE SHE'D GOTTEN MUCH SLEEP.
MAYBE SHE HAD A FIGHT WITH HER PARENTS!
DID YOU NOTICE ANYTHING ELSE ABOUT HER?
ANYTHING DIFFERENT?
LET ME SEE... I COMMENTED THAT SHE WAS UP VERY EARLY.

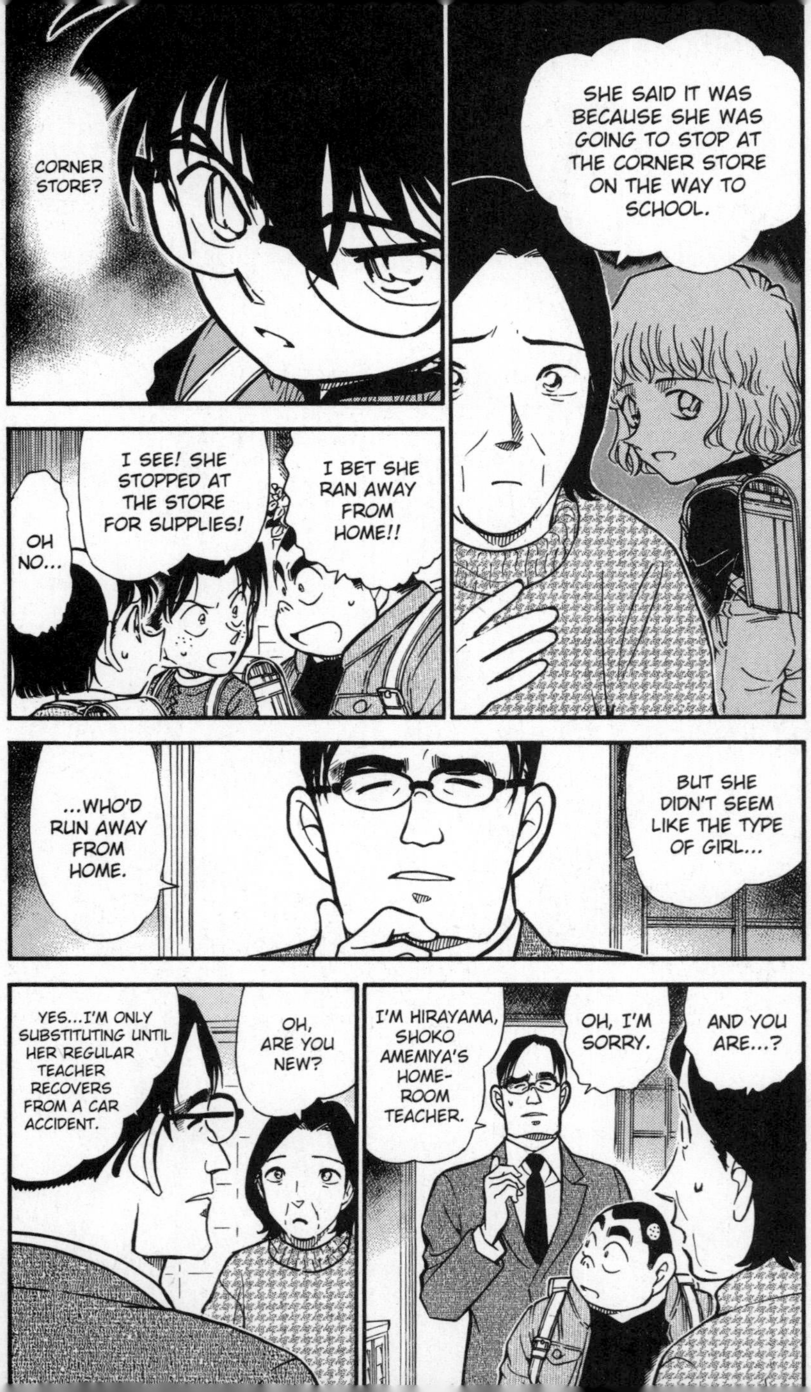
SHE SAID IT WAS BECAUSE SHE WAS GOING TO STOP AT THE CORNER STORE ON THE WAY TO SCHOOL.
CORNER STORE?
I BET SHE RAN AWAY FROM HOME!!
I SEE! SHE STOPPED AT THE STORE FOR SUPPLIES!
OH NO...
BUT SHE DIDN'T SEEM LIKE THE TYPE OF GIRL...
...WHO'D RUN AWAY FROM HOME.
AND YOU ARE...?
OH, I'M SORRY.
I'M HIRAYAMA, SHOKO AMEMIYA'S HOME-ROOM TEACHER.
OH, ARE YOU NEW?
YES...I'M ONLY SUBSTITUTING UNTIL HER REGULAR TEACHER RECOVERS FROM A CAR ACCIDENT.

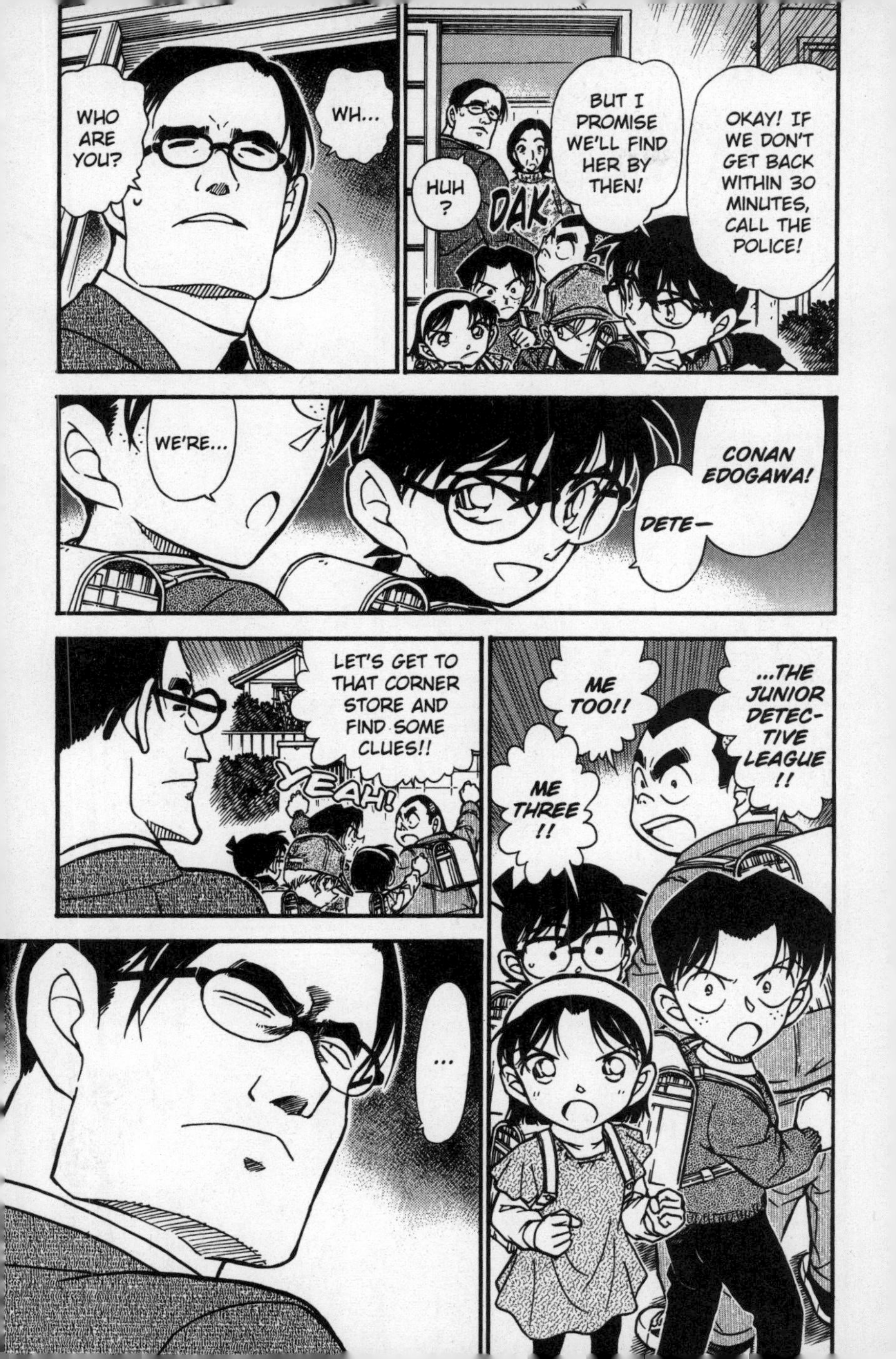
OKAY! IF WE DON'T GET BACK WITHIN 30 MINUTES, CALL THE POLICE!
BUT I PROMISE WE'LL FIND HER BY THEN!
DAK
HUH?
WH...
WHO ARE YOU?
CONAN EDOGAWA!
DETE—
WE'RE...
...THE JUNIOR DETECTIVE LEAGUE!!
ME TOO!!
ME THREE!!
LET'S GET TO THAT CORNER STORE AND FIND SOME CLUES!!
YEAH!
...

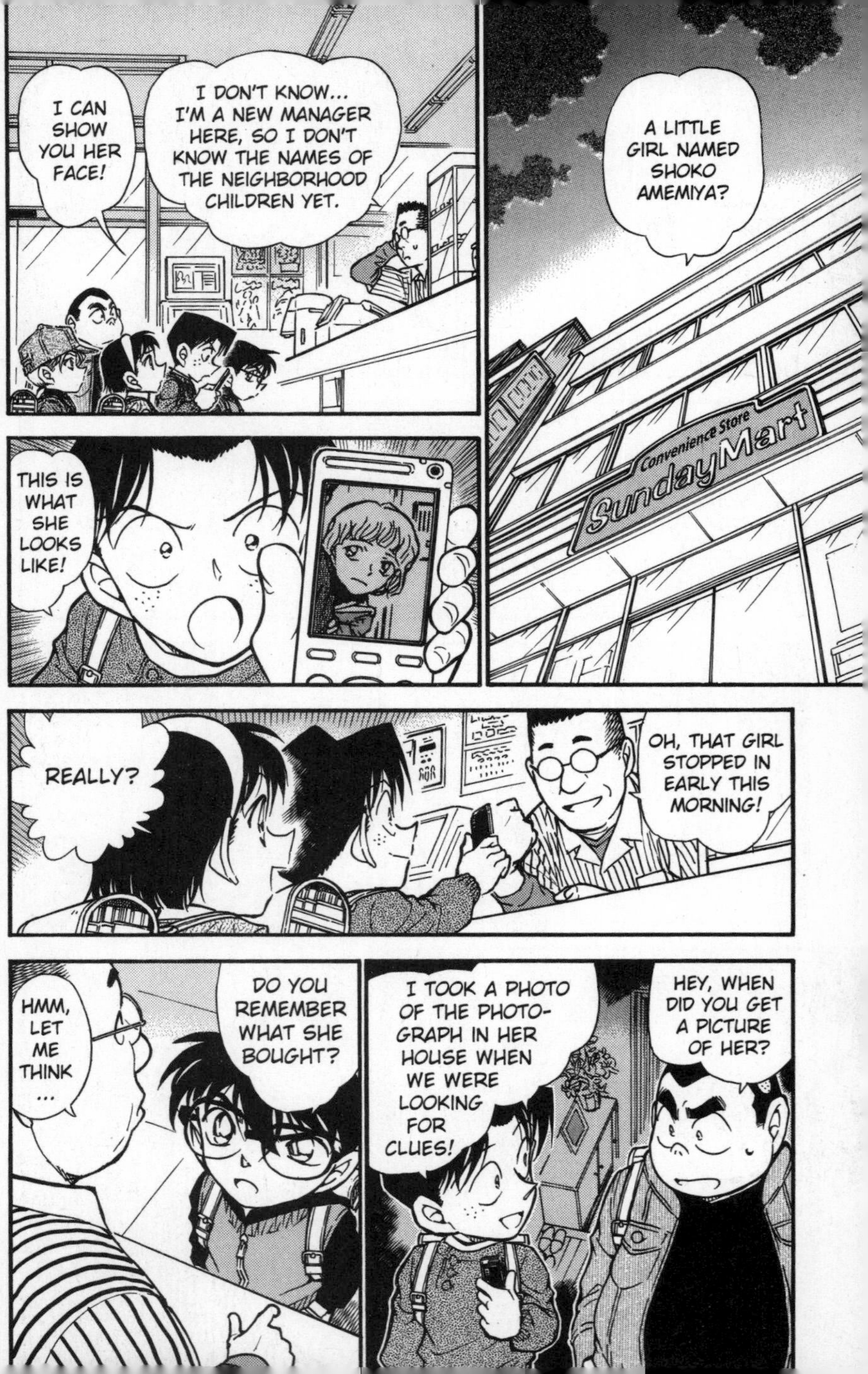
A LITTLE GIRL NAMED SHOKO AMEMIYA?
Convenience Store
SundayMart
I DON'T KNOW... I'M A NEW MANAGER HERE, SO I DON'T KNOW THE NAMES OF THE NEIGHBORHOOD CHILDREN YET.
I CAN SHOW YOU HER FACE!
THIS IS WHAT SHE LOOKS LIKE!
OH, THAT GIRL STOPPED IN EARLY THIS MORNING!
REALLY?
HEY, WHEN DID YOU GET A PICTURE OF HER?
I TOOK A PHOTO OF THE PHOTO-GRAPH IN HER HOUSE WHEN WE WERE LOOKING FOR CLUES!
DO YOU REMEMBER WHAT SHE BOUGHT?
HMM, LET ME THINK ...

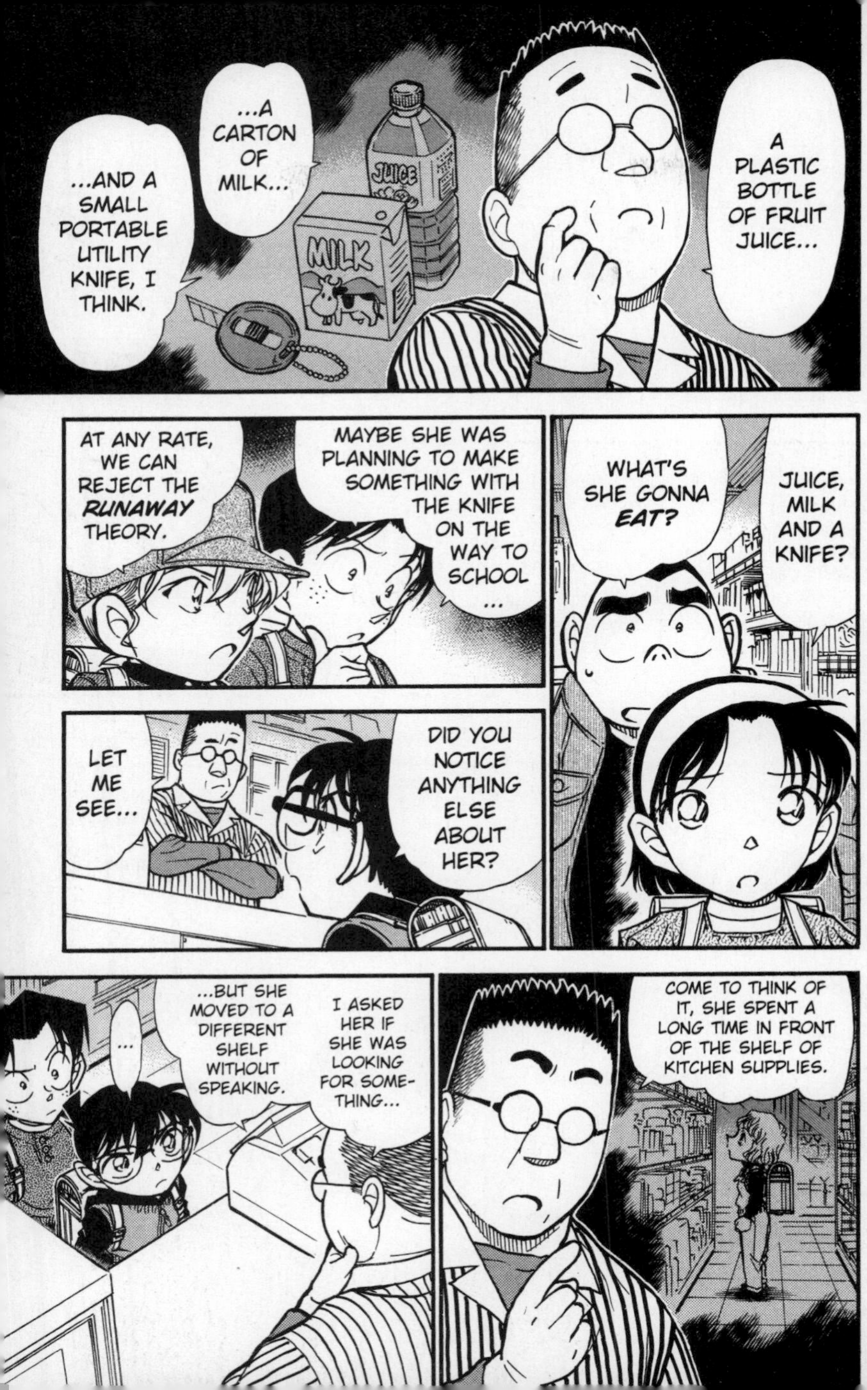
A PLASTIC BOTTLE OF FRUIT JUICE...
...A CARTON OF MILK...
...AND A SMALL PORTABLE UTILITY KNIFE, I THINK.
JUICE
MILK
JUICE, MILK AND A KNIFE?
WHAT'S SHE GONNA *EAT?*
MAYBE SHE WAS PLANNING TO MAKE SOMETHING WITH THE KNIFE ON THE WAY TO SCHOOL...
AT ANY RATE, WE CAN REJECT THE *RUNAWAY* THEORY.
DID YOU NOTICE ANYTHING ELSE ABOUT HER?
LET ME SEE...
COME TO THINK OF IT, SHE SPENT A LONG TIME IN FRONT OF THE SHELF OF KITCHEN SUPPLIES.
I ASKED HER IF SHE WAS LOOKING FOR SOMETHING...
...BUT SHE MOVED TO A DIFFERENT SHELF WITHOUT SPEAKING.
...

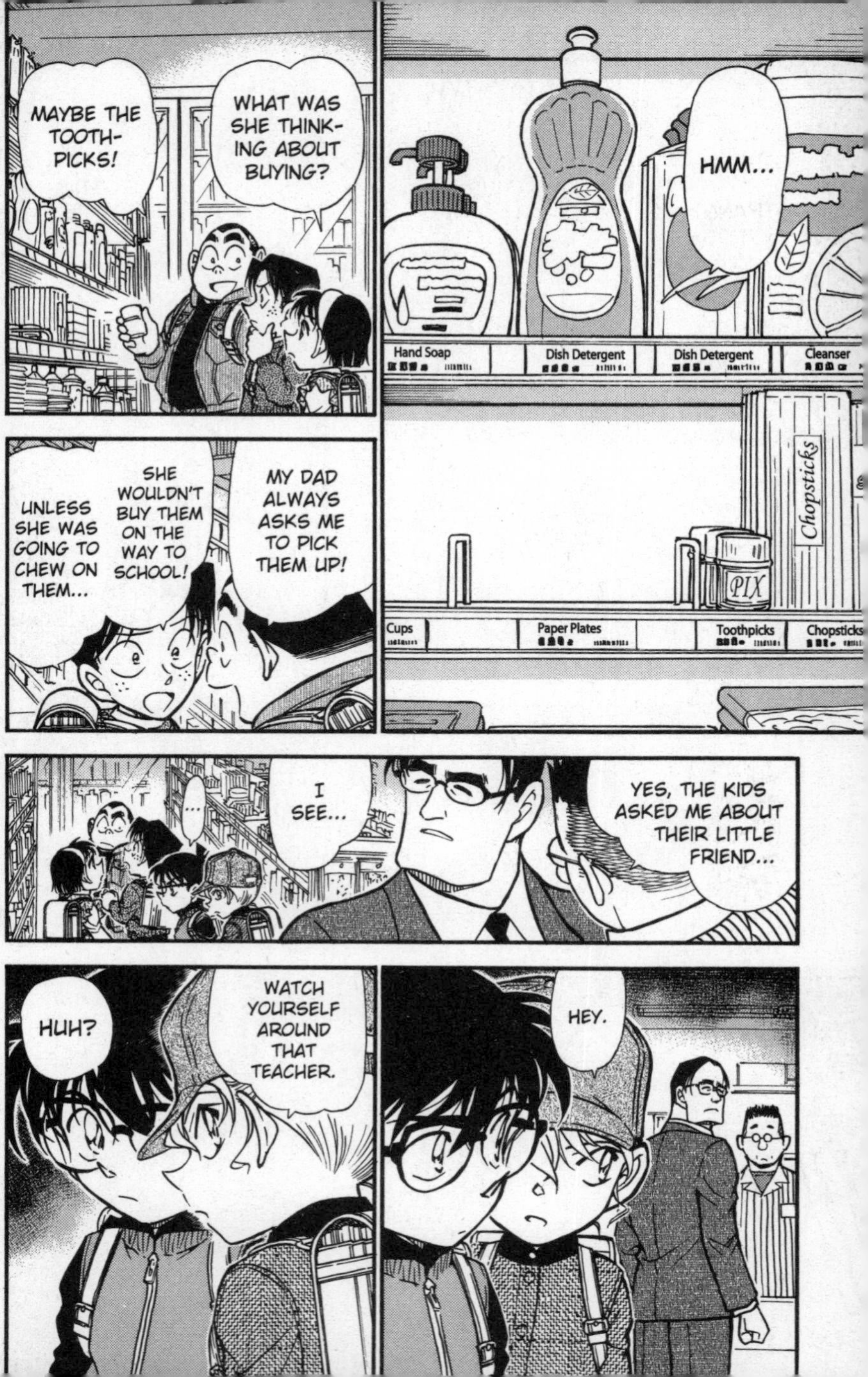
HMM...
Hand Soap
Dish Detergent
Dish Detergent
Cleanser
Chopsticks
PIX
Cups
Paper Plates
Toothpicks
Chopsticks
WHAT WAS SHE THINKING-ING ABOUT BUYING?
MAYBE THE TOOTH-PICKS!
MY DAD ALWAYS ASKS ME TO PICK THEM UP!
SHE WOULDN'T BUY THEM ON THE WAY TO SCHOOL!
UNLESS SHE WAS GOING TO CHEW ON THEM...
YES, THE KIDS ASKED ME ABOUT THEIR LITTLE FRIEND...
I SEE...
...
HEY.
WATCH YOURSELF AROUND THAT TEACHER.
HUH?

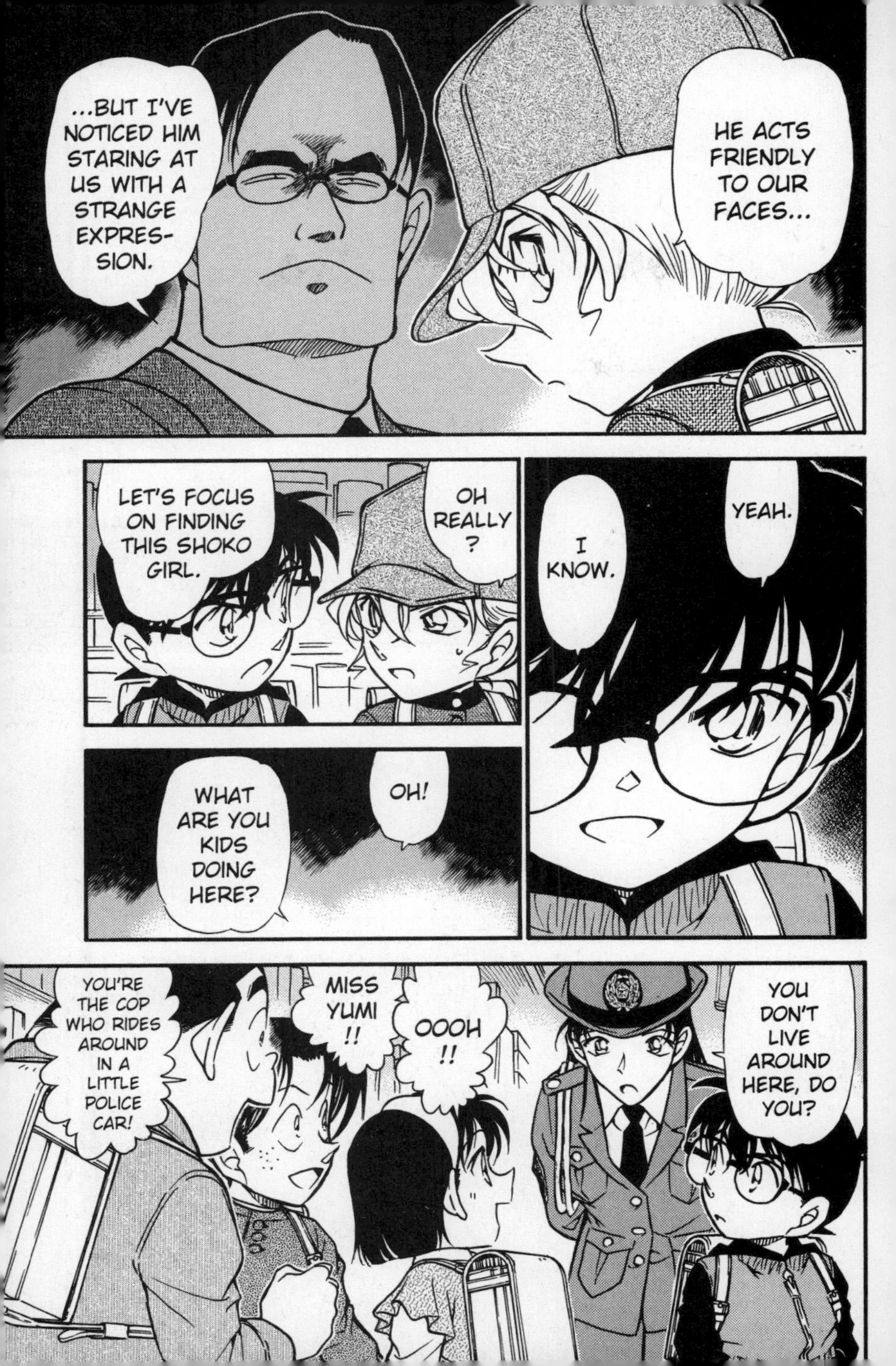

HE ACTS FRIENDLY TO OUR FACES...
...BUT I'VE NOTICED HIM STARING AT US WITH A STRANGE EXPRESSION.
YEAH.
I KNOW.
OH REALLY?
LET'S FOCUS ON FINDING THIS SHOKO GIRL.
OH!
WHAT ARE YOU KIDS DOING HERE?
YOU DON'T LIVE AROUND HERE, DO YOU?
OOOH!!
MISS YUMI!!
YOU'RE THE COP WHO RIDES AROUND IN A LITTLE POLICE CAR!

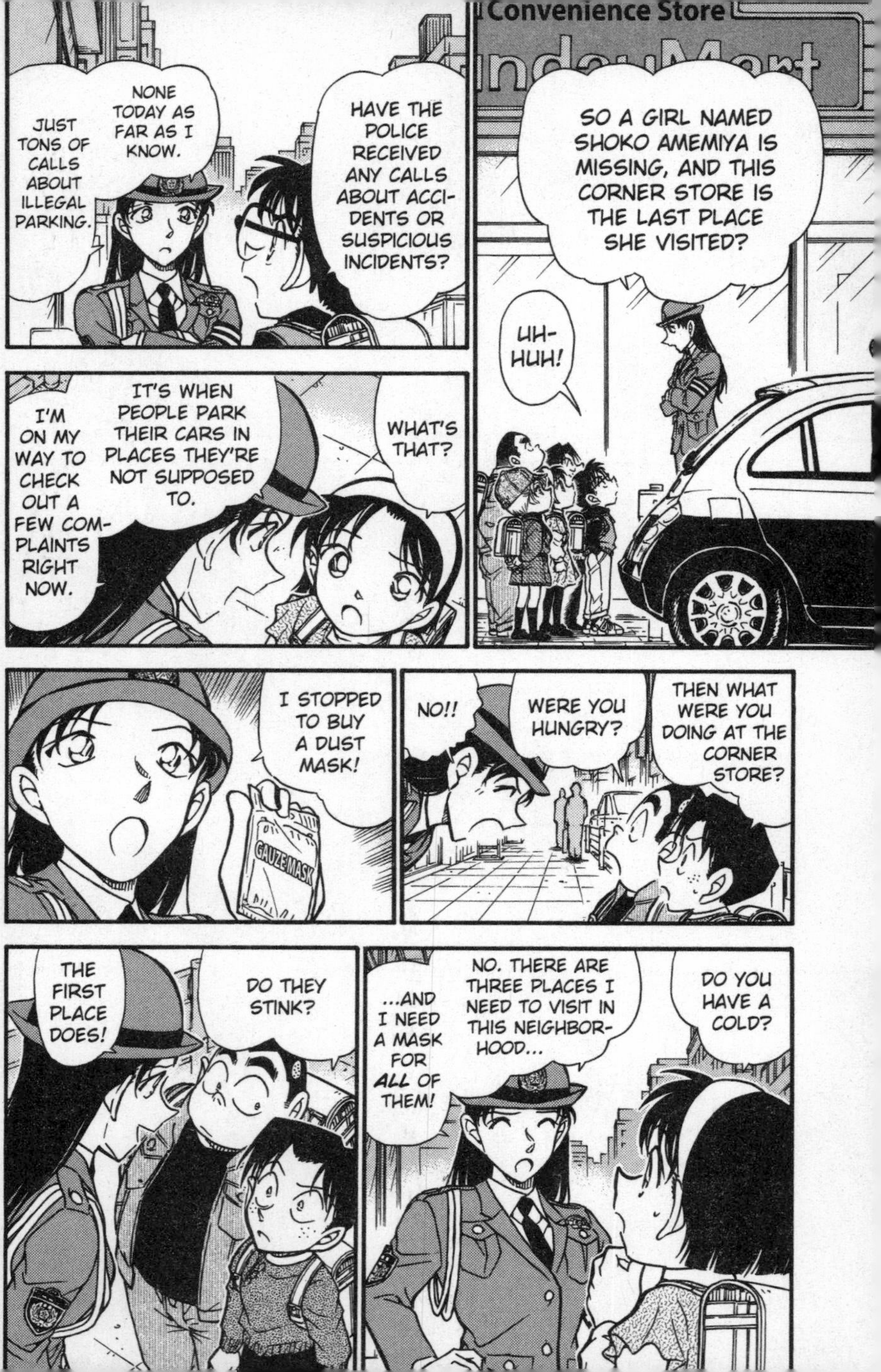
Convenience Store
SO A GIRL NAMED SHOKO AMEMIYA IS MISSING, AND THIS CORNER STORE IS THE LAST PLACE SHE VISITED?
UH-HUH!
HAVE THE POLICE RECEIVED ANY CALLS ABOUT ACCI-DENTS OR SUSPICIOUS INCIDENTS?
NONE TODAY AS FAR AS I KNOW.
JUST TONS OF CALLS ABOUT ILLEGAL PARKING.
WHAT'S THAT?
IT'S WHEN PEOPLE PARK THEIR CARS IN PLACES THEY'RE NOT SUPPOSED TO.
I'M ON MY WAY TO CHECK OUT A FEW COM-PLAINTS RIGHT NOW.
THEN WHAT WERE YOU DOING AT THE CORNER STORE?
WERE YOU HUNGRY?
NO!!
I STOPPED TO BUY A DUST MASK!
GAUZE MASK
DO YOU HAVE A COLD?
NO. THERE ARE THREE PLACES I NEED TO VISIT IN THIS NEIGHBOR-HOOD...
...AND I NEED A MASK FOR **ALL** OF THEM!
DO THEY STINK?
THE FIRST PLACE DOES!

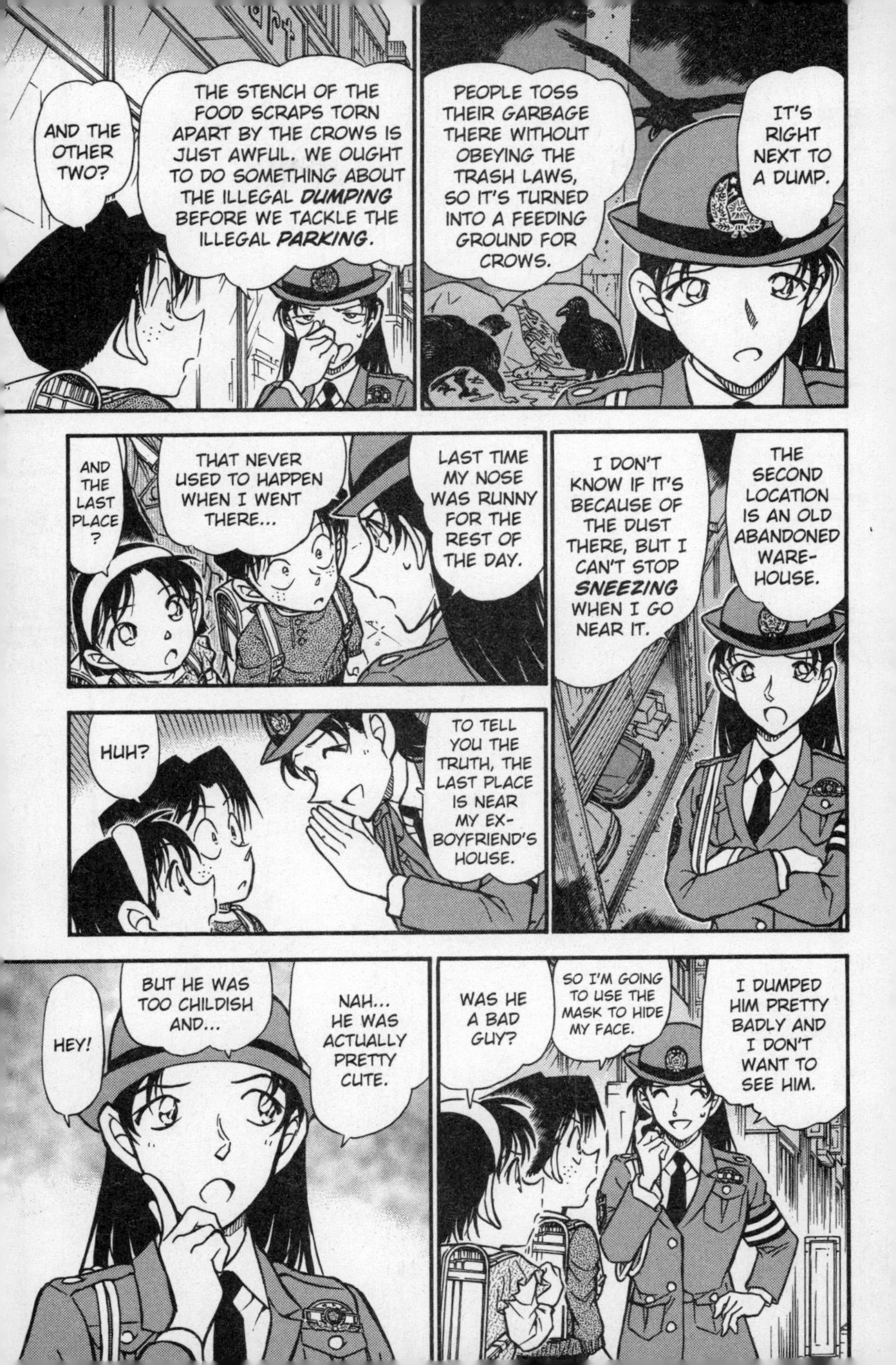
IT'S RIGHT NEXT TO A DUMP.
PEOPLE TOSS THEIR GARBAGE THERE WITHOUT OBEYING THE TRASH LAWS, SO IT'S TURNED INTO A FEEDING GROUND FOR CROWS.
THE STENCH OF THE FOOD SCRAPS TORN APART BY THE CROWS IS JUST AWFUL. WE OUGHT TO DO SOMETHING ABOUT THE ILLEGAL *DUMPING* BEFORE WE TACKLE THE ILLEGAL *PARKING*.
AND THE OTHER TWO?
THE SECOND LOCATION IS AN OLD ABANDONED WARE-HOUSE.
I DON'T KNOW IF IT'S BECAUSE OF THE DUST THERE, BUT I CAN'T STOP **SNEEZING** WHEN I GO NEAR IT.
LAST TIME MY NOSE WAS RUNNY FOR THE REST OF THE DAY.
THAT NEVER USED TO HAPPEN WHEN I WENT THERE...
AND THE LAST PLACE?
TO TELL YOU THE TRUTH, THE LAST PLACE IS NEAR MY EX-BOYFRIEND'S HOUSE.
HUH?
I DUMPED HIM PRETTY BADLY AND I DON'T WANT TO SEE HIM.
SO I'M GOING TO USE THE MASK TO HIDE MY FACE.
WAS HE A BAD GUY?
NAH... HE WAS ACTUALLY PRETTY CUTE.
BUT HE WAS TOO CHILDISH AND...
HEY!

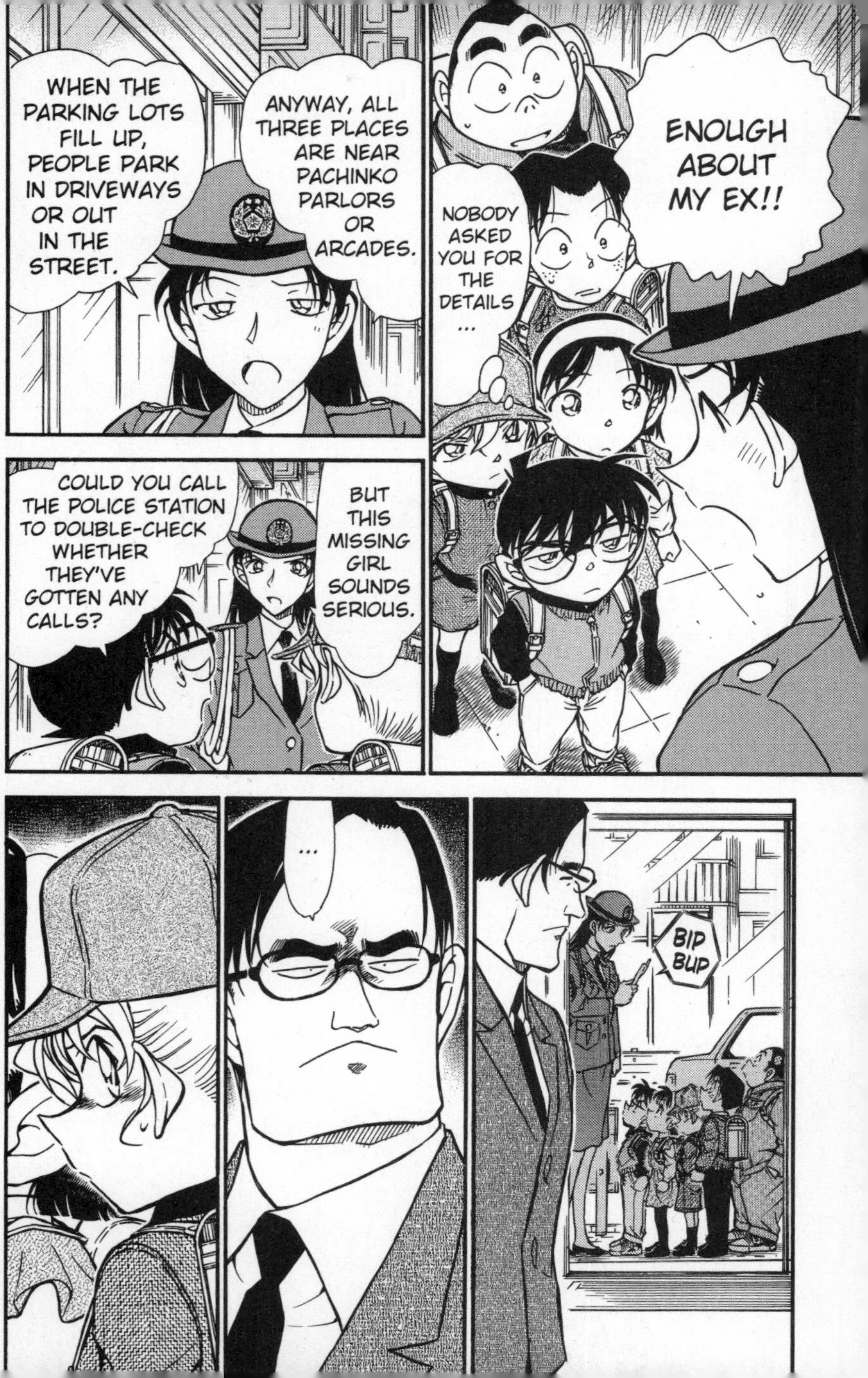
ENOUGH ABOUT MY EX!!
NOBODY ASKED YOU FOR THE DETAILS ...
ANYWAY, ALL THREE PLACES ARE NEAR PACHINKO PARLORS OR ARCADES.
WHEN THE PARKING LOTS FILL UP, PEOPLE PARK IN DRIVEWAYS OR OUT IN THE STREET.
BUT THIS MISSING GIRL SOUNDS SERIOUS.
COULD YOU CALL THE POLICE STATION TO DOUBLE-CHECK WHETHER THEY'VE GOTTEN ANY CALLS?
BIP BUP
...

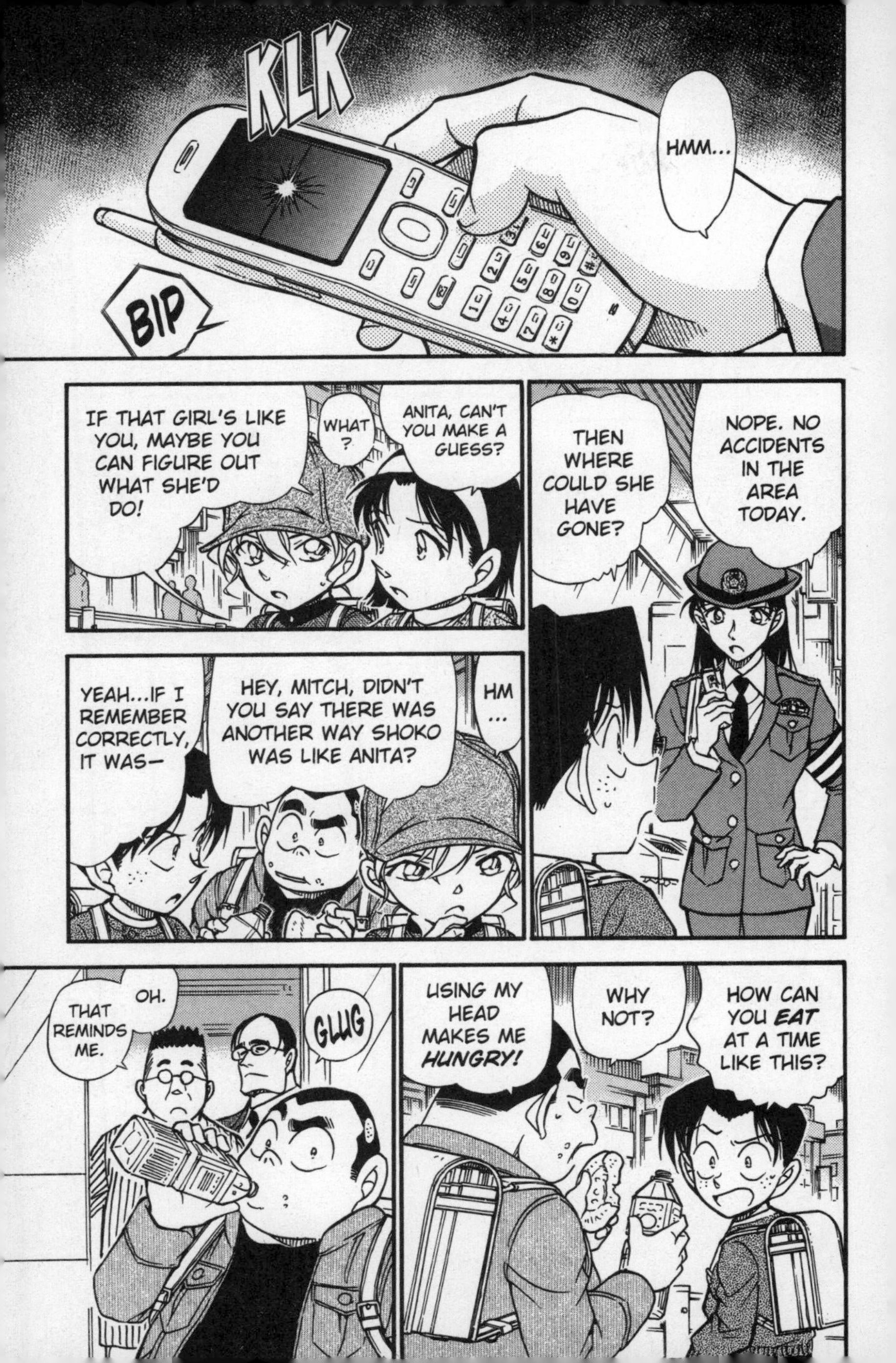
HMM...
KLK
BIP
NOPE. NO ACCIDENTS IN THE AREA TODAY.
THEN WHERE COULD SHE HAVE GONE?
ANITA, CAN'T YOU MAKE A GUESS?
WHAT?
IF THAT GIRL'S LIKE YOU, MAYBE YOU CAN FIGURE OUT WHAT SHE'D DO!
HM...
HEY, MITCH, DIDN'T YOU SAY THERE WAS ANOTHER WAY SHOKO WAS LIKE ANITA?
YEAH...IF I REMEMBER CORRECTLY, IT WAS—
HOW CAN YOU *EAT* AT A TIME LIKE THIS?
WHY NOT?
USING MY HEAD MAKES ME *HUNGRY!*
GLUG
OH. THAT REMINDS ME.

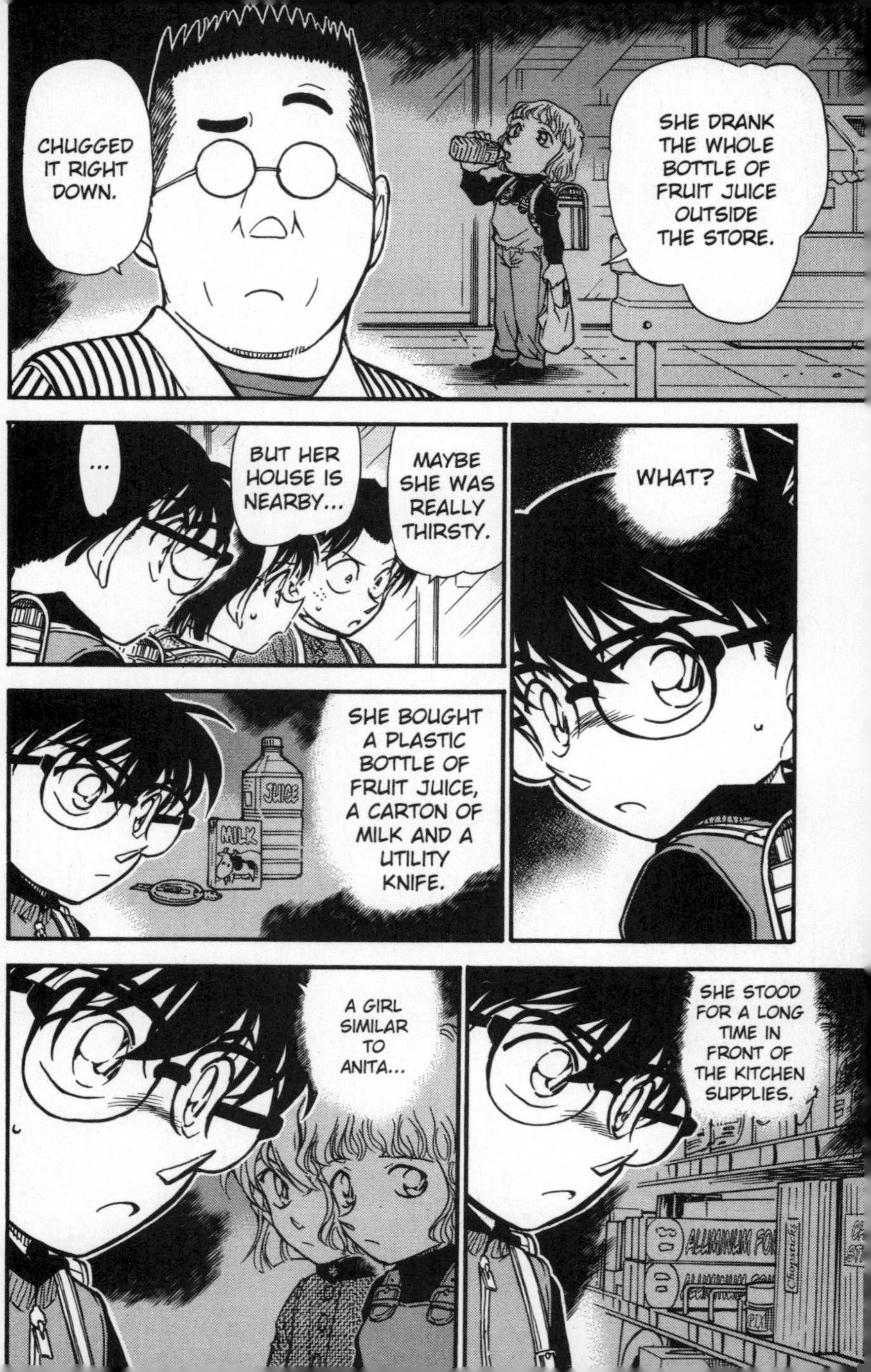
SHE DRANK THE WHOLE BOTTLE OF FRUIT JUICE OUTSIDE THE STORE.
CHUGGED IT RIGHT DOWN.
MAYBE SHE WAS REALLY THIRSTY.
BUT HER HOUSE IS NEARBY...
...
WHAT?
SHE BOUGHT A PLASTIC BOTTLE OF FRUIT JUICE, A CARTON OF MILK AND A UTILITY KNIFE.
JUICE
MILK
SHE STOOD FOR A LONG TIME IN FRONT OF THE KITCHEN SUPPLIES.
ALUMINUM FOI
Chopsticks
A GIRL SIMILAR TO ANITA...

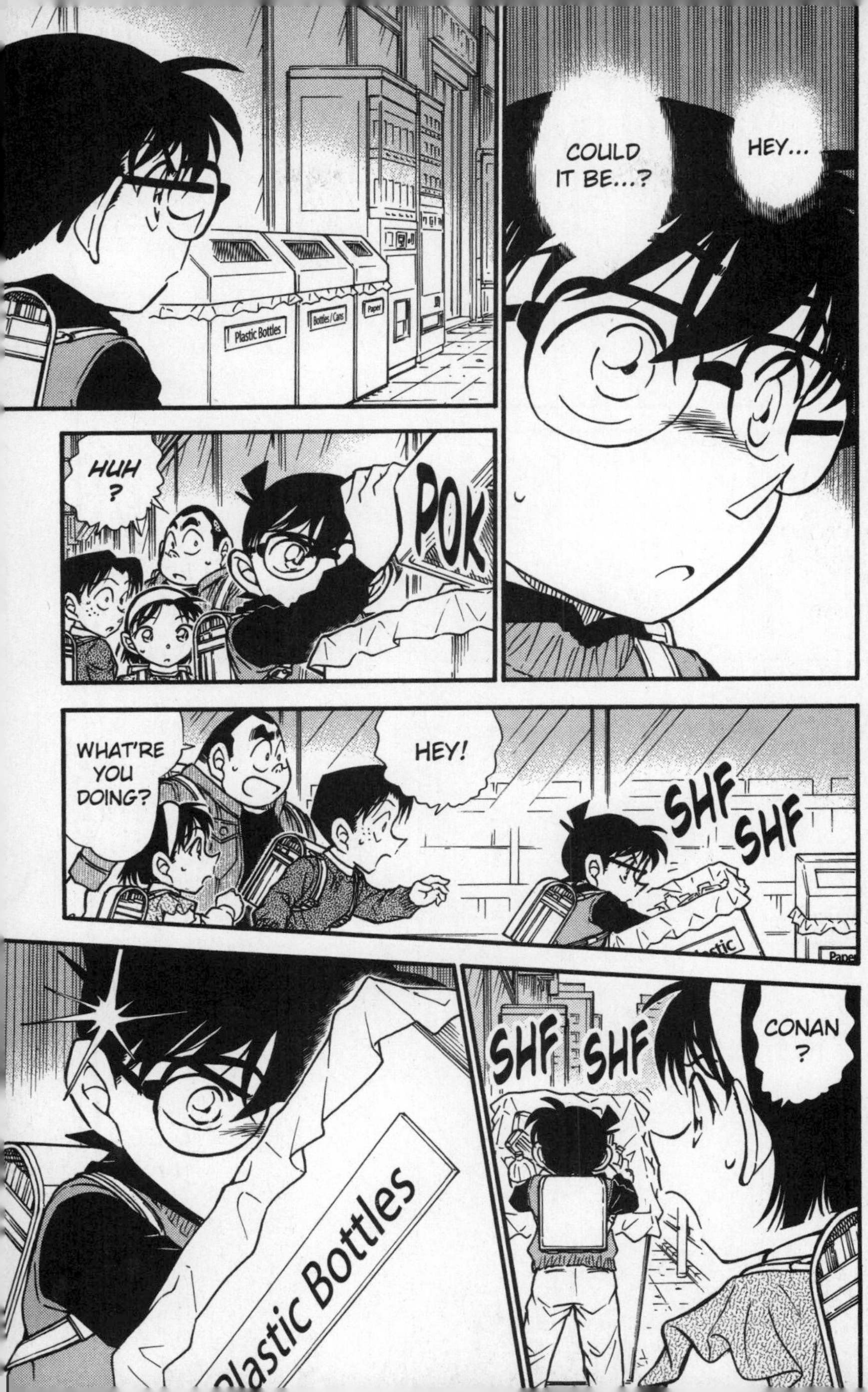

HEY...
COULD IT BE...?
Plastic Bottles
Bottles / Cans
Paper
HUH ?
POK
SHF SHF
HEY!
WHAT'RE YOU DOING?
Paper
CONAN ?
SHF SHF
Plastic Bottles

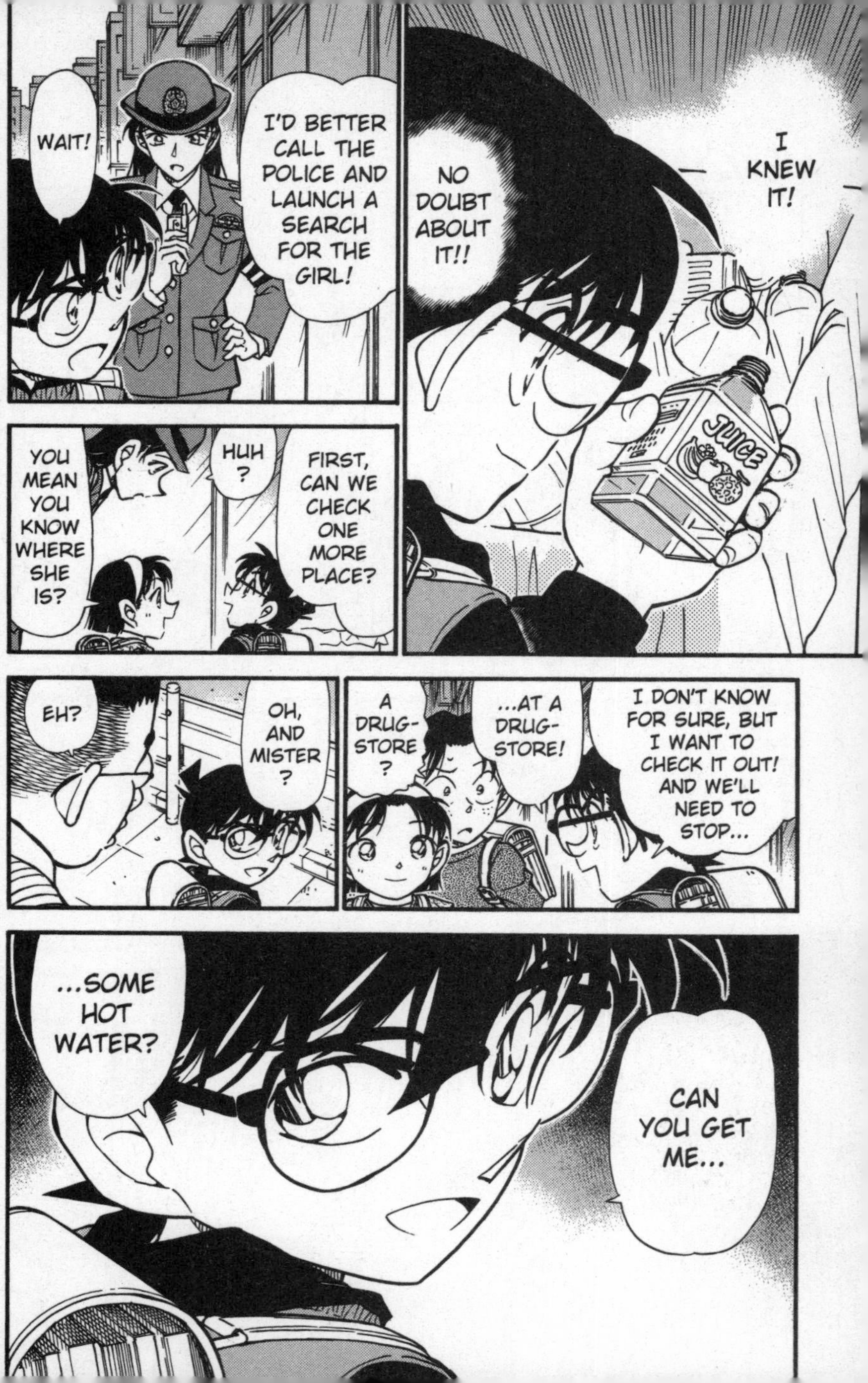
I KNEW IT!
NO DOUBT ABOUT IT!!
I'D BETTER CALL THE POLICE AND LAUNCH A SEARCH FOR THE GIRL!
WAIT!
FIRST, CAN WE CHECK ONE MORE PLACE?
HUH?
YOU MEAN YOU KNOW WHERE SHE IS?
I DON'T KNOW FOR SURE, BUT I WANT TO CHECK IT OUT! AND WE'LL NEED TO STOP...
...AT A DRUG-STORE!
A DRUG-STORE?
OH, AND MISTER?
EH?
CAN YOU GET ME...
...SOME HOT WATER?

FILE 7: THE SECRET ROUTE ②

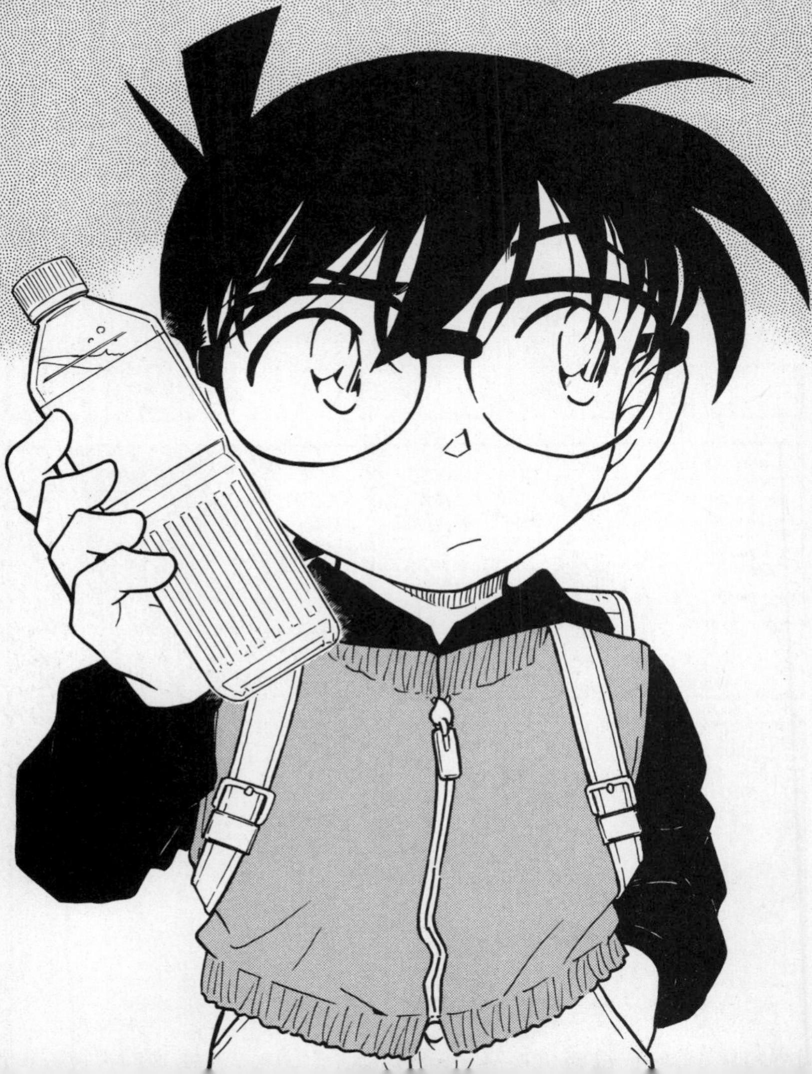

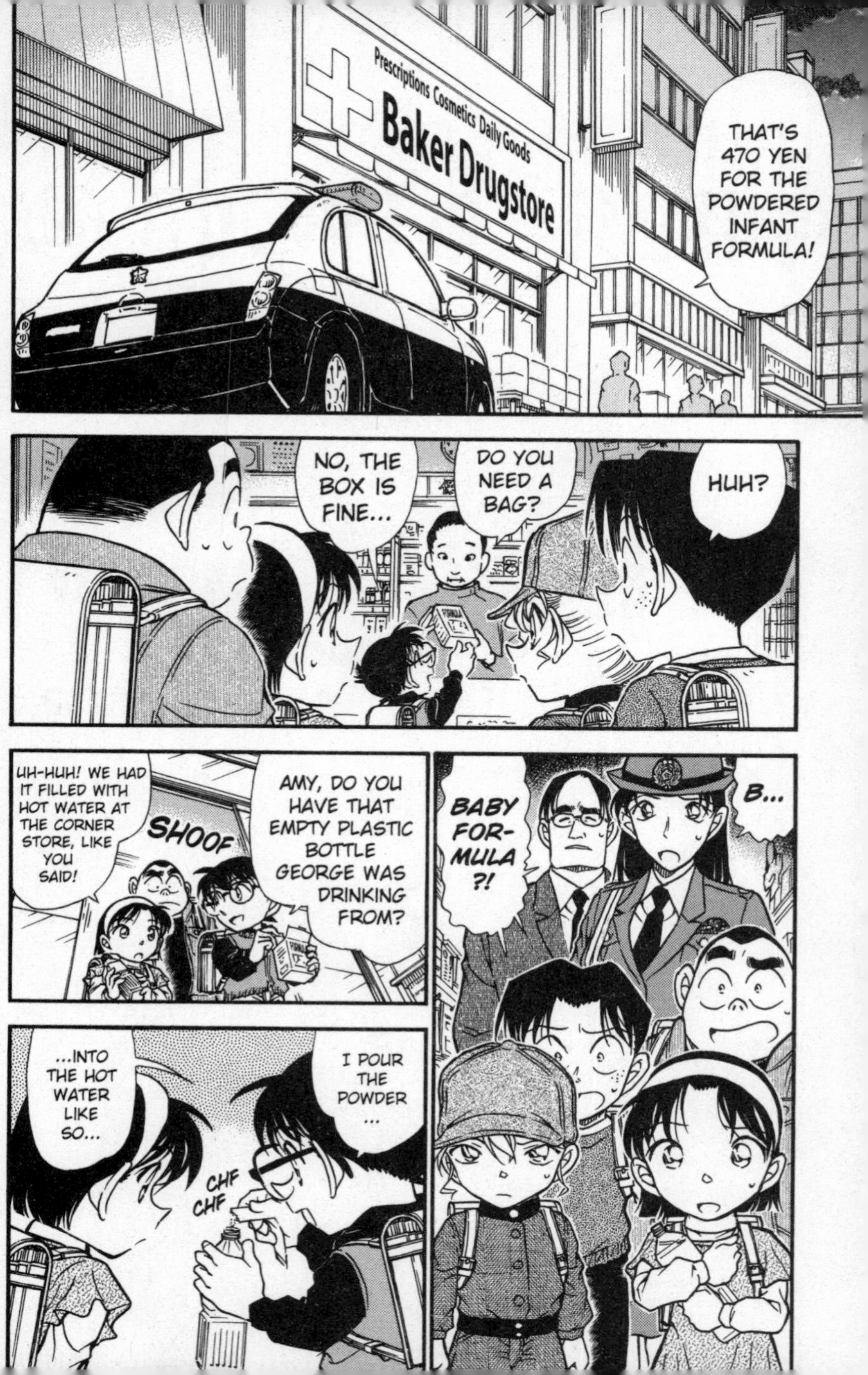
Prescriptions Cosmetics Daily Goods
Baker Drugstore
THAT'S 470 YEN FOR THE POWDERED INFANT FORMULA!
HUH?
DO YOU NEED A BAG?
NO, THE BOX IS FINE...
B...
BABY FOR-MULA?!
AMY, DO YOU HAVE THAT EMPTY PLASTIC BOTTLE GEORGE WAS DRINKING FROM?
SHOOF
UH-HUH! WE HAD IT FILLED WITH HOT WATER AT THE CORNER STORE, LIKE YOU SAID!
I POUR THE POWDER ...
...INTO THE HOT WATER LIKE SO...
CHF CHF

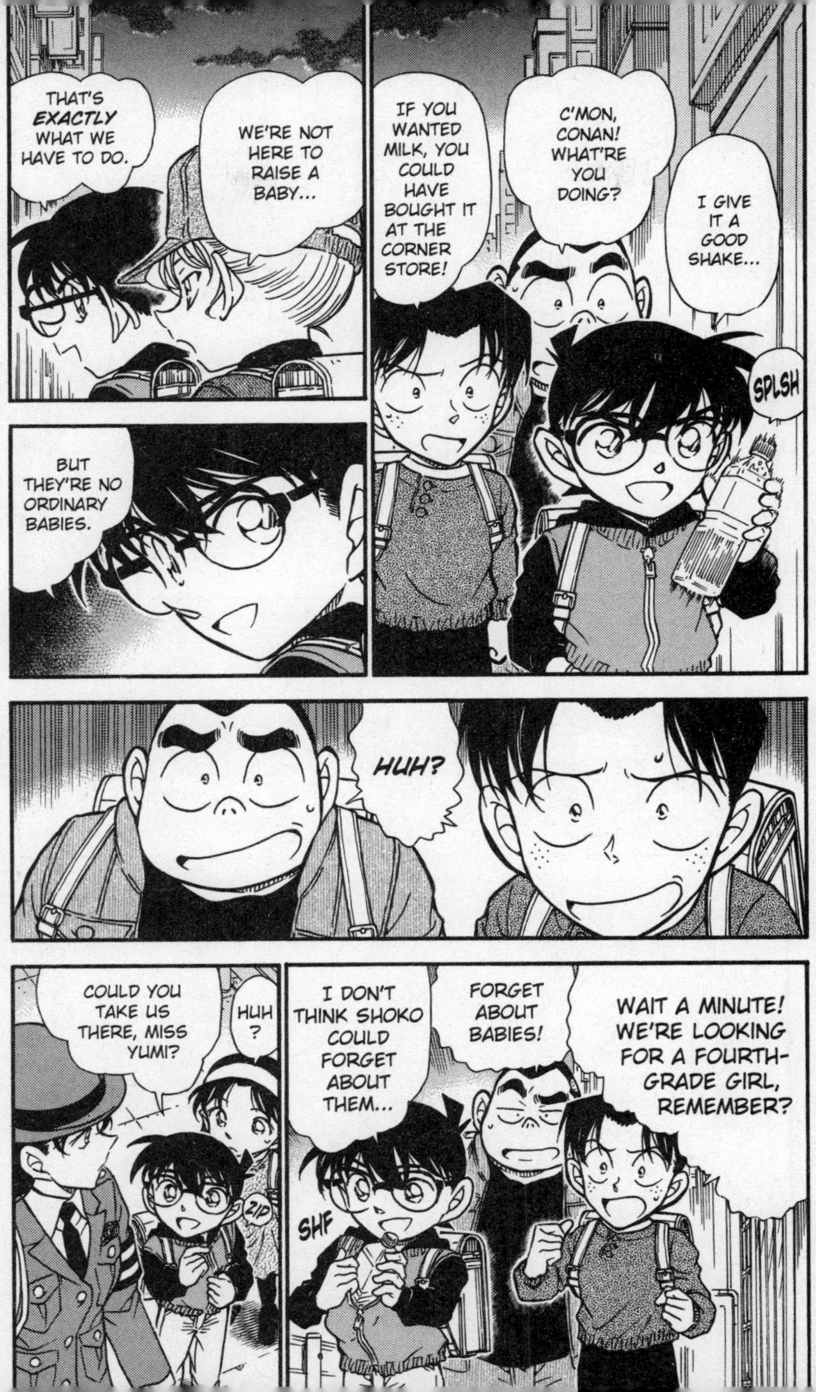
C'MON, CONAN! WHAT'RE YOU DOING?
I GIVE IT A GOOD SHAKE...
SPLSH
IF YOU WANTED MILK, YOU COULD HAVE BOUGHT IT AT THE CORNER STORE!
WE'RE NOT HERE TO RAISE A BABY...
THAT'S *EXACTLY* WHAT WE HAVE TO DO.
BUT THEY'RE NO ORDINARY BABIES.
HUH?
WAIT A MINUTE! WE'RE LOOKING FOR A FOURTH-GRADE GIRL, REMEMBER?
FORGET ABOUT BABIES!
I DON'T THINK SHOKO COULD FORGET ABOUT THEM...
SHF
HUH ?
COULD YOU TAKE US THERE, MISS YUMI?
ZIP

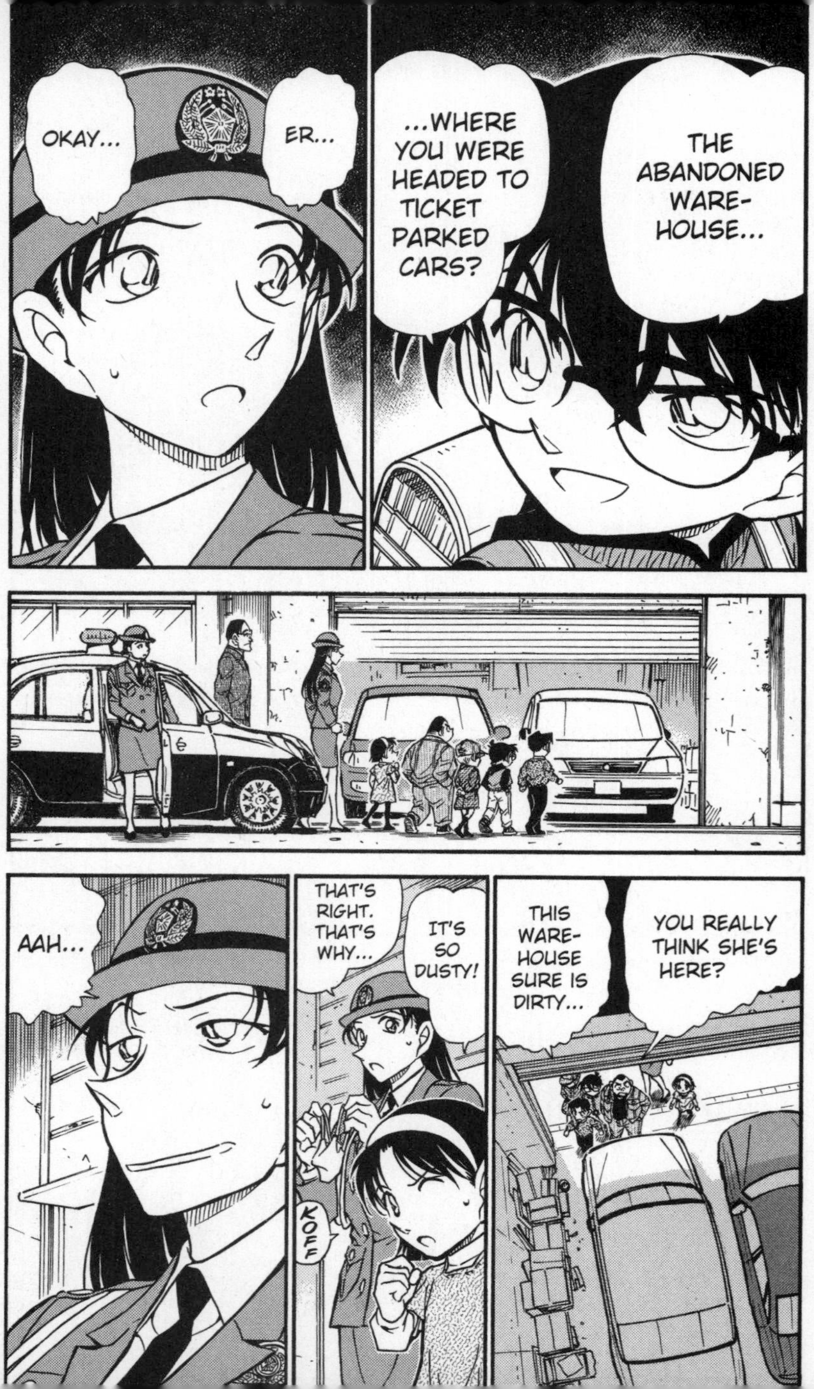
THE ABANDONED WARE-HOUSE...
...WHERE YOU WERE HEADED TO TICKET PARKED CARS?
ER...
OKAY...
YOU REALLY THINK SHE'S HERE?
THIS WARE-HOUSE SURE IS DIRTY...
IT'S SO DUSTY!
THAT'S RIGHT. THAT'S WHY...
KOFF
AAH...

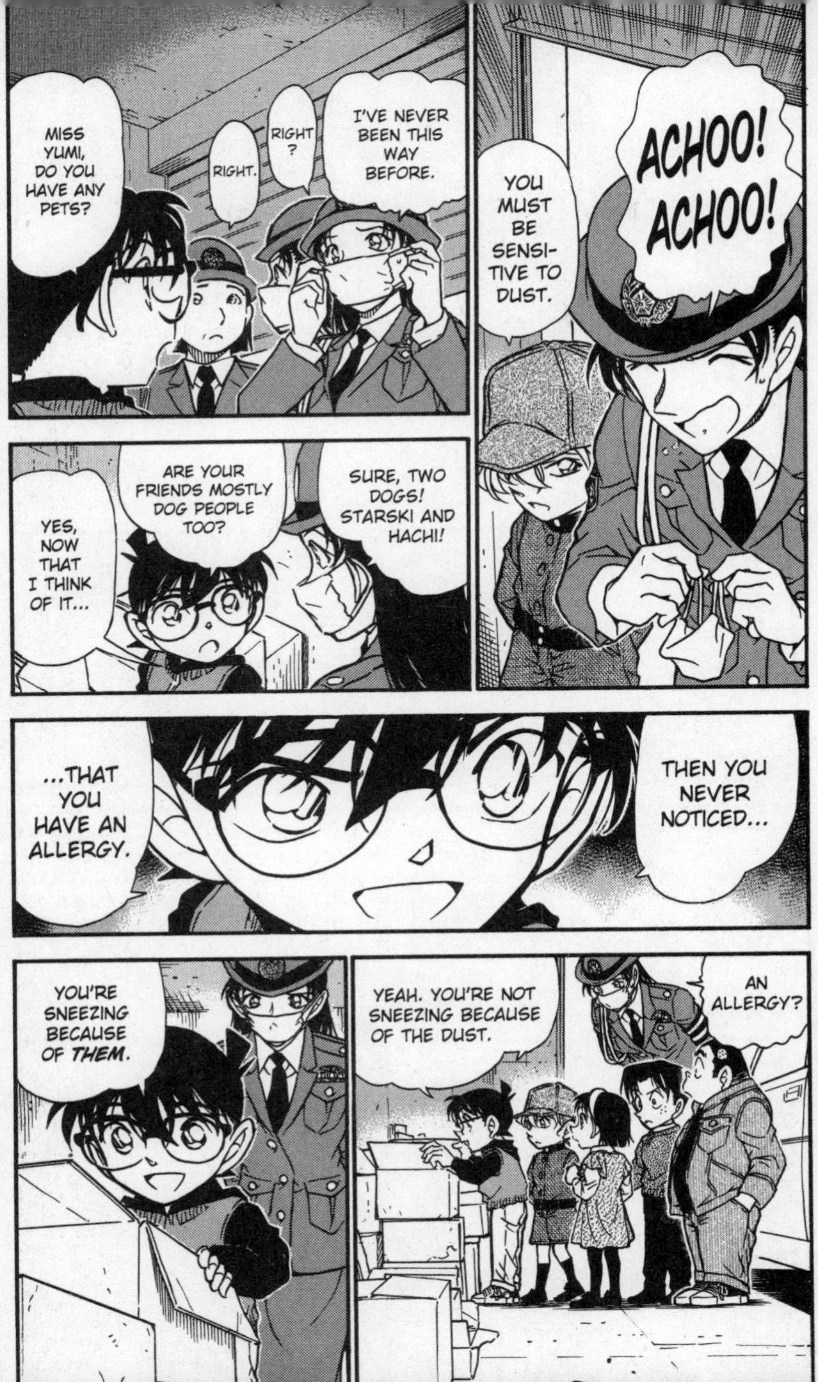
ACHOO! ACHOO!
YOU MUST BE SENSI-TIVE TO DUST.
I'VE NEVER BEEN THIS WAY BEFORE.
RIGHT?
RIGHT.
MISS YUMI, DO YOU HAVE ANY PETS?
SURE, TWO DOGS! STARSKI AND HACHI!
ARE YOUR FRIENDS MOSTLY DOG PEOPLE TOO?
YES, NOW THAT I THINK OF IT...
THEN YOU NEVER NOTICED...
...THAT YOU HAVE AN ALLERGY.
AN ALLERGY?
YEAH. YOU'RE NOT SNEEZING BECAUSE OF THE DUST.
YOU'RE SNEEZING BECAUSE OF *THEM*.

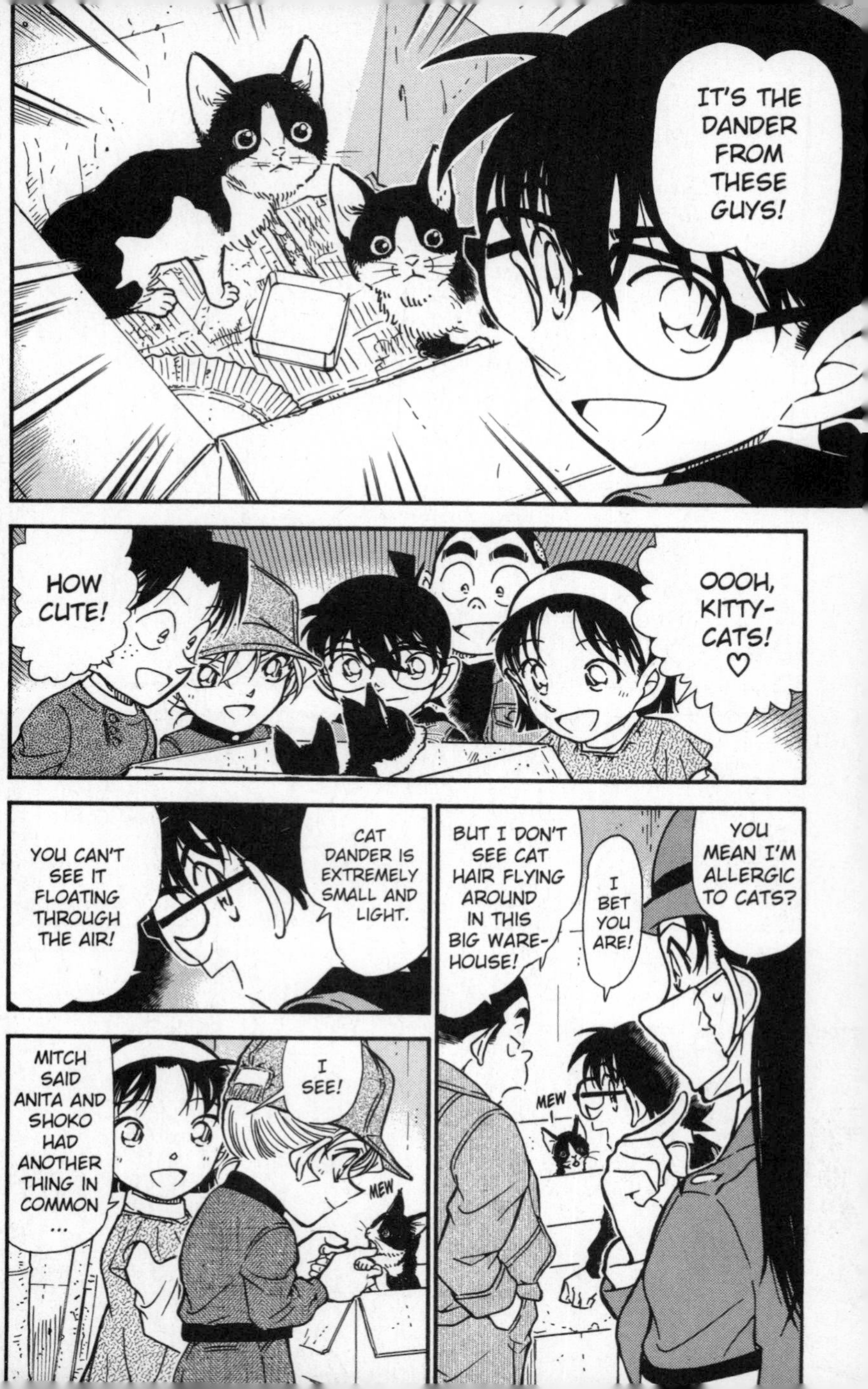
IT'S THE DANDER FROM THESE GUYS!
OOOH, KITTY-CATS! ♡
HOW CUTE!
YOU MEAN I'M ALLERGIC TO CATS?
I BET YOU ARE!
BUT I DON'T SEE CAT HAIR FLYING AROUND IN THIS BIG WARE-HOUSE!
MEW
CAT DANDER IS EXTREMELY SMALL AND LIGHT.
YOU CAN'T SEE IT FLOATING THROUGH THE AIR!
I SEE!
MITCH SAID ANITA AND SHOKO HAD ANOTHER THING IN COMMON ...
MEW

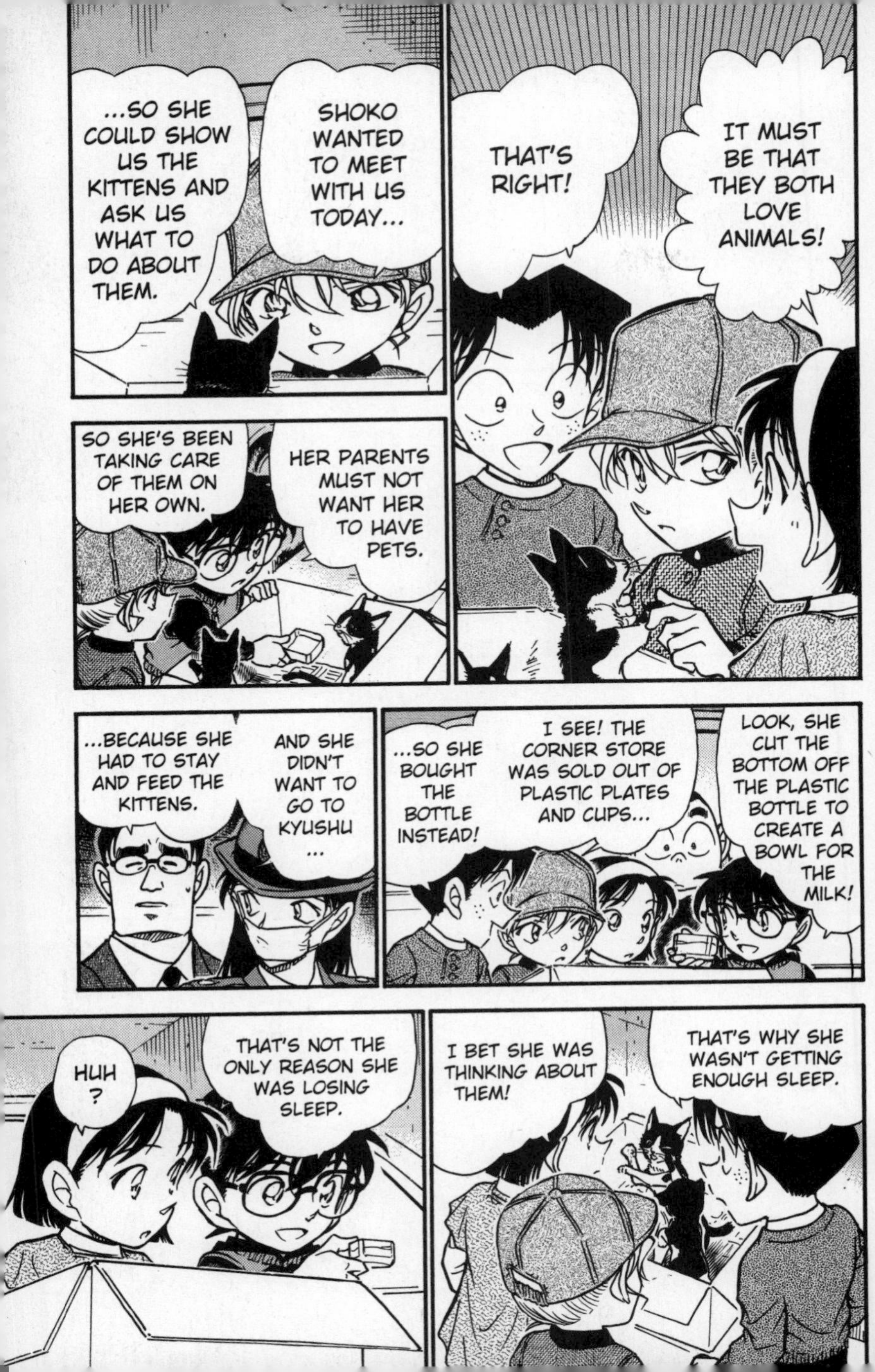
IT MUST BE THAT THEY BOTH LOVE ANIMALS!
THAT'S RIGHT!
SHOKO WANTED TO MEET WITH US TODAY...
...SO SHE COULD SHOW US THE KITTENS AND ASK US WHAT TO DO ABOUT THEM.
HER PARENTS MUST NOT WANT HER TO HAVE PETS.
SO SHE'S BEEN TAKING CARE OF THEM ON HER OWN.
LOOK, SHE CUT THE BOTTOM OFF THE PLASTIC BOTTLE TO CREATE A BOWL FOR THE MILK!
I SEE! THE CORNER STORE WAS SOLD OUT OF PLASTIC PLATES AND CUPS...
...SO SHE BOUGHT THE BOTTLE INSTEAD!
AND SHE DIDN'T WANT TO GO TO KYUSHU ...
...BECAUSE SHE HAD TO STAY AND FEED THE KITTENS.
THAT'S WHY SHE WASN'T GETTING ENOUGH SLEEP.
I BET SHE WAS THINKING ABOUT THEM!
THAT'S NOT THE ONLY REASON SHE WAS LOSING SLEEP.
HUH ?

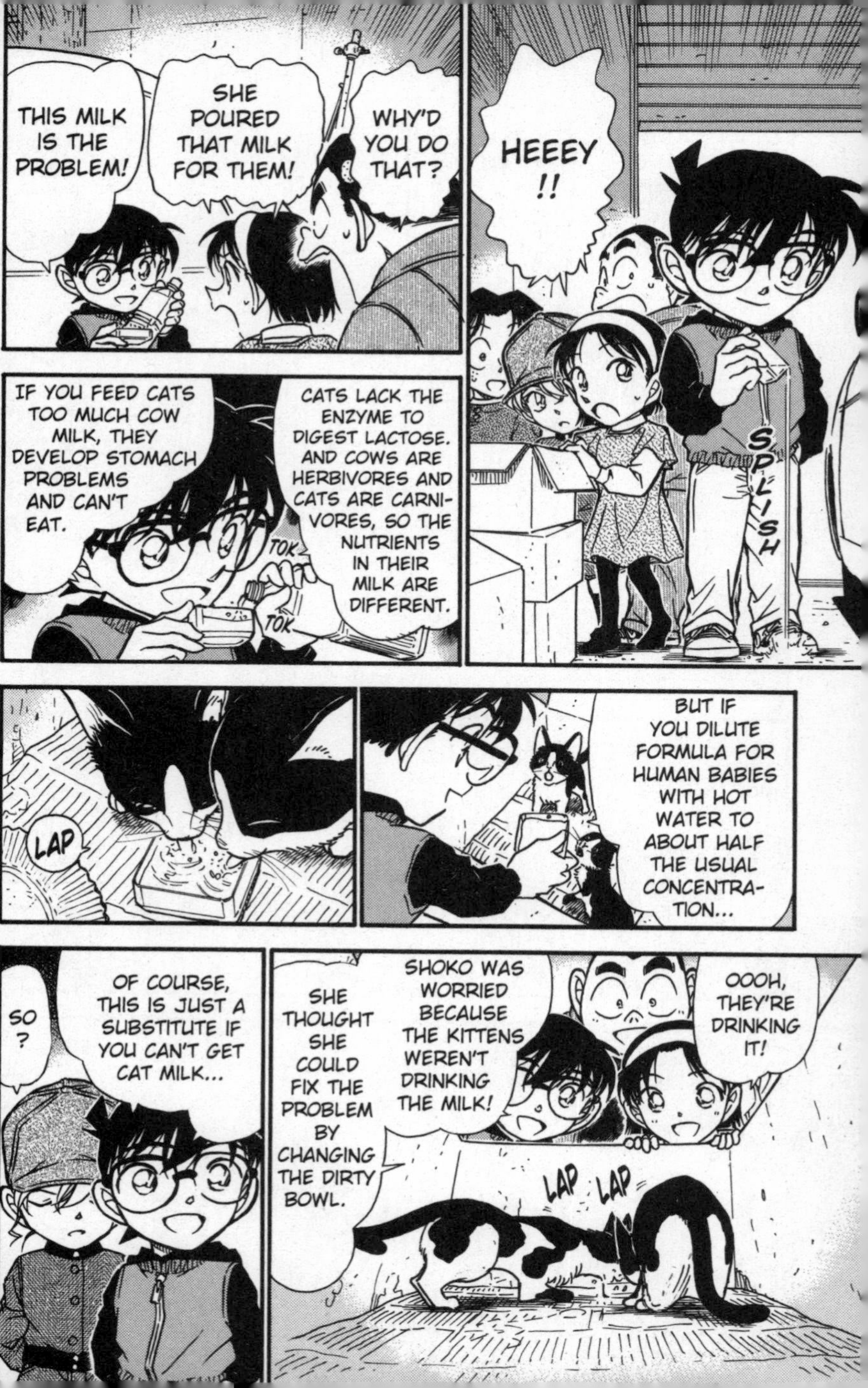
HEEEY !!
SPLISH
WHY'D YOU DO THAT?
SHE POURED THAT MILK FOR THEM!
THIS MILK IS THE PROBLEM!
CATS LACK THE ENZYME TO DIGEST LACTOSE. AND COWS ARE HERBIVORES AND CATS ARE CARNIVORES, SO THE NUTRIENTS IN THEIR MILK ARE DIFFERENT.
IF YOU FEED CATS TOO MUCH COW MILK, THEY DEVELOP STOMACH PROBLEMS AND CAN'T EAT.
TOK
TOK
BUT IF YOU DILUTE FORMULA FOR HUMAN BABIES WITH HOT WATER TO ABOUT HALF THE USUAL CONCENTRATION...
LAP
OOOH, THEY'RE DRINKING IT!
SHOKO WAS WORRIED BECAUSE THE KITTENS WEREN'T DRINKING THE MILK!
SHE THOUGHT SHE COULD FIX THE PROBLEM BY CHANGING THE DIRTY BOWL.
LAP LAP
OF COURSE, THIS IS JUST A SUBSTITUTE IF YOU CAN'T GET CAT MILK...
SO ?

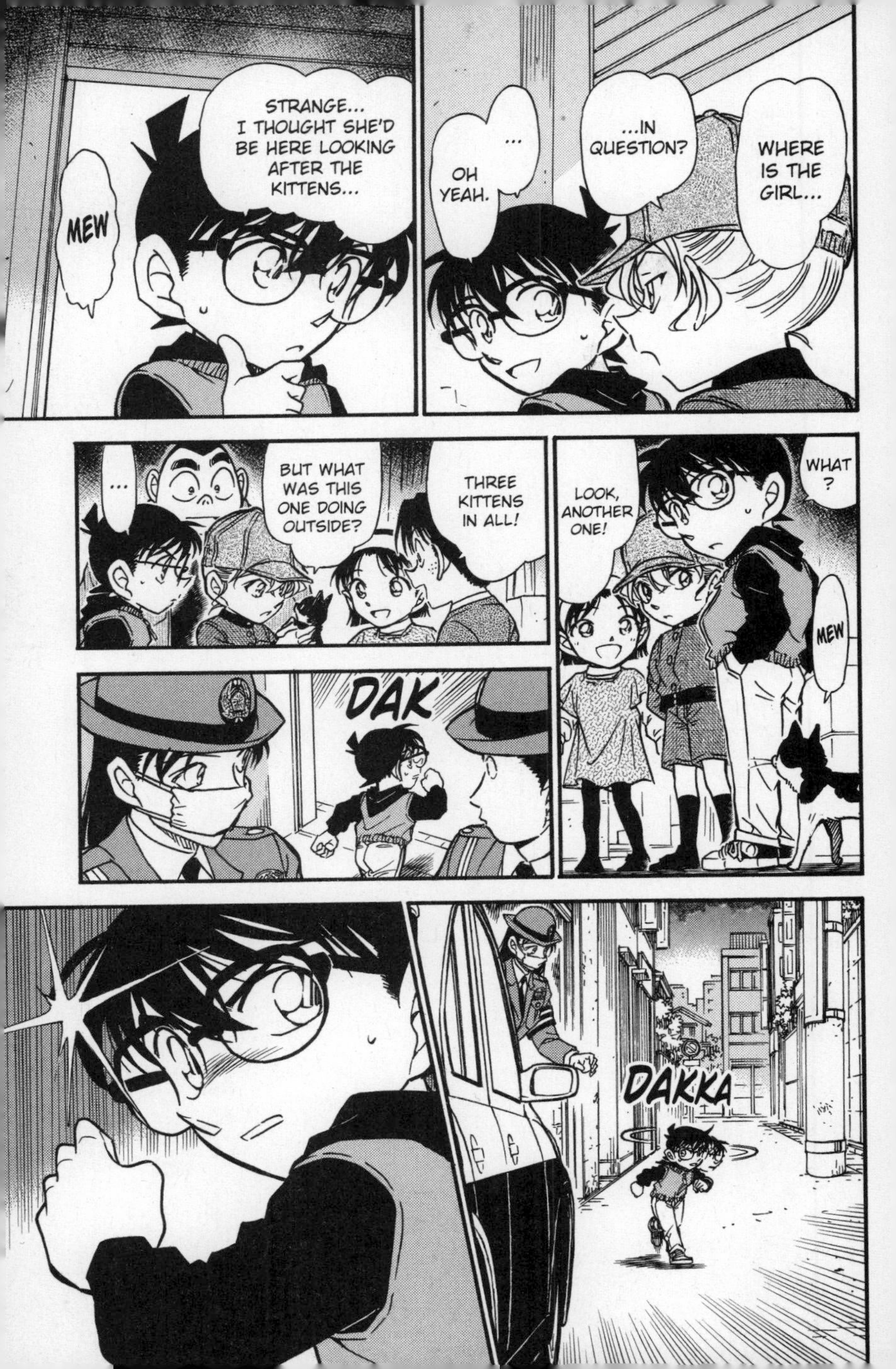
WHERE IS THE GIRL...
...IN QUESTION?
...
OH YEAH.
STRANGE... I THOUGHT SHE'D BE HERE LOOKING AFTER THE KITTENS...
MEW
WHAT?
LOOK, ANOTHER ONE!
MEW
THREE KITTENS IN ALL!
BUT WHAT WAS THIS ONE DOING OUTSIDE?
...
DAK
DAKKA

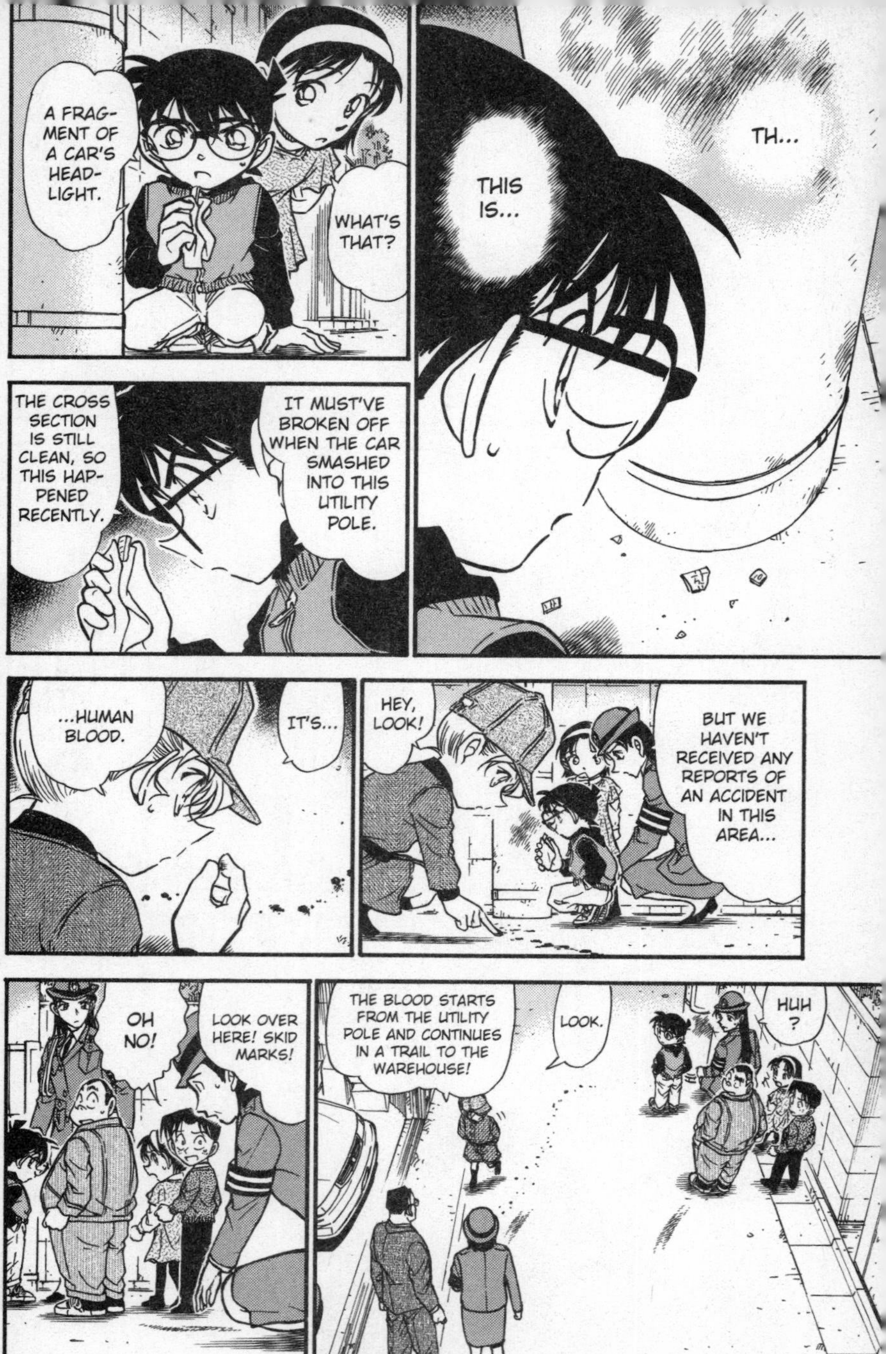
TH...
THIS IS...
WHAT'S THAT?
A FRAG-MENT OF A CAR'S HEAD-LIGHT.
IT MUST'VE BROKEN OFF WHEN THE CAR SMASHED INTO THIS UTILITY POLE.
THE CROSS SECTION IS STILL CLEAN, SO THIS HAP-PENED RECENTLY.
BUT WE HAVEN'T RECEIVED ANY REPORTS OF AN ACCIDENT IN THIS AREA...
HEY, LOOK!
IT'S...
...HUMAN BLOOD.
HUH?
LOOK.
THE BLOOD STARTS FROM THE UTILITY POLE AND CONTINUES IN A TRAIL TO THE WAREHOUSE!
LOOK OVER HERE! SKID MARKS!
OH NO!

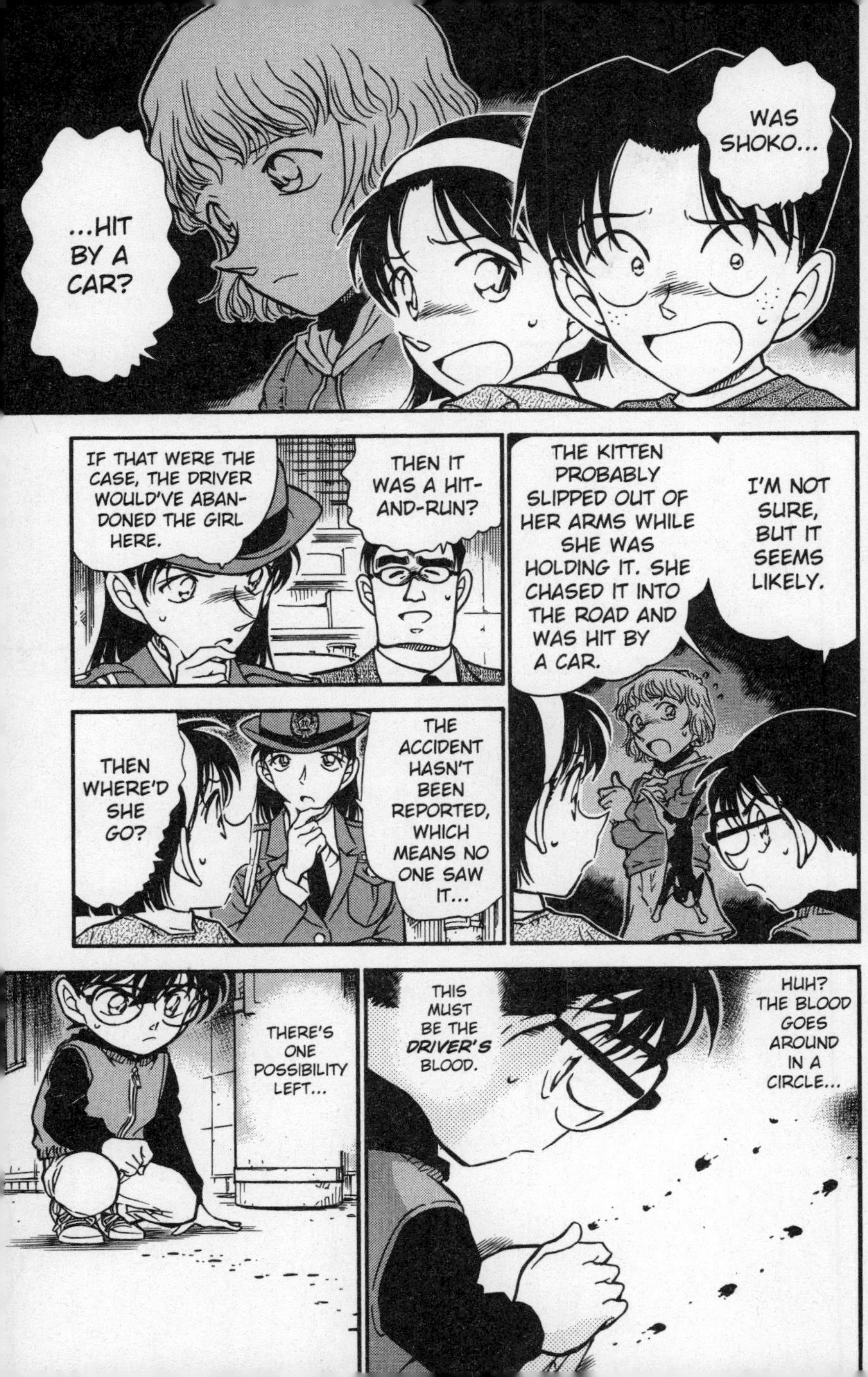
WAS SHOKO...
...HIT BY A CAR?
I'M NOT SURE, BUT IT SEEMS LIKELY.
THE KITTEN PROBABLY SLIPPED OUT OF HER ARMS WHILE SHE WAS HOLDING IT. SHE CHASED IT INTO THE ROAD AND WAS HIT BY A CAR.
THEN IT WAS A HIT-AND-RUN?
IF THAT WERE THE CASE, THE DRIVER WOULD'VE ABANDONED THE GIRL HERE.
THE ACCIDENT HASN'T BEEN REPORTED, WHICH MEANS NO ONE SAW IT...
THEN WHERE'D SHE GO?
HUH? THE BLOOD GOES AROUND IN A CIRCLE...
THIS MUST BE THE *DRIVER'S* BLOOD.
THERE'S ONE POSSIBILITY LEFT...

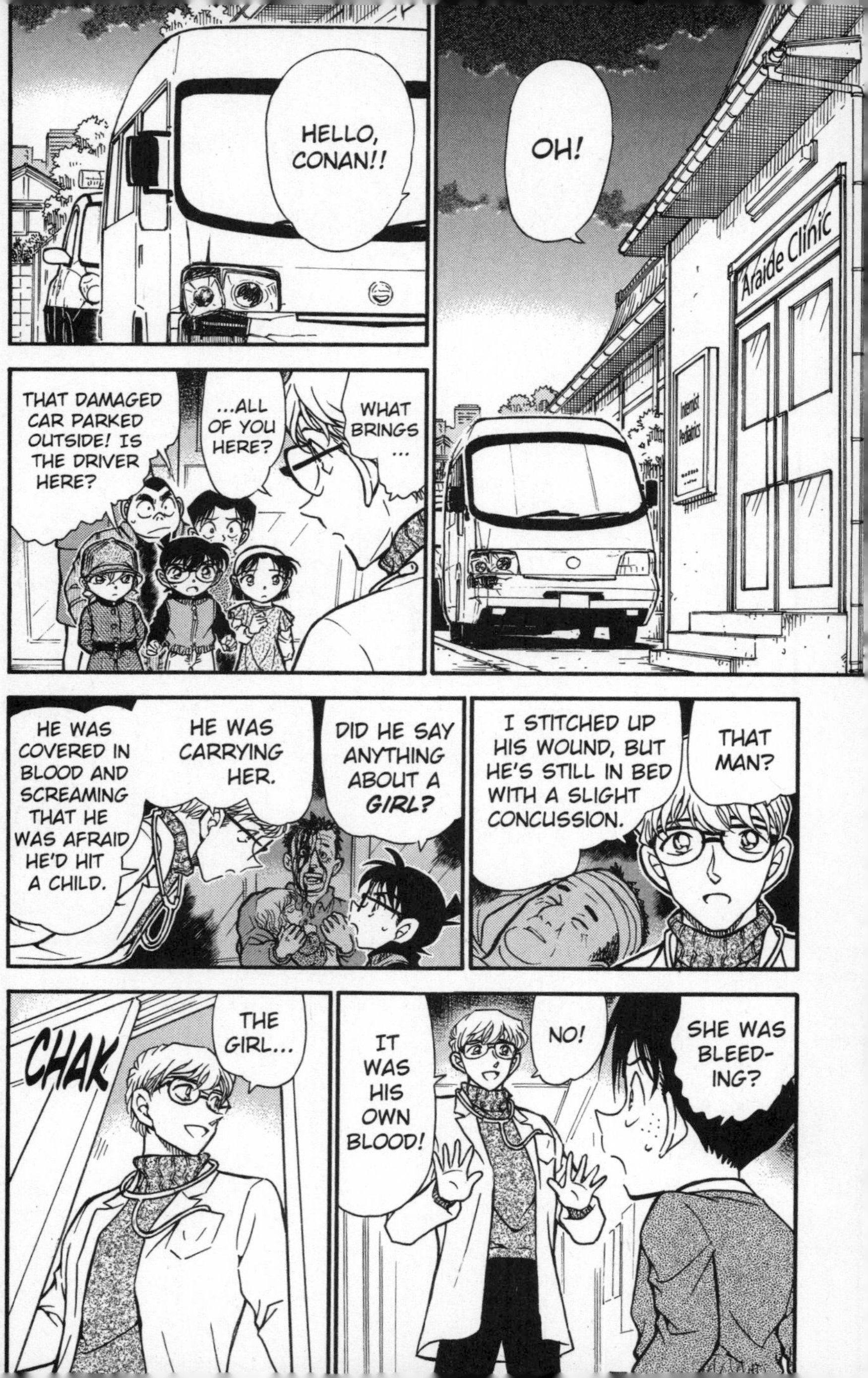
OH!
Araide Clinic
Internist
Pediatrics
HELLO, CONAN!!
WHAT BRINGS...
...ALL OF YOU HERE?
THAT DAMAGED CAR PARKED OUTSIDE! IS THE DRIVER HERE?
THAT MAN?
I STITCHED UP HIS WOUND, BUT HE'S STILL IN BED WITH A SLIGHT CONCUSSION.
DID HE SAY ANYTHING ABOUT A *GIRL?*
HE WAS CARRYING HER.
HE WAS COVERED IN BLOOD AND SCREAMING THAT HE WAS AFRAID HE'D HIT A CHILD.
SHE WAS BLEED-ING?
NO!
IT WAS HIS OWN BLOOD!
THE GIRL...
CHAK

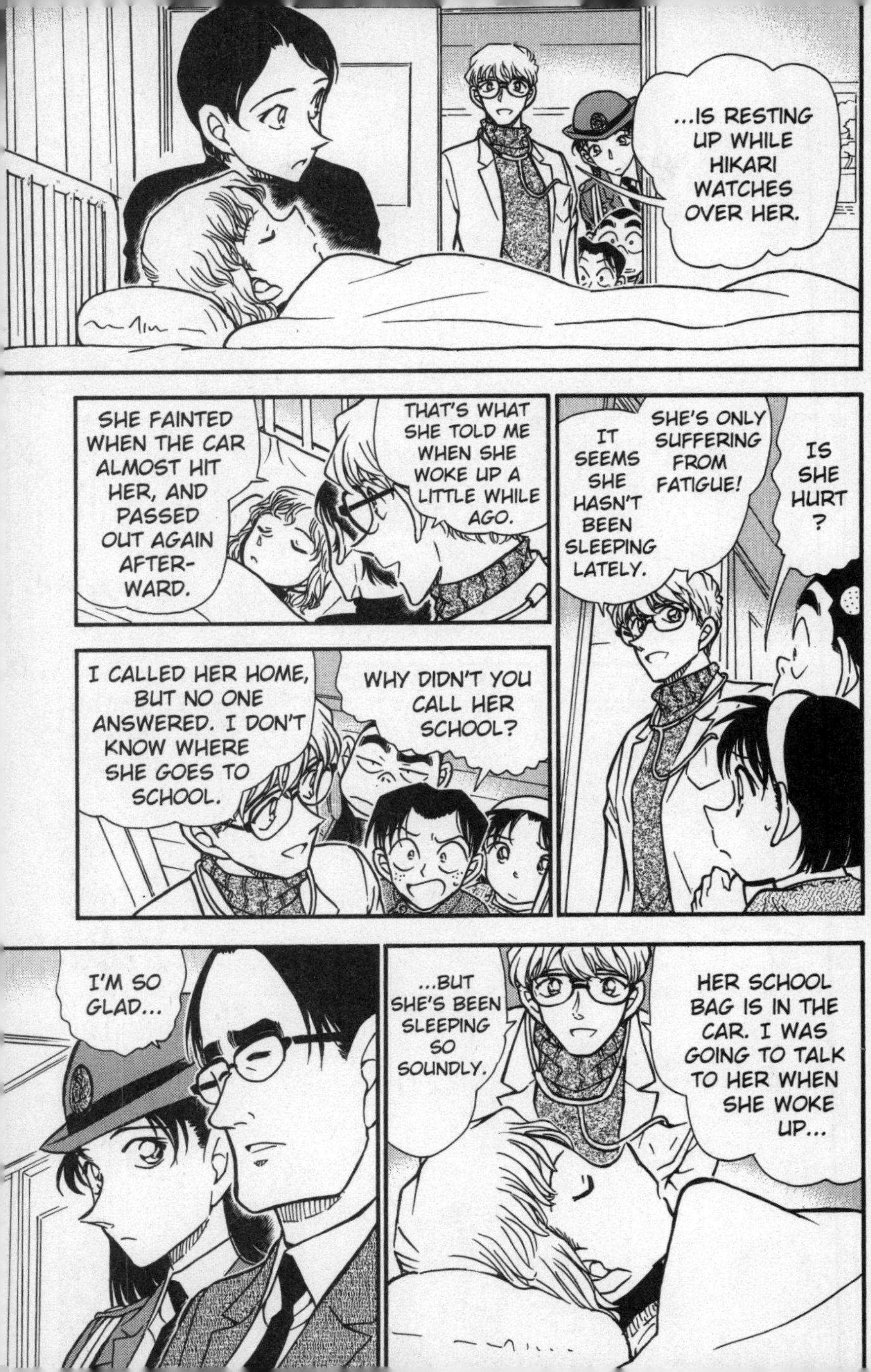
...IS RESTING UP WHILE HIKARI WATCHES OVER HER.
IS SHE HURT?
SHE'S ONLY SUFFERING FROM FATIGUE!
IT SEEMS SHE HASN'T BEEN SLEEPING LATELY.
THAT'S WHAT SHE TOLD ME WHEN SHE WOKE UP A LITTLE WHILE AGO.
SHE FAINTED WHEN THE CAR ALMOST HIT HER, AND PASSED OUT AGAIN AFTER-WARD.
WHY DIDN'T YOU CALL HER SCHOOL?
I CALLED HER HOME, BUT NO ONE ANSWERED. I DON'T KNOW WHERE SHE GOES TO SCHOOL.
HER SCHOOL BAG IS IN THE CAR. I WAS GOING TO TALK TO HER WHEN SHE WOKE UP...
...BUT SHE'S BEEN SLEEPING SO SOUNDLY.
I'M SO GLAD...

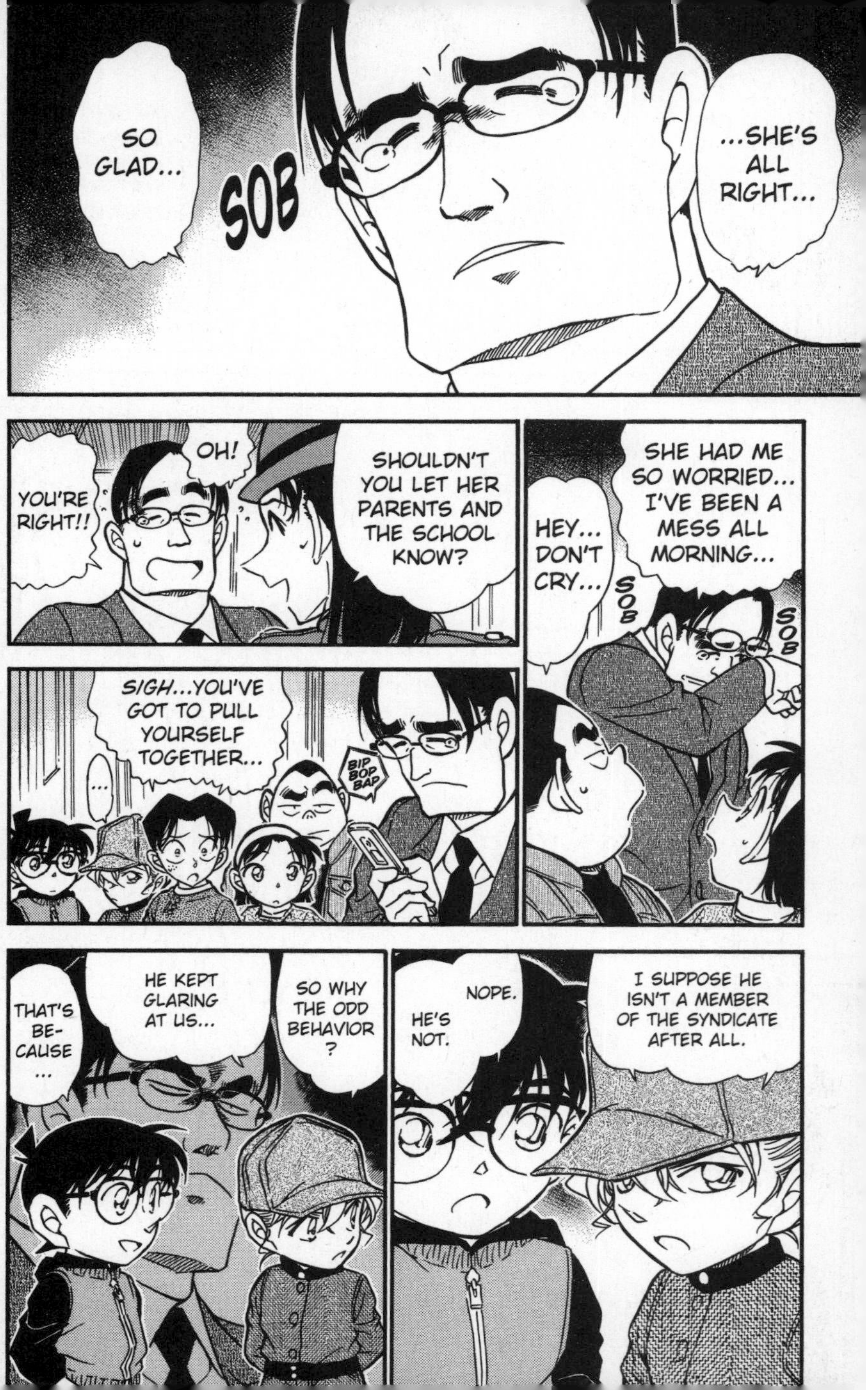
...SHE'S ALL RIGHT...
SOB
SO GLAD...
SHE HAD ME SO WORRIED... I'VE BEEN A MESS ALL MORNING...
HEY... DON'T CRY...
SOB
SOB
SHOULDN'T YOU LET HER PARENTS AND THE SCHOOL KNOW?
OH!
YOU'RE RIGHT!!
SIGH...YOU'VE GOT TO PULL YOURSELF TOGETHER...
BIP BOP BAP
...
I SUPPOSE HE ISN'T A MEMBER OF THE SYNDICATE AFTER ALL.
NOPE.
HE'S NOT.
SO WHY THE ODD BEHAVIOR?
HE KEPT GLARING AT US...
THAT'S BE-CAUSE ...

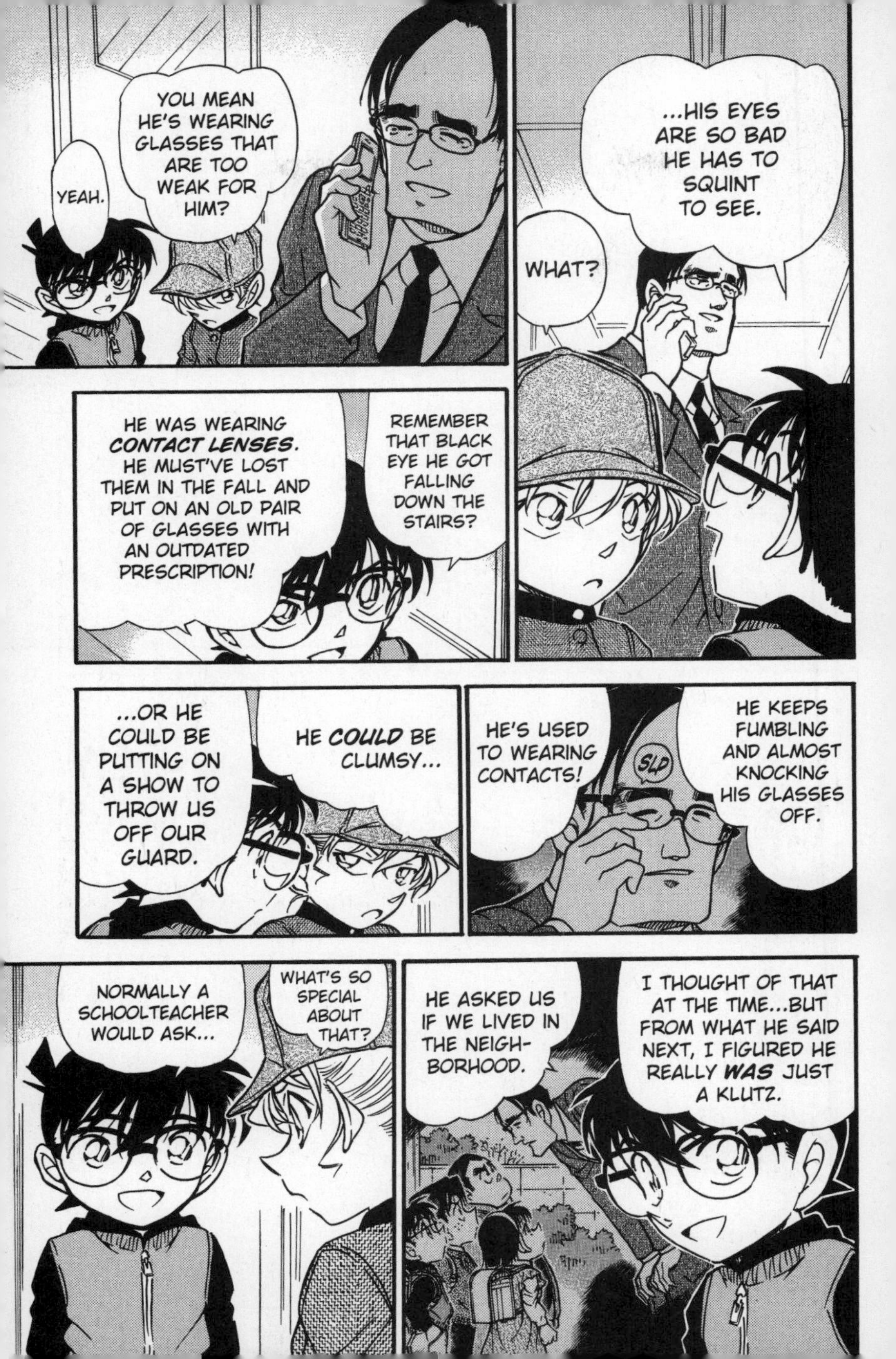
...HIS EYES ARE SO BAD HE HAS TO SQUINT TO SEE.
WHAT?
YOU MEAN HE'S WEARING GLASSES THAT ARE TOO WEAK FOR HIM?
YEAH.
REMEMBER THAT BLACK EYE HE GOT FALLING DOWN THE STAIRS?
HE WAS WEARING ***CONTACT LENSES.*** HE MUST'VE LOST THEM IN THE FALL AND PUT ON AN OLD PAIR OF GLASSES WITH AN OUTDATED PRESCRIPTION!
HE KEEPS FUMBLING AND ALMOST KNOCKING HIS GLASSES OFF.
SLP
HE'S USED TO WEARING CONTACTS!
HE ***COULD*** BE CLUMSY...
...OR HE COULD BE PUTTING ON A SHOW TO THROW US OFF OUR GUARD.
I THOUGHT OF THAT AT THE TIME...BUT FROM WHAT HE SAID NEXT, I FIGURED HE REALLY ***WAS*** JUST A KLUTZ.
HE ASKED US IF WE LIVED IN THE NEIGH-BORHOOD.
WHAT'S SO SPECIAL ABOUT THAT?
NORMALLY A SCHOOLTEACHER WOULD ASK...

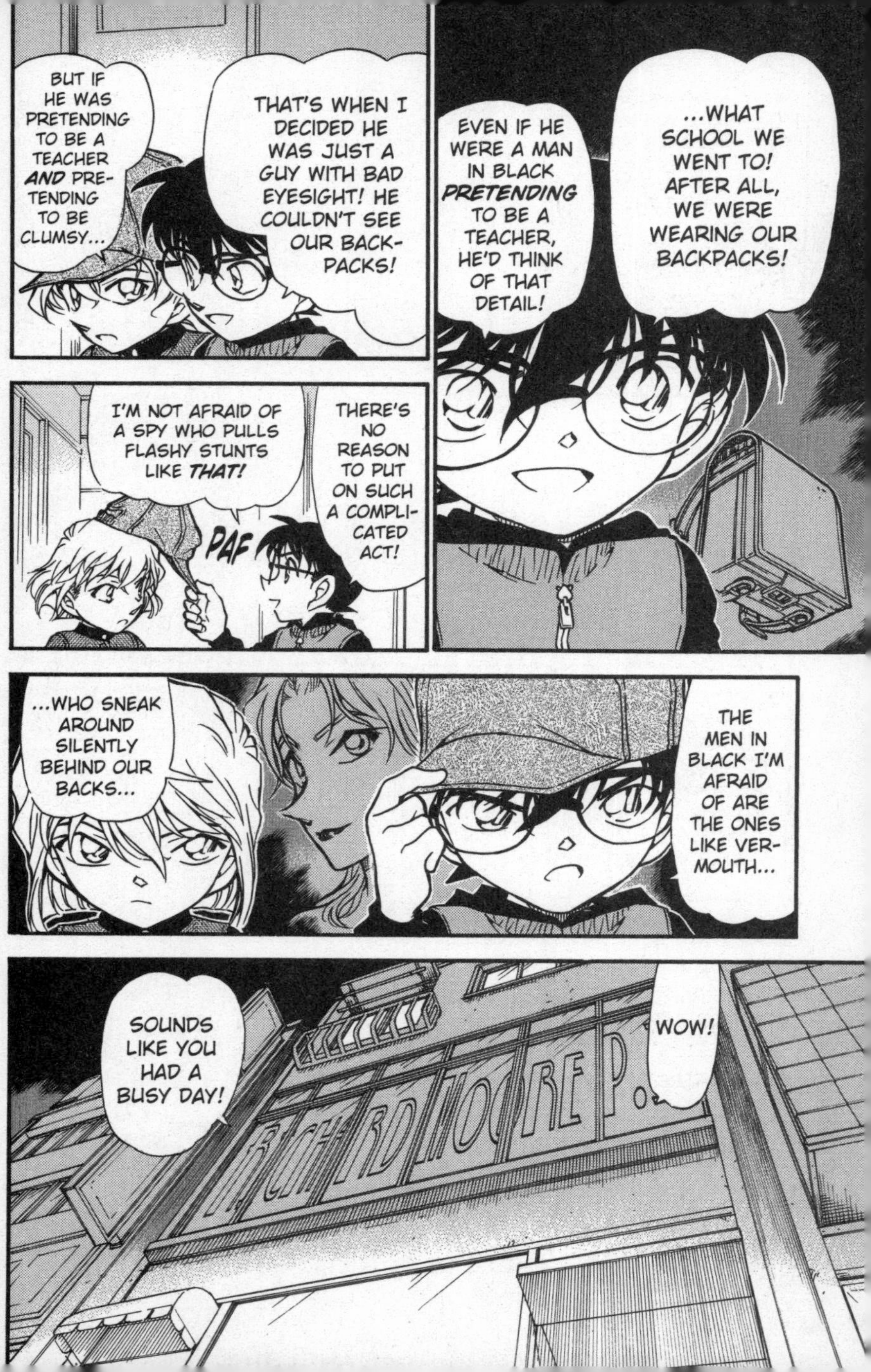

...WHAT SCHOOL WE WENT TO! AFTER ALL, WE WERE WEARING OUR BACKPACKS!
EVEN IF HE WERE A MAN IN BLACK PRETENDING TO BE A TEACHER, HE'D THINK OF THAT DETAIL!
THAT'S WHEN I DECIDED HE WAS JUST A GUY WITH BAD EYESIGHT! HE COULDN'T SEE OUR BACK-PACKS!
BUT IF HE WAS PRETENDING TO BE A TEACHER AND PRE-TENDING TO BE CLUMSY...
THERE'S NO REASON TO PUT ON SUCH A COMPLI-CATED ACT!
I'M NOT AFRAID OF A SPY WHO PULLS FLASHY STUNTS LIKE THAT!
PAF
THE MEN IN BLACK I'M AFRAID OF ARE THE ONES LIKE VER-MOUTH...
...WHO SNEAK AROUND SILENTLY BEHIND OUR BACKS...
WOW!
SOUNDS LIKE YOU HAD A BUSY DAY!

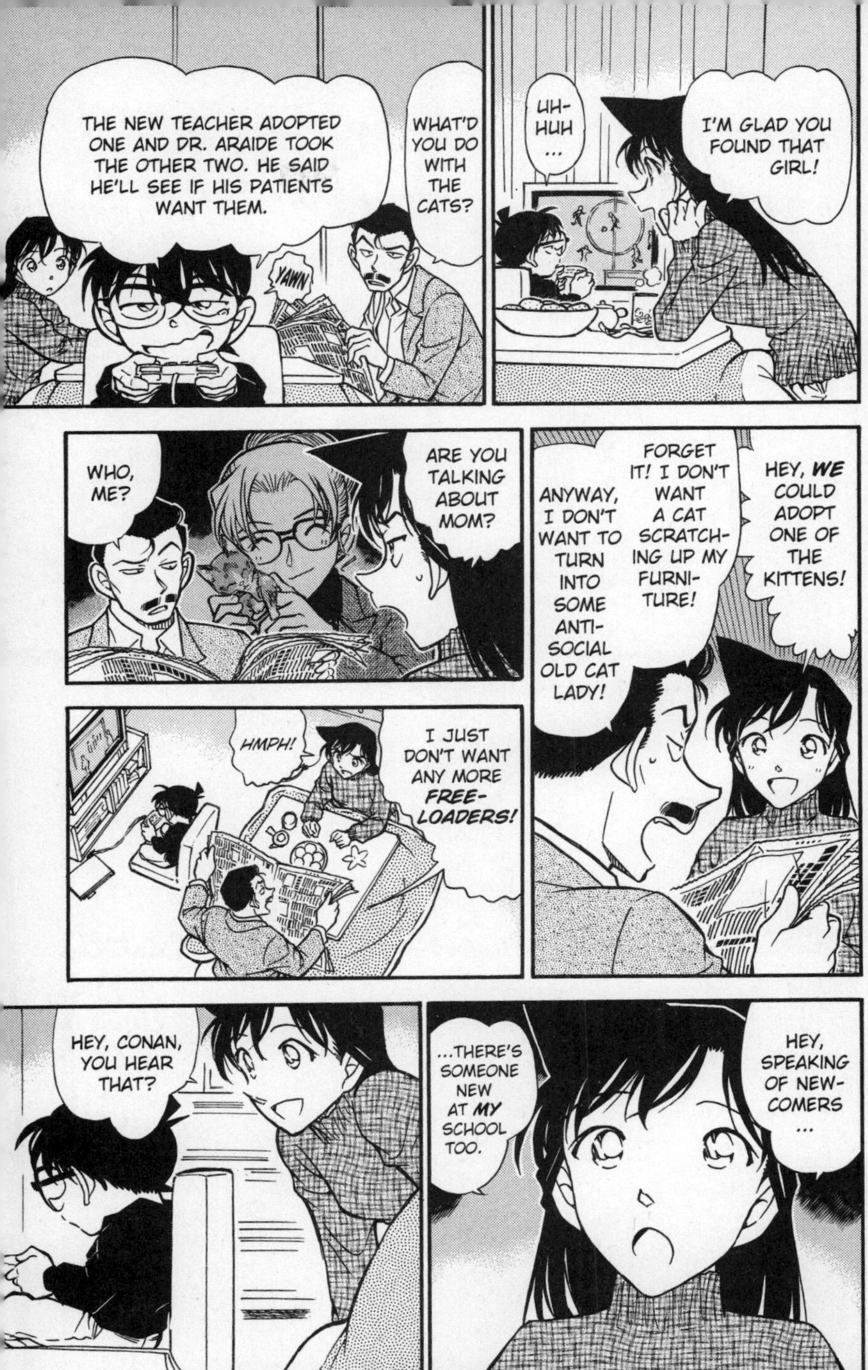

I'M GLAD YOU FOUND THAT GIRL!
UH-HUH ...
WHAT'D YOU DO WITH THE CATS?
THE NEW TEACHER ADOPTED ONE AND DR. ARAIDE TOOK THE OTHER TWO. HE SAID HE'LL SEE IF HIS PATIENTS WANT THEM.
YAWN
HEY, **WE** COULD ADOPT ONE OF THE KITTENS!
FORGET IT! I DON'T WANT A CAT SCRATCHING UP MY FURNITURE!
ANYWAY, I DON'T WANT TO TURN INTO SOME ANTI-SOCIAL OLD CAT LADY!
ARE YOU TALKING ABOUT MOM?
WHO, ME?
I JUST DON'T WANT ANY MORE ***FREE-LOADERS!***
HMPH!
HEY, SPEAKING OF NEW-COMERS ...
...THERE'S SOMEONE NEW AT ***MY*** SCHOOL TOO.
HEY, CONAN, YOU HEAR THAT?

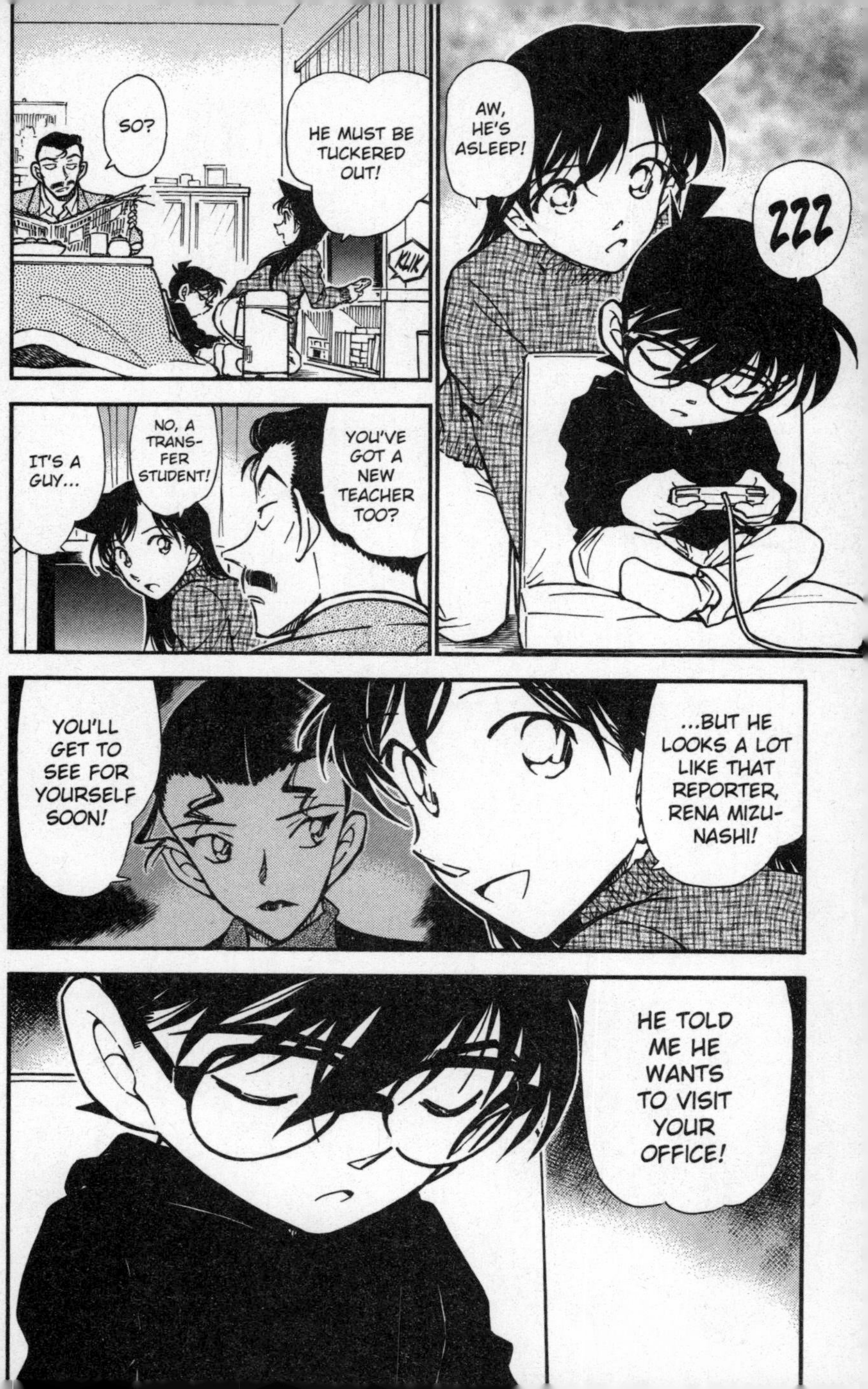
AW, HE'S ASLEEP!
ZZZ
HE MUST BE TUCKERED OUT!
KLIK
SO?
YOU'VE GOT A NEW TEACHER TOO?
NO, A TRANS-FER STUDENT!
IT'S A GUY...
...BUT HE LOOKS A LOT LIKE THAT REPORTER, RENA MIZU-NASHI!
YOU'LL GET TO SEE FOR YOURSELF SOON!
HE TOLD ME HE WANTS TO VISIT YOUR OFFICE!

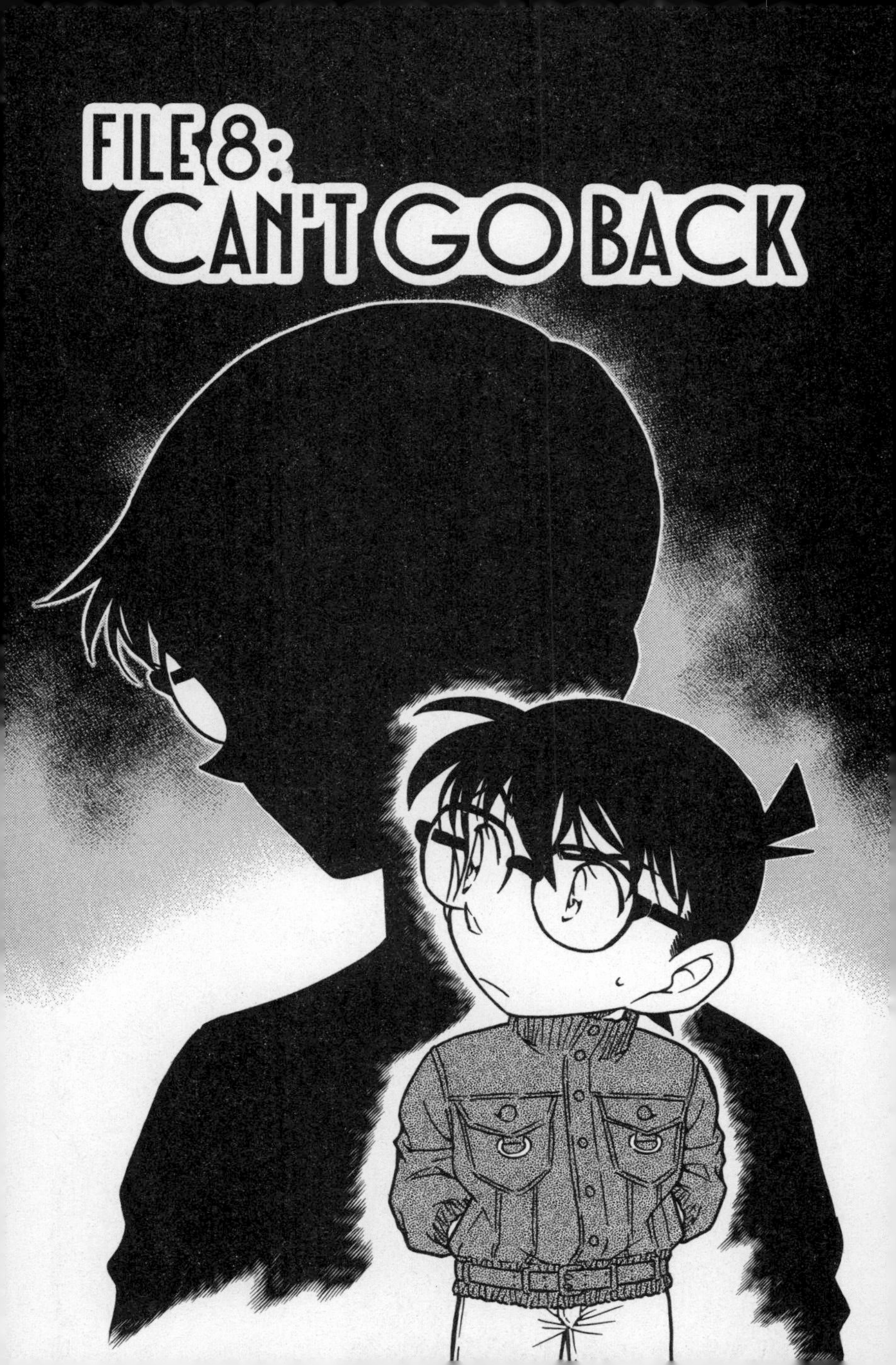
FILE 8:
CAN'T GO BACK

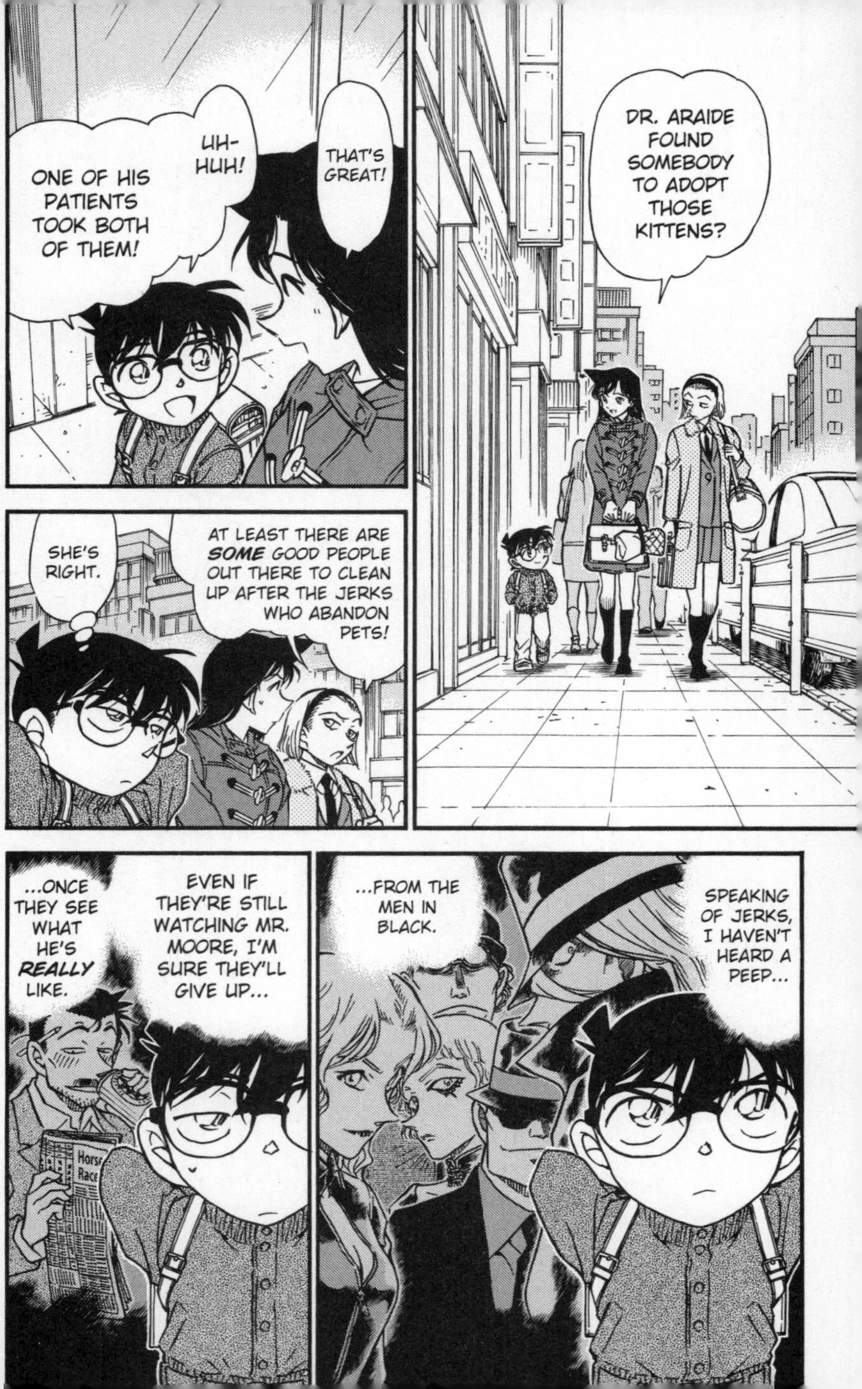
DR. ARAIDE FOUND SOMEBODY TO ADOPT THOSE KITTENS?
THAT'S GREAT!
UH-HUH!
ONE OF HIS PATIENTS TOOK BOTH OF THEM!
AT LEAST THERE ARE *SOME* GOOD PEOPLE OUT THERE TO CLEAN UP AFTER THE JERKS WHO ABANDON PETS!
SHE'S RIGHT.
SPEAKING OF JERKS, I HAVEN'T HEARD A PEEP...
...FROM THE MEN IN BLACK.
EVEN IF THEY'RE STILL WATCHING MR. MOORE, I'M SURE THEY'LL GIVE UP...
...ONCE THEY SEE WHAT HE'S *REALLY* LIKE.
Horse Race

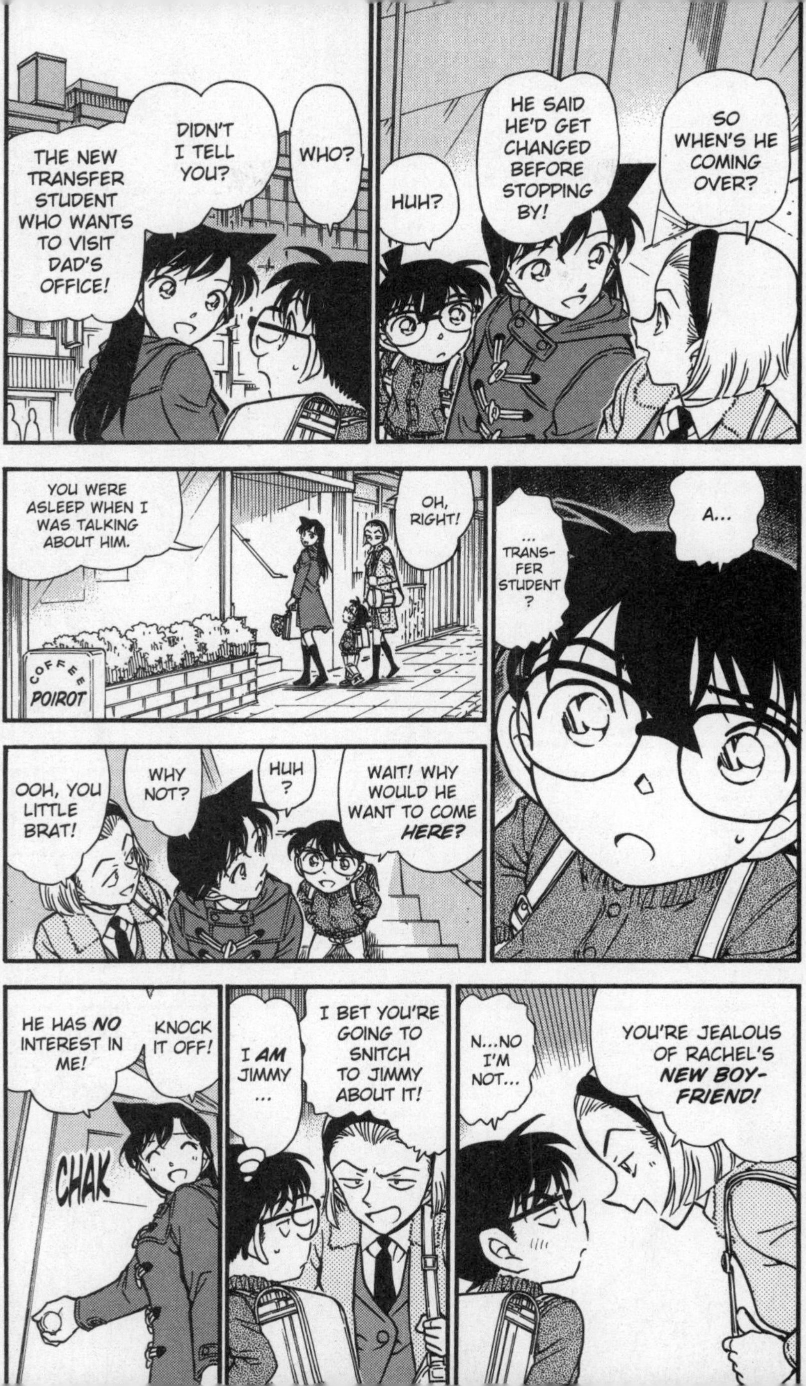
SO WHEN'S HE COMING OVER?
HE SAID HE'D GET CHANGED BEFORE STOPPING BY!
HUH?
WHO?
DIDN'T I TELL YOU?
THE NEW TRANSFER STUDENT WHO WANTS TO VISIT DAD'S OFFICE!
A...
...TRANSFER-STUDENT?
OH, RIGHT!
YOU WERE ASLEEP WHEN I WAS TALKING ABOUT HIM.
COFFEE POIROT
WAIT! WHY WOULD HE WANT TO COME *HERE?*
HUH?
WHY NOT?
OOH, YOU LITTLE BRAT!
YOU'RE JEALOUS OF RACHEL'S *NEW BOY-FRIEND!*
N...NO I'M NOT...
I BET YOU'RE GOING TO SNITCH TO JIMMY ABOUT IT!
I *AM* JIMMY...
KNOCK IT OFF!
HE HAS *NO* INTEREST IN ME!
CHAK

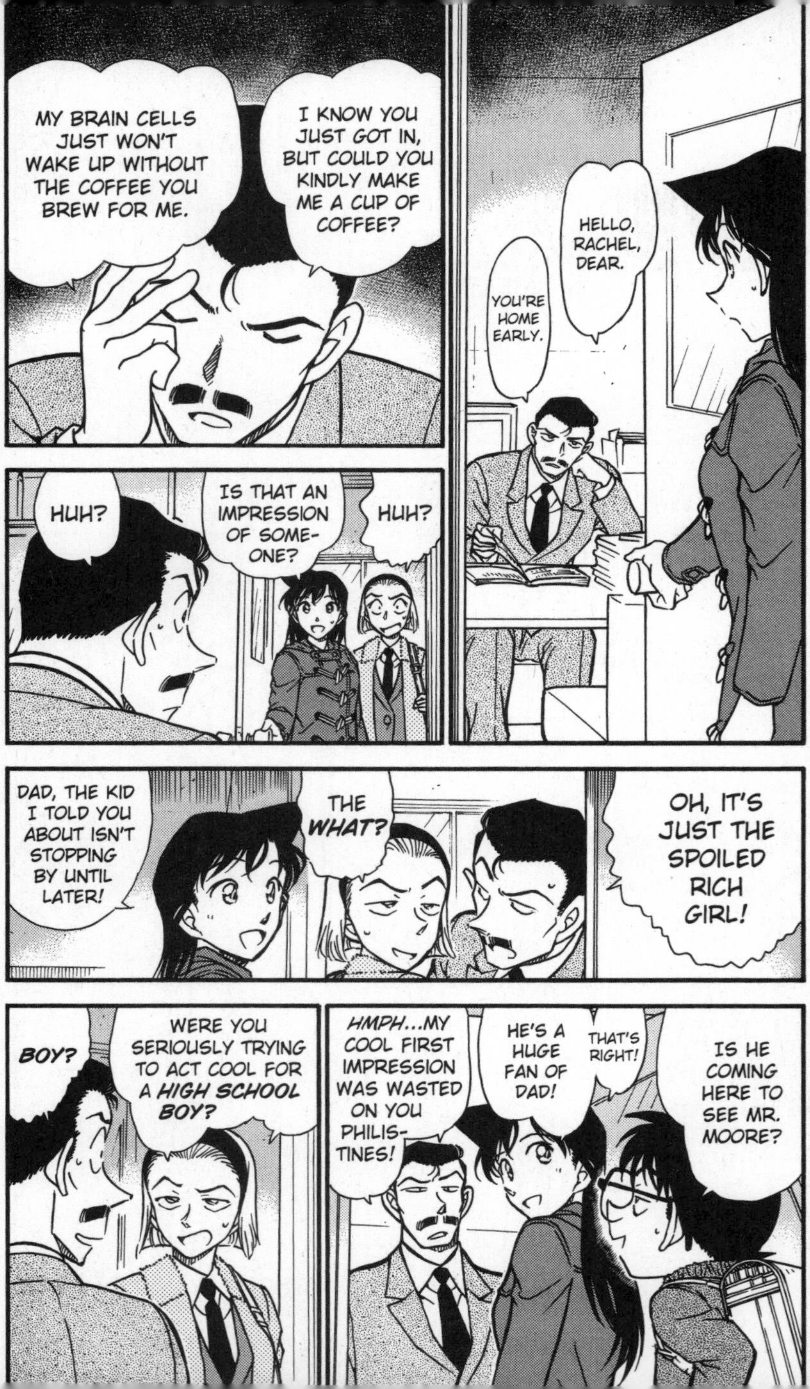
HELLO, RACHEL, DEAR.
YOU'RE HOME EARLY.
I KNOW YOU JUST GOT IN, BUT COULD YOU KINDLY MAKE ME A CUP OF COFFEE?
MY BRAIN CELLS JUST WON'T WAKE UP WITHOUT THE COFFEE YOU BREW FOR ME.
HUH?
IS THAT AN IMPRESSION OF SOME-ONE?
HUH?
OH, IT'S JUST THE SPOILED RICH GIRL!
THE *WHAT?*
DAD, THE KID I TOLD YOU ABOUT ISN'T STOPPING BY UNTIL LATER!
IS HE COMING HERE TO SEE MR. MOORE?
THAT'S RIGHT!
HE'S A HUGE FAN OF DAD!
HMPH...MY COOL FIRST IMPRESSION WAS WASTED ON YOU PHILIS-TINES!
WERE YOU SERIOUSLY TRYING TO ACT COOL FOR A ***HIGH SCHOOL BOY?***
BOY?

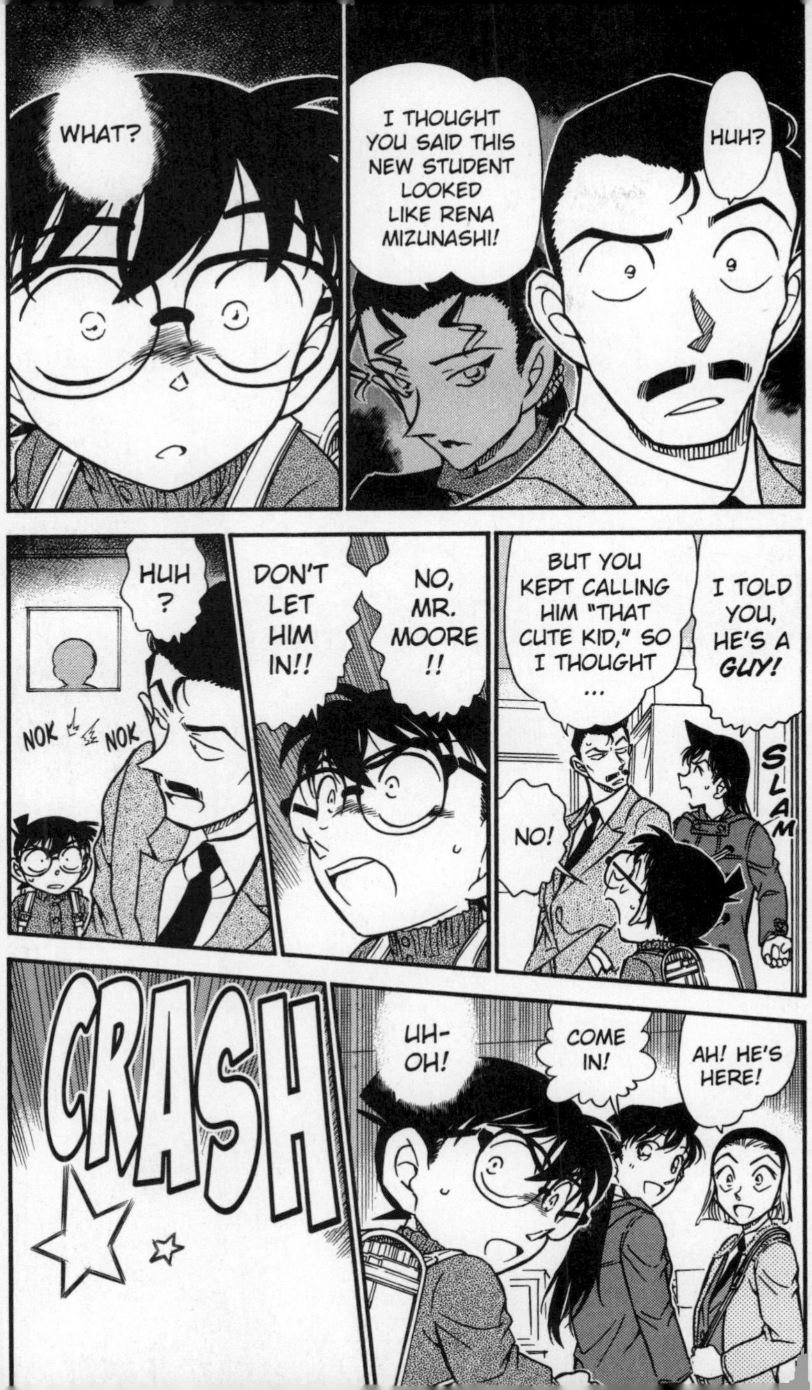
HUH?
I THOUGHT YOU SAID THIS NEW STUDENT LOOKED LIKE RENA MIZUNASHI!
WHAT?
I TOLD YOU, HE'S A *GUY!*
BUT YOU KEPT CALLING HIM "THAT CUTE KID," SO I THOUGHT ...
SLAM
NO!
NO, MR. MOORE!!
DON'T LET HIM IN!!
HUH ?
NOK NOK
AH! HE'S HERE!
COME IN!
UH-OH!
CRASH

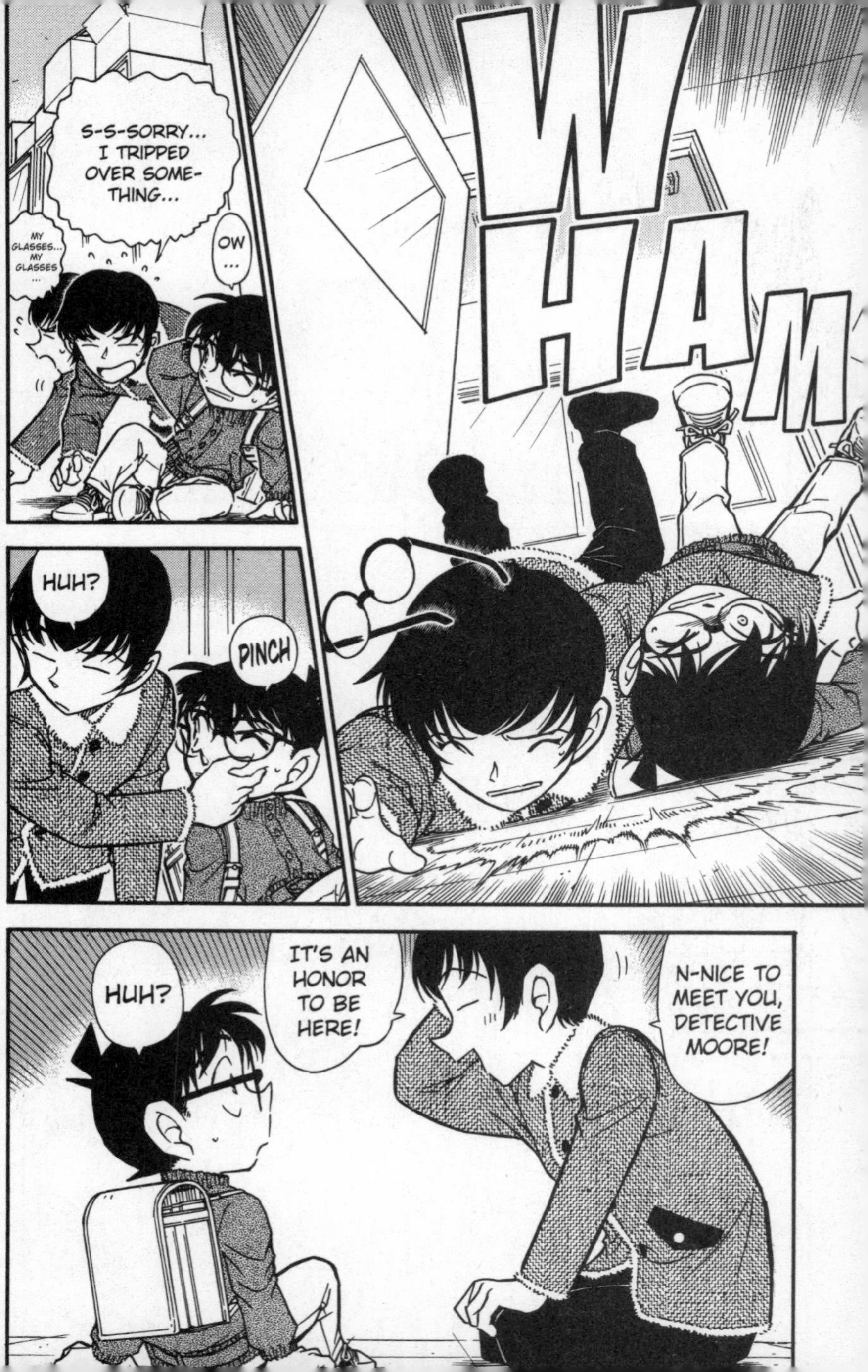
WHAM
S-S-SORRY... I TRIPPED OVER SOME-THING...
OW ...
MY GLASSES... MY GLASSES ...
HUH?
PINCH
N-NICE TO MEET YOU, DETECTIVE MOORE!
IT'S AN HONOR TO BE HERE!
HUH?

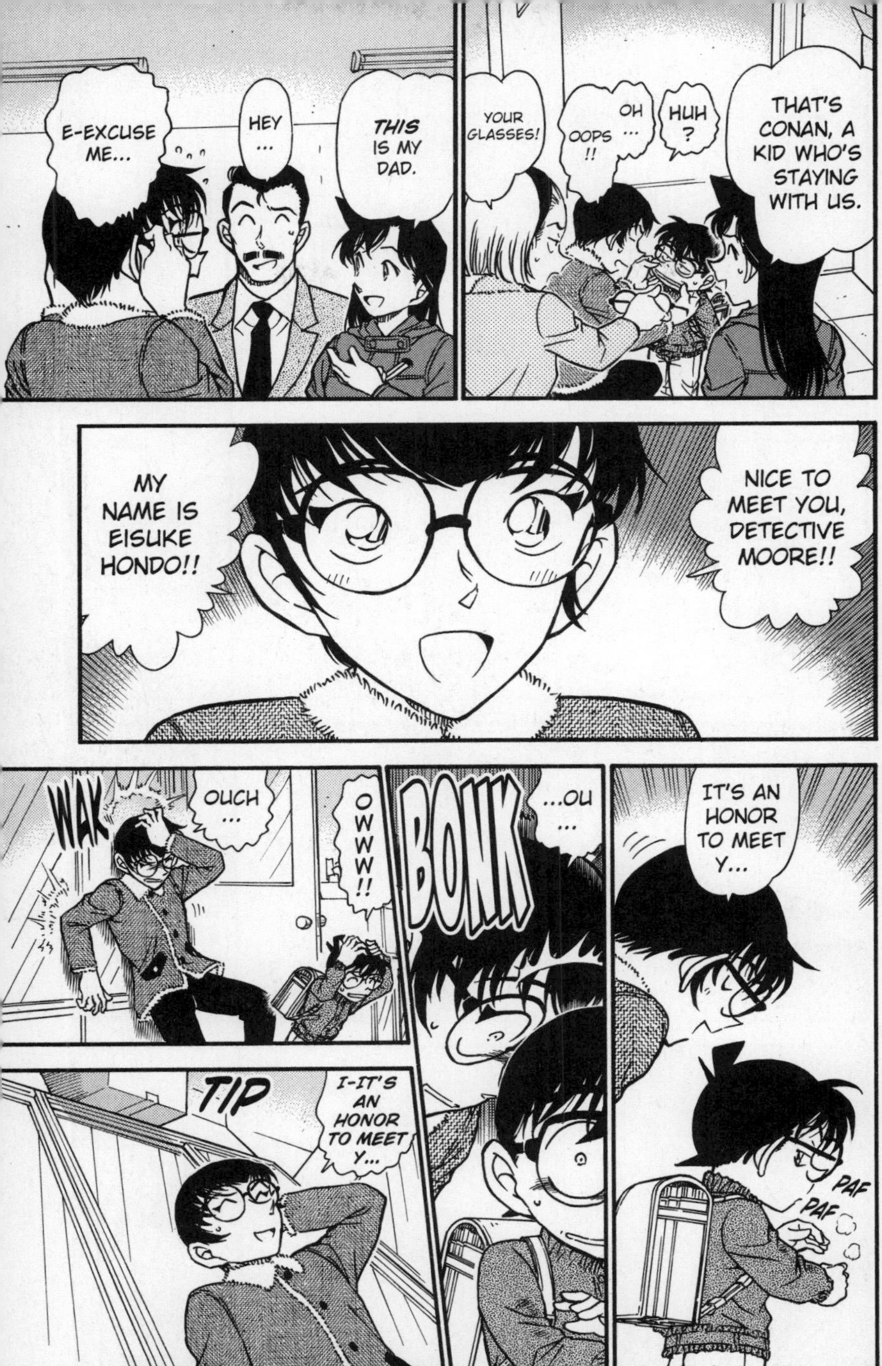
THAT'S CONAN, A KID WHO'S STAYING WITH US.
HUH?
OH...
OOPS!!
YOUR GLASSES!
THIS IS MY DAD.
HEY...
E-EXCUSE ME...
NICE TO MEET YOU, DETECTIVE MOORE!!
MY NAME IS EISUKE HONDO!!
IT'S AN HONOR TO MEET Y...
PAF
PAF
...OU...
BONK
OWWW!!
OUCH...
WAK
TIP
I-IT'S AN HONOR TO MEET Y...

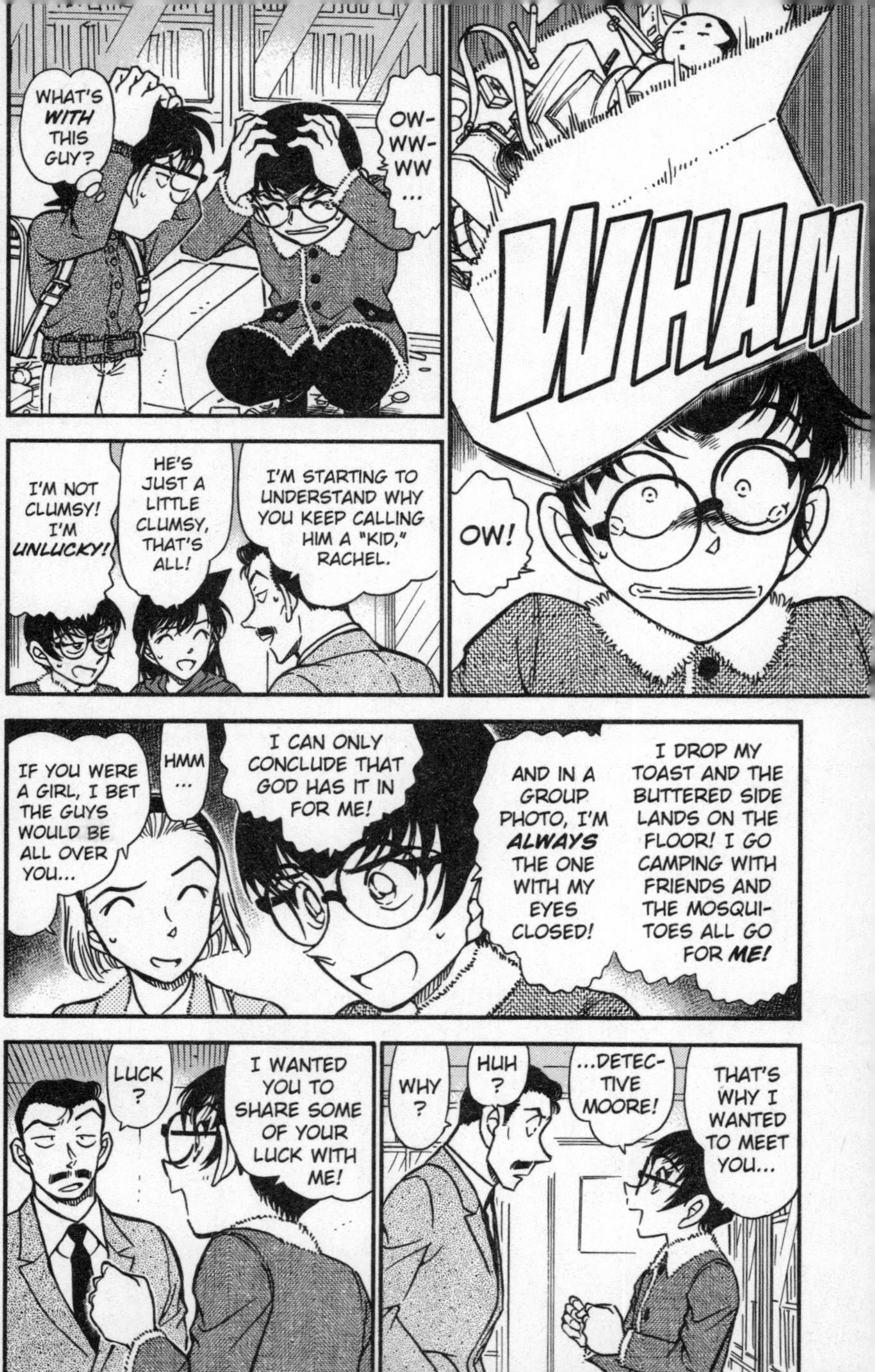
WHAM
OW!
OW-WW-WW...
WHAT'S WITH THIS GUY?
I'M STARTING TO UNDERSTAND WHY YOU KEEP CALLING HIM A "KID," RACHEL.
HE'S JUST A LITTLE CLUMSY, THAT'S ALL!
I'M NOT CLUMSY! I'M UNLUCKY!
I DROP MY TOAST AND THE BUTTERED SIDE LANDS ON THE FLOOR! I GO CAMPING WITH FRIENDS AND THE MOSQUITOES ALL GO FOR ME!
AND IN A GROUP PHOTO, I'M ALWAYS THE ONE WITH MY EYES CLOSED!
I CAN ONLY CONCLUDE THAT GOD HAS IT IN FOR ME!
HMM...
IF YOU WERE A GIRL, I BET THE GUYS WOULD BE ALL OVER YOU...
THAT'S WHY I WANTED TO MEET YOU...
...DETECTIVE MOORE!
HUH?
WHY?
I WANTED YOU TO SHARE SOME OF YOUR LUCK WITH ME!
LUCK?

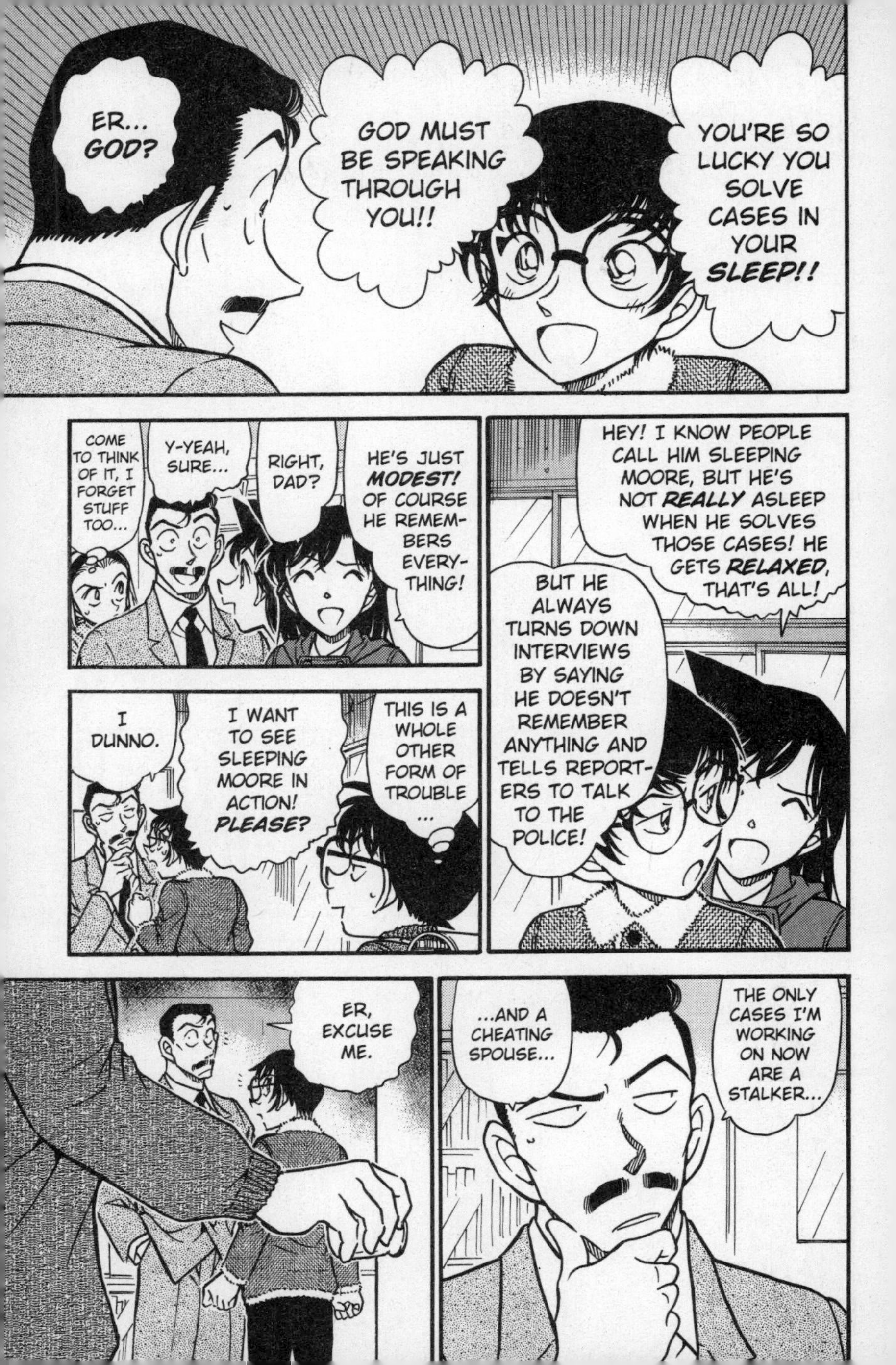
YOU'RE SO LUCKY YOU SOLVE CASES IN YOUR SLEEP!!
GOD MUST BE SPEAKING THROUGH YOU!!
ER... GOD?
HEY! I KNOW PEOPLE CALL HIM SLEEPING MOORE, BUT HE'S NOT REALLY ASLEEP WHEN HE SOLVES THOSE CASES! HE GETS RELAXED, THAT'S ALL!
BUT HE ALWAYS TURNS DOWN INTERVIEWS BY SAYING HE DOESN'T REMEMBER ANYTHING AND TELLS REPORTERS TO TALK TO THE POLICE!
HE'S JUST MODEST! OF COURSE HE REMEMBERS EVERYTHING!
RIGHT, DAD?
Y-YEAH, SURE...
COME TO THINK OF IT, I FORGET STUFF TOO...
THIS IS A WHOLE OTHER FORM OF TROUBLE...
I WANT TO SEE SLEEPING MOORE IN ACTION! PLEASE?
I DUNNO.
THE ONLY CASES I'M WORKING ON NOW ARE A STALKER...
...AND A CHEATING SPOUSE...
ER, EXCUSE ME.

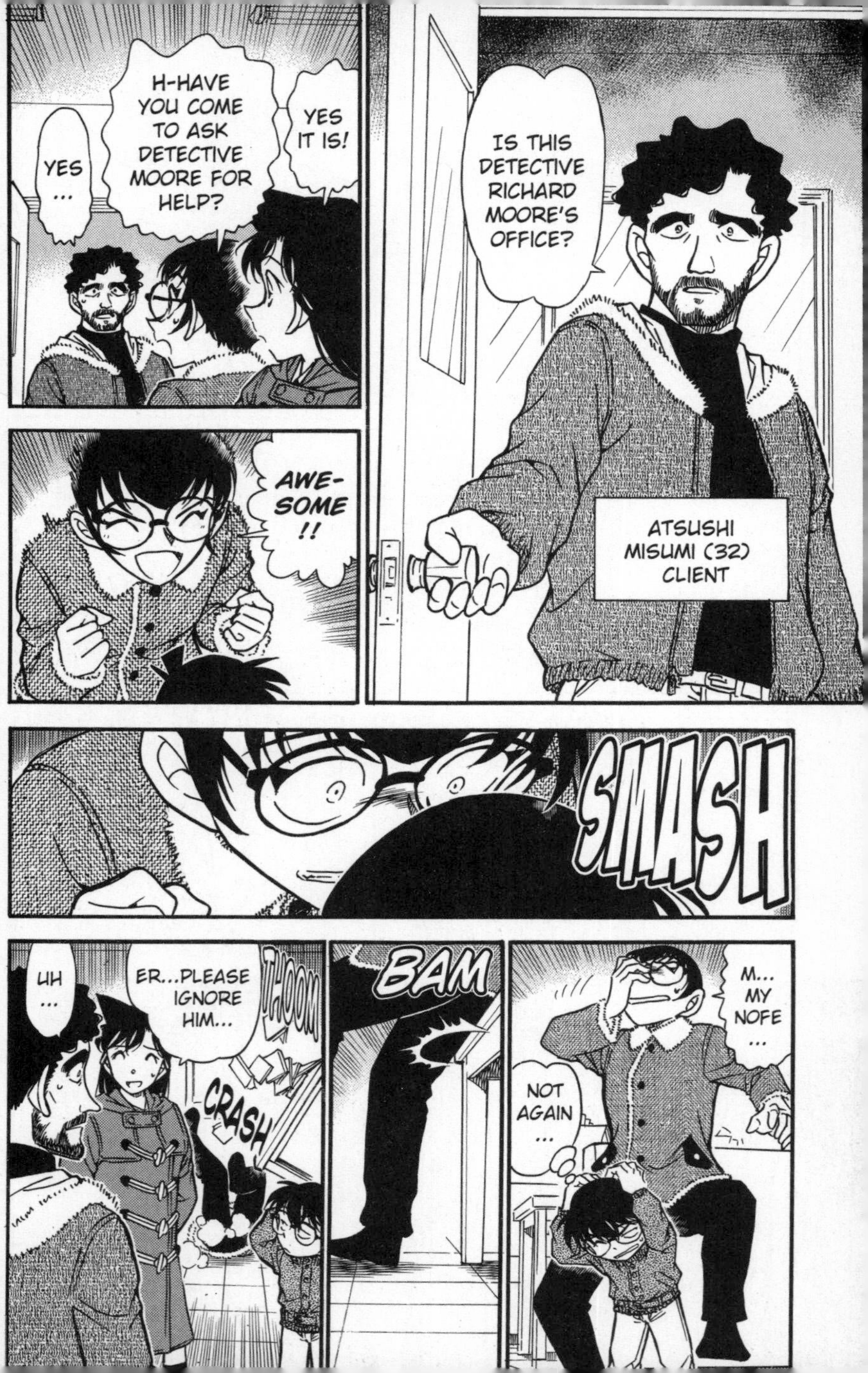

IS THIS DETECTIVE RICHARD MOORE'S OFFICE?
ATSUSHI MISUMI (32) CLIENT
YES IT IS!
H-HAVE YOU COME TO ASK DETECTIVE MOORE FOR HELP?
YES ...
AWE-SOME !!
SMASH
M... MY NOFE ...
NOT AGAIN ...
BAM
THOOM
ER...PLEASE IGNORE HIM...
CRASH
UH ...

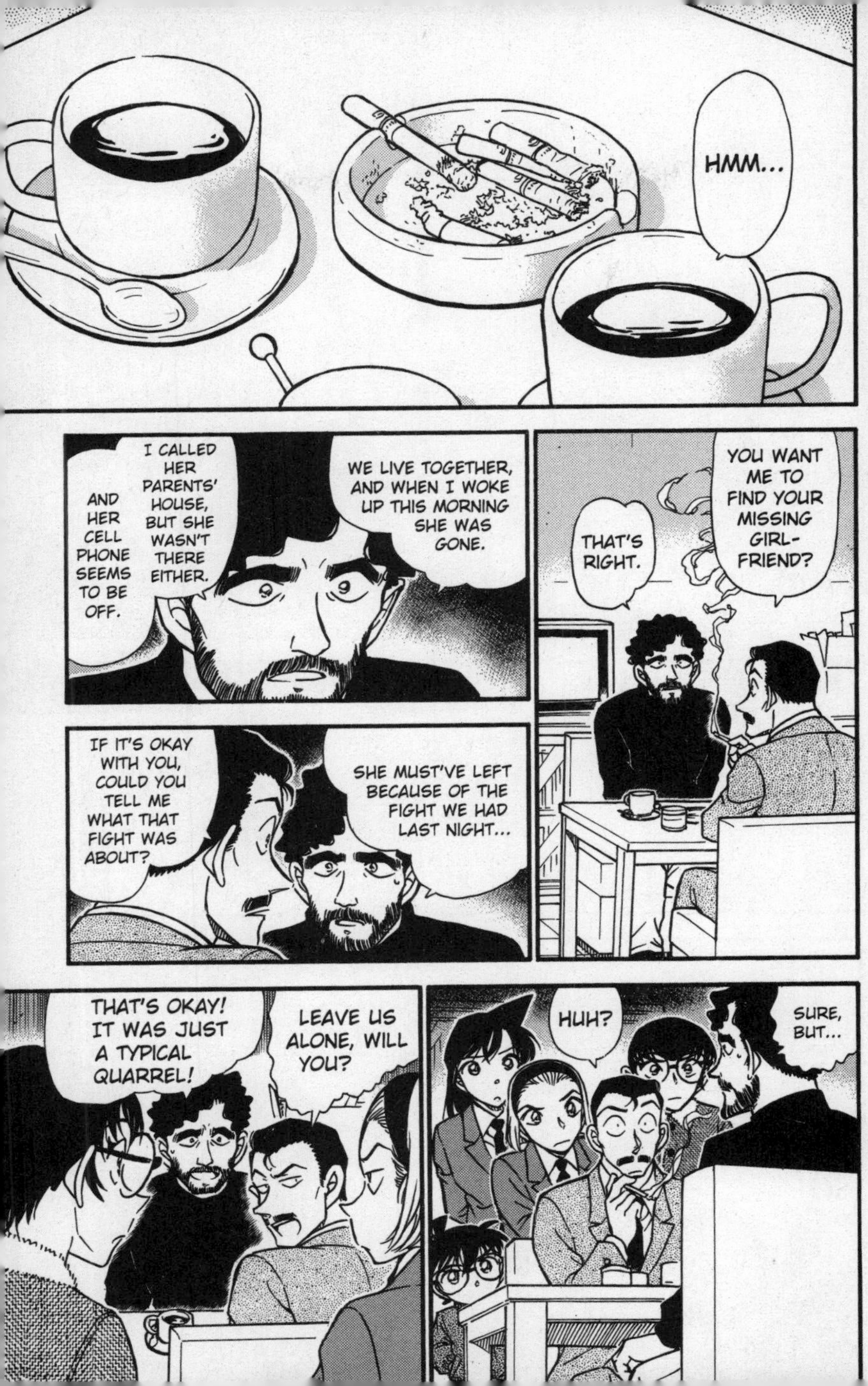
HMM...
YOU WANT ME TO FIND YOUR MISSING GIRL-FRIEND?
THAT'S RIGHT.
WE LIVE TOGETHER, AND WHEN I WOKE UP THIS MORNING SHE WAS GONE.
I CALLED HER PARENTS' HOUSE, BUT SHE WASN'T THERE EITHER.
AND HER CELL PHONE SEEMS TO BE OFF.
SHE MUST'VE LEFT BECAUSE OF THE FIGHT WE HAD LAST NIGHT...
IF IT'S OKAY WITH YOU, COULD YOU TELL ME WHAT THAT FIGHT WAS ABOUT?
SURE, BUT...
HUH?
LEAVE US ALONE, WILL YOU?
THAT'S OKAY! IT WAS JUST A TYPICAL QUARREL!

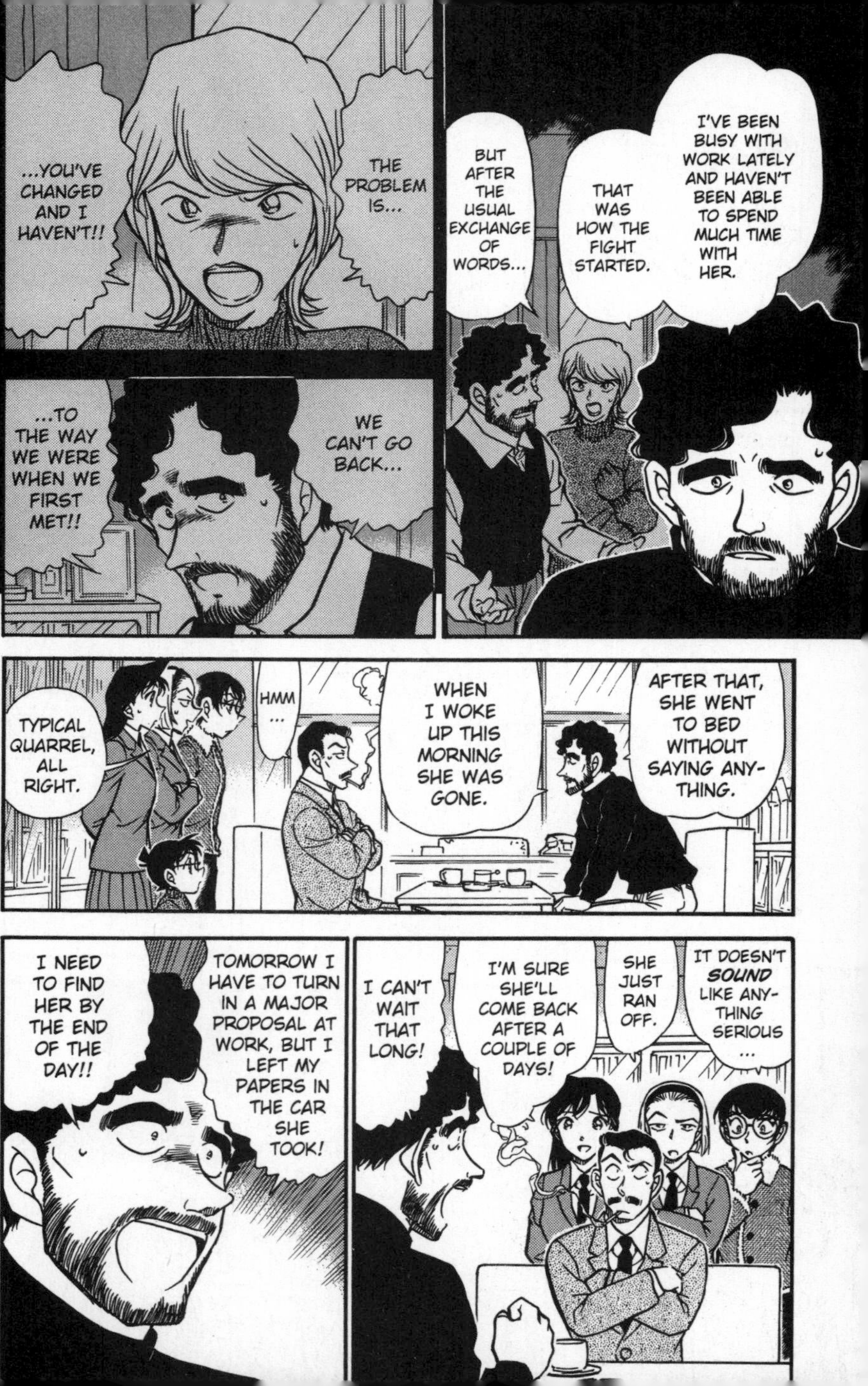
I'VE BEEN BUSY WITH WORK LATELY AND HAVEN'T BEEN ABLE TO SPEND MUCH TIME WITH HER.
THAT WAS HOW THE FIGHT STARTED.
BUT AFTER THE USUAL EXCHANGE OF WORDS...
THE PROBLEM IS...
...YOU'VE CHANGED AND I HAVEN'T!!
WE CAN'T GO BACK...
...TO THE WAY WE WERE WHEN WE FIRST MET!!
AFTER THAT, SHE WENT TO BED WITHOUT SAYING ANY-THING.
WHEN I WOKE UP THIS MORNING SHE WAS GONE.
HMM...
TYPICAL QUARREL, ALL RIGHT.
IT DOESN'T *SOUND* LIKE ANY-THING SERIOUS...
SHE JUST RAN OFF.
I'M SURE SHE'LL COME BACK AFTER A COUPLE OF DAYS!
I CAN'T WAIT THAT LONG!
TOMORROW I HAVE TO TURN IN A MAJOR PROPOSAL AT WORK, BUT I LEFT MY PAPERS IN THE CAR SHE TOOK!
I NEED TO FIND HER BY THE END OF THE DAY!!

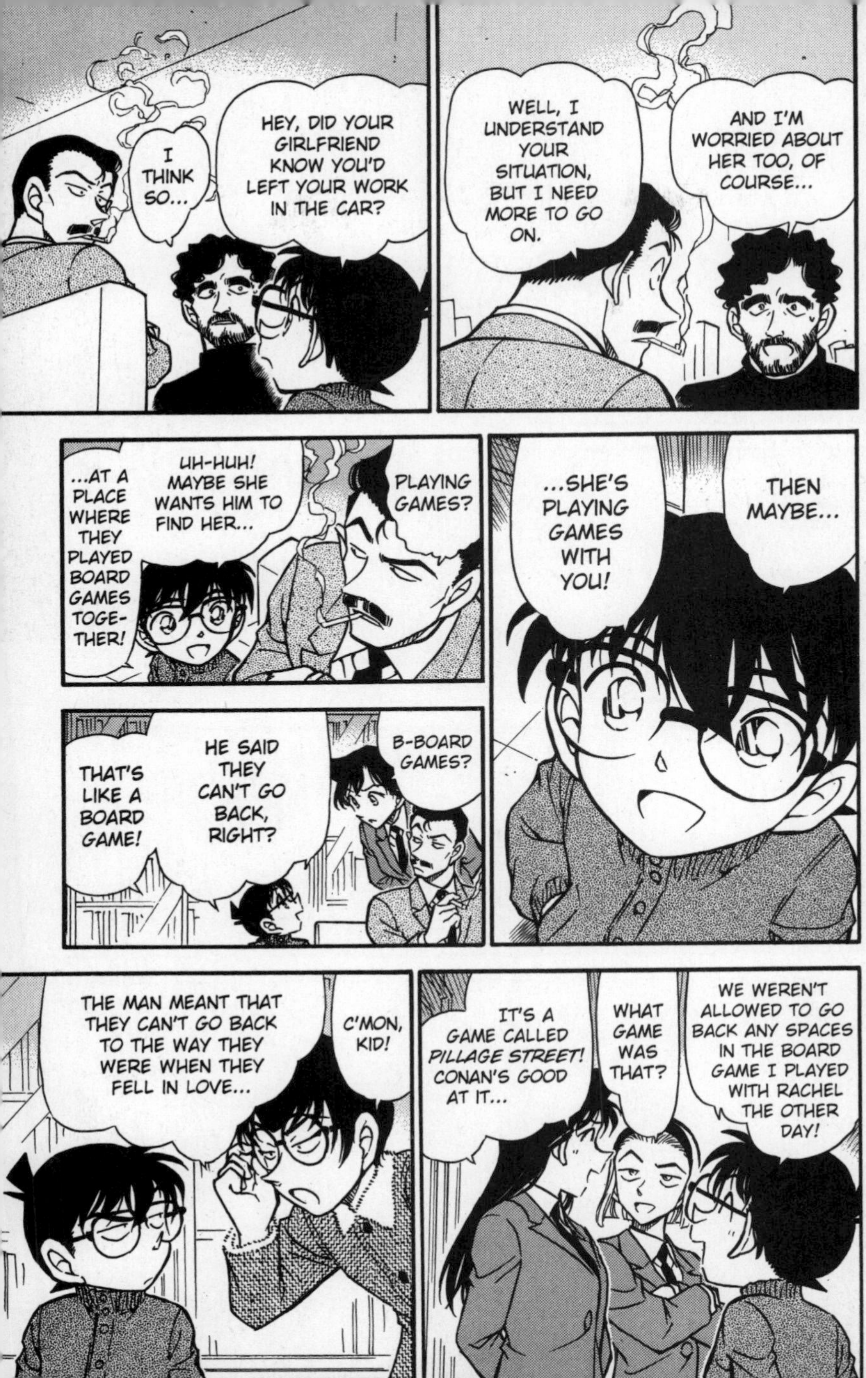
AND I'M WORRIED ABOUT HER TOO, OF COURSE...
WELL, I UNDERSTAND YOUR SITUATION, BUT I NEED MORE TO GO ON.
HEY, DID YOUR GIRLFRIEND KNOW YOU'D LEFT YOUR WORK IN THE CAR?
I THINK SO...
THEN MAYBE...
...SHE'S PLAYING GAMES WITH YOU!
PLAYING GAMES?
UH-HUH! MAYBE SHE WANTS HIM TO FIND HER...
...AT A PLACE WHERE THEY PLAYED BOARD GAMES TOGE-THER!
B-BOARD GAMES?
HE SAID THEY CAN'T GO BACK, RIGHT?
THAT'S LIKE A BOARD GAME!
WE WEREN'T ALLOWED TO GO BACK ANY SPACES IN THE BOARD GAME I PLAYED WITH RACHEL THE OTHER DAY!
WHAT GAME WAS THAT?
IT'S A GAME CALLED *PILLAGE STREET*! CONAN'S GOOD AT IT...
C'MON, KID!
THE MAN MEANT THAT THEY CAN'T GO BACK TO THE WAY THEY WERE WHEN THEY FELL IN LOVE...

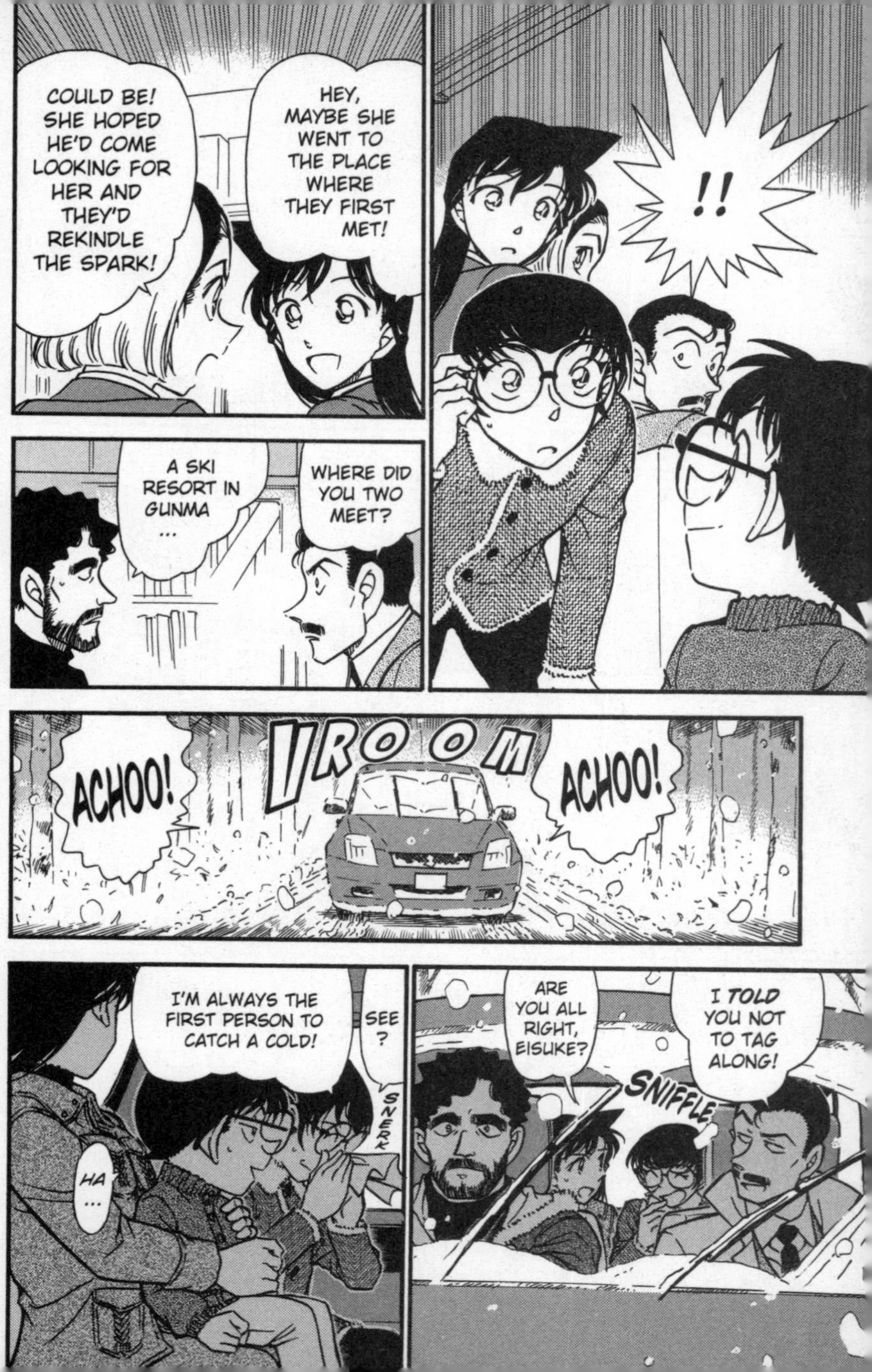
!!
HEY, MAYBE SHE WENT TO THE PLACE WHERE THEY FIRST MET!
COULD BE! SHE HOPED HE'D COME LOOKING FOR HER AND THEY'D REKINDLE THE SPARK!
WHERE DID YOU TWO MEET?
A SKI RESORT IN GUNMA ...
ACHOO!
VROOM
ACHOO!
I *TOLD* YOU NOT TO TAG ALONG!
SNIFFLE
ARE YOU ALL RIGHT, EISUKE?
SEE?
SNERK
I'M ALWAYS THE FIRST PERSON TO CATCH A COLD!
HA ...

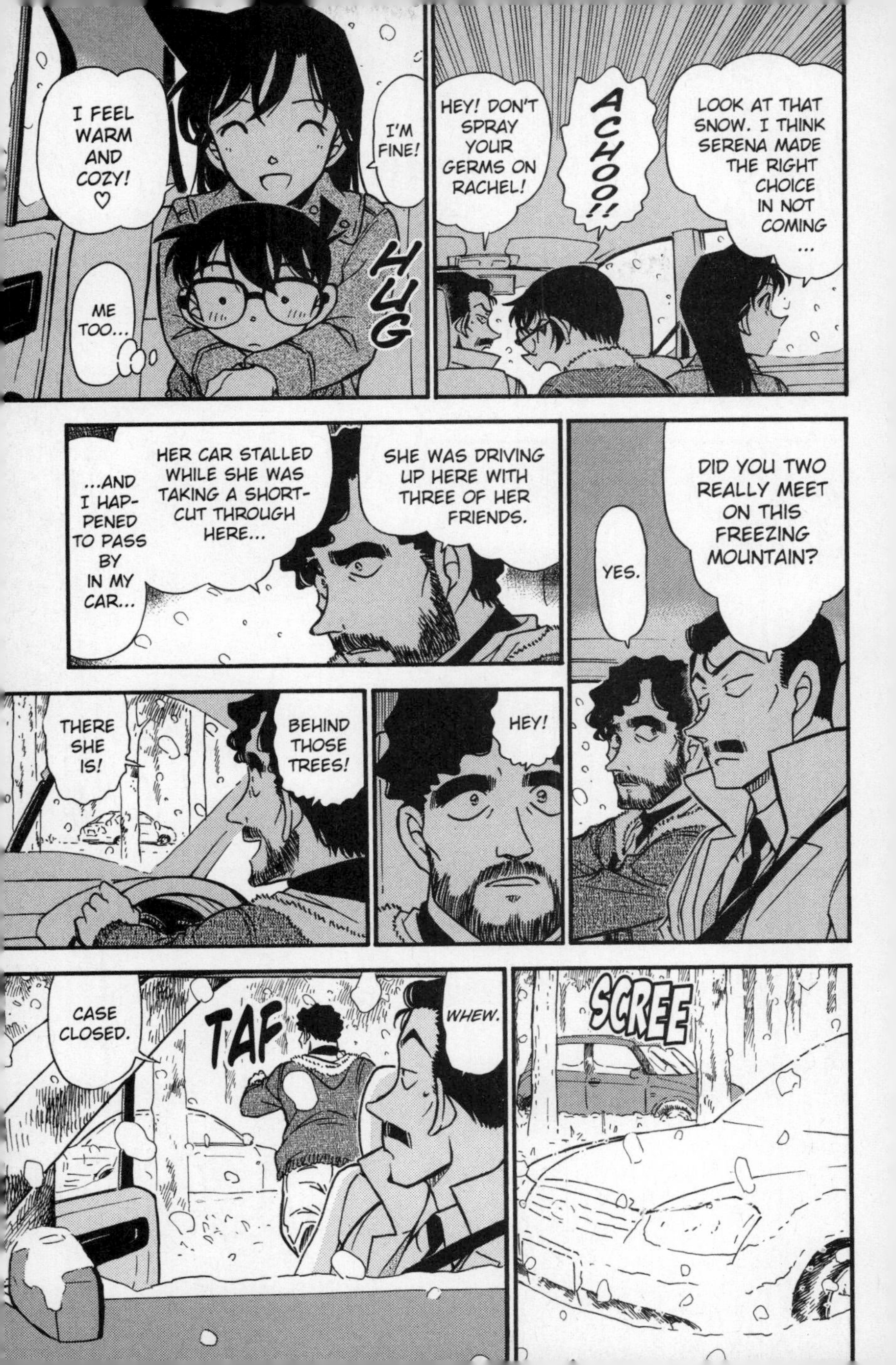
LOOK AT THAT SNOW. I THINK SERENA MADE THE RIGHT CHOICE IN NOT COMING...
ACHOO!!
HEY! DON'T SPRAY YOUR GERMS ON RACHEL!
I'M FINE!
I FEEL WARM AND COZY! ♡
HUG
ME TOO...
DID YOU TWO REALLY MEET ON THIS FREEZING MOUNTAIN?
YES.
SHE WAS DRIVING UP HERE WITH THREE OF HER FRIENDS.
HER CAR STALLED WHILE SHE WAS TAKING A SHORT-CUT THROUGH HERE...
...AND I HAPPENED TO PASS BY IN MY CAR...
HEY!
BEHIND THOSE TREES!
THERE SHE IS!
SCREE
WHEW.
TAF
CASE CLOSED.

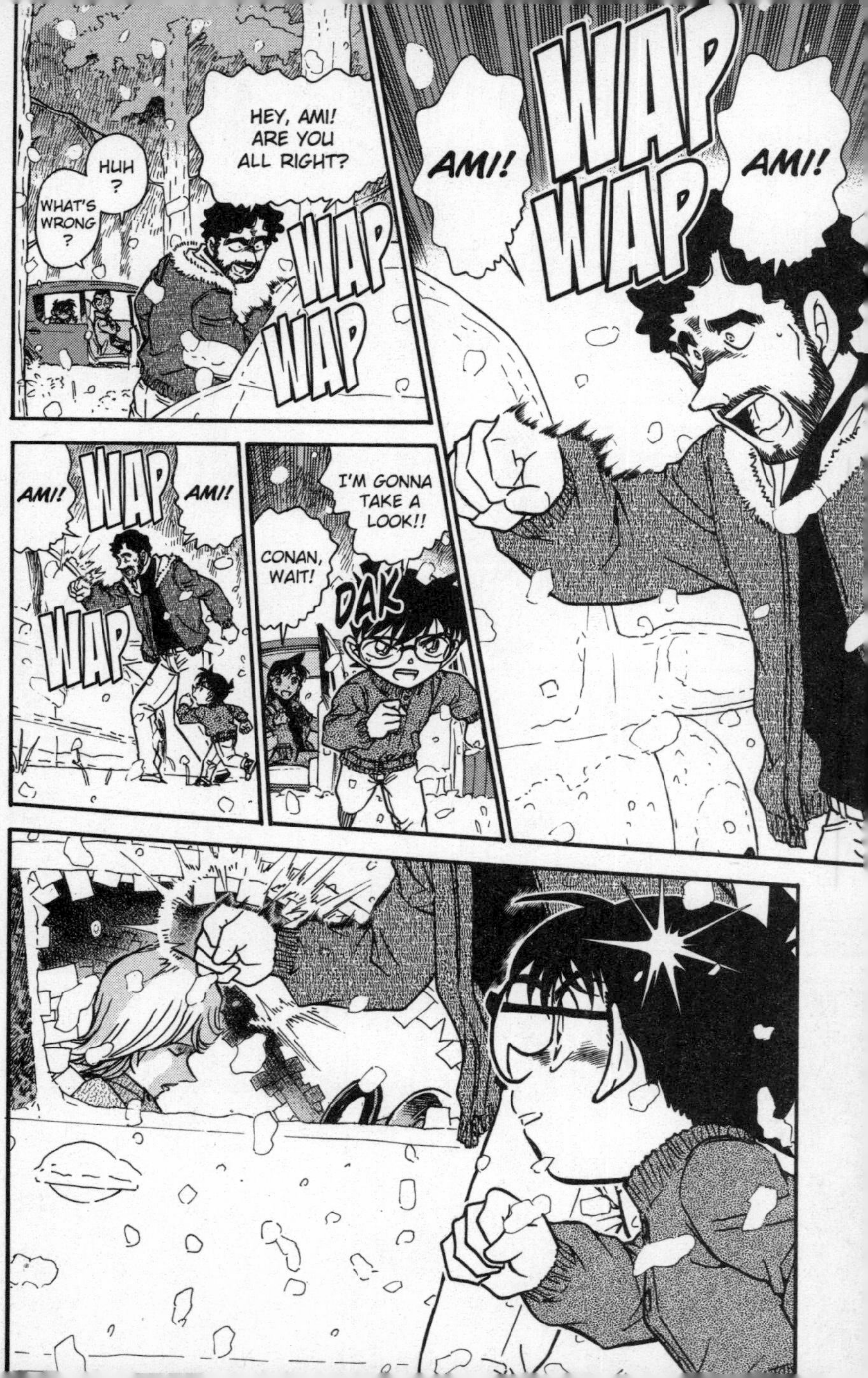
AMI!
WAP WAP
AMI!
HEY, AMI! ARE YOU ALL RIGHT?
HUH?
WHAT'S WRONG?
WAP WAP
I'M GONNA TAKE A LOOK!!
CONAN, WAIT!
DAK
AMI!
WAP
AMI!
WAP

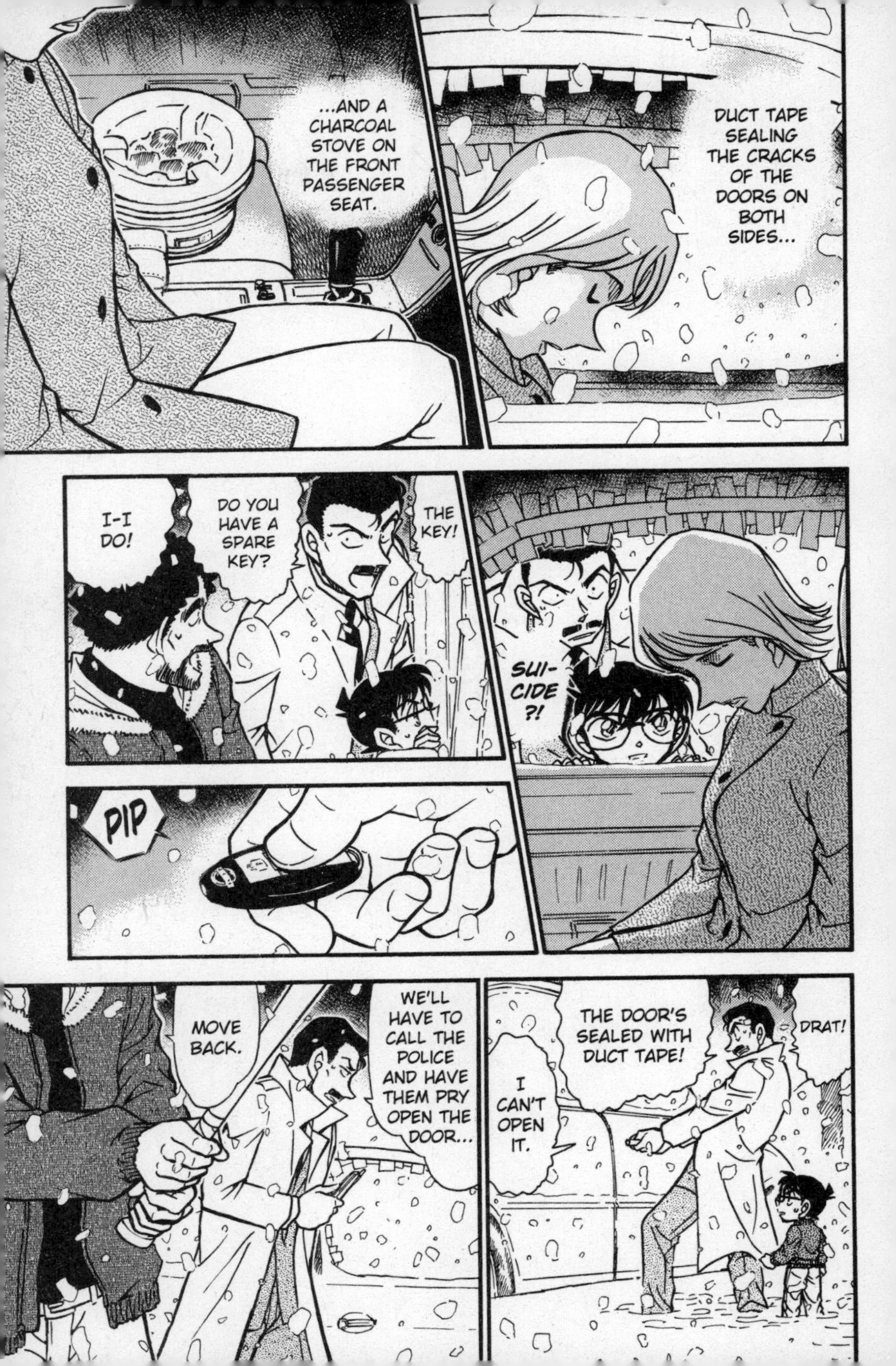
DUCT TAPE SEALING THE CRACKS OF THE DOORS ON BOTH SIDES...
...AND A CHARCOAL STOVE ON THE FRONT PASSENGER SEAT.
SUI-CIDE?!
THE KEY!
DO YOU HAVE A SPARE KEY?
I-I DO!
PIP
DRAT!
THE DOOR'S SEALED WITH DUCT TAPE!
I CAN'T OPEN IT.
WE'LL HAVE TO CALL THE POLICE AND HAVE THEM PRY OPEN THE DOOR...
MOVE BACK.

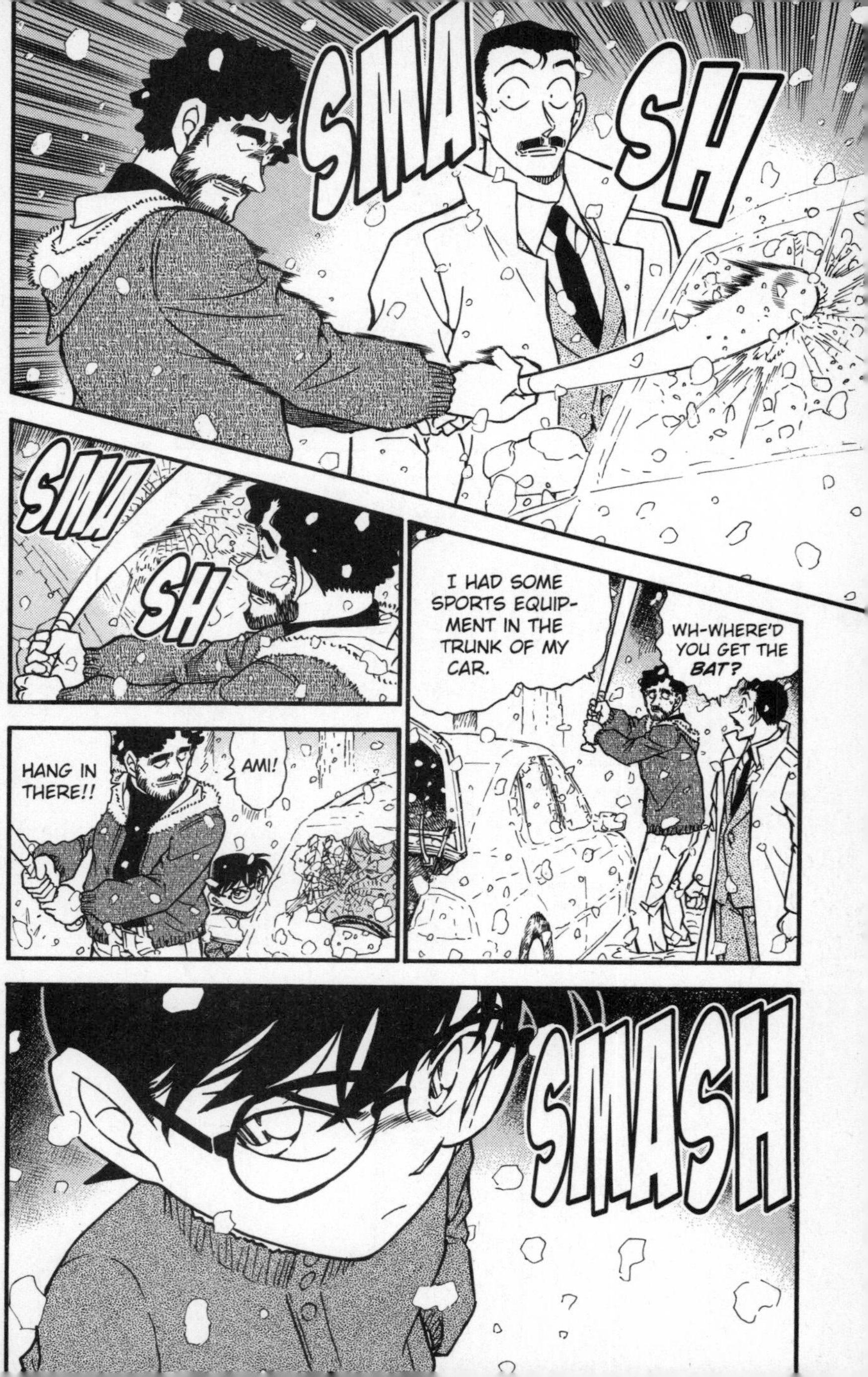
SMASH
WH-WHERE'D YOU GET THE BAT?
I HAD SOME SPORTS EQUIPMENT IN THE TRUNK OF MY CAR.
SMASH
AMI!
HANG IN THERE!!
SMASH

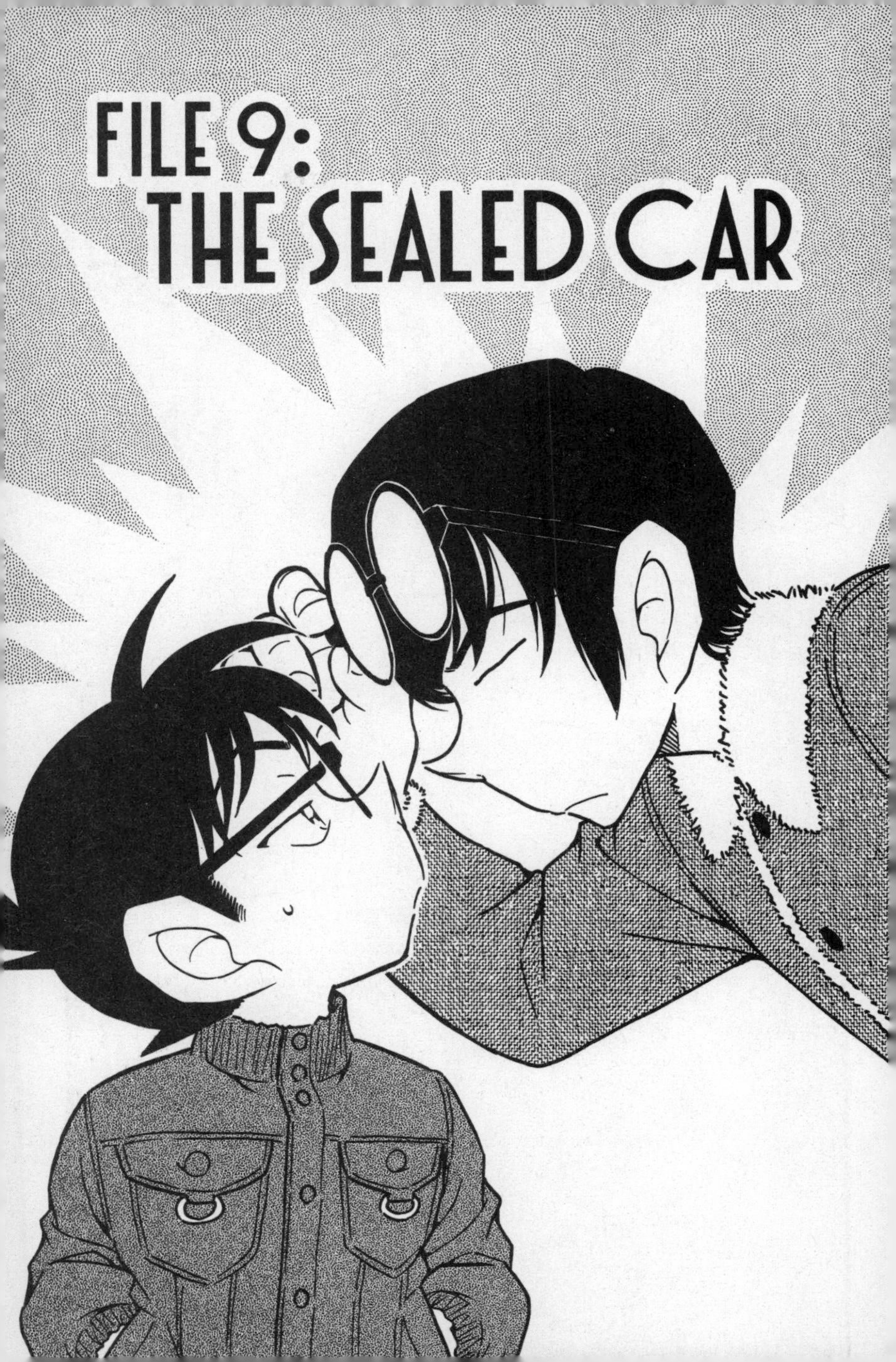
FILE 9:
THE SEALED CAR

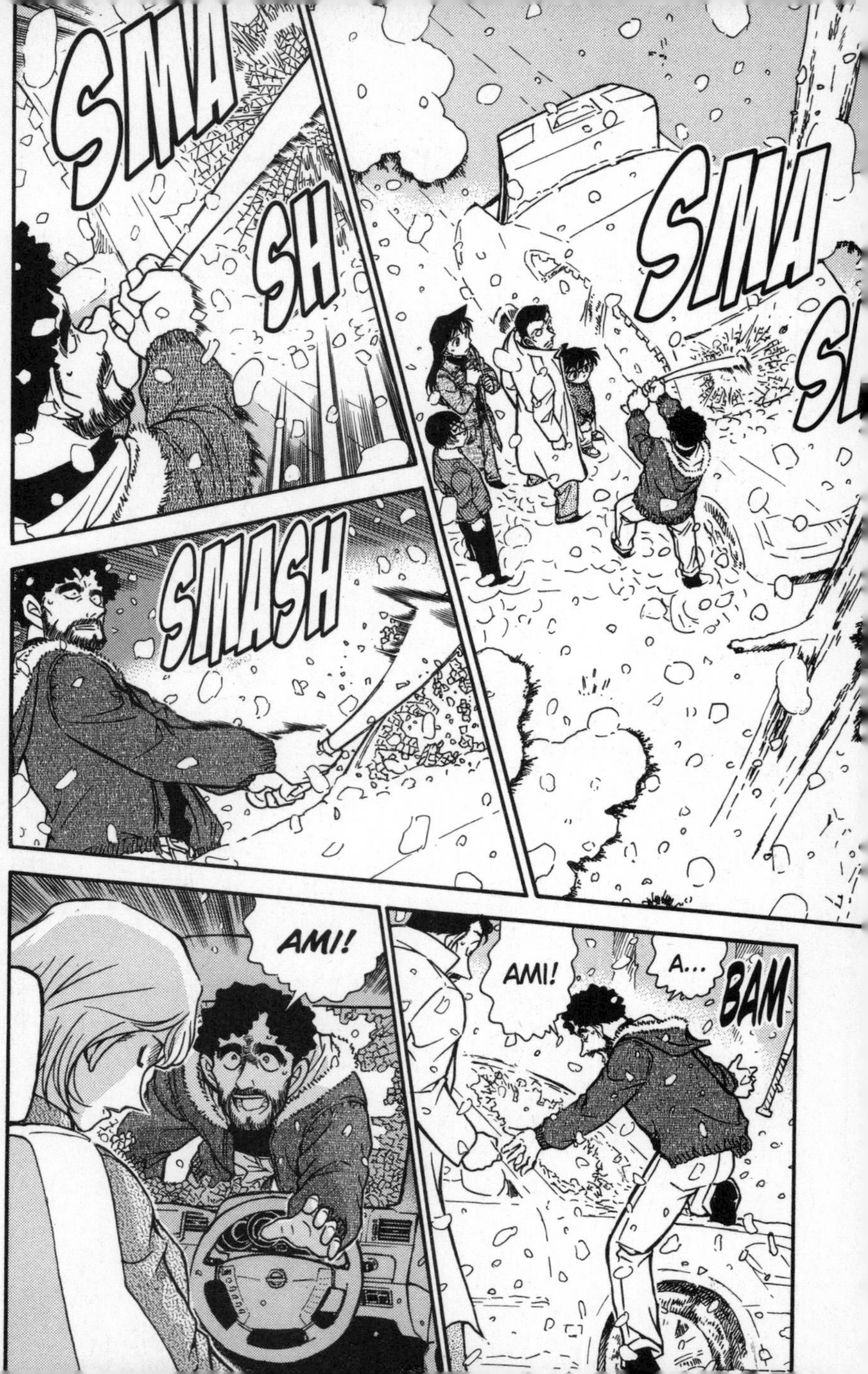
SMA
SMA
SH
SMASH
BAM
A...
AMI!
AMI!

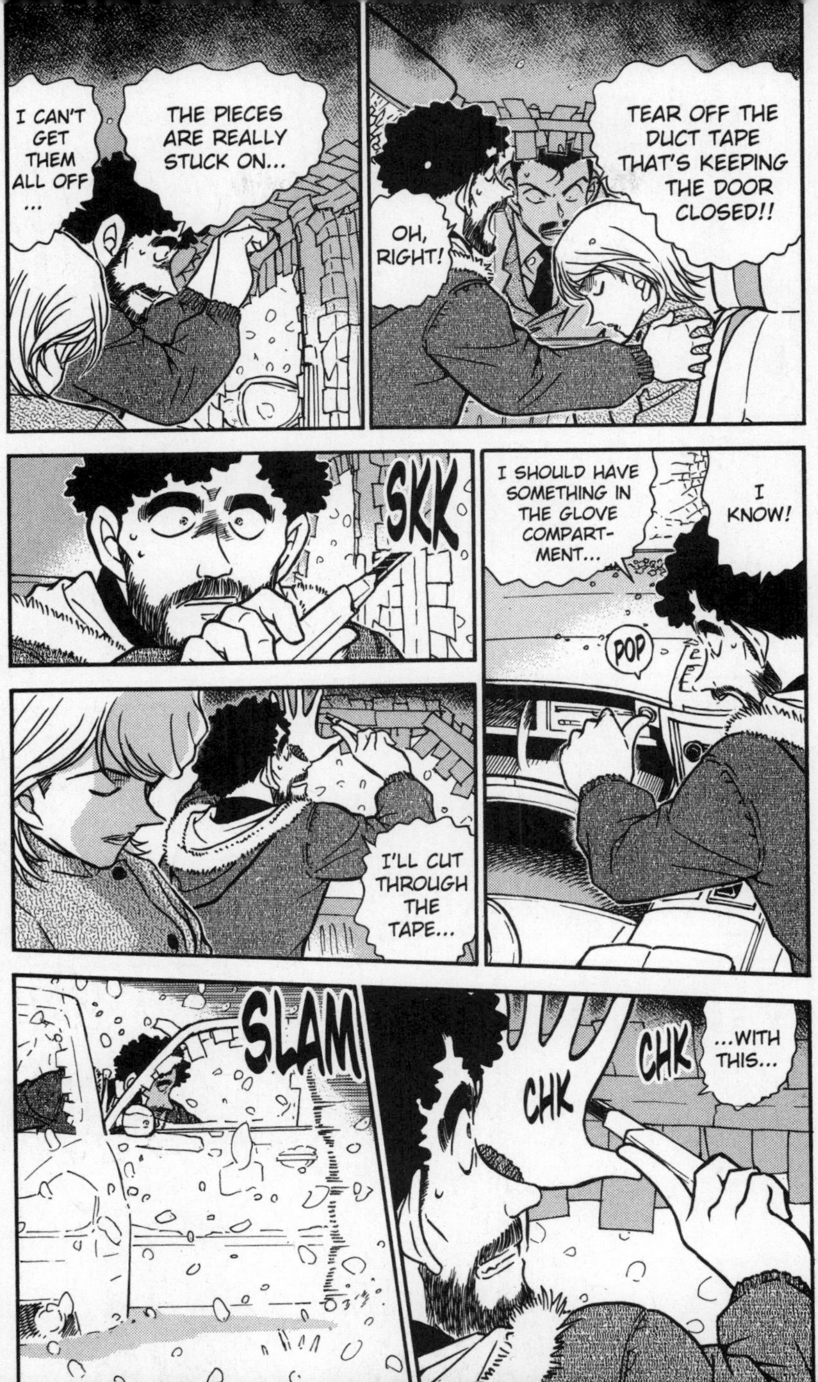
TEAR OFF THE DUCT TAPE THAT'S KEEPING THE DOOR CLOSED!!
OH, RIGHT!
THE PIECES ARE REALLY STUCK ON...
I CAN'T GET THEM ALL OFF ...
I KNOW!
I SHOULD HAVE SOMETHING IN THE GLOVE COMPART-MENT...
POP
SKK
I'LL CUT THROUGH THE TAPE...
...WITH THIS...
CHK
CHK
SLAM

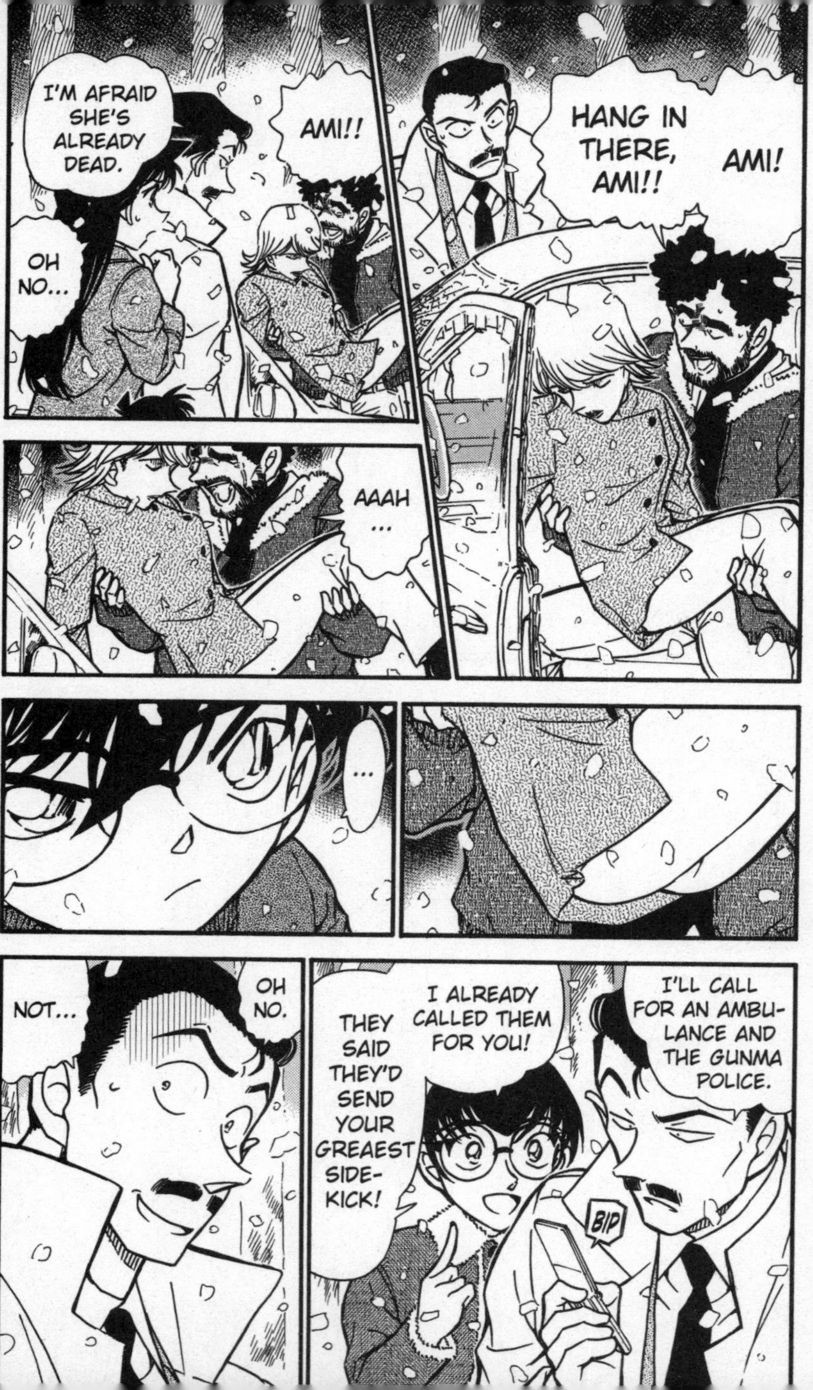
AMI!
HANG IN THERE, AMI!!
AMI!!
I'M AFRAID SHE'S ALREADY DEAD.
OH NO...
AAAH ...
...
I'LL CALL FOR AN AMBULANCE AND THE GUNMA POLICE.
BIP
I ALREADY CALLED THEM FOR YOU!
THEY SAID THEY'D SEND YOUR GREAEST SIDE-KICK!
OH NO.
NOT...

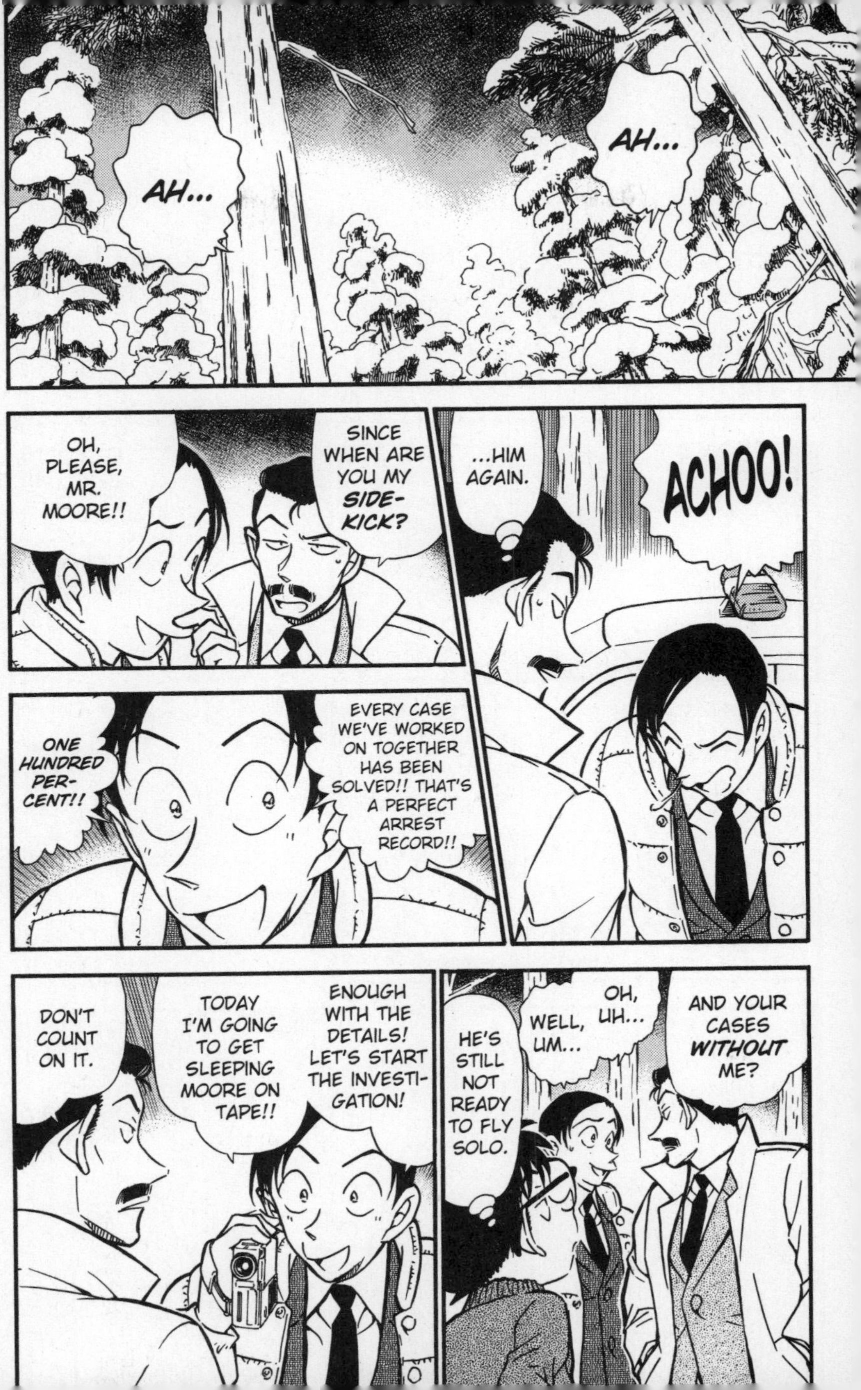
AH...
AH...
ACHOO!
...HIM AGAIN.
SINCE WHEN ARE YOU MY SIDE-KICK?
OH, PLEASE, MR. MOORE!!
EVERY CASE WE'VE WORKED ON TOGETHER HAS BEEN SOLVED!! THAT'S A PERFECT ARREST RECORD!!
ONE HUNDRED PER-CENT!!
AND YOUR CASES WITHOUT ME?
OH, UH...
WELL, UM...
HE'S STILL NOT READY TO FLY SOLO.
ENOUGH WITH THE DETAILS! LET'S START THE INVESTI-GATION!
TODAY I'M GOING TO GET SLEEPING MOORE ON TAPE!!
DON'T COUNT ON IT.

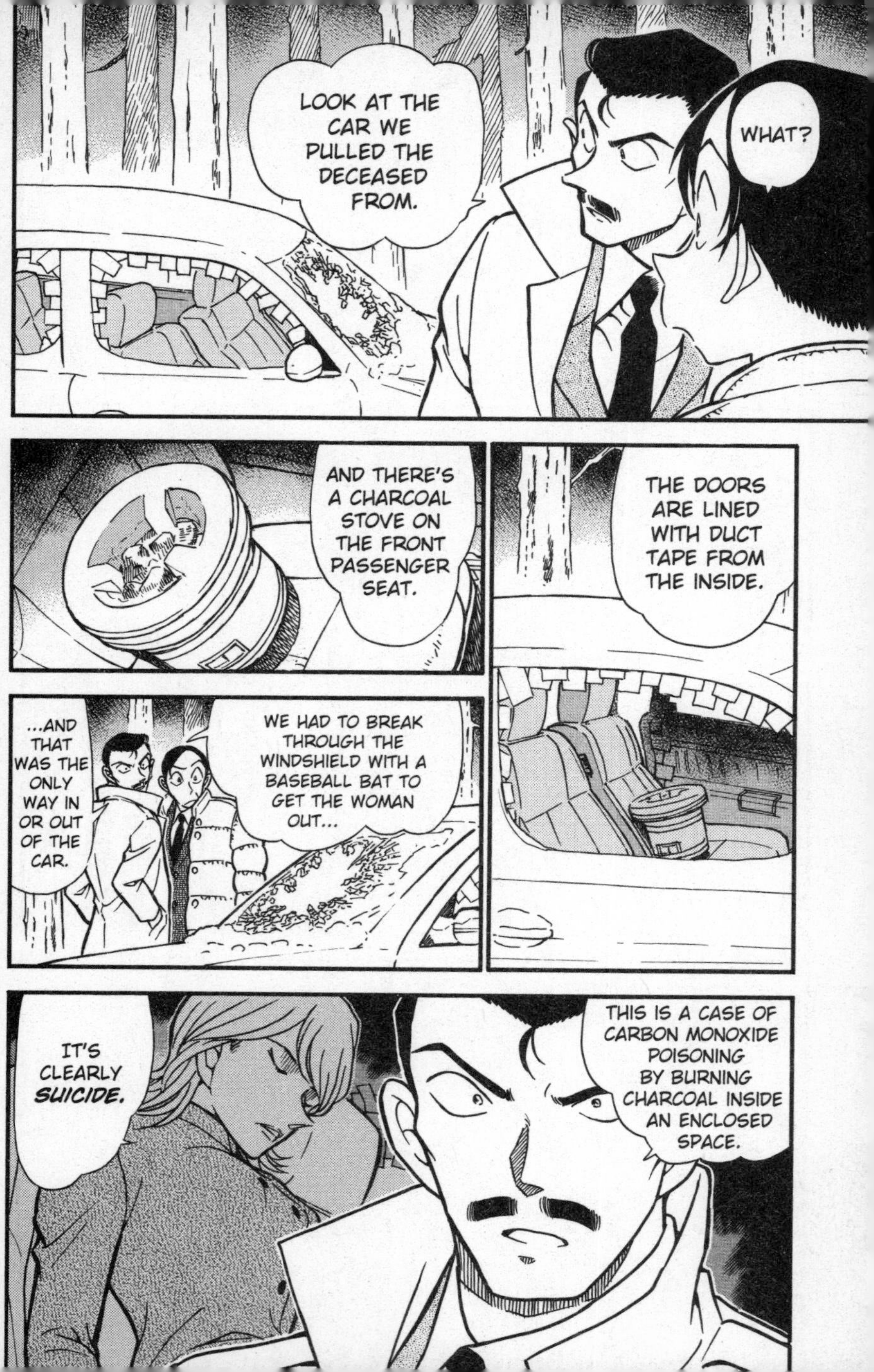
WHAT?
LOOK AT THE CAR WE PULLED THE DECEASED FROM.
THE DOORS ARE LINED WITH DUCT TAPE FROM THE INSIDE.
AND THERE'S A CHARCOAL STOVE ON THE FRONT PASSENGER SEAT.
WE HAD TO BREAK THROUGH THE WINDSHIELD WITH A BASEBALL BAT TO GET THE WOMAN OUT...
...AND THAT WAS THE ONLY WAY IN OR OUT OF THE CAR.
THIS IS A CASE OF CARBON MONOXIDE POISONING BY BURNING CHARCOAL INSIDE AN ENCLOSED SPACE.
IT'S CLEARLY *SUICIDE.*

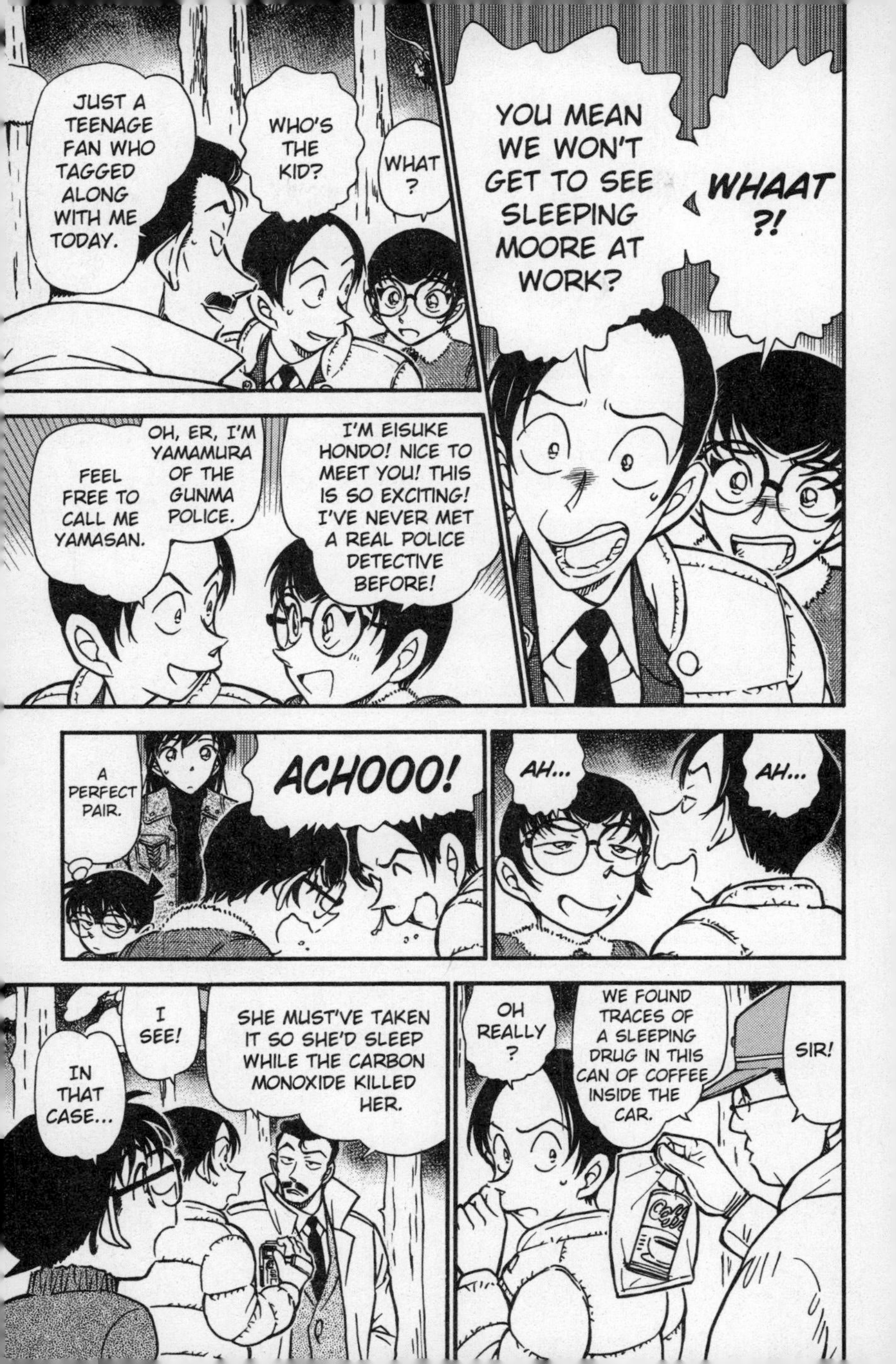
WHAAT ?!
YOU MEAN WE WON'T GET TO SEE SLEEPING MOORE AT WORK?
WHAT ?
WHO'S THE KID?
JUST A TEENAGE FAN WHO TAGGED ALONG WITH ME TODAY.
I'M EISUKE HONDO! NICE TO MEET YOU! THIS IS SO EXCITING! I'VE NEVER MET A REAL POLICE DETECTIVE BEFORE!
OH, ER, I'M YAMAMURA OF THE GUNMA POLICE.
FEEL FREE TO CALL ME YAMASAN.
AH...
AH...
ACHOOO!
A PERFECT PAIR.
SIR!
WE FOUND TRACES OF A SLEEPING DRUG IN THIS CAN OF COFFEE INSIDE THE CAR.
OH REALLY ?
SHE MUST'VE TAKEN IT SO SHE'D SLEEP WHILE THE CARBON MONOXIDE KILLED HER.
I SEE!
IN THAT CASE...

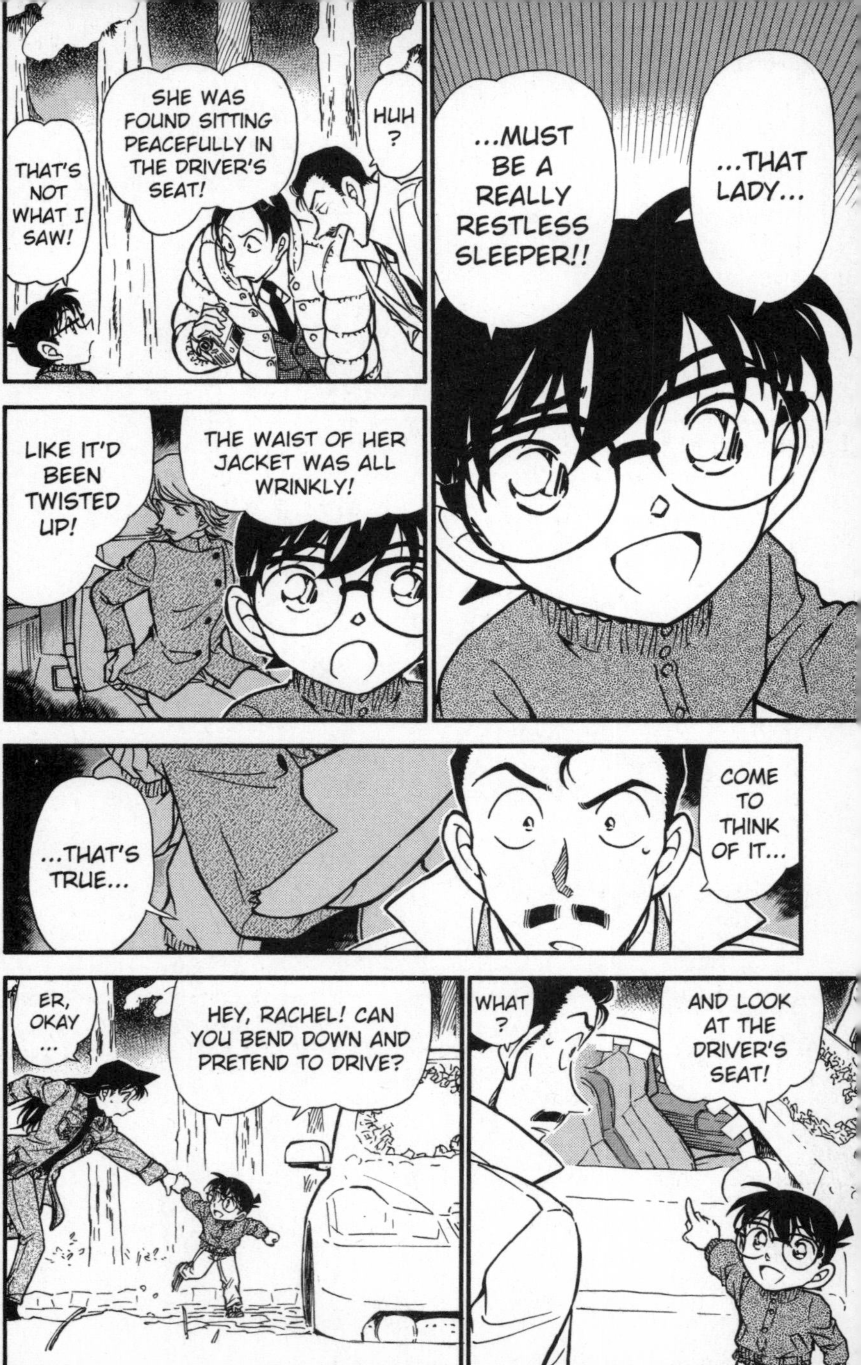
...THAT LADY...
...MUST BE A REALLY RESTLESS SLEEPER!!
HUH?
SHE WAS FOUND SITTING PEACEFULLY IN THE DRIVER'S SEAT!
THAT'S NOT WHAT I SAW!
THE WAIST OF HER JACKET WAS ALL WRINKLY!
LIKE IT'D BEEN TWISTED UP!
COME TO THINK OF IT...
...THAT'S TRUE...
AND LOOK AT THE DRIVER'S SEAT!
WHAT?
HEY, RACHEL! CAN YOU BEND DOWN AND PRETEND TO DRIVE?
ER, OKAY...

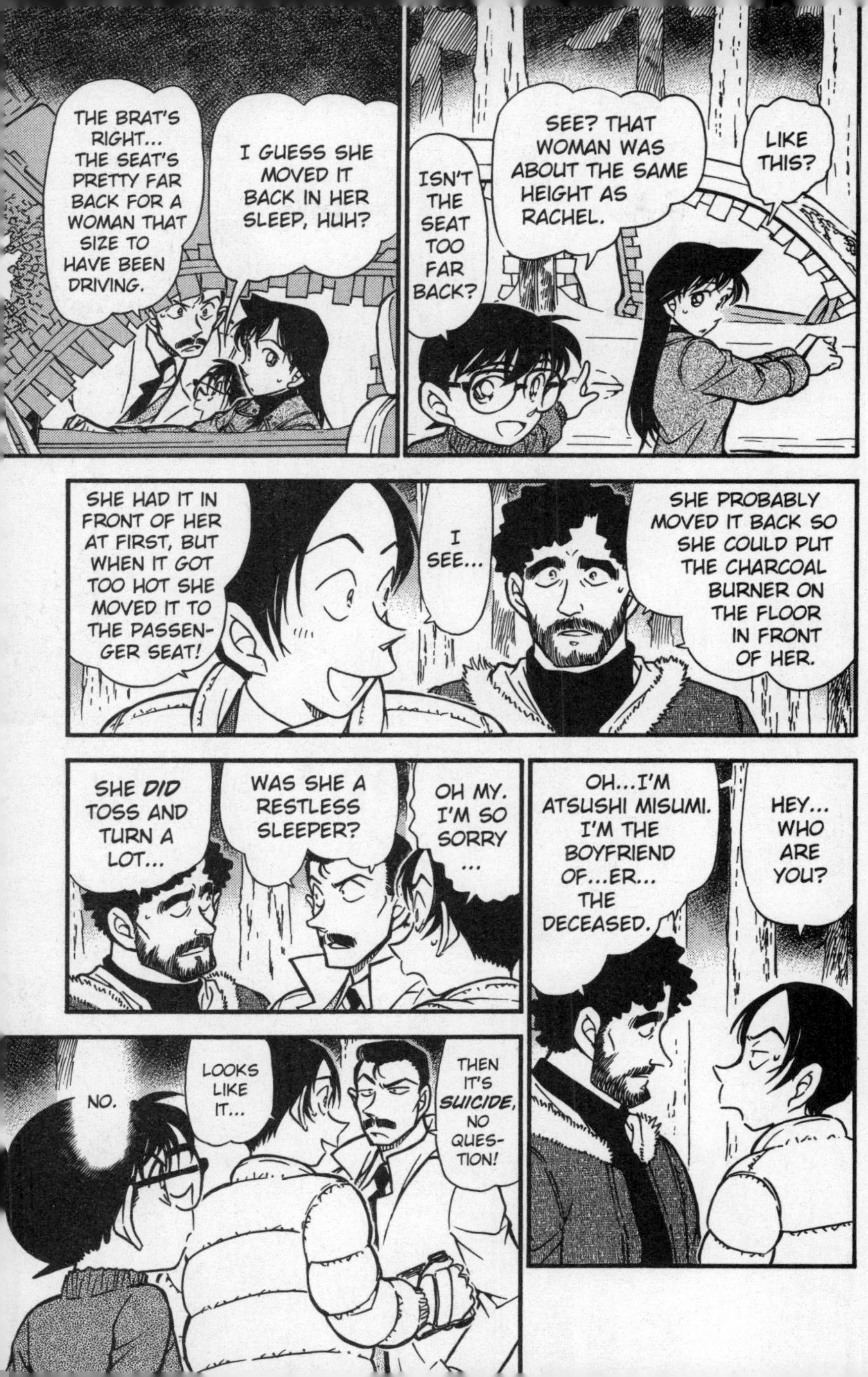
LIKE THIS?
SEE? THAT WOMAN WAS ABOUT THE SAME HEIGHT AS RACHEL.
ISN'T THE SEAT TOO FAR BACK?
I GUESS SHE MOVED IT BACK IN HER SLEEP, HUH?
THE BRAT'S RIGHT... THE SEAT'S PRETTY FAR BACK FOR A WOMAN THAT SIZE TO HAVE BEEN DRIVING.
SHE PROBABLY MOVED IT BACK SO SHE COULD PUT THE CHARCOAL BURNER ON THE FLOOR IN FRONT OF HER.
I SEE...
SHE HAD IT IN FRONT OF HER AT FIRST, BUT WHEN IT GOT TOO HOT SHE MOVED IT TO THE PASSENGER SEAT!
HEY... WHO ARE YOU?
OH...I'M ATSUSHI MISUMI. I'M THE BOYFRIEND OF...ER... THE DECEASED.
OH MY. I'M SO SORRY ...
WAS SHE A RESTLESS SLEEPER?
SHE *DID* TOSS AND TURN A LOT...
THEN IT'S *SUICIDE*, NO QUESTION!
LOOKS LIKE IT...
NO.

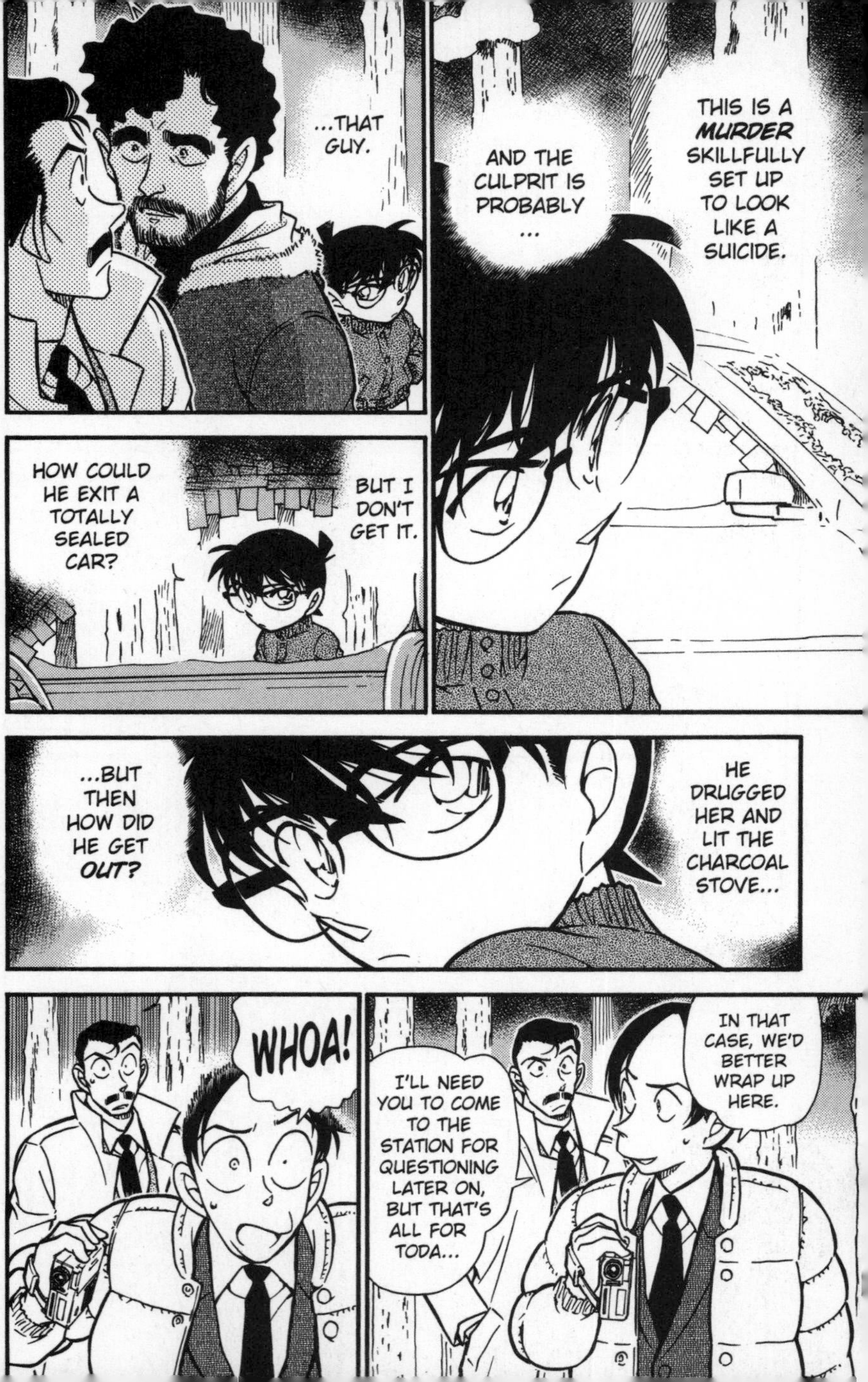
THIS IS A MURDER SKILLFULLY SET UP TO LOOK LIKE A SUICIDE.
AND THE CULPRIT IS PROBABLY ...
...THAT GUY.
BUT I DON'T GET IT.
HOW COULD HE EXIT A TOTALLY SEALED CAR?
HE DRUGGED HER AND LIT THE CHARCOAL STOVE...
...BUT THEN HOW DID HE GET OUT?
IN THAT CASE, WE'D BETTER WRAP UP HERE.
I'LL NEED YOU TO COME TO THE STATION FOR QUESTIONING LATER ON, BUT THAT'S ALL FOR TODA...
WHOA!

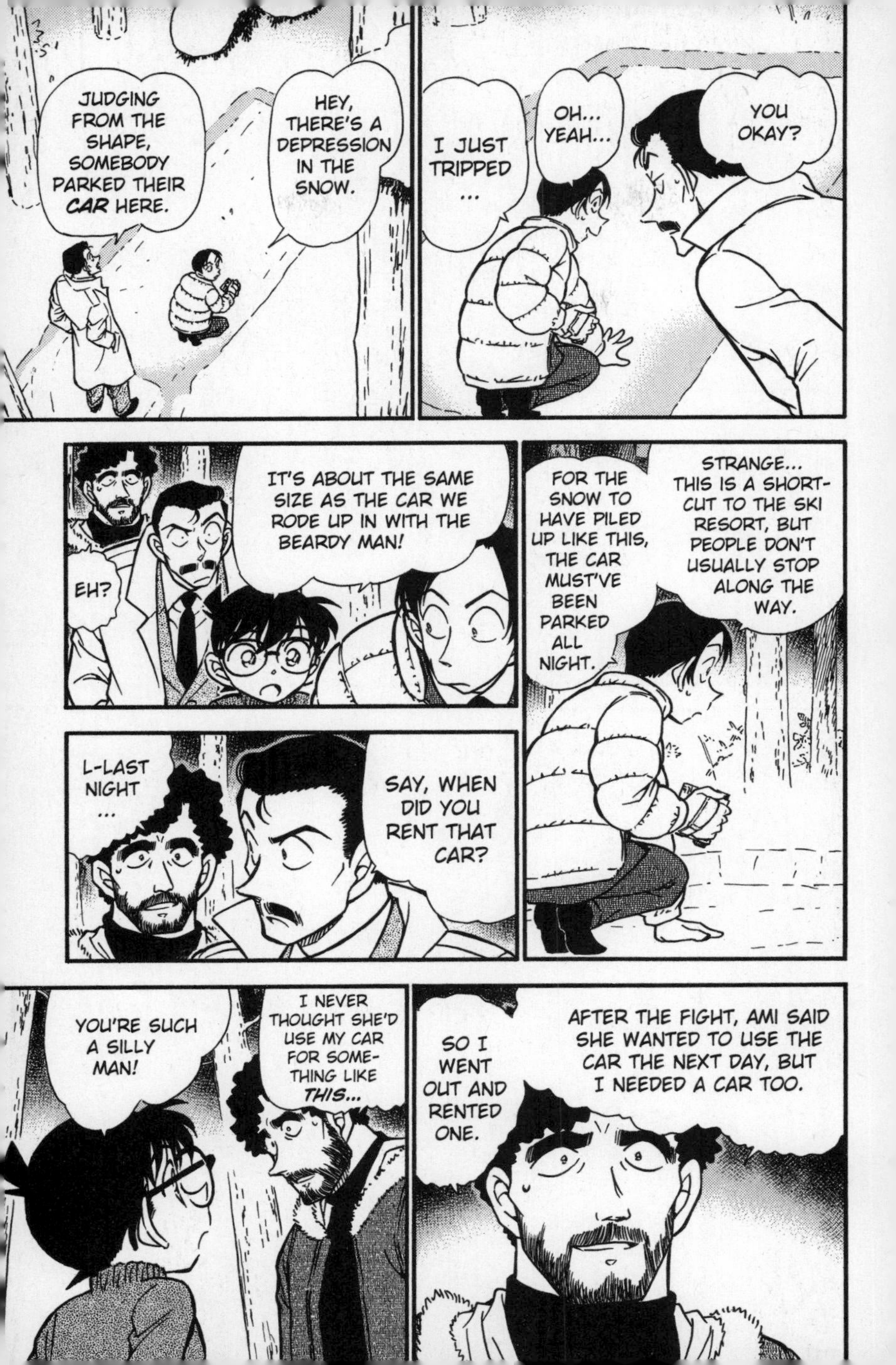
YOU OKAY?
OH... YEAH...
I JUST TRIPPED ...
HEY, THERE'S A DEPRESSION IN THE SNOW.
JUDGING FROM THE SHAPE, SOMEBODY PARKED THEIR CAR HERE.
STRANGE... THIS IS A SHORT-CUT TO THE SKI RESORT, BUT PEOPLE DON'T USUALLY STOP ALONG THE WAY.
FOR THE SNOW TO HAVE PILED UP LIKE THIS, THE CAR MUST'VE BEEN PARKED ALL NIGHT.
IT'S ABOUT THE SAME SIZE AS THE CAR WE RODE UP IN WITH THE BEARDY MAN!
EH?
SAY, WHEN DID YOU RENT THAT CAR?
L-LAST NIGHT ...
AFTER THE FIGHT, AMI SAID SHE WANTED TO USE THE CAR THE NEXT DAY, BUT I NEEDED A CAR TOO.
SO I WENT OUT AND RENTED ONE.
I NEVER THOUGHT SHE'D USE MY CAR FOR SOME-THING LIKE THIS...
YOU'RE SUCH A SILLY MAN!

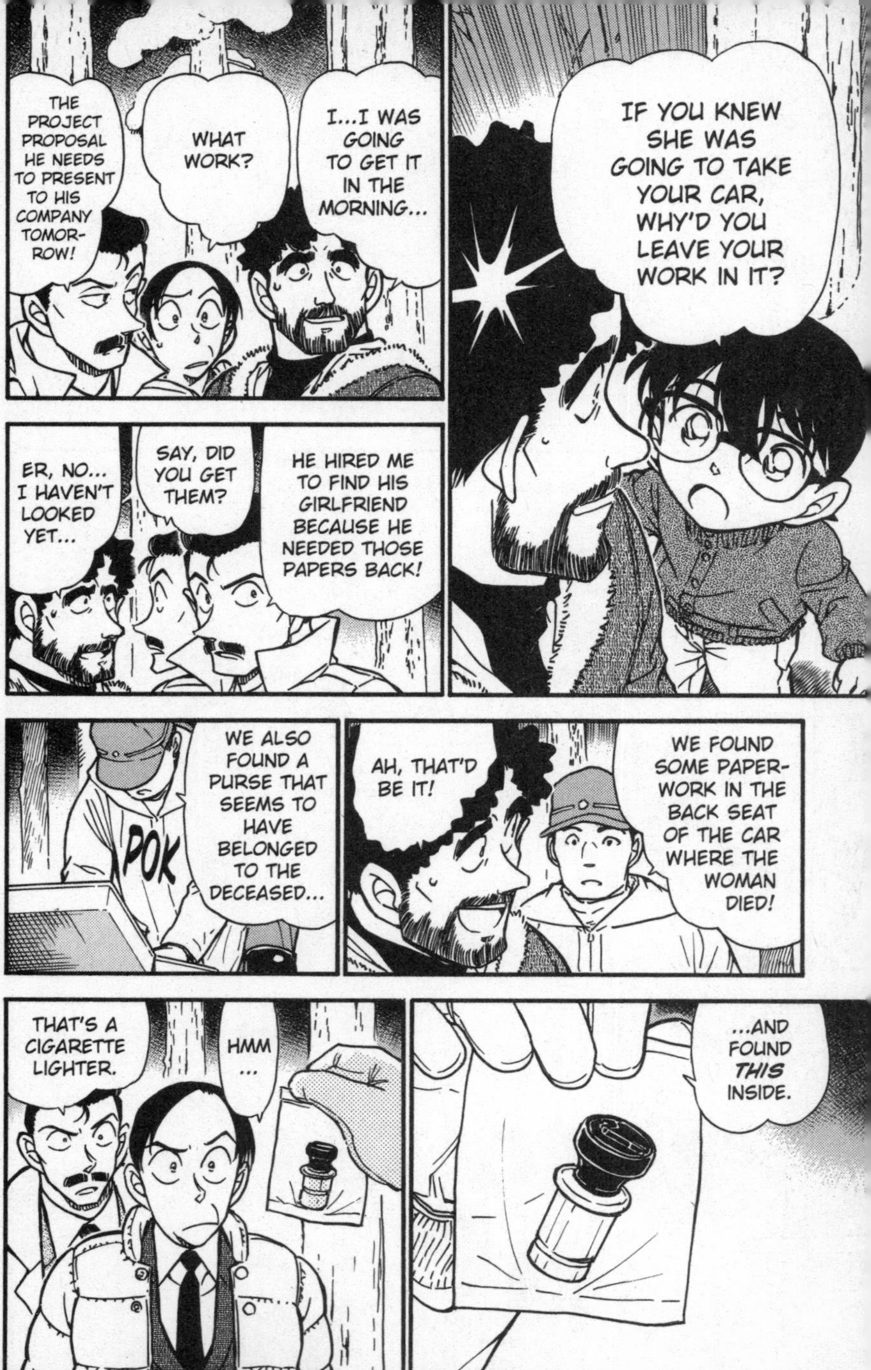

IF YOU KNEW SHE WAS GOING TO TAKE YOUR CAR, WHY'D YOU LEAVE YOUR WORK IN IT?
I...I WAS GOING TO GET IT IN THE MORNING...
WHAT WORK?
THE PROJECT PROPOSAL HE NEEDS TO PRESENT TO HIS COMPANY TOMORROW!
HE HIRED ME TO FIND HIS GIRLFRIEND BECAUSE HE NEEDED THOSE PAPERS BACK!
SAY, DID YOU GET THEM?
ER, NO... I HAVEN'T LOOKED YET...
WE FOUND SOME PAPERWORK IN THE BACK SEAT OF THE CAR WHERE THE WOMAN DIED!
AH, THAT'D BE IT!
WE ALSO FOUND A PURSE THAT SEEMS TO HAVE BELONGED TO THE DECEASED...
POK
...AND FOUND *THIS* INSIDE.
HMM ...
THAT'S A CIGARETTE LIGHTER.

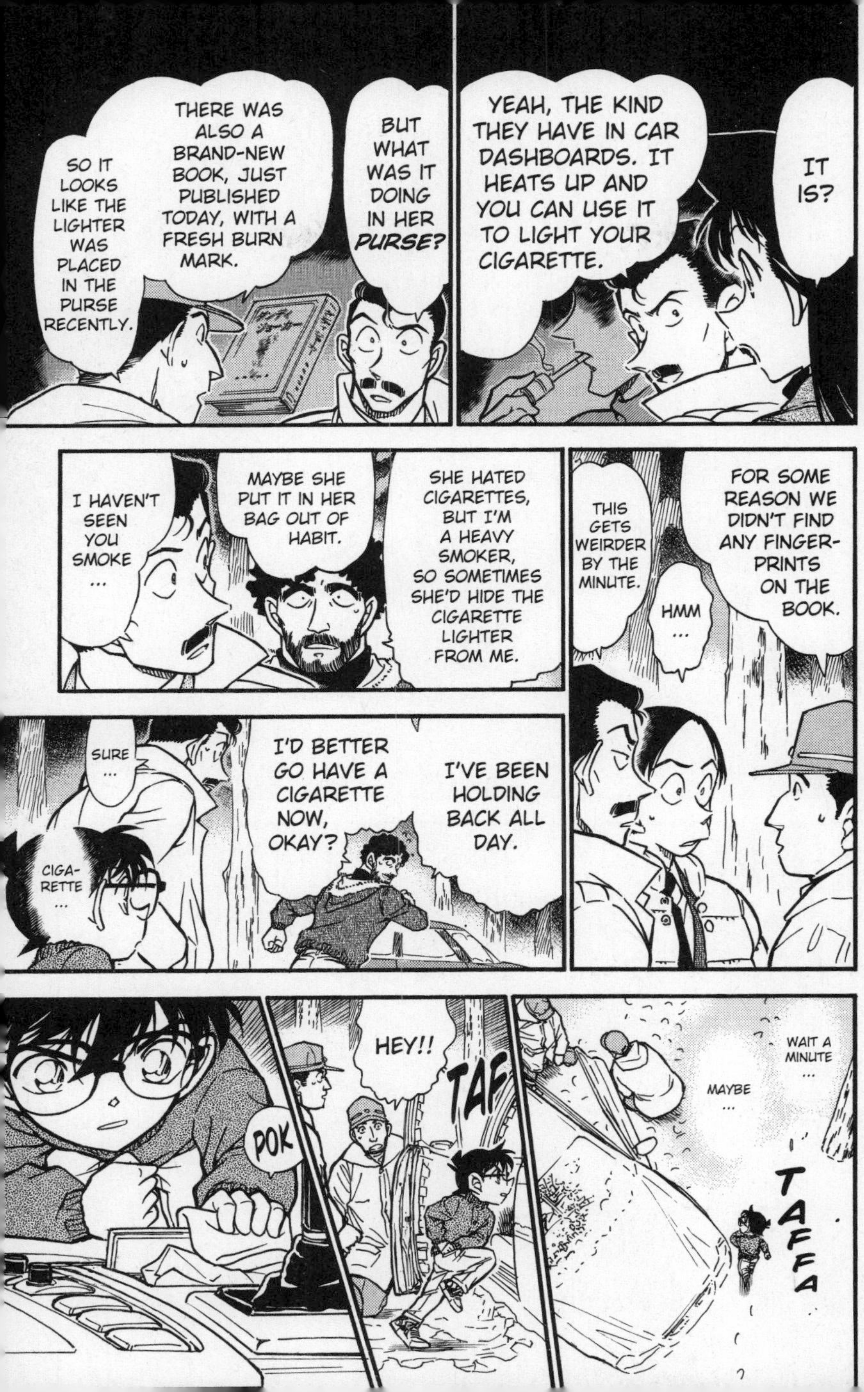
IT IS?
YEAH, THE KIND THEY HAVE IN CAR DASHBOARDS. IT HEATS UP AND YOU CAN USE IT TO LIGHT YOUR CIGARETTE.
BUT WHAT WAS IT DOING IN HER PURSE?
THERE WAS ALSO A BRAND-NEW BOOK, JUST PUBLISHED TODAY, WITH A FRESH BURN MARK.
SO IT LOOKS LIKE THE LIGHTER WAS PLACED IN THE PURSE RECENTLY.
FOR SOME REASON WE DIDN'T FIND ANY FINGER-PRINTS ON THE BOOK.
THIS GETS WEIRDER BY THE MINUTE.
HMM ...
SHE HATED CIGARETTES, BUT I'M A HEAVY SMOKER, SO SOMETIMES SHE'D HIDE THE CIGARETTE LIGHTER FROM ME.
MAYBE SHE PUT IT IN HER BAG OUT OF HABIT.
I HAVEN'T SEEN YOU SMOKE ...
I'VE BEEN HOLDING BACK ALL DAY.
I'D BETTER GO HAVE A CIGARETTE NOW, OKAY?
SURE ...
CIGA-RETTE ...
WAIT A MINUTE ...
MAYBE ...
TAFFA
HEY!!
TAF
POK

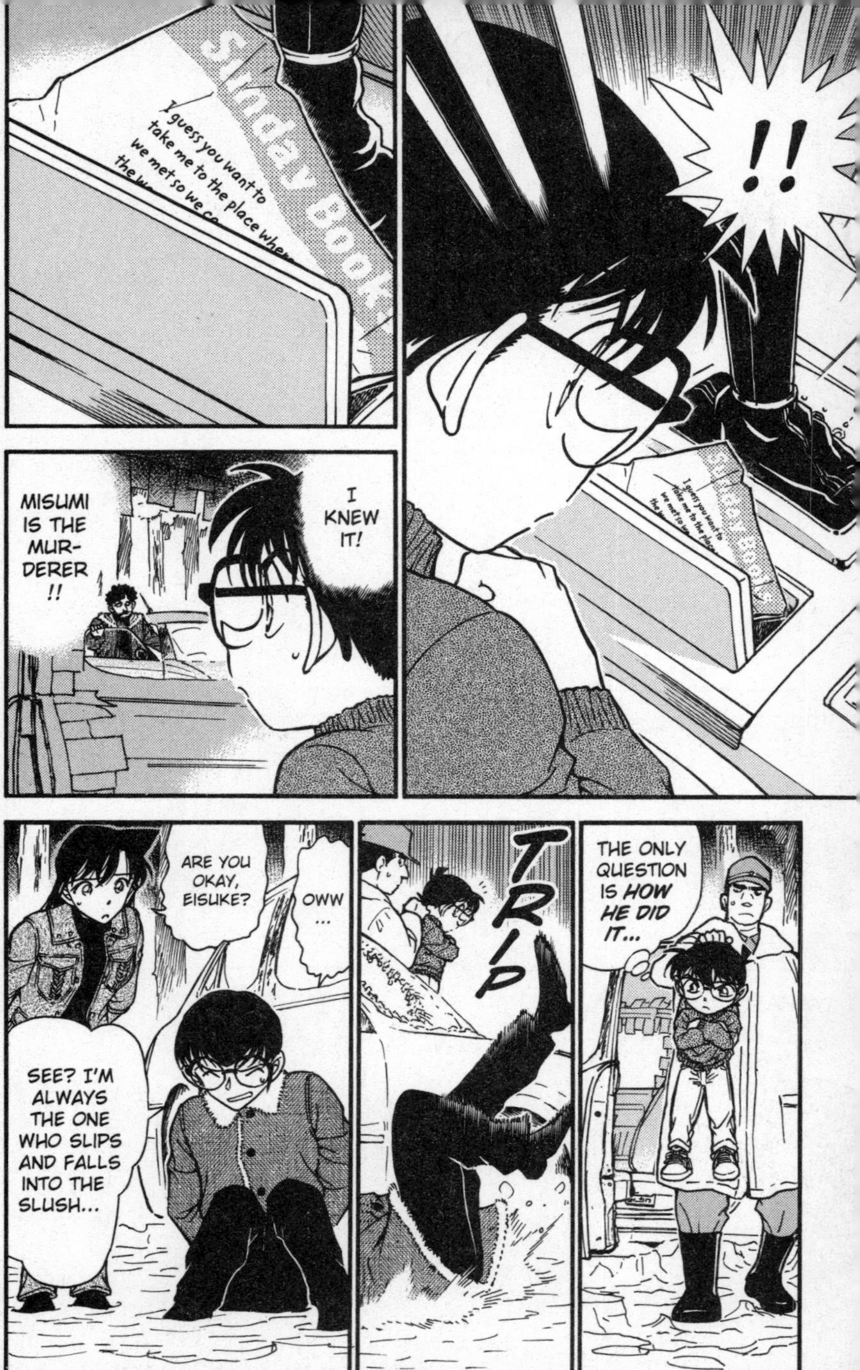
!!
Sunday Book
I guess you want to
take me to the place where
we met so we ca
I KNEW IT!
MISUMI IS THE MURDERER!!
THE ONLY QUESTION IS *HOW HE DID IT*...
TRIP
ARE YOU OKAY, EISUKE?
OWW...
SEE? I'M ALWAYS THE ONE WHO SLIPS AND FALLS INTO THE SLUSH...

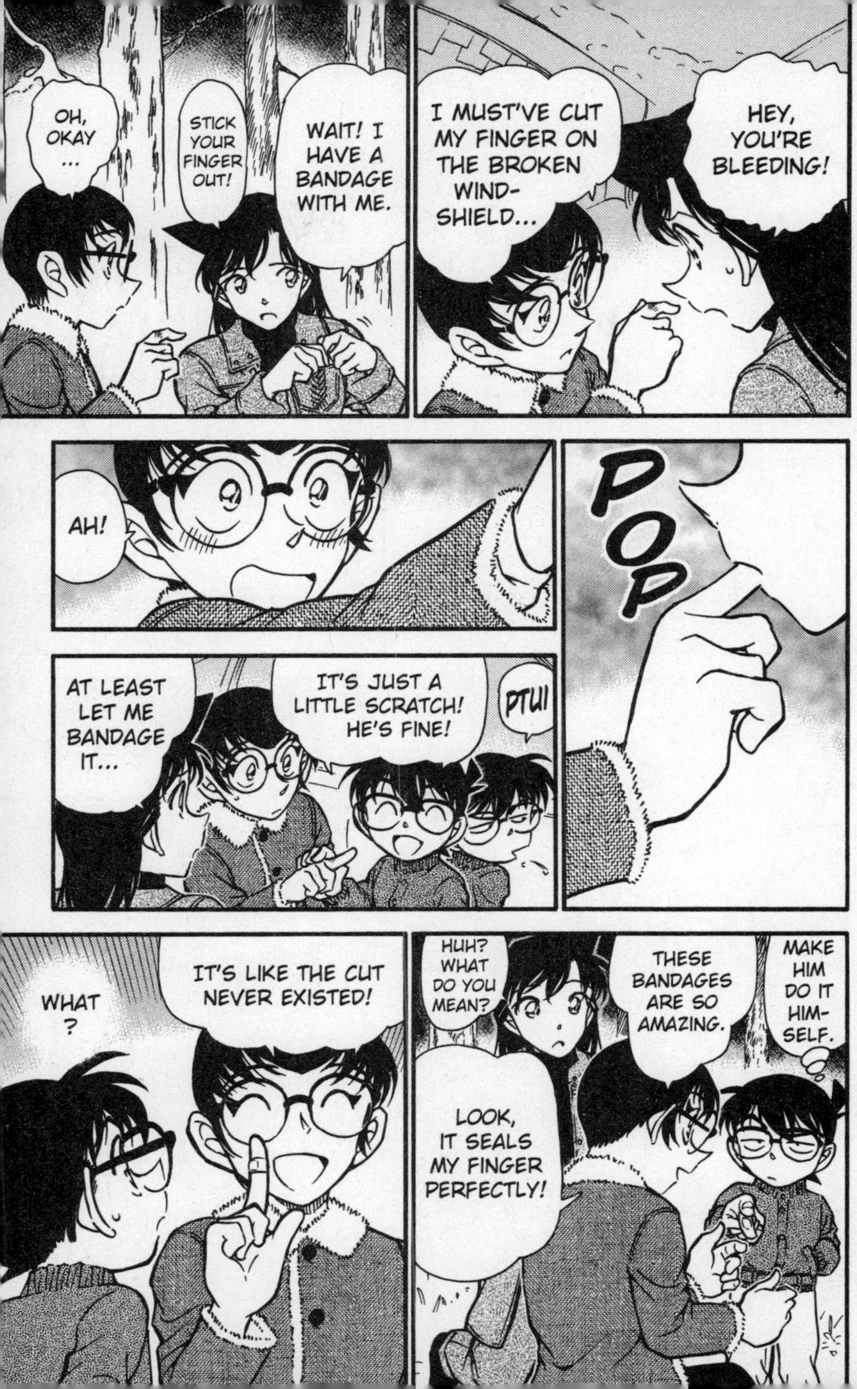
HEY, YOU'RE BLEEDING!
I MUST'VE CUT MY FINGER ON THE BROKEN WIND-SHIELD...
WAIT! I HAVE A BANDAGE WITH ME.
STICK YOUR FINGER OUT!
OH, OKAY ...
POP
AH!
PTUI
IT'S JUST A LITTLE SCRATCH! HE'S FINE!
AT LEAST LET ME BANDAGE IT...
MAKE HIM DO IT HIM-SELF.
THESE BANDAGES ARE SO AMAZING.
HUH? WHAT DO YOU MEAN?
LOOK, IT SEALS MY FINGER PERFECTLY!
IT'S LIKE THE CUT NEVER EXISTED!
WHAT ?

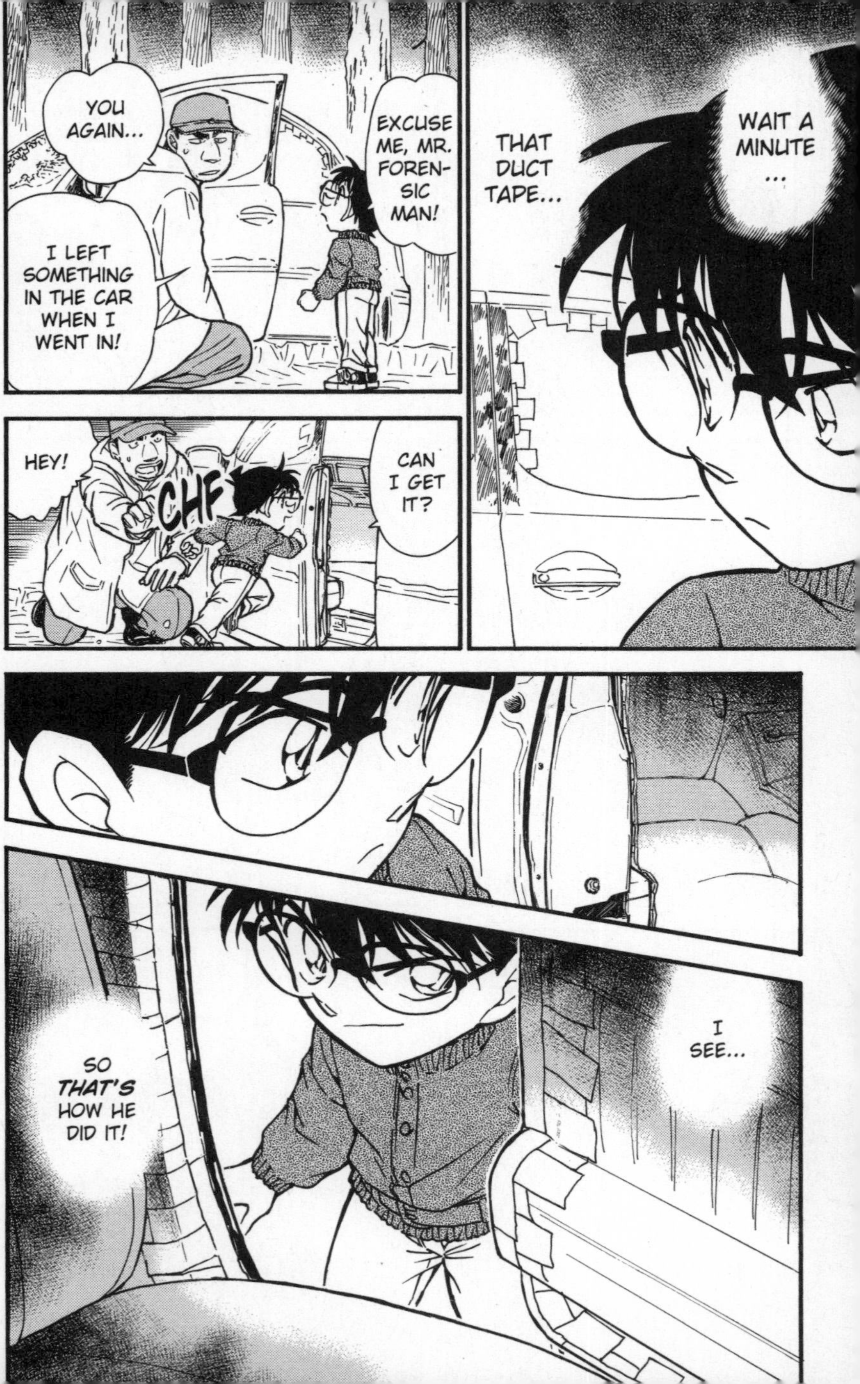
WAIT A MINUTE ...
THAT DUCT TAPE...
EXCUSE ME, MR. FORENSIC MAN!
YOU AGAIN...
I LEFT SOMETHING IN THE CAR WHEN I WENT IN!
CAN I GET IT?
CHF
HEY!
I SEE...
SO *THAT'S* HOW HE DID IT!

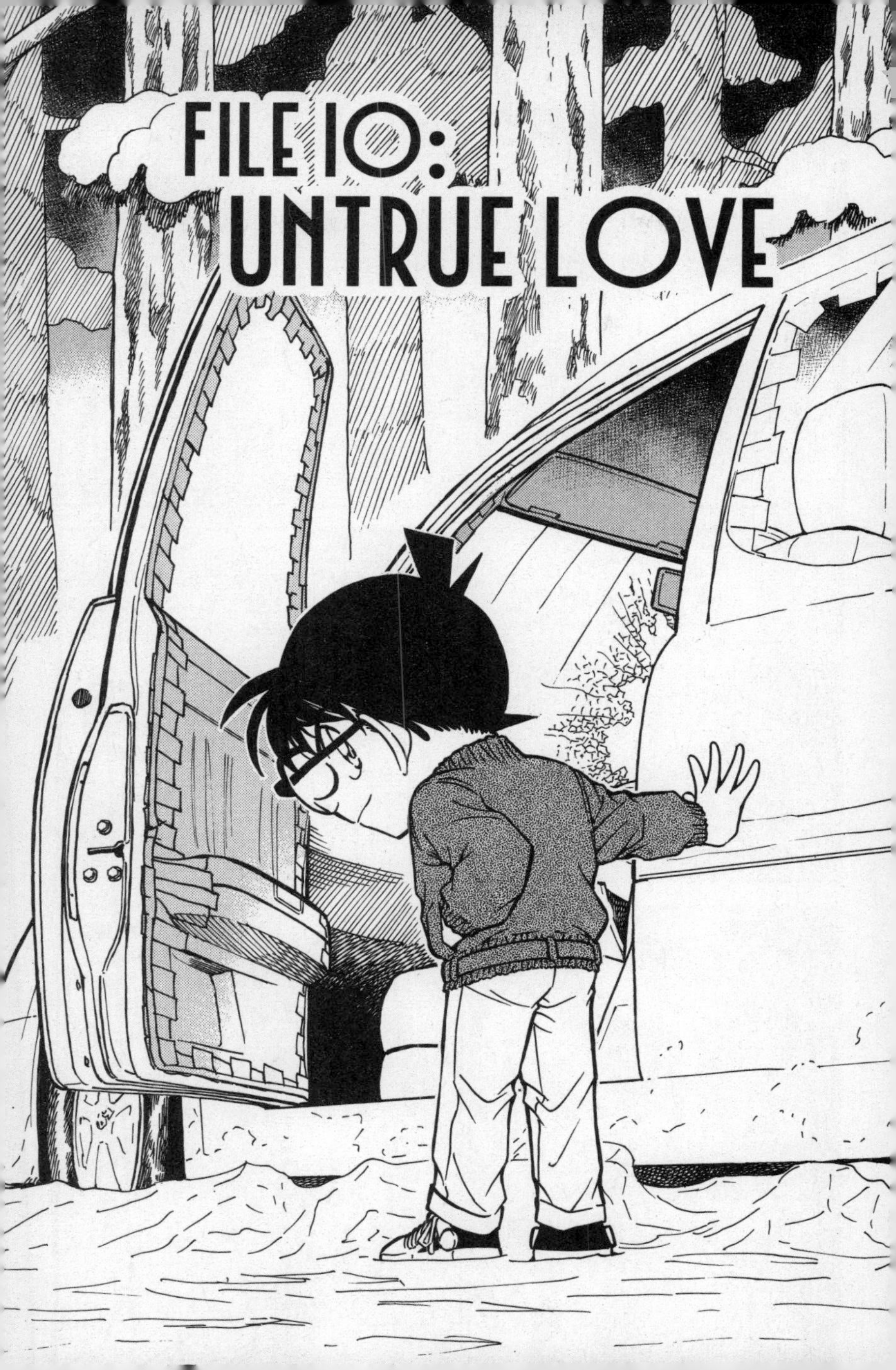
FILE 10:
UNTRUE LOVE

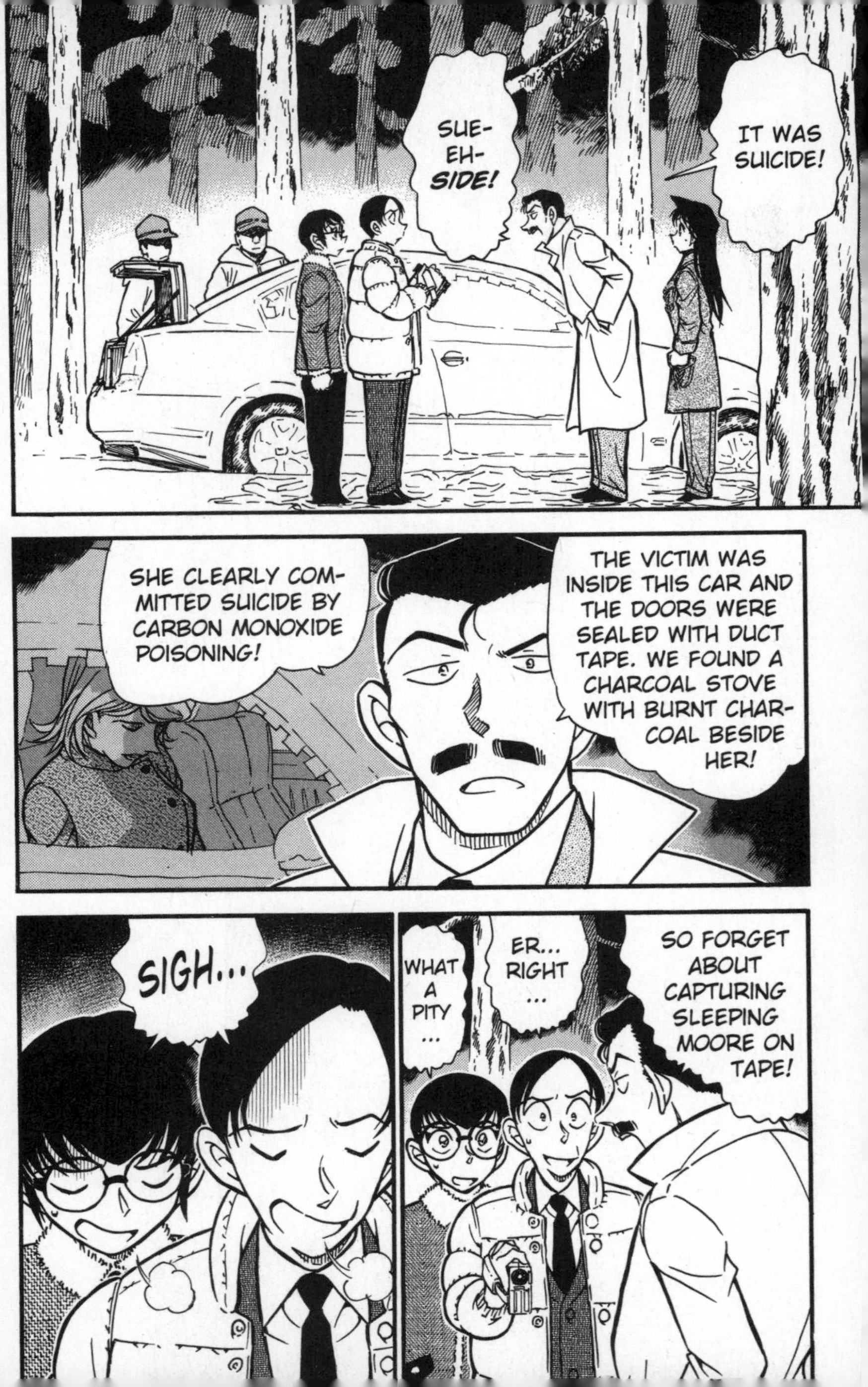
IT WAS SUICIDE!
SUE-EH-SIDE!
THE VICTIM WAS INSIDE THIS CAR AND THE DOORS WERE SEALED WITH DUCT TAPE. WE FOUND A CHARCOAL STOVE WITH BURNT CHARCOAL BESIDE HER!
SHE CLEARLY COMMITTED SUICIDE BY CARBON MONOXIDE POISONING!
SO FORGET ABOUT CAPTURING SLEEPING MOORE ON TAPE!
ER... RIGHT...
WHAT A PITY...
SIGH...

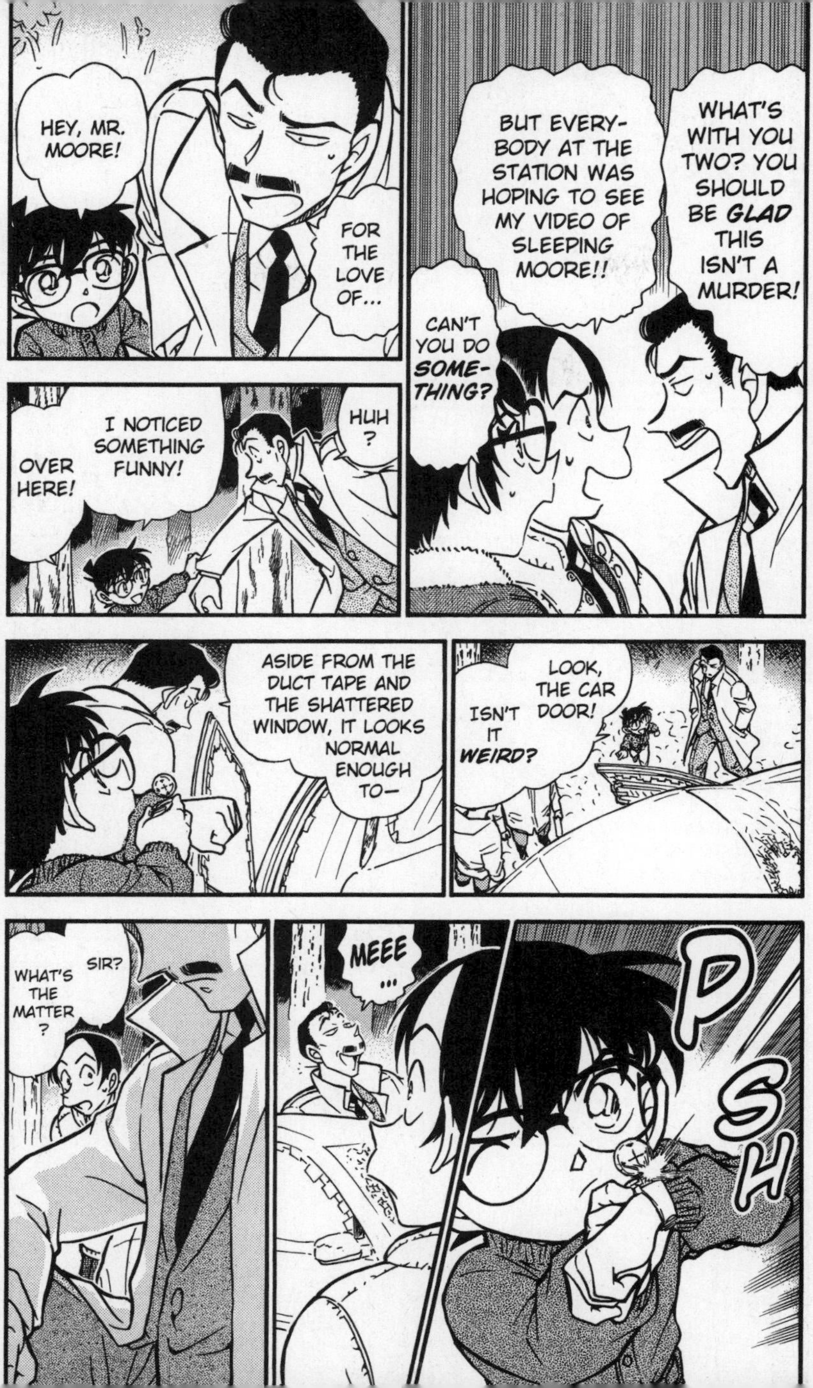
WHAT'S WITH YOU TWO? YOU SHOULD BE **GLAD** THIS ISN'T A MURDER!
BUT EVERYBODY AT THE STATION WAS HOPING TO SEE MY VIDEO OF SLEEPING MOORE!!
CAN'T YOU DO **SOMETHING?**
HEY, MR. MOORE!
FOR THE LOVE OF...
HUH?
I NOTICED SOMETHING FUNNY!
OVER HERE!
LOOK, THE CAR DOOR!
ISN'T IT **WEIRD?**
ASIDE FROM THE DUCT TAPE AND THE SHATTERED WINDOW, IT LOOKS NORMAL ENOUGH TO—
PSSH
MEEE...
SIR?
WHAT'S THE MATTER?

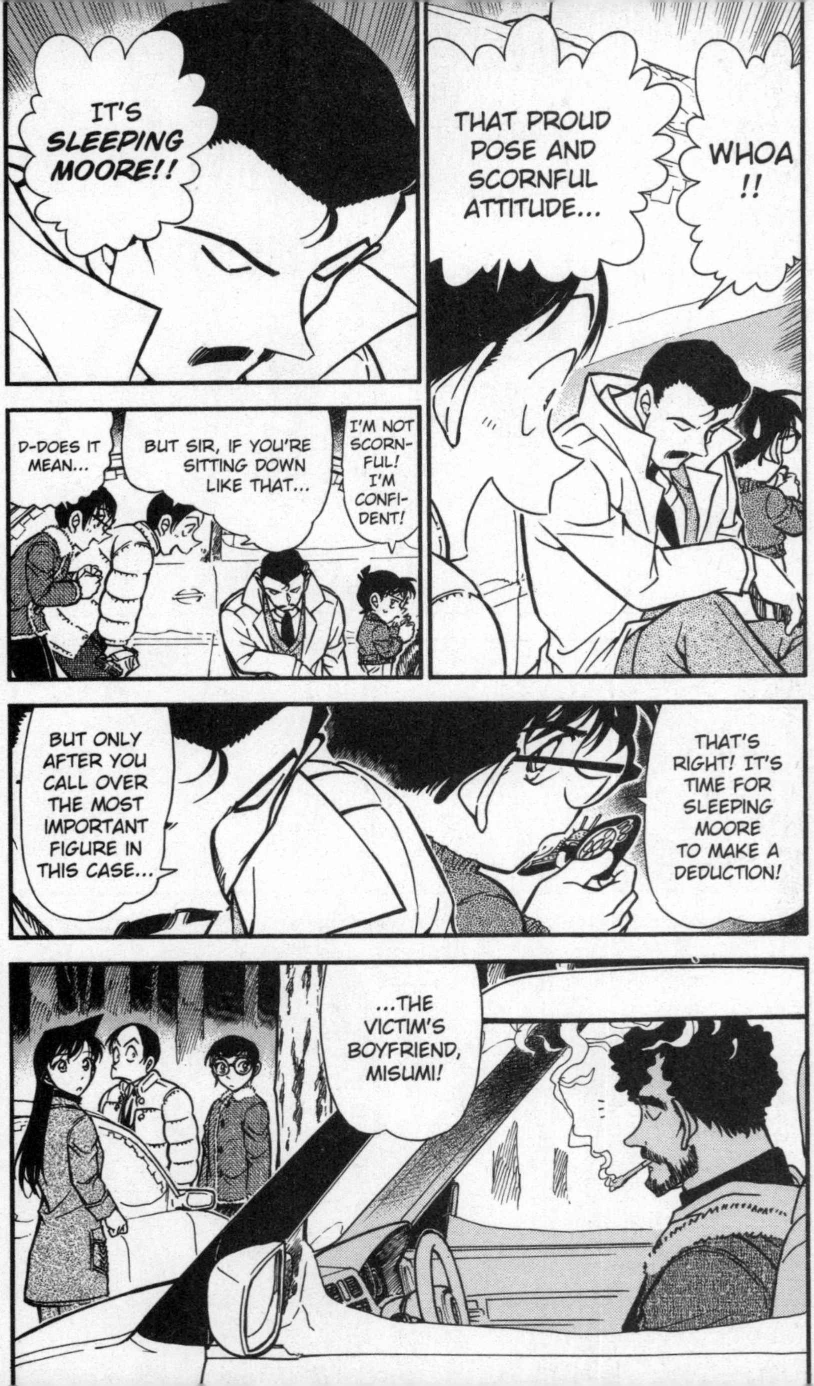
WHOA !!
THAT PROUD POSE AND SCORNFUL ATTITUDE...
IT'S SLEEPING MOORE!!
I'M NOT SCORNFUL! I'M CONFIDENT!
BUT SIR, IF YOU'RE SITTING DOWN LIKE THAT...
D-DOES IT MEAN...
THAT'S RIGHT! IT'S TIME FOR SLEEPING MOORE TO MAKE A DEDUCTION!
BUT ONLY AFTER YOU CALL OVER THE MOST IMPORTANT FIGURE IN THIS CASE...
...THE VICTIM'S BOYFRIEND, MISUMI!

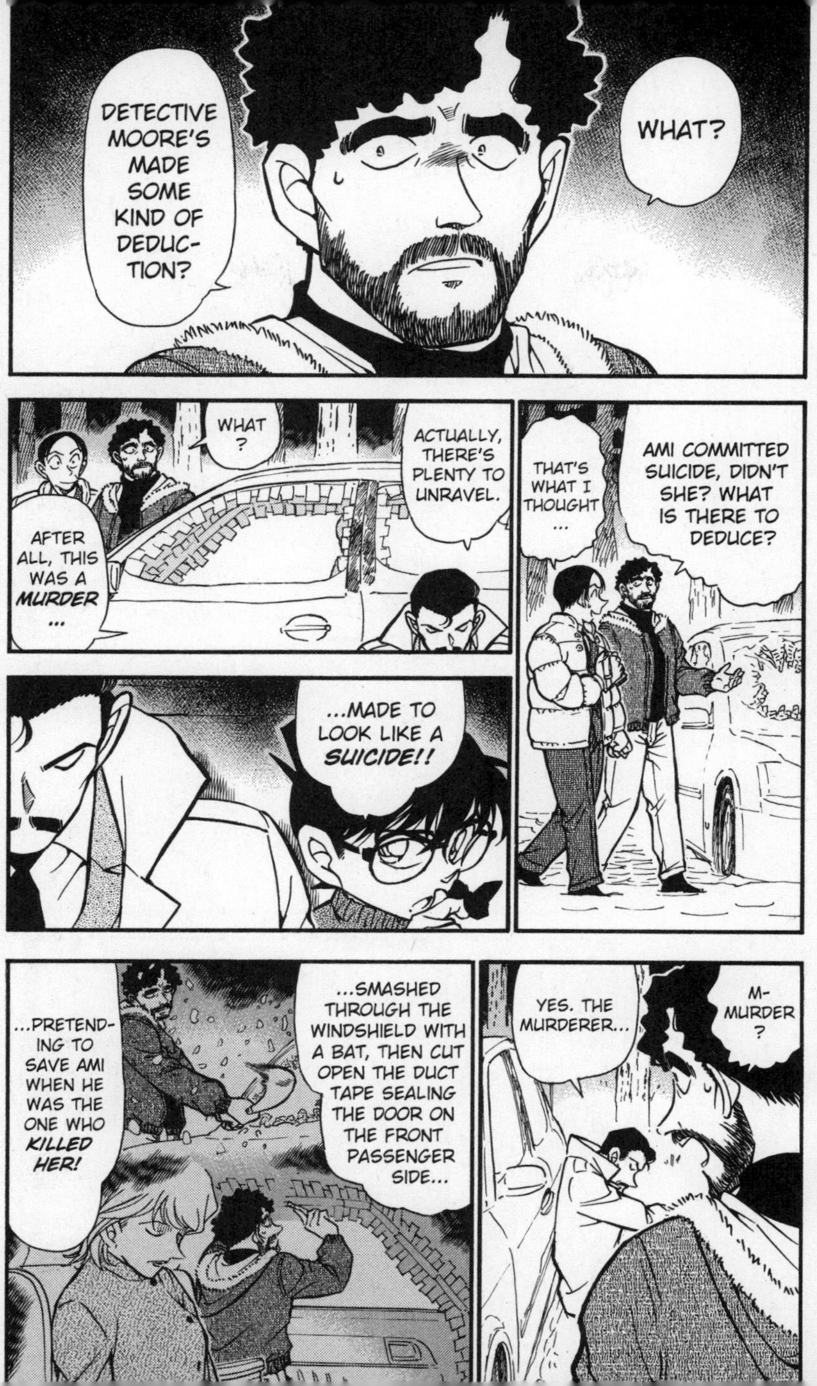
WHAT?
DETECTIVE MOORE'S MADE SOME KIND OF DEDUCTION?
AMI COMMITTED SUICIDE, DIDN'T SHE? WHAT IS THERE TO DEDUCE?
THAT'S WHAT I THOUGHT...
ACTUALLY, THERE'S PLENTY TO UNRAVEL.
WHAT?
AFTER ALL, THIS WAS A MURDER...
...MADE TO LOOK LIKE A SUICIDE!!
M-MURDER?
YES. THE MURDERER...
...SMASHED THROUGH THE WINDSHIELD WITH A BAT, THEN CUT OPEN THE DUCT TAPE SEALING THE DOOR ON THE FRONT PASSENGER SIDE...
...PRETENDING TO SAVE AMI WHEN HE WAS THE ONE WHO KILLED HER!

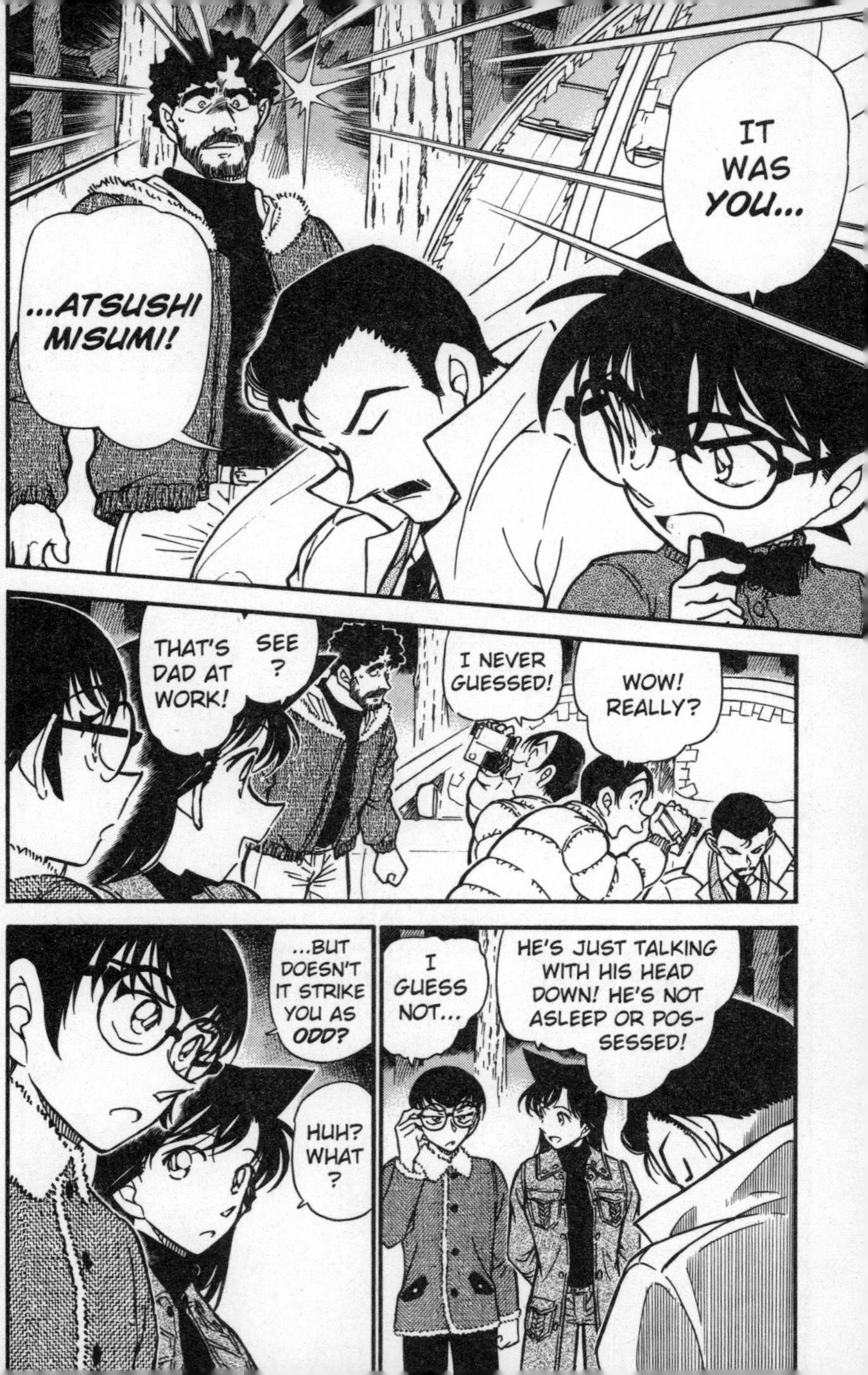
IT WAS YOU...
...ATSUSHI MISUMI!
WOW! REALLY?
I NEVER GUESSED!
SEE?
THAT'S DAD AT WORK!
HE'S JUST TALKING WITH HIS HEAD DOWN! HE'S NOT ASLEEP OR POS-SESSED!
I GUESS NOT...
...BUT DOESN'T IT STRIKE YOU AS ODD?
HUH? WHAT?

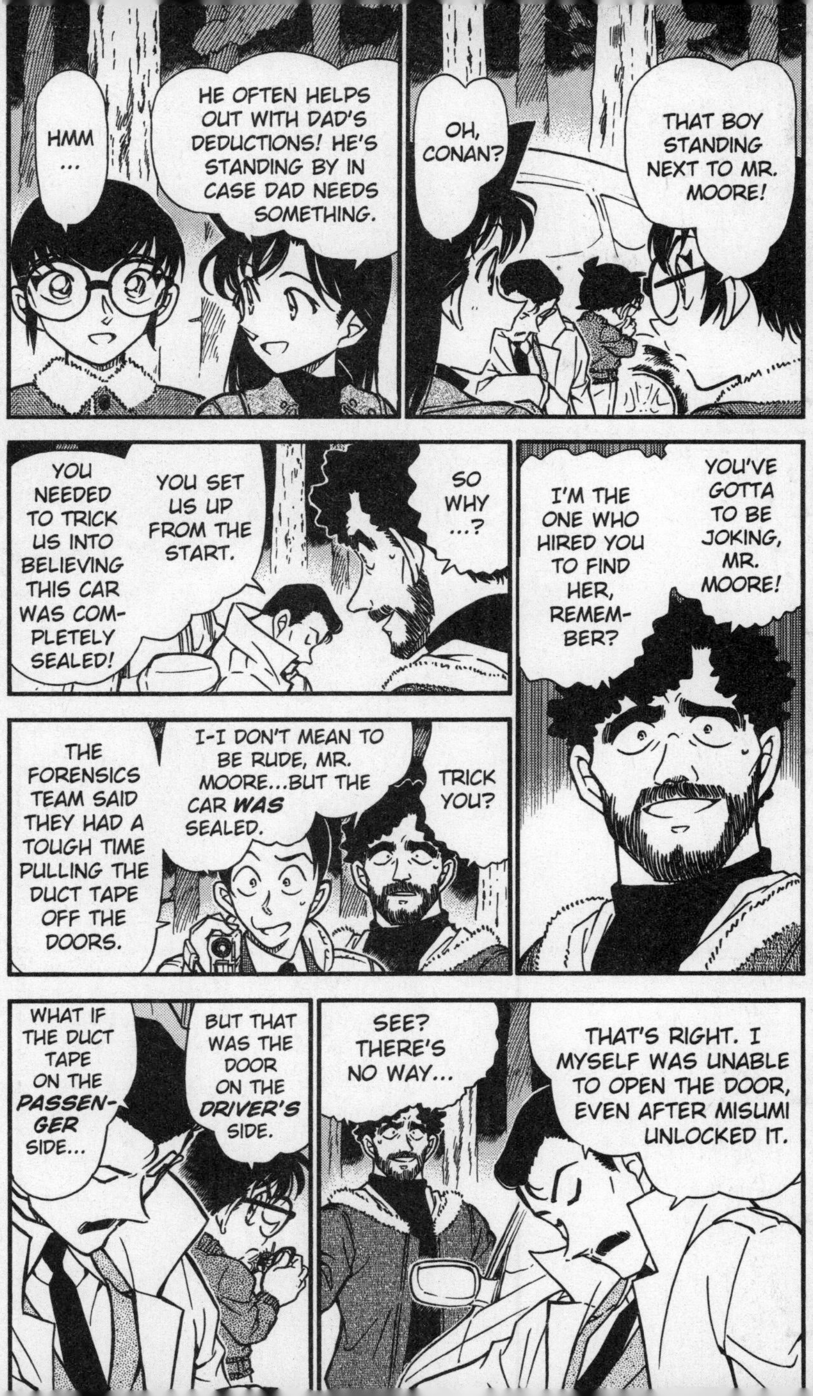
THAT BOY STANDING NEXT TO MR. MOORE!
OH, CONAN?
HE OFTEN HELPS OUT WITH DAD'S DEDUCTIONS! HE'S STANDING BY IN CASE DAD NEEDS SOMETHING.
HMM ...
YOU'VE GOTTA TO BE JOKING, MR. MOORE!
I'M THE ONE WHO HIRED YOU TO FIND HER, REMEMBER?
SO WHY ...?
YOU SET US UP FROM THE START.
YOU NEEDED TO TRICK US INTO BELIEVING THIS CAR WAS COMPLETELY SEALED!
TRICK YOU?
I-I DON'T MEAN TO BE RUDE, MR. MOORE...BUT THE CAR *WAS* SEALED.
THE FORENSICS TEAM SAID THEY HAD A TOUGH TIME PULLING THE DUCT TAPE OFF THE DOORS.
THAT'S RIGHT. I MYSELF WAS UNABLE TO OPEN THE DOOR, EVEN AFTER MISUMI UNLOCKED IT.
SEE? THERE'S NO WAY...
BUT THAT WAS THE DOOR ON THE *DRIVER'S* SIDE.
WHAT IF THE DUCT TAPE ON THE *PASSENGER* SIDE...

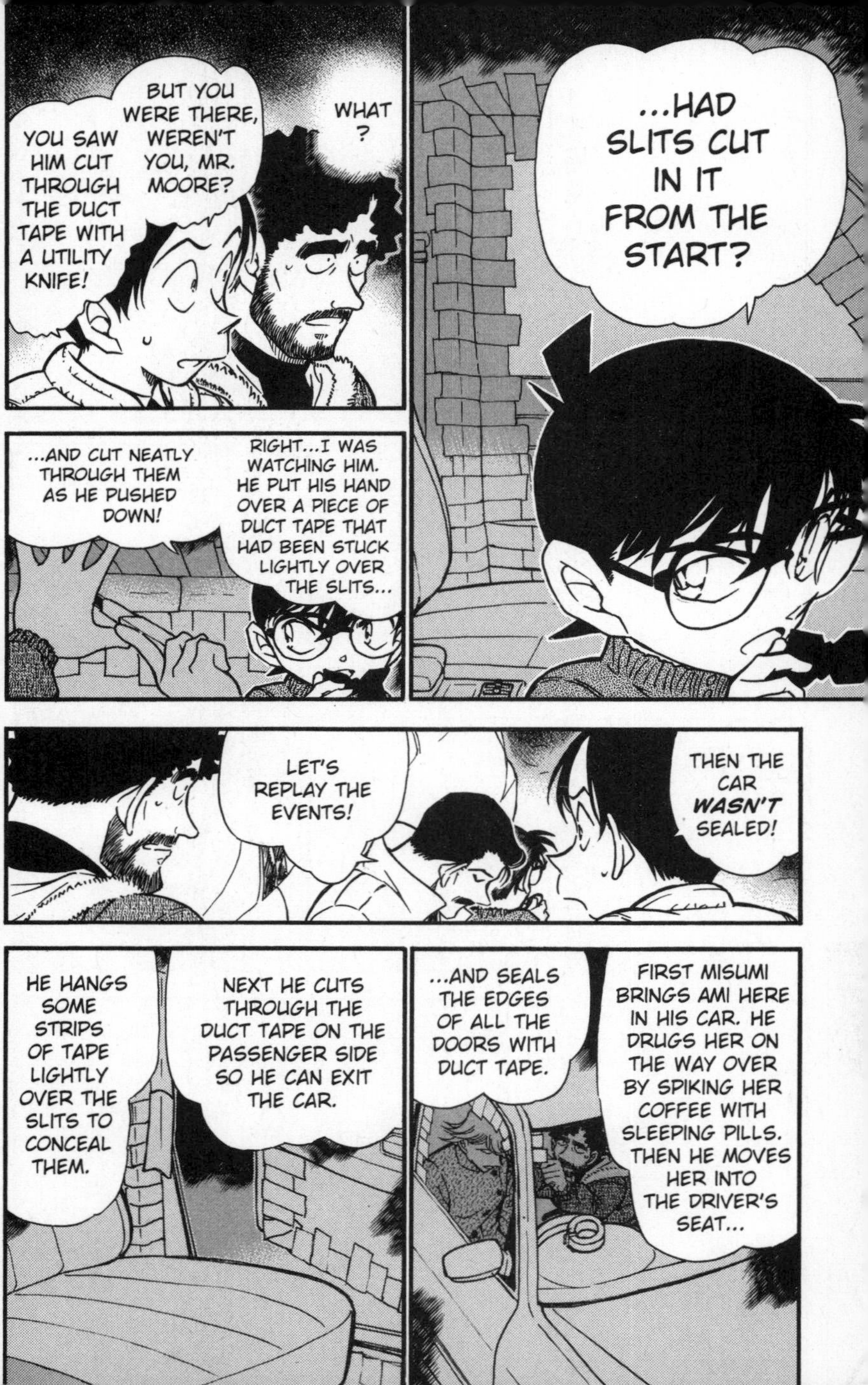
...HAD SLITS CUT IN IT FROM THE START?
WHAT?
BUT YOU WERE THERE, WEREN'T YOU, MR. MOORE?
YOU SAW HIM CUT THROUGH THE DUCT TAPE WITH A UTILITY KNIFE!
RIGHT...I WAS WATCHING HIM. HE PUT HIS HAND OVER A PIECE OF DUCT TAPE THAT HAD BEEN STUCK LIGHTLY OVER THE SLITS...
...AND CUT NEATLY THROUGH THEM AS HE PUSHED DOWN!
THEN THE CAR *WASN'T* SEALED!
LET'S REPLAY THE EVENTS!
FIRST MISUMI BRINGS AMI HERE IN HIS CAR. HE DRUGS HER ON THE WAY OVER BY SPIKING HER COFFEE WITH SLEEPING PILLS. THEN HE MOVES HER INTO THE DRIVER'S SEAT...
...AND SEALS THE EDGES OF ALL THE DOORS WITH DUCT TAPE.
NEXT HE CUTS THROUGH THE DUCT TAPE ON THE PASSENGER SIDE SO HE CAN EXIT THE CAR.
HE HANGS SOME STRIPS OF TAPE LIGHTLY OVER THE SLITS TO CONCEAL THEM.

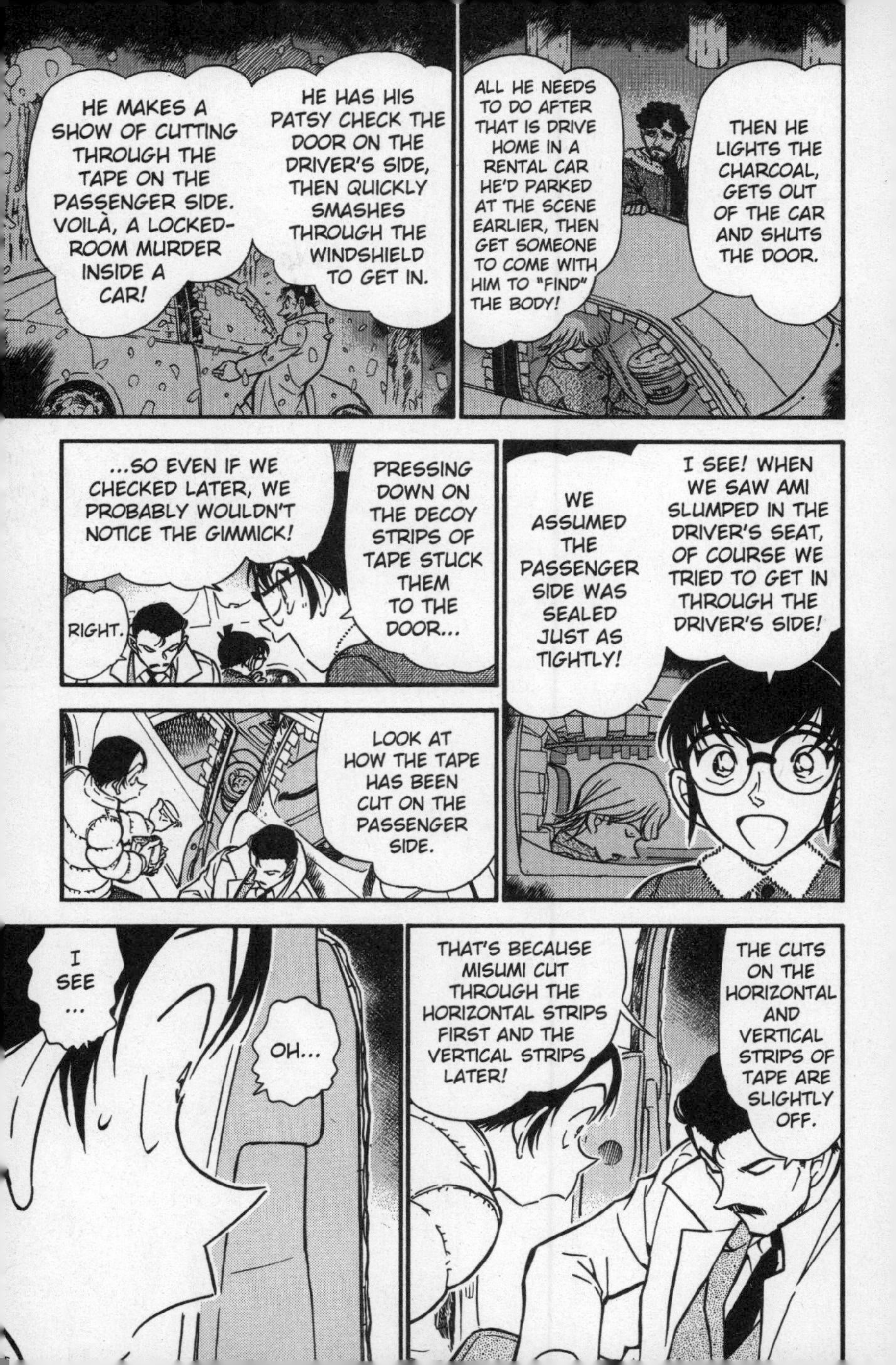
THEN HE LIGHTS THE CHARCOAL, GETS OUT OF THE CAR AND SHUTS THE DOOR.
ALL HE NEEDS TO DO AFTER THAT IS DRIVE HOME IN A RENTAL CAR HE'D PARKED AT THE SCENE EARLIER, THEN GET SOMEONE TO COME WITH HIM TO "FIND" THE BODY!
HE HAS HIS PATSY CHECK THE DOOR ON THE DRIVER'S SIDE, THEN QUICKLY SMASHES THROUGH THE WINDSHIELD TO GET IN.
HE MAKES A SHOW OF CUTTING THROUGH THE TAPE ON THE PASSENGER SIDE. VOILÀ, A LOCKED-ROOM MURDER INSIDE A CAR!
I SEE! WHEN WE SAW AMI SLUMPED IN THE DRIVER'S SEAT, OF COURSE WE TRIED TO GET IN THROUGH THE DRIVER'S SIDE!
WE ASSUMED THE PASSENGER SIDE WAS SEALED JUST AS TIGHTLY!
PRESSING DOWN ON THE DECOY STRIPS OF TAPE STUCK THEM TO THE DOOR...
...SO EVEN IF WE CHECKED LATER, WE PROBABLY WOULDN'T NOTICE THE GIMMICK!
RIGHT.
LOOK AT HOW THE TAPE HAS BEEN CUT ON THE PASSENGER SIDE.
THE CUTS ON THE HORIZONTAL AND VERTICAL STRIPS OF TAPE ARE SLIGHTLY OFF.
THAT'S BECAUSE MISUMI CUT THROUGH THE HORIZONTAL STRIPS FIRST AND THE VERTICAL STRIPS LATER!
I SEE ...
OH...

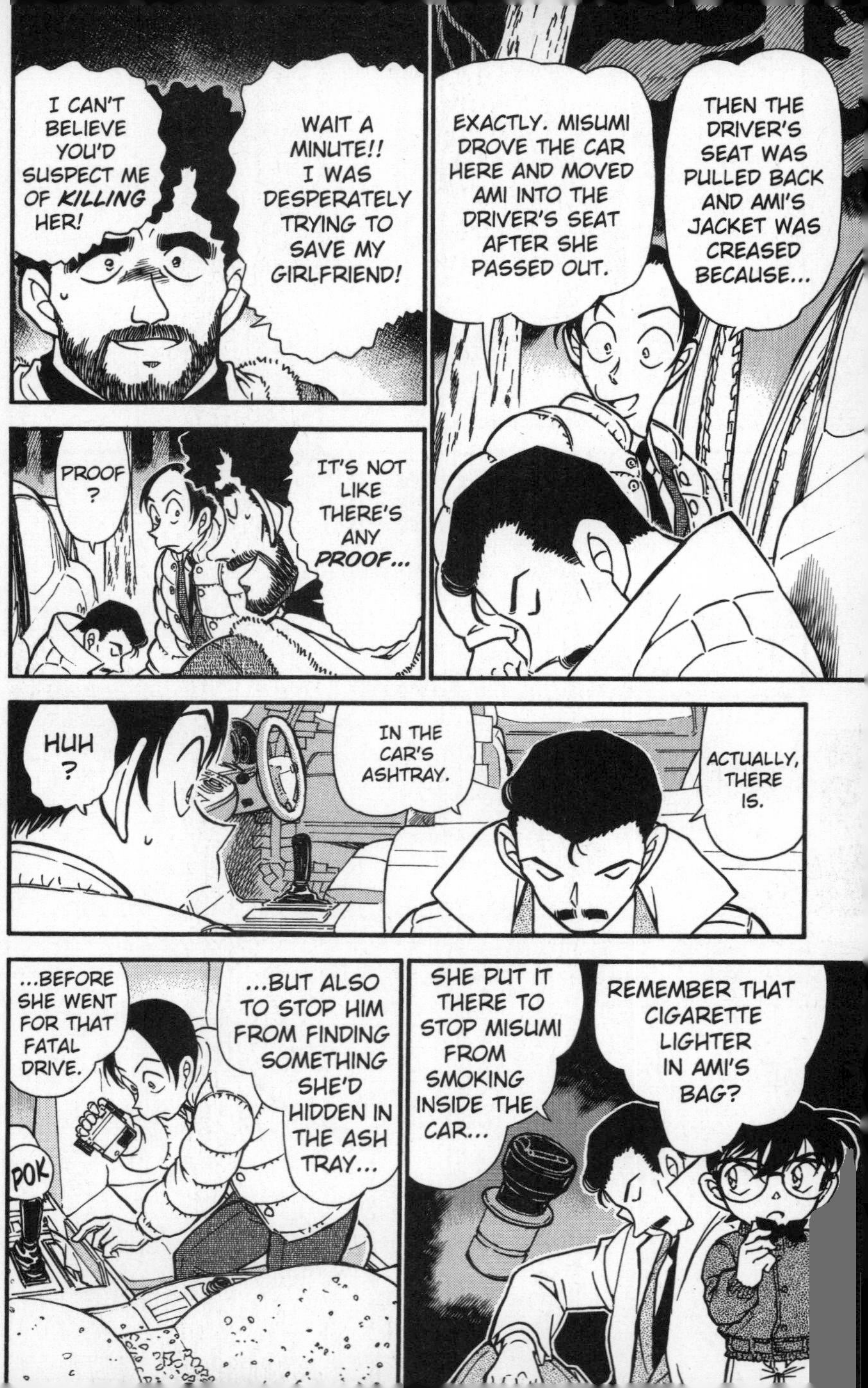
THEN THE DRIVER'S SEAT WAS PULLED BACK AND AMI'S JACKET WAS CREASED BECAUSE...
EXACTLY. MISUMI DROVE THE CAR HERE AND MOVED AMI INTO THE DRIVER'S SEAT AFTER SHE PASSED OUT.
WAIT A MINUTE!! I WAS DESPERATELY TRYING TO SAVE MY GIRLFRIEND!
I CAN'T BELIEVE YOU'D SUSPECT ME OF *KILLING* HER!
IT'S NOT LIKE THERE'S ANY *PROOF*...
PROOF?
ACTUALLY, THERE IS.
IN THE CAR'S ASHTRAY.
HUH?
REMEMBER THAT CIGARETTE LIGHTER IN AMI'S BAG?
SHE PUT IT THERE TO STOP MISUMI FROM SMOKING INSIDE THE CAR...
...BUT ALSO TO STOP HIM FROM FINDING SOMETHING SHE'D HIDDEN IN THE ASH TRAY...
...BEFORE SHE WENT FOR THAT FATAL DRIVE.
POK

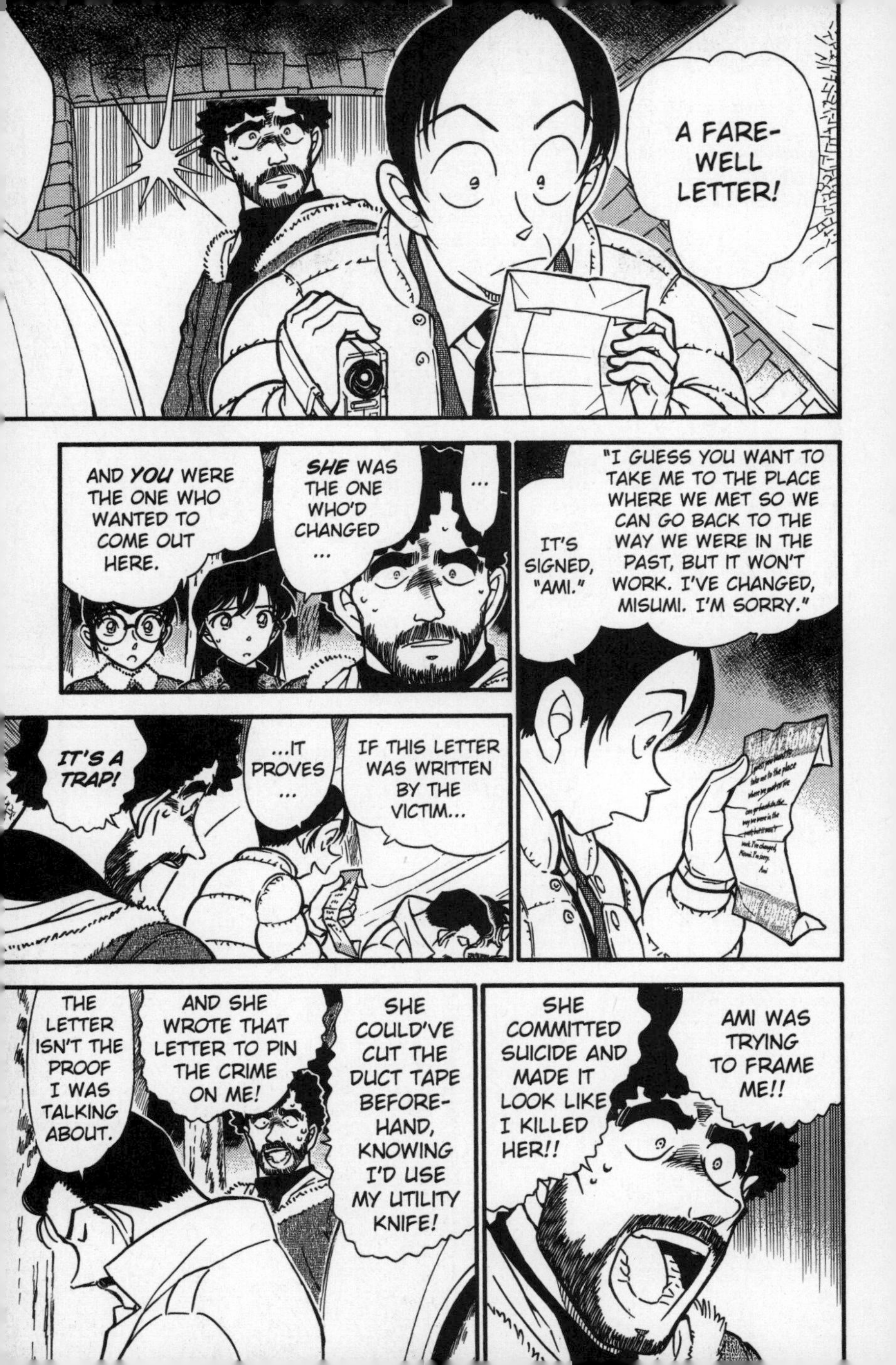
A FARE-WELL LETTER!
"I GUESS YOU WANT TO TAKE ME TO THE PLACE WHERE WE MET SO WE CAN GO BACK TO THE WAY WE WERE IN THE PAST, BUT IT WON'T WORK. I'VE CHANGED, MISUMI. I'M SORRY."
IT'S SIGNED, "AMI."
...
SHE WAS THE ONE WHO'D CHANGED ...
AND *YOU* WERE THE ONE WHO WANTED TO COME OUT HERE.
IF THIS LETTER WAS WRITTEN BY THE VICTIM...
...IT PROVES ...
IT'S A TRAP!
AMI WAS TRYING TO FRAME ME!!
SHE COMMITTED SUICIDE AND MADE IT LOOK LIKE I KILLED HER!!
SHE COULD'VE CUT THE DUCT TAPE BEFORE-HAND, KNOWING I'D USE MY UTILITY KNIFE!
AND SHE WROTE THAT LETTER TO PIN THE CRIME ON ME!
THE LETTER ISN'T THE PROOF I WAS TALKING ABOUT.

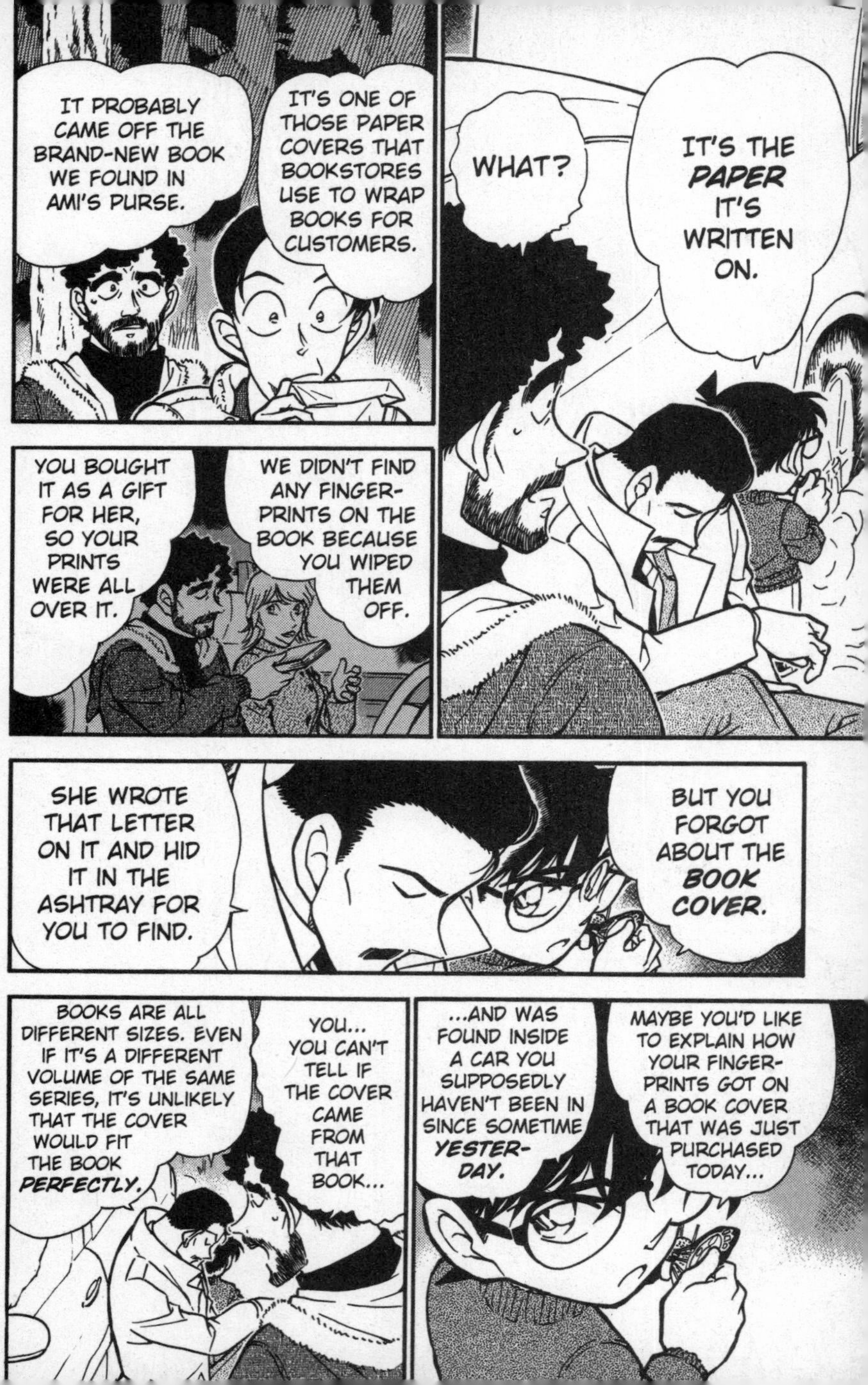
IT'S THE PAPER IT'S WRITTEN ON.
WHAT?
IT'S ONE OF THOSE PAPER COVERS THAT BOOKSTORES USE TO WRAP BOOKS FOR CUSTOMERS.
IT PROBABLY CAME OFF THE BRAND-NEW BOOK WE FOUND IN AMI'S PURSE.
WE DIDN'T FIND ANY FINGER-PRINTS ON THE BOOK BECAUSE YOU WIPED THEM OFF.
YOU BOUGHT IT AS A GIFT FOR HER, SO YOUR PRINTS WERE ALL OVER IT.
BUT YOU FORGOT ABOUT THE BOOK COVER.
SHE WROTE THAT LETTER ON IT AND HID IT IN THE ASHTRAY FOR YOU TO FIND.
MAYBE YOU'D LIKE TO EXPLAIN HOW YOUR FINGER-PRINTS GOT ON A BOOK COVER THAT WAS JUST PURCHASED TODAY...
...AND WAS FOUND INSIDE A CAR YOU SUPPOSEDLY HAVEN'T BEEN IN SINCE SOMETIME YESTER-DAY.
YOU... YOU CAN'T TELL IF THE COVER CAME FROM THAT BOOK...
BOOKS ARE ALL DIFFERENT SIZES. EVEN IF IT'S A DIFFERENT VOLUME OF THE SAME SERIES, IT'S UNLIKELY THAT THE COVER WOULD FIT THE BOOK PERFECTLY.

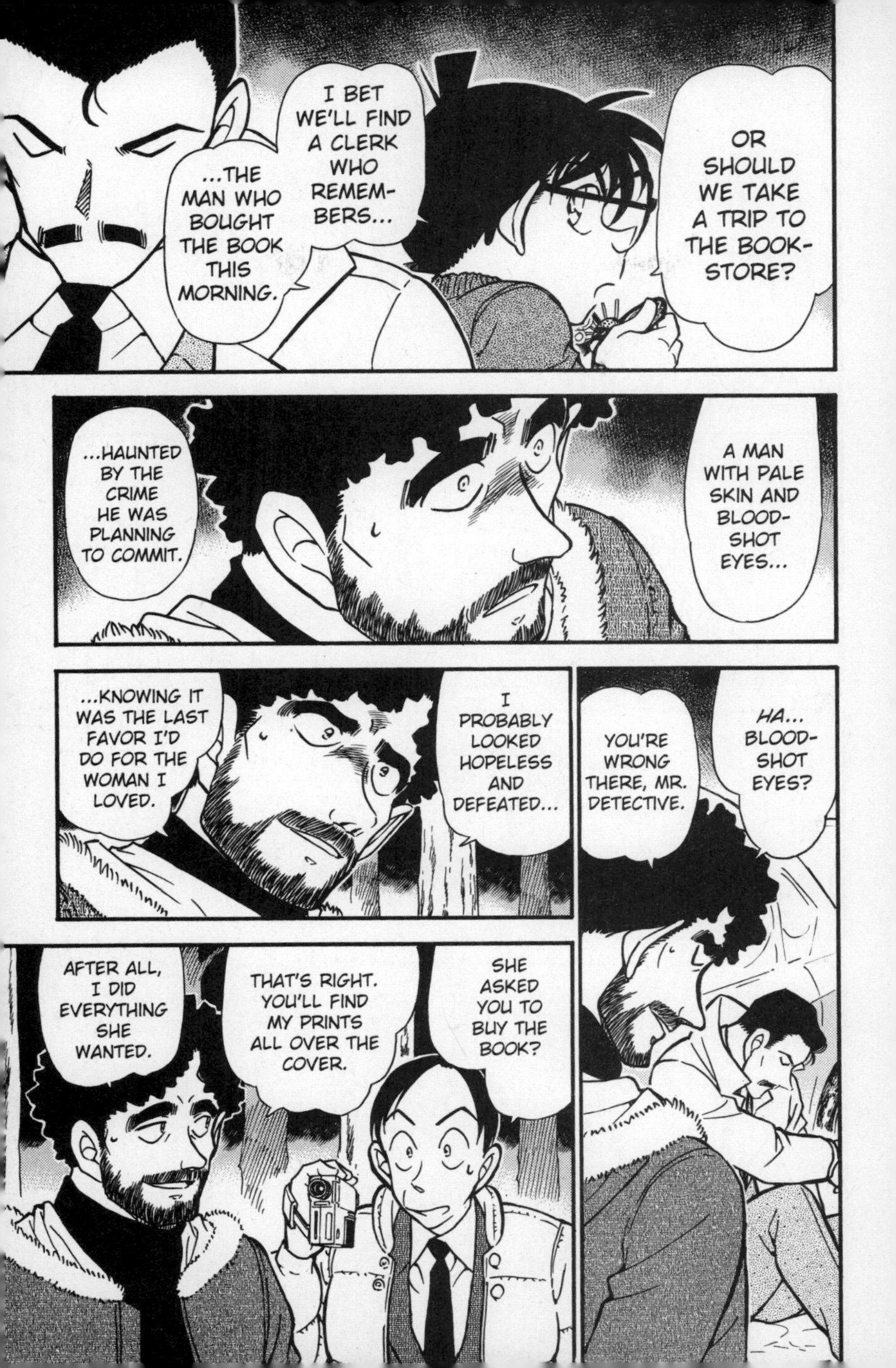
OR SHOULD WE TAKE A TRIP TO THE BOOK-STORE?
I BET WE'LL FIND A CLERK WHO REMEMBERS...
...THE MAN WHO BOUGHT THE BOOK THIS MORNING.
A MAN WITH PALE SKIN AND BLOOD-SHOT EYES...
...HAUNTED BY THE CRIME HE WAS PLANNING TO COMMIT.
HA... BLOOD-SHOT EYES?
YOU'RE WRONG THERE, MR. DETECTIVE.
I PROBABLY LOOKED HOPELESS AND DEFEATED...
...KNOWING IT WAS THE LAST FAVOR I'D DO FOR THE WOMAN I LOVED.
SHE ASKED YOU TO BUY THE BOOK?
THAT'S RIGHT. YOU'LL FIND MY PRINTS ALL OVER THE COVER.
AFTER ALL, I DID EVERYTHING SHE WANTED.

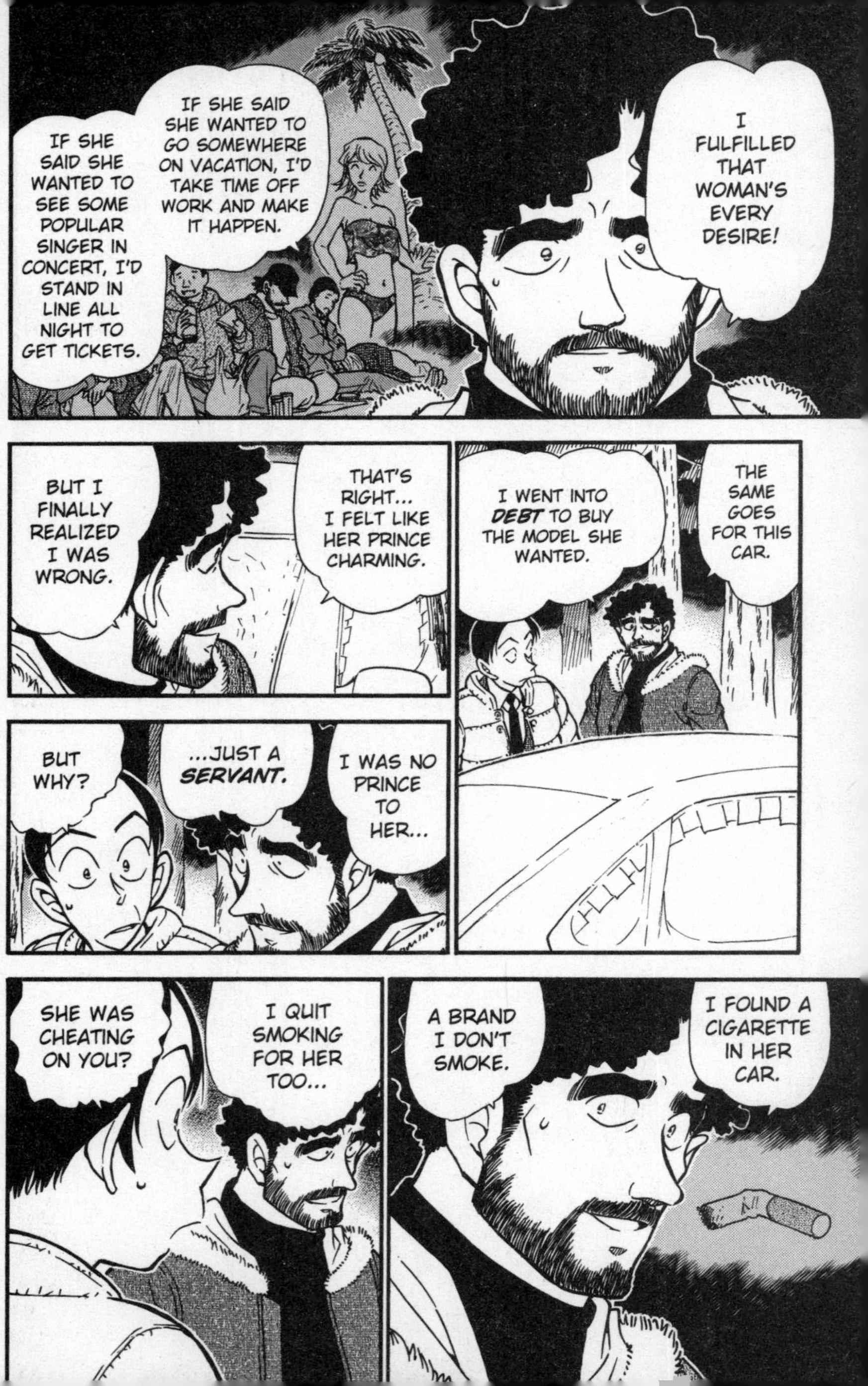
I FULFILLED THAT WOMAN'S EVERY DESIRE!
IF SHE SAID SHE WANTED TO GO SOMEWHERE ON VACATION, I'D TAKE TIME OFF WORK AND MAKE IT HAPPEN.
IF SHE SAID SHE WANTED TO SEE SOME POPULAR SINGER IN CONCERT, I'D STAND IN LINE ALL NIGHT TO GET TICKETS.
THE SAME GOES FOR THIS CAR.
I WENT INTO DEBT TO BUY THE MODEL SHE WANTED.
THAT'S RIGHT... I FELT LIKE HER PRINCE CHARMING.
BUT I FINALLY REALIZED I WAS WRONG.
I WAS NO PRINCE TO HER...
...JUST A SERVANT.
BUT WHY?
I FOUND A CIGARETTE IN HER CAR.
A BRAND I DON'T SMOKE.
I QUIT SMOKING FOR HER TOO...
SHE WAS CHEATING ON YOU?

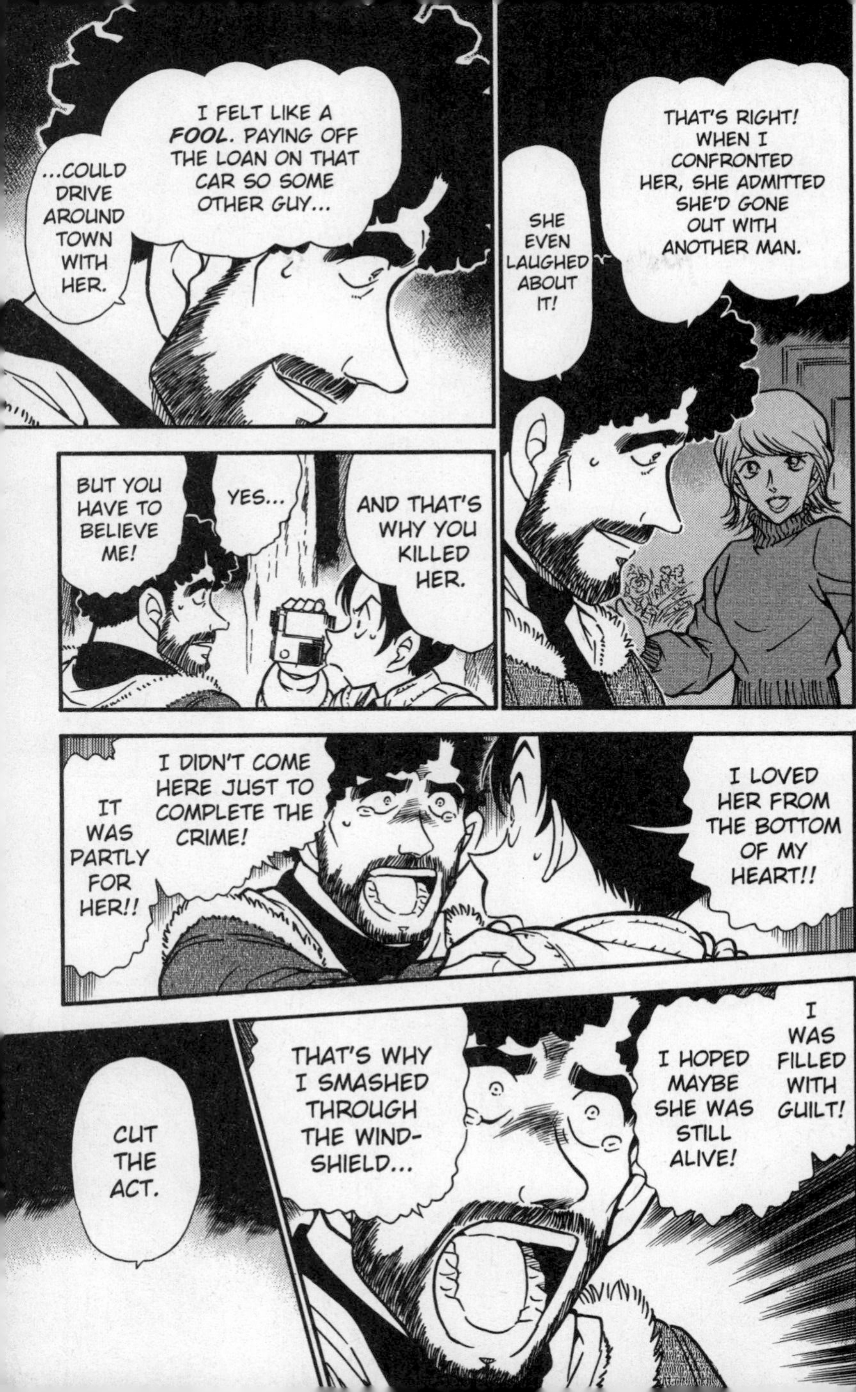

THAT'S RIGHT! WHEN I CONFRONTED HER, SHE ADMITTED SHE'D GONE OUT WITH ANOTHER MAN.
SHE EVEN LAUGHED ABOUT IT!
I FELT LIKE A *FOOL*. PAYING OFF THE LOAN ON THAT CAR SO SOME OTHER GUY...
...COULD DRIVE AROUND TOWN WITH HER.
AND THAT'S WHY YOU KILLED HER.
YES...
BUT YOU HAVE TO BELIEVE ME!
I LOVED HER FROM THE BOTTOM OF MY HEART!!
I DIDN'T COME HERE JUST TO COMPLETE THE CRIME!
IT WAS PARTLY FOR HER!!
I WAS FILLED WITH GUILT!
I HOPED MAYBE SHE WAS STILL ALIVE!
THAT'S WHY I SMASHED THROUGH THE WIND-SHIELD...
CUT THE ACT.

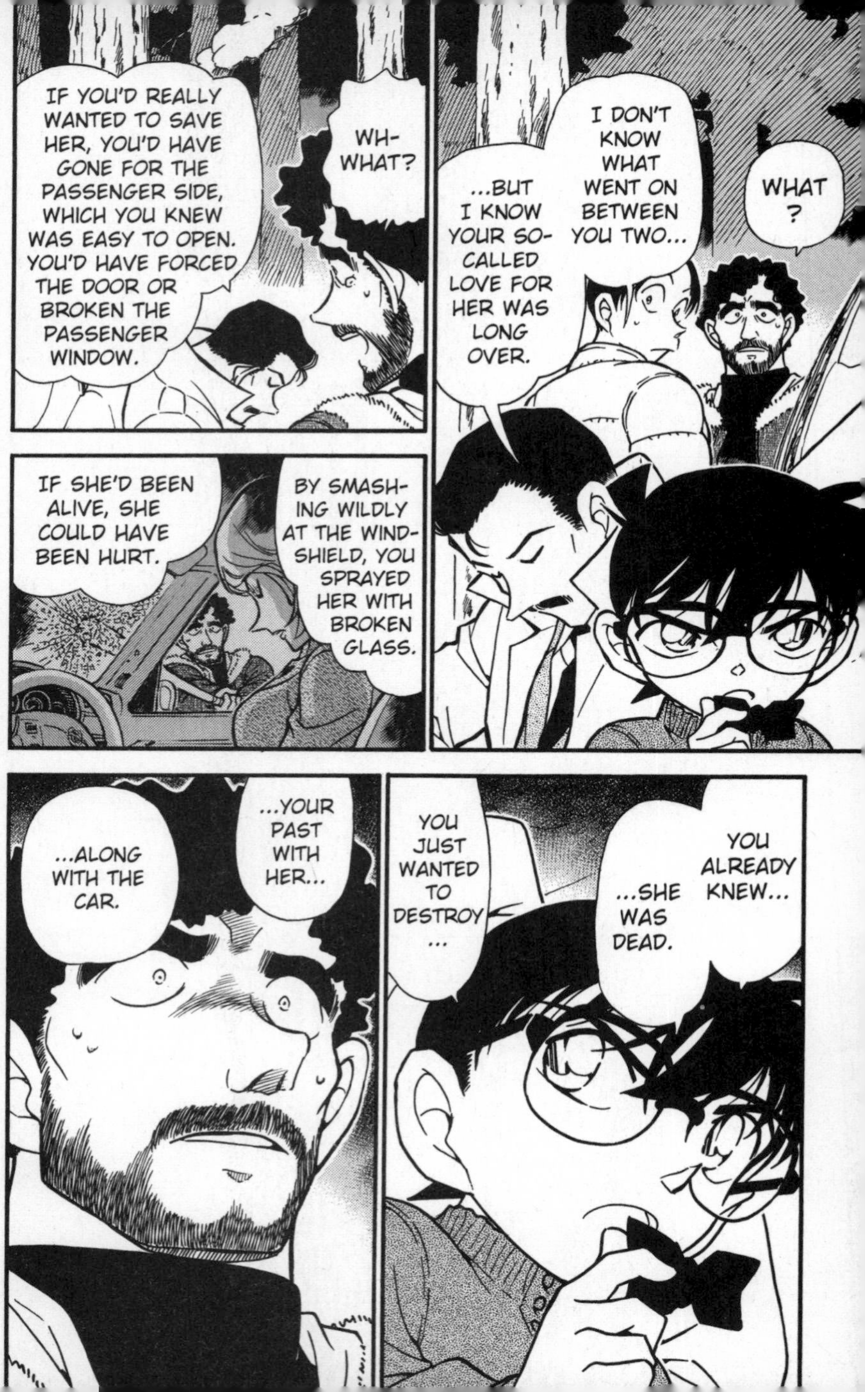
I DON'T KNOW WHAT WENT ON BETWEEN YOU TWO...
...BUT I KNOW YOUR SO-CALLED LOVE FOR HER WAS LONG OVER.
WHAT ?
IF YOU'D REALLY WANTED TO SAVE HER, YOU'D HAVE GONE FOR THE PASSENGER SIDE, WHICH YOU KNEW WAS EASY TO OPEN. YOU'D HAVE FORCED THE DOOR OR BROKEN THE PASSENGER WINDOW.
WH-WHAT?
BY SMASHING WILDLY AT THE WINDSHIELD, YOU SPRAYED HER WITH BROKEN GLASS.
IF SHE'D BEEN ALIVE, SHE COULD HAVE BEEN HURT.
YOU ALREADY KNEW...
...SHE WAS DEAD.
YOU JUST WANTED TO DESTROY...
...YOUR PAST WITH HER...
...ALONG WITH THE CAR.

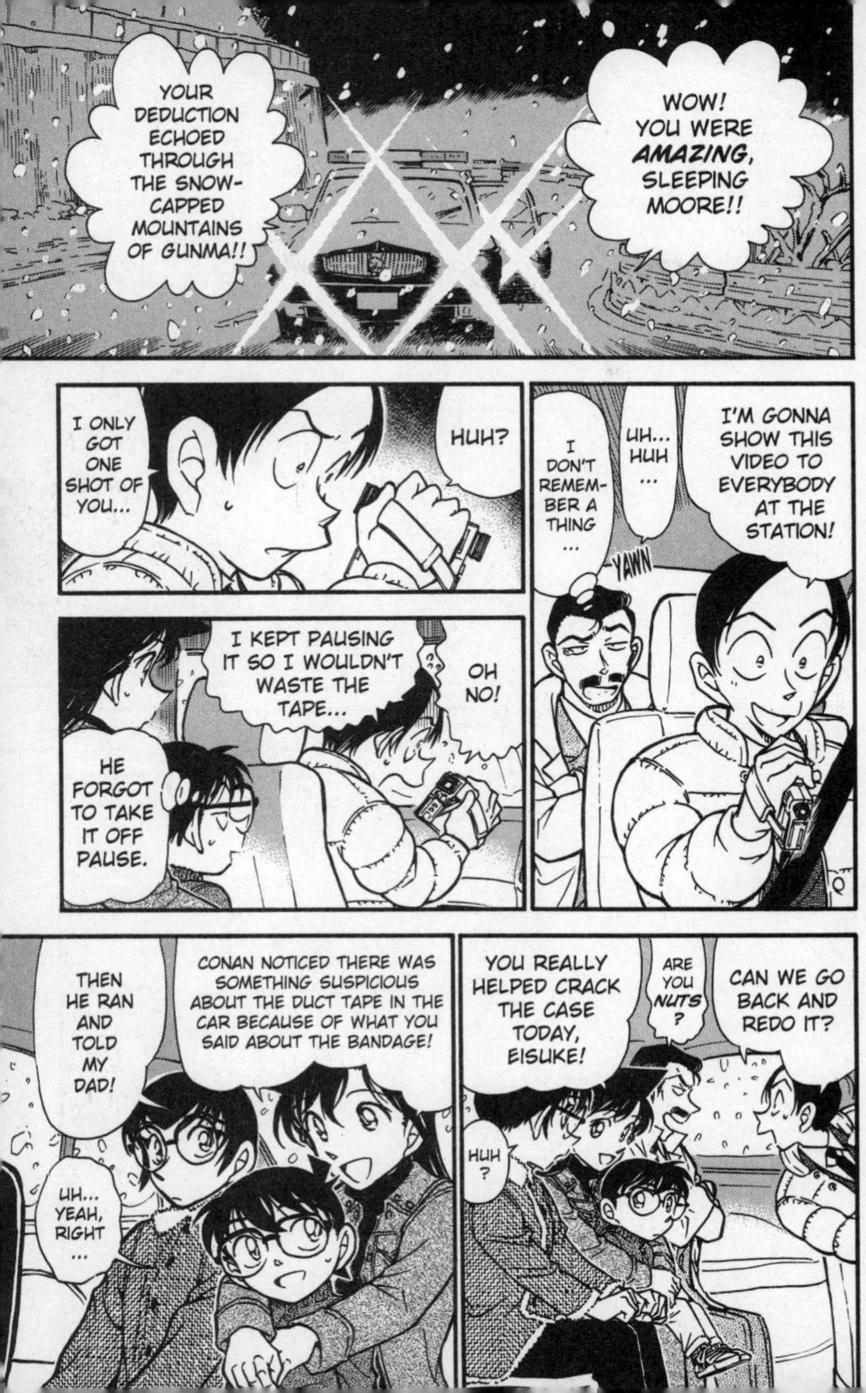
WOW! YOU WERE AMAZING, SLEEPING MOORE!!
YOUR DEDUCTION ECHOED THROUGH THE SNOW-CAPPED MOUNTAINS OF GUNMA!!
I'M GONNA SHOW THIS VIDEO TO EVERYBODY AT THE STATION!
UH... HUH...
YAWN
I DON'T REMEMBER A THING...
HUH?
I ONLY GOT ONE SHOT OF YOU...
OH NO!
I KEPT PAUSING IT SO I WOULDN'T WASTE THE TAPE...
HE FORGOT TO TAKE IT OFF PAUSE.
CAN WE GO BACK AND REDO IT?
ARE YOU NUTS?
YOU REALLY HELPED CRACK THE CASE TODAY, EISUKE!
HUH?
CONAN NOTICED THERE WAS SOMETHING SUSPICIOUS ABOUT THE DUCT TAPE IN THE CAR BECAUSE OF WHAT YOU SAID ABOUT THE BANDAGE!
THEN HE RAN AND TOLD MY DAD!
UH... YEAH, RIGHT...

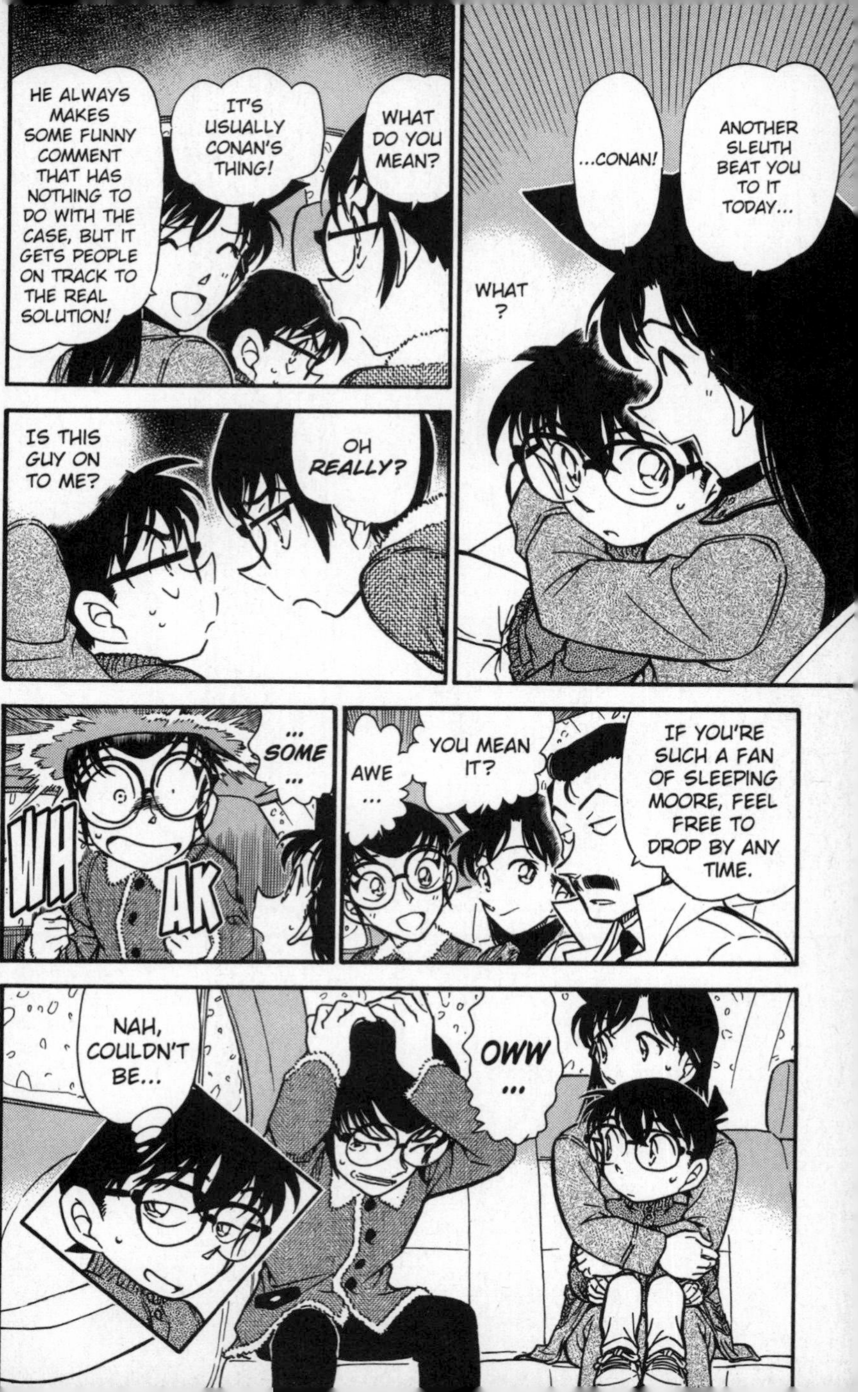
ANOTHER SLEUTH BEAT YOU TO IT TODAY...
...CONAN!
WHAT ?
WHAT DO YOU MEAN?
IT'S USUALLY CONAN'S THING!
HE ALWAYS MAKES SOME FUNNY COMMENT THAT HAS NOTHING TO DO WITH THE CASE, BUT IT GETS PEOPLE ON TRACK TO THE REAL SOLUTION!
OH *REALLY?*
IS THIS GUY ON TO ME?
IF YOU'RE SUCH A FAN OF SLEEPING MOORE, FEEL FREE TO DROP BY ANY TIME.
YOU MEAN IT?
AWE ...
... *SOME* ...
WH
AK
OWW ...
NAH, COULDN'T BE...

500th Chapter Celebration

Case Closed

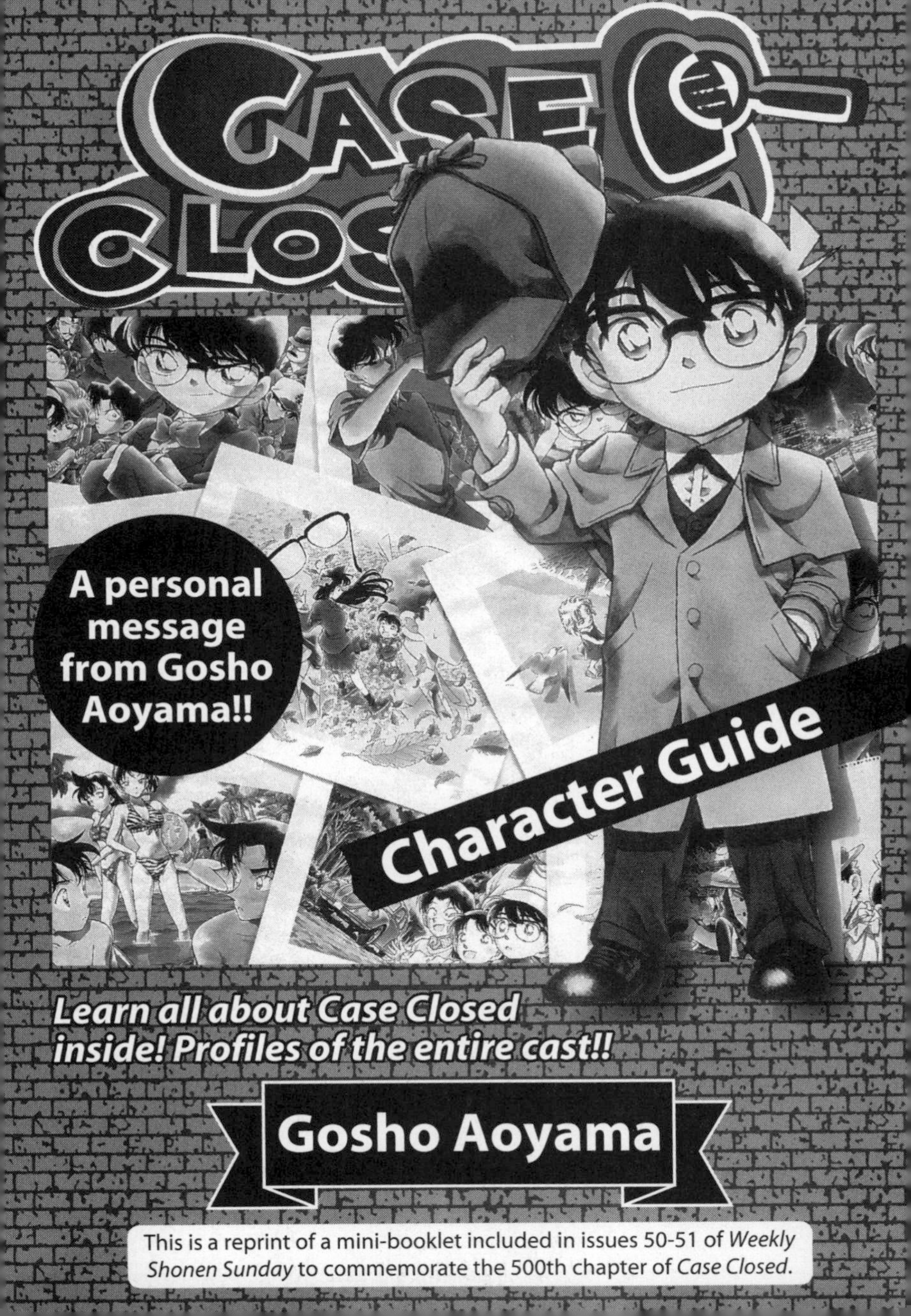
A personal message from Gosho Aoyama!!
Character Guide

Learn all about Case Closed inside! Profiles of the entire cast!!

Gosho Aoyama

This is a reprint of a mini-booklet included in issues 50-51 of *Weekly Shonen Sunday* to commemorate the 500th chapter of *Case Closed*.

Gosho Aoyama's Profile

500 chapters!

The star of *Shonen Sunday* magazine leaves all others in the dust!

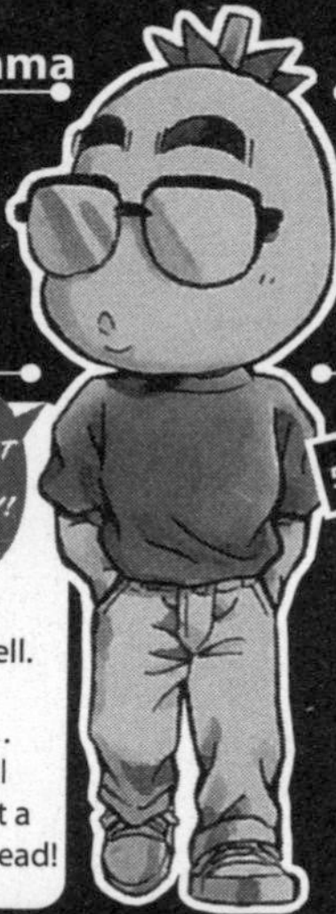
DON'T BE SILLY!

Name: Gosho Aoyama

Blood-type: B

Gender: Male

Height: 5'7"

Birthday: June 21

Favorite Phrase: "Don't be silly."

He likes the Yomiuri Giants and curry. He doesn't like natto (fermented soybeans) or raisins. He's the same height as Jimmy Kudo, and he practices kendo like Harley Hartwell. There are rumors that he already knows the ending of *Case Closed*… so if you want to find out what will happen in the final chapter, invent a machine that will look inside his head!

500th Chapter Mini Interview!!!

Favorite storyline? The bombing case in volumes 36–37.
Favorite cover illustration? The cover of volume 37.
Happiest moment so far? When *Case Closed* became an animated movie. I was thrilled!
Toughest experience? All the color illustrations I had to draw when *Case Closed* was animated...

Helloooo, Aoyama here.
Wow, *Case Closed* has reached its 500th chapter. ♪ I'm so surprised! I couldn't have done it without all you readers and your support for this crazy murder-mystery romantic comedy manga!
Thank you very much. ♥
To show my gratitude, I drew the first wraparound cover ever for *Shonen Sunday*, the magazine in which *Case Closed* runs.
Hope you're surprised too…

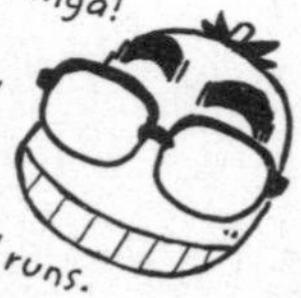

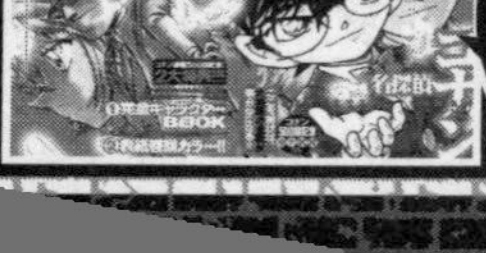

The first issue of *Shonen Sunday* with a wraparound cover!

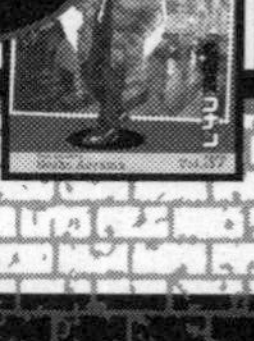

My Best Cover

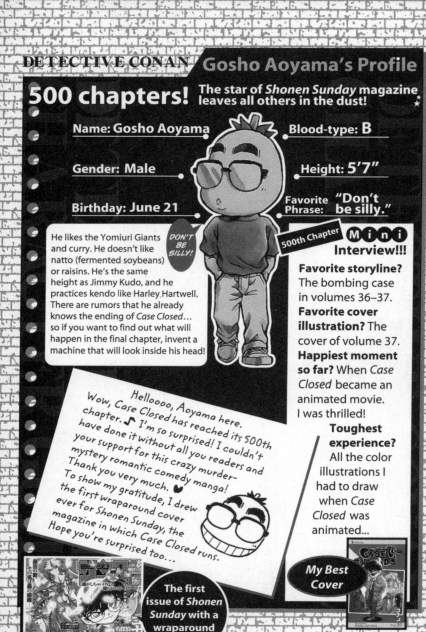

CHARACTER GUIDE

The Detective with Two Faces!

A mystery geek who lives for codes and deductions!

Aiming to Become the Modern-Day Holmes

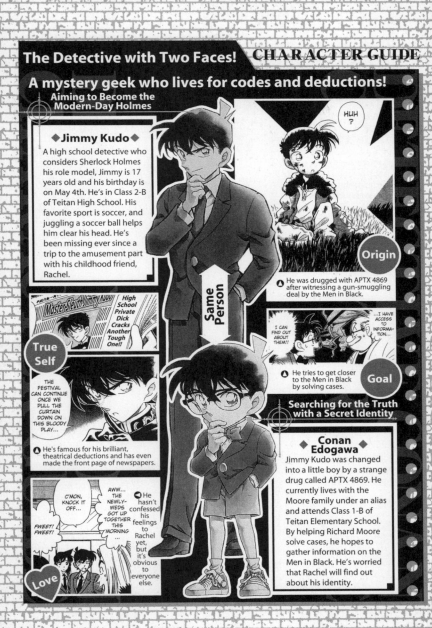

◆Jimmy Kudo◆

A high school detective who considers Sherlock Holmes his role model, Jimmy is 17 years old and his birthday is on May 4th. He's in Class 2-B of Teitan High School. His favorite sport is soccer, and juggling a soccer ball helps him clear his head. He's been missing ever since a trip to the amusement part with his childhood friend, Rachel.

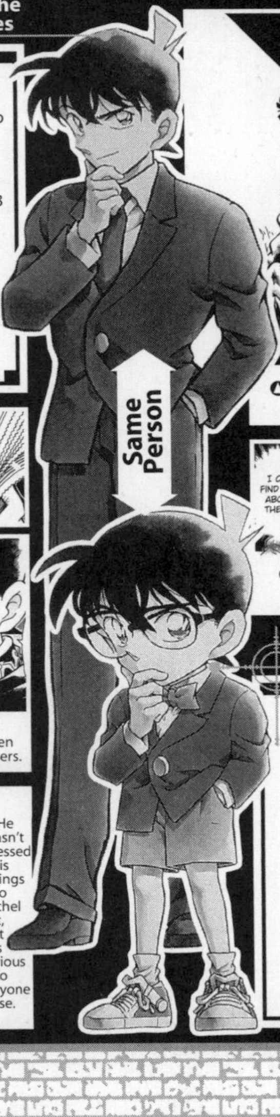
Same Person

Origin

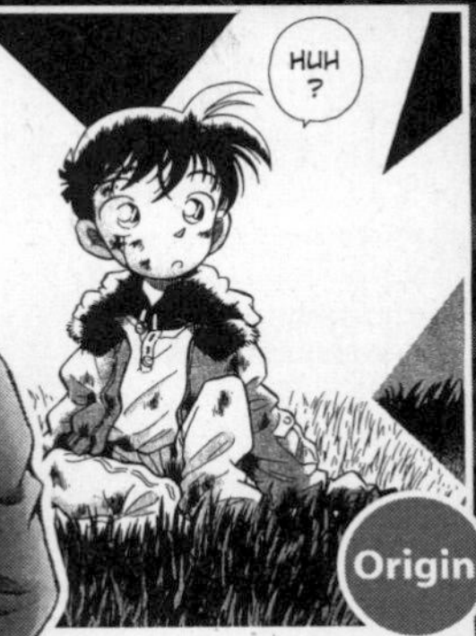
HUH ?

▲ He was drugged with APTX 4869 after witnessing a gun-smuggling deal by the Men in Black.

True Self

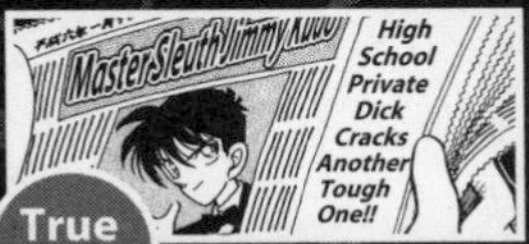
Master Sleuth Jimmy Kudo
High School Private Dick Cracks Another Tough One!!

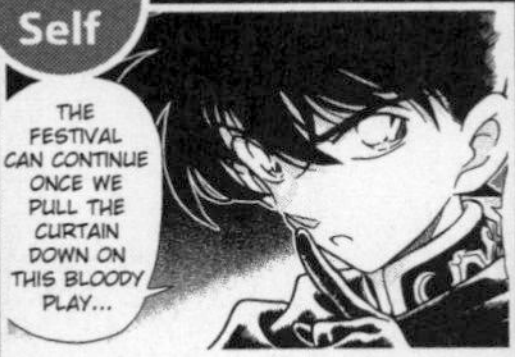
THE FESTIVAL CAN CONTINUE ONCE WE PULL THE CURTAIN DOWN ON THIS BLOODY PLAY...

▲ He's famous for his brilliant, theatrical deductions and has even made the front page of newspapers.

Goal

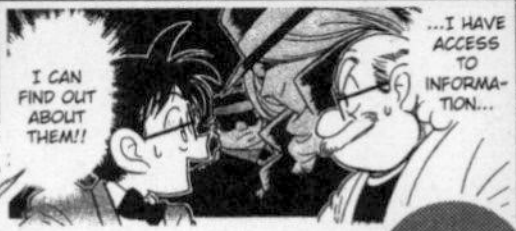
...I HAVE ACCESS TO INFORMATION...
I CAN FIND OUT ABOUT THEM!!

▲ He tries to get closer to the Men in Black by solving cases.

Love

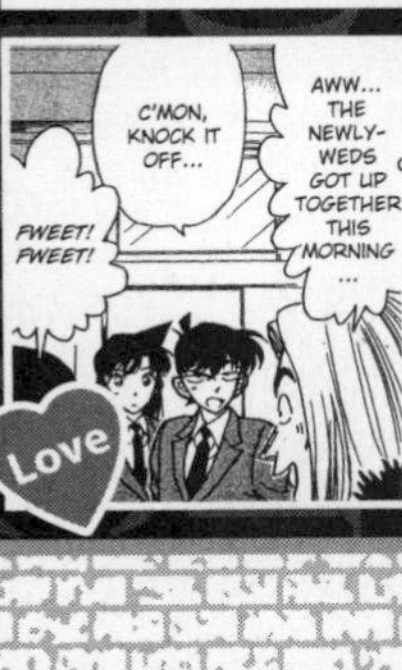
AWW... THE NEWLYWEDS GOT UP TOGETHER THIS MORNING...
C'MON, KNOCK IT OFF...
FWEET! FWEET!

◀ He hasn't confessed his feelings to Rachel yet, but it's obvious to everyone else.

Searching for the Truth with a Secret Identity

◆Conan Edogawa◆

Jimmy Kudo was changed into a little boy by a strange drug called APTX 4869. He currently lives with the Moore family under an alias and attends Class 1-B of Teitan Elementary School. By helping Richard Moore solve cases, he hopes to gather information on the Men in Black. He's worried that Rachel will find out about his identity.

DETECTIVE CONAN CHARACTER GUIDE

Always Ready for an Adventure: The Junior Detective League!

Conan's eager friends! Together they can solve any case…right?

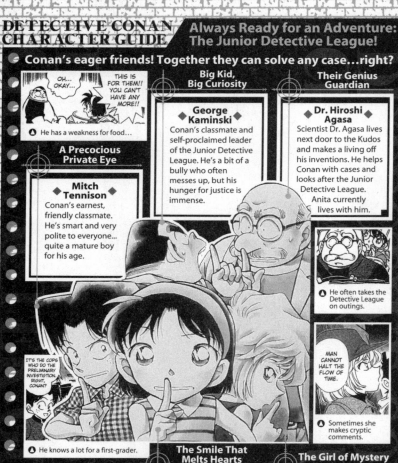

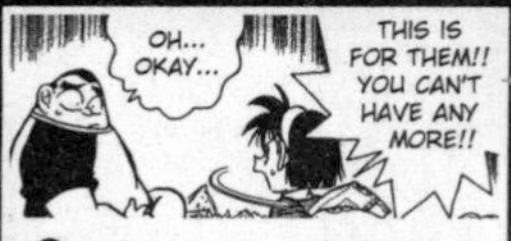
THIS IS FOR THEM!! YOU CAN'T HAVE ANY MORE!!
OH... OKAY...

He has a weakness for food…

Big Kid, Big Curiosity

◆ George Kaminski ◆

Conan's classmate and self-proclaimed leader of the Junior Detective League. He's a bit of a bully who often messes up, but his hunger for justice is immense.

Their Genius Guardian

◆ Dr. Hiroshi Agasa ◆

Scientist Dr. Agasa lives next door to the Kudos and makes a living off his inventions. He helps Conan with cases and looks after the Junior Detective League. Anita currently lives with him.

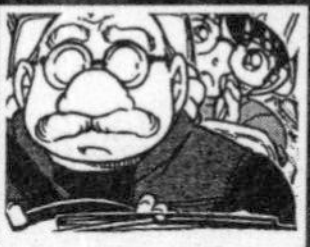

He often takes the Detective League on outings.

A Precocious Private Eye

◆ Mitch Tennison ◆

Conan's earnest, friendly classmate. He's smart and very polite to everyone... quite a mature boy for his age.

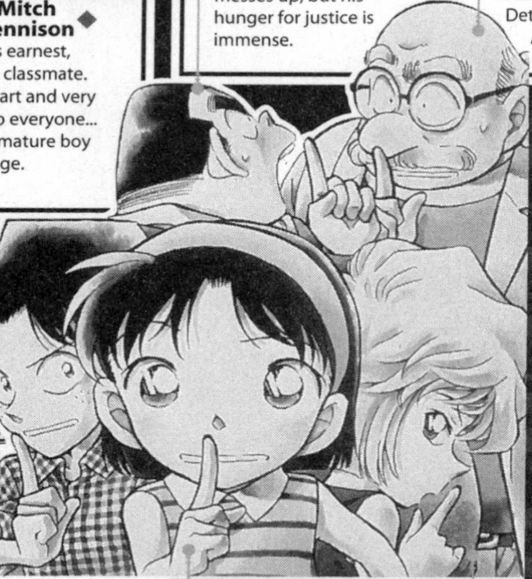

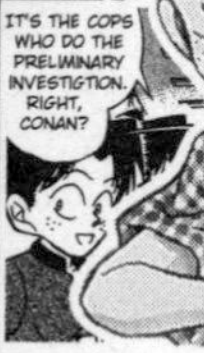
IT'S THE COPS WHO DO THE PRELIMINARY INVESTIGTION. RIGHT, CONAN?

He knows a lot for a first-grader.

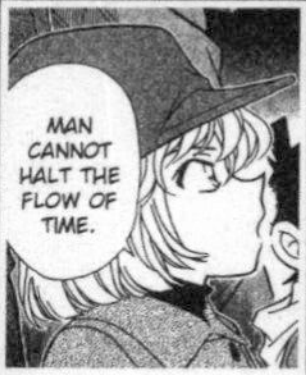
MAN CANNOT HALT THE FLOW OF TIME.

Sometimes she makes cryptic comments.

The Smile That Melts Hearts

◆ Amy Yeager ◆

A sweet, generous member of the Detective League. She's kind to everyone around her but especially likes Conan.

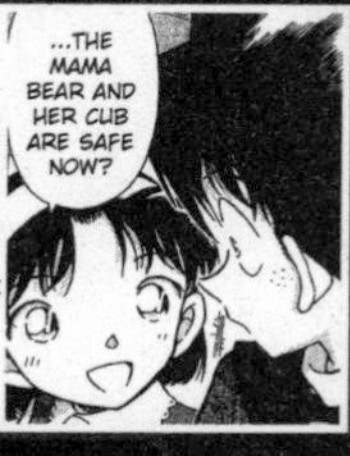
...THE MAMA BEAR AND HER CUB ARE SAFE NOW?

She lightens the mood with her innocent remarks.

The Girl of Mystery

◆ Anita Hailey ◆

A scientist who turned herself into a little girl with APTX 4869 to escape from the Men in Black. She's currently working on a cure while Dr. Agasa covers for her.

Conan's Trusty...

Secret Gadgets +1

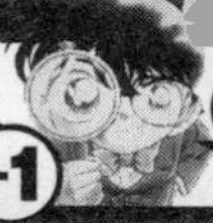

Dr. Agasa's Gadgets!

Here are all the super (and super-strange) inventions created by Dr. Agasa for Conan

Voice Modulating Bow Tie

FILE——006

A gadget Conan can't do without. He can change his voice by turning the dial.

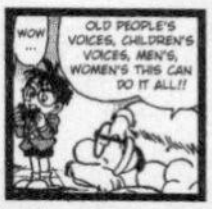
OLD PEOPLE'S VOICES, CHILDREN'S VOICES, MEN'S, WOMEN'S THIS CAN DO IT ALL!!
WOW ...

Super Sneakers

FILE——010

They stimulate the pressure points of the feet for a power boost. Conan uses his soccer skills to take criminals down!

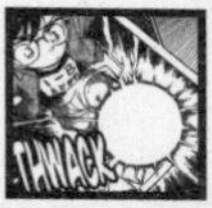
THWACK

Homing Glasses

FILE——013

By raising an antenna on his glasses, Conan can track a transmitter.

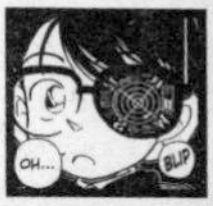
BLIP
OH...

Button Transmitter

FILE——013/252

A mini transmitter. When not using it, Conan hides it under his button.

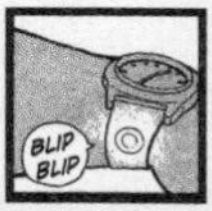
BLIP BLIP

Stretchy Suspenders

FILE——018

They stretch and contract with the push of a button and are strong enough to lift heavy objects.

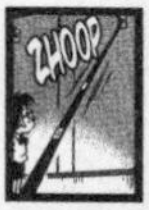
ZHOOP

Sleeping Dart Watch

FILE——024

Capable of shooting one sleeping dart to instantaneously knock a target out. A must-have for Conan!

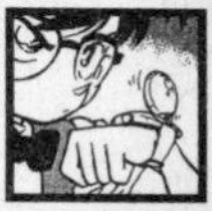

Detective League Badge

FILE——056

The sign of a member of the Junior Detective League, it's also a useful device that works as a transmitter and transceiver.

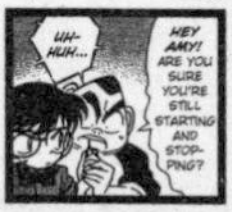
HEY AMY! ARE YOU SURE YOU'RE STILL STARTING AND STOP-PING?
UH-HUH...

Bento Box Fax

FILE——069

A combination fax machine and bento box. The food inside is real.

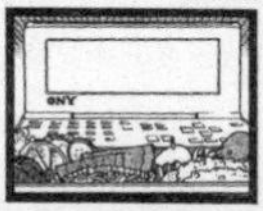

Turbo Skateboard

FILE——082

A speedy solar-powered skateboard. Since its first appearance, it's been refined with a rechargeable battery.

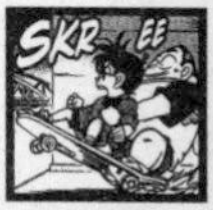
SKR
EE

Button-Size Speaker

FILE——110

A speaker Conan uses to enhance the voice from his Voice Modulating Bow Tie. It can be stuck anywhere.

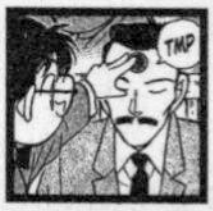
TMP

Voice Reco-Changer

FILE——111

A pen Dr. Agasa designed for a toy company. Using the same technology as the Voice Modulating Bow Tie, it can record voices as well as change the sound of a voice.

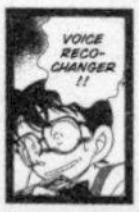
VOICE RECO-CHANGER !!

Mobile Phone Earring

FILE——140

A cell phone in the shape of an earring. It can also receive transmissions from the Voice Modulating Bow Tie.

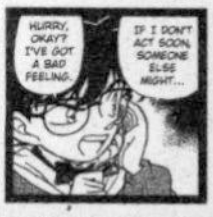
IF I DON'T ACT SOON, SOMEONE ELSE MIGHT...
HURRY, OKAY? I'VE GOT A BAD FEELING.

Watch Flashlight

FILE——200

A gadget all members of the Junior Detective League carry. It has a flashlight so you don't have to be afraid of the dark!

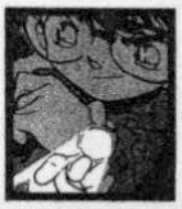

Voice-Changing Mask

FILE——255

This has the same functions as Conan's bow tie. Anita used it to pose as Conan.

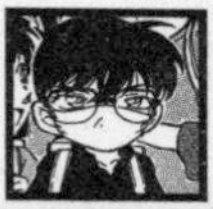

Instant Ball Belt

FILE——380

Turn the dial and a ball pops out!

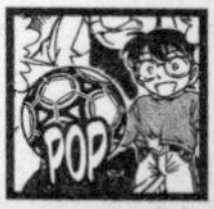
POP

DETECTIVE CONAN

Waiting for Jimmy Kudo

Friends, family, rivals...all those who await his return!

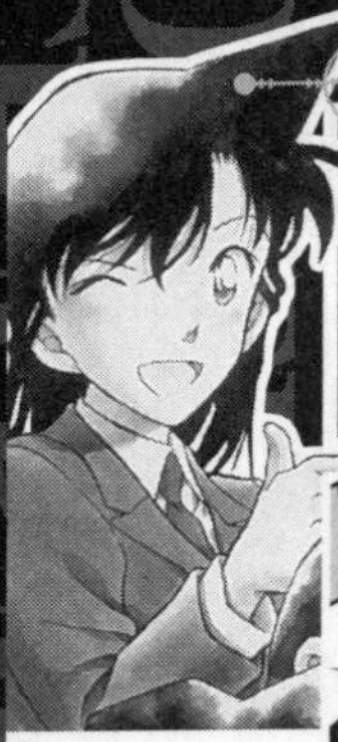

The Strong-Hearted Superheroine

◆ Rachel Moore ◆

Jimmy's childhood friend, a high-school karate champ, has been taking care of her dad since her parents separated.

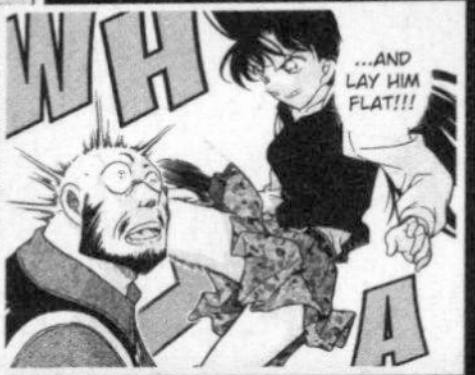

WH
...AND LAY HIM FLAT!!!
A

▶ The captain of the Karate Club. She always ranks at the top in tournaments.

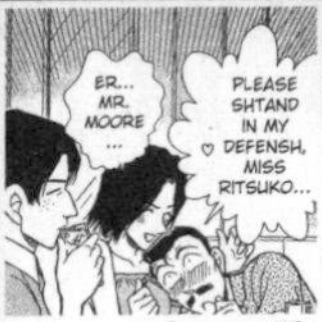

PLEASE SHTAND IN MY DEFENSH, MISS RITSUKO...
ER... MR. MOORE ...

▲ He loves liquor, gambling and beautiful women.

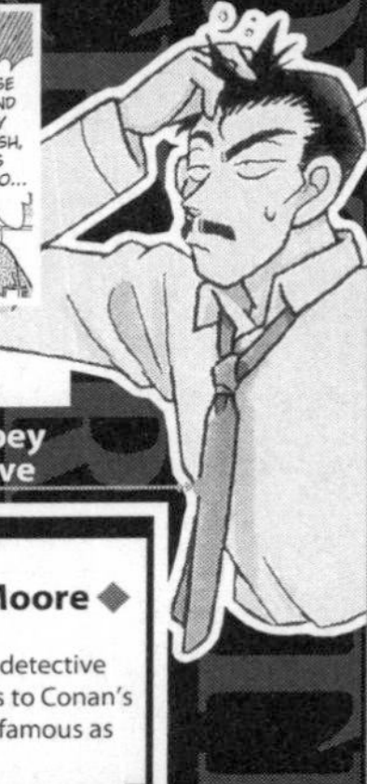

The Dopey Detective

◆ Richard Moore ◆

Rachel's father is a detective and ex-cop. Thanks to Conan's help, he's become famous as "Sleeping Moore."

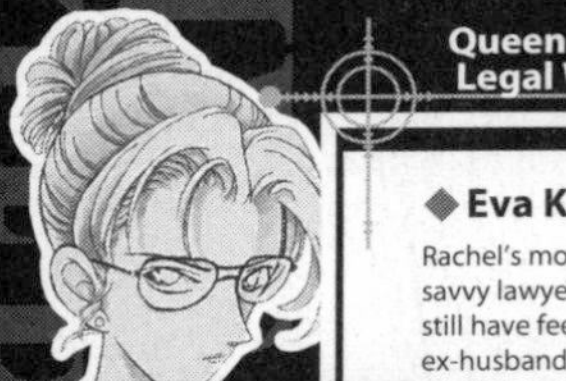

Queen of the Legal World

◆ Eva Kaden ◆

Rachel's mother is a savvy lawyer. Does she still have feelings for her ex-husband Richard?

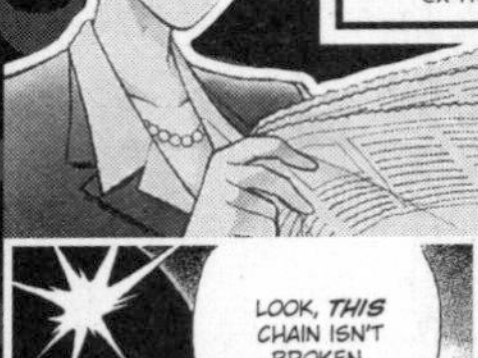

LOOK, *THIS* CHAIN ISN'T BROKEN, IS IT?

▲ Eva did her own sleuthing to prove her husband's innocence!

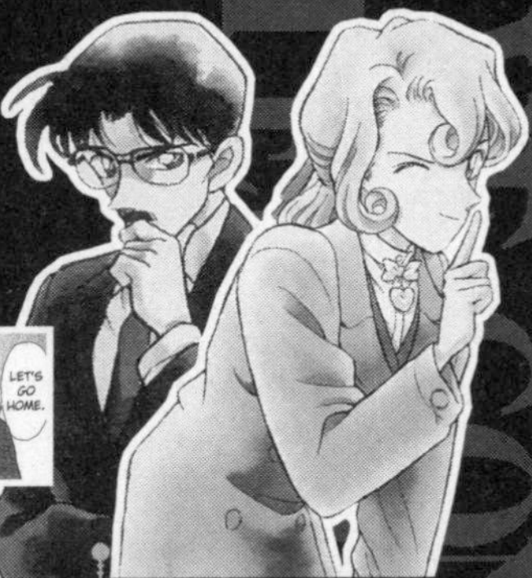

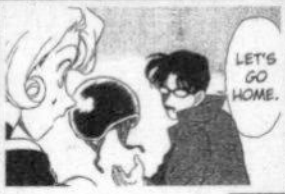

LET'S GO HOME.

▲ They still get into spats.

The Nonchalant Novelist

◆ Booker Kudo ◆

Jimmy's father, a brilliant mystery novelist, is famous for his Night Baron series.

The Sweetheart of the Stage

◆ Vivian Kudo ◆

Jimmy's mother was internationally renowned as an actress before she retired. She's skilled at disguise.

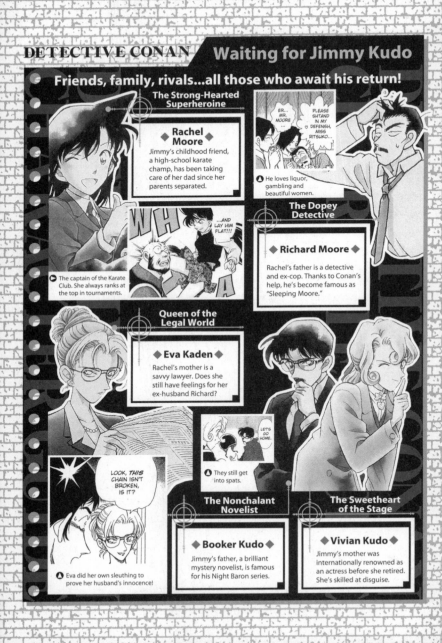

Waiting for Jimmy Kudo CHARACTER GUIDE

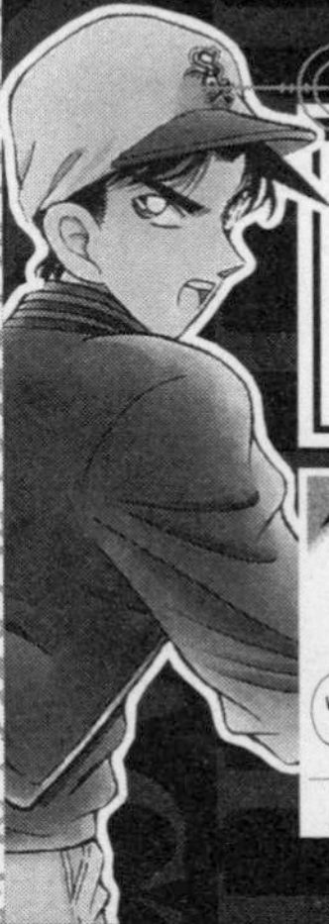

The White Knight of the West

◆ Harley Hartwell ◆

Teen detective Harley is a student at Kaiho High School and practices kendo. Since Jimmy's transformation, they've gradually changed from rivals to friends.

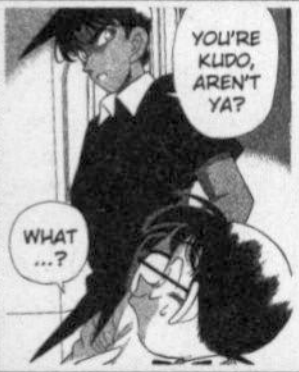
YOU'RE KUDO, AREN'T YA?
WHAT ...?

◀ He cleverly deduced Conan's true identity.

▶ She once suspected that Rachel and Harley were an item.

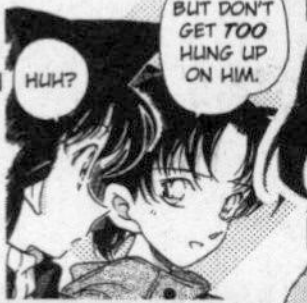
BUT DON'T GET TOO HUNG UP ON HIM.
HUH?

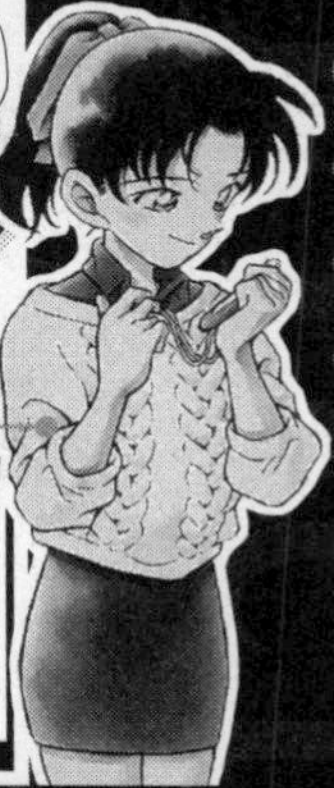

The Girl Next Door in Osaka

◆ Kazuha Toyama ◆

Harley's childhood friend is an Aikido expert. She often gets involved in cases with Harley.

The Demure Doctor

◆ Tomoaki Araide ◆

Dr. Araide, the school doctor at Teitan High, is trusted by all the students.

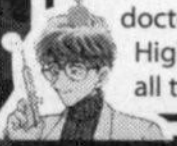

The Chivalrous Champ

◆ Makoto Kyogoku ◆

The captain of the Haido High School Karate Club, Makoto is devoted to Serena.

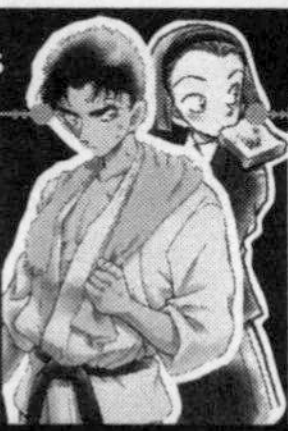

The Poor Little Rich Girl

◆ Serena Sebastian ◆

Rachel's boy-crazy best friend is the wealthy heiress to the Sebastian Conglomerate.

The Children's Hero

◆ Samurai Kid ◆

This fictional super-hero is popular with Conan's friends.

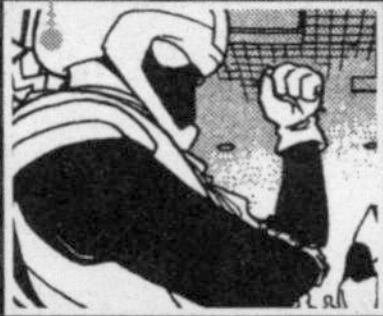

The Cute Idol

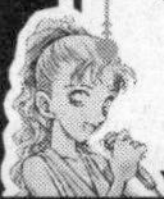

◆ Yoko Okino ◆

Richard is a huge fan of this pop singer.

The Literary Hero

◆ Night Baron ◆

The mysterious protagonist of Booker's detective novels.

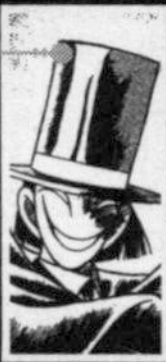

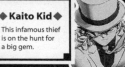

The Modern-Day Lupin III

◆ Kaito Kid ◆

This infamous thief is on the hunt for a big gem.

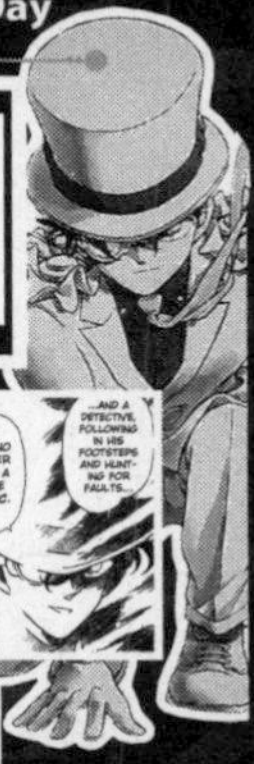

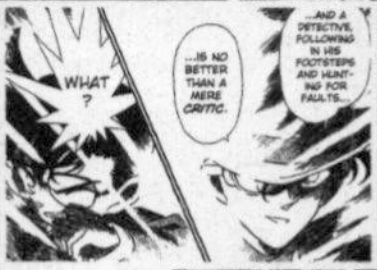
...AND A DETECTIVE, FOLLOWING IN HIS FOOTSTEPS AND HUNTING FOR FAULTS...
...IS NO BETTER THAN A MERE CRITIC.
WHAT ?

▲ He sees Conan as his opposite number.

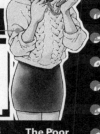

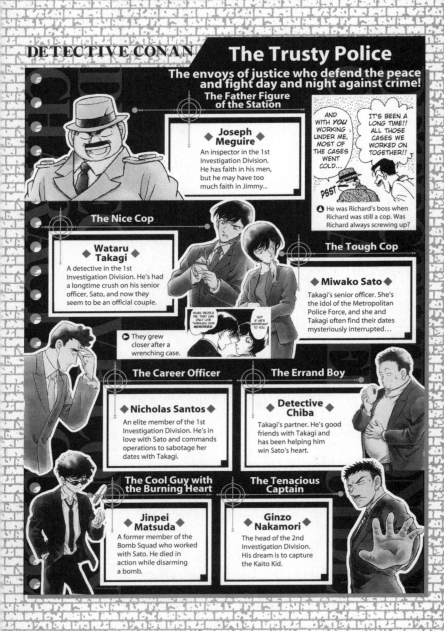

DETECTIVE CONAN The Trusty Police

The envoys of justice who defend the peace and fight day and night against crime!

The Father Figure of the Station

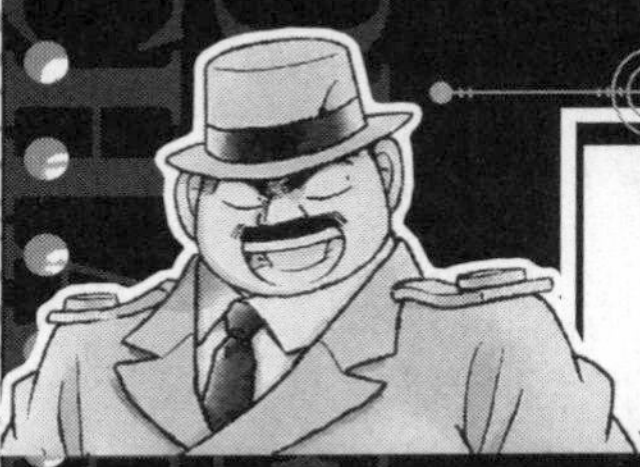

◆ Joseph Meguire ◆

An inspector in the 1st Investigation Division. He has faith in his men, but he may have too much faith in Jimmy...

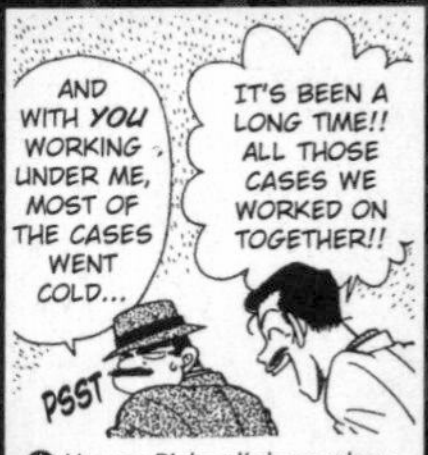
IT'S BEEN A LONG TIME!! ALL THOSE CASES WE WORKED ON TOGETHER!!
AND WITH *YOU* WORKING UNDER ME, MOST OF THE CASES WENT COLD...
PSST

▲ He was Richard's boss when Richard was still a cop. Was Richard always screwing up?

The Nice Cop

◆ Wataru Takagi ◆

A detective in the 1st Investigation Division. He's had a longtime crush on his senior officer, Sato, and now they seem to be an official couple.

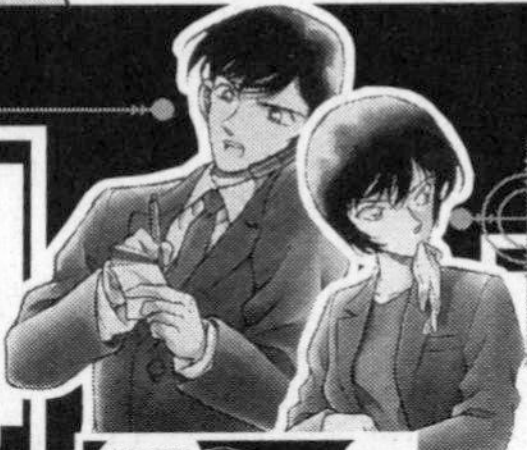

The Tough Cop

◆ Miwako Sato ◆

Takagi's senior officer. She's the idol of the Metropolitan Police Force, and she and Takagi often find their dates mysteriously interrupted…

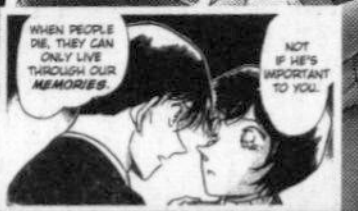
NOT IF HE'S IMPORTANT TO YOU.
WHEN PEOPLE DIE, THEY CAN ONLY LIVE THROUGH OUR *MEMORIES.*

► They grew closer after a wrenching case.

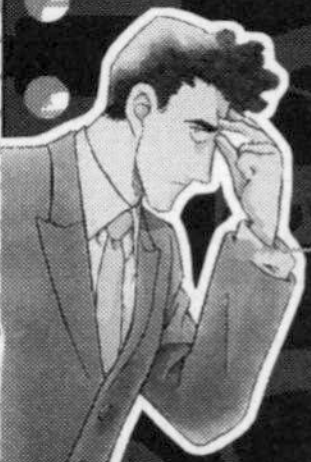

The Career Officer

◆ Nicholas Santos ◆

An elite member of the 1st Investigation Division. He's in love with Sato and commands operations to sabotage her dates with Takagi.

The Errand Boy

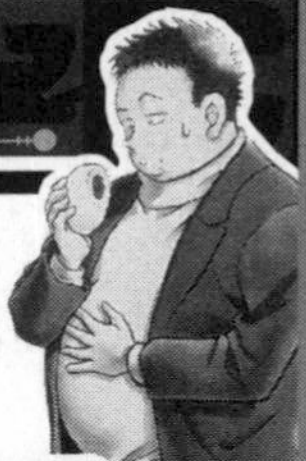

◆ Detective Chiba ◆

Takagi's partner. He's good friends with Takagi and has been helping him win Sato's heart.

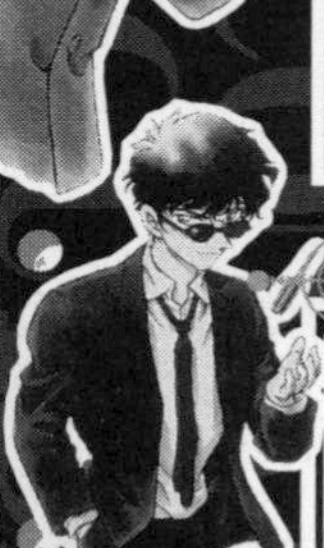

The Cool Guy with the Burning Heart

◆ Jinpei Matsuda ◆

A former member of the Bomb Squad who worked with Sato. He died in action while disarming a bomb.

The Tenacious Captain

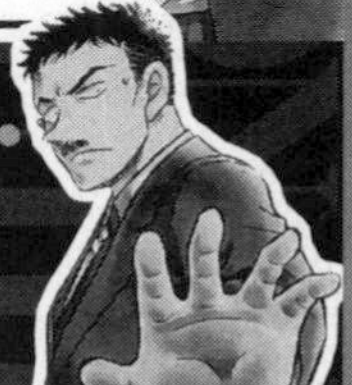

◆ Ginzo Nakamori ◆

The head of the 2nd Investigation Division. His dream is to capture the Kaito Kid.

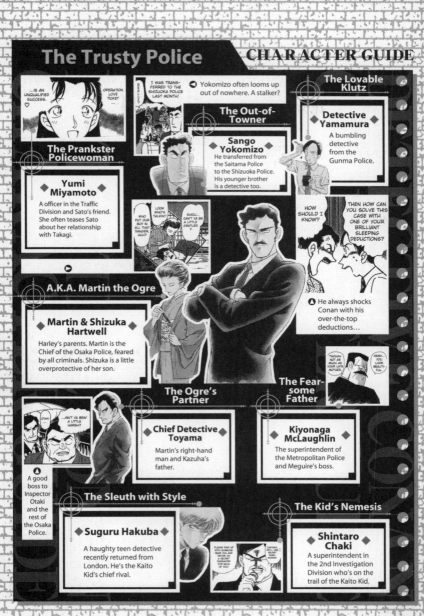

The Trusty Police

CHARACTER GUIDE

OPERATION LOVE TICKET ...
...IS AN UNQUALIFIED SUCCESS. ♡

The Prankster Policewoman

◆ **Yumi Miyamoto** ◆

A officer in the Traffic Division and Sato's friend. She often teases Sato about her relationship with Takagi.

I WAS TRANSFERRED TO THE SHIZUOKA POLICE LAST MONTH!
REALLY?

◀ Yokomizo often looms up out of nowhere. A stalker?

The Out-of-Towner

◆ **Sango Yokomizo** ◆

He transferred from the Saitama Police to the Shizuoka Police. His younger brother is a detective too.

The Lovable Klutz

◆ **Detective Yamamura** ◆

A bumbling detective from the Gunma Police.

SHIZU... CAN'T YA BE A LITTLE GENTLER ?
LOOK WHO'S TALKIN'!
WHO PUT OUR BOY IN ALL THAT DANGER, HUH?

▶

THEN HOW CAN YOU SOLVE THIS CASE WITH ONE OF YOUR BRILLIANT SLEEPING DEDUCTIONS?
HOW SHOULD I KNOW?

▲ He always shocks Conan with his over-the-top deductions...

A.K.A. Martin the Ogre

◆ **Martin & Shizuka Hartwell** ◆

Harley's parents. Martin is the Chief of the Osaka Police, feared by all criminals. Shizuka is a little overprotective of her son.

YEAH... YOU LOOK BEAUTIFUL.
THOUGH NOT AS MUCH AS YOUR LATE MOTHER.

The Fearsome Father

◆ **Kiyonaga McLaughlin** ◆

The superintendent of the Metropolitan Police and Meguire's boss.

...AIN'T YA BEIN' A LITTLE HARSH?
OTAKI ...

▲ A good boss to Inspector Otaki and the rest of the Osaka Police.

The Ogre's Partner

◆ **Chief Detective Toyama** ◆

Martin's right-hand man and Kazuha's father.

The Sleuth with Style

◆ **Suguru Hakuba** ◆

A haughty teen detective recently returned from London. He's the Kaito Kid's chief rival.

INSTEAD, WE'LL USE SECRET PASSWORDS!
PLEASE PAIR UP WITH SOMEONE NEAR YOU AND DECIDE ON A SECRET PASSWORD FOR EACH OF YOU!

The Kid's Nemesis

◆ **Shintaro Chaki** ◆

A superintendent in the 2nd Investigation Division who's on the trail of the Kaito Kid.

The Men in Black

A massive crime syndicate that controls the underworld!

These are the known members of an international organization responsible for countless crimes.

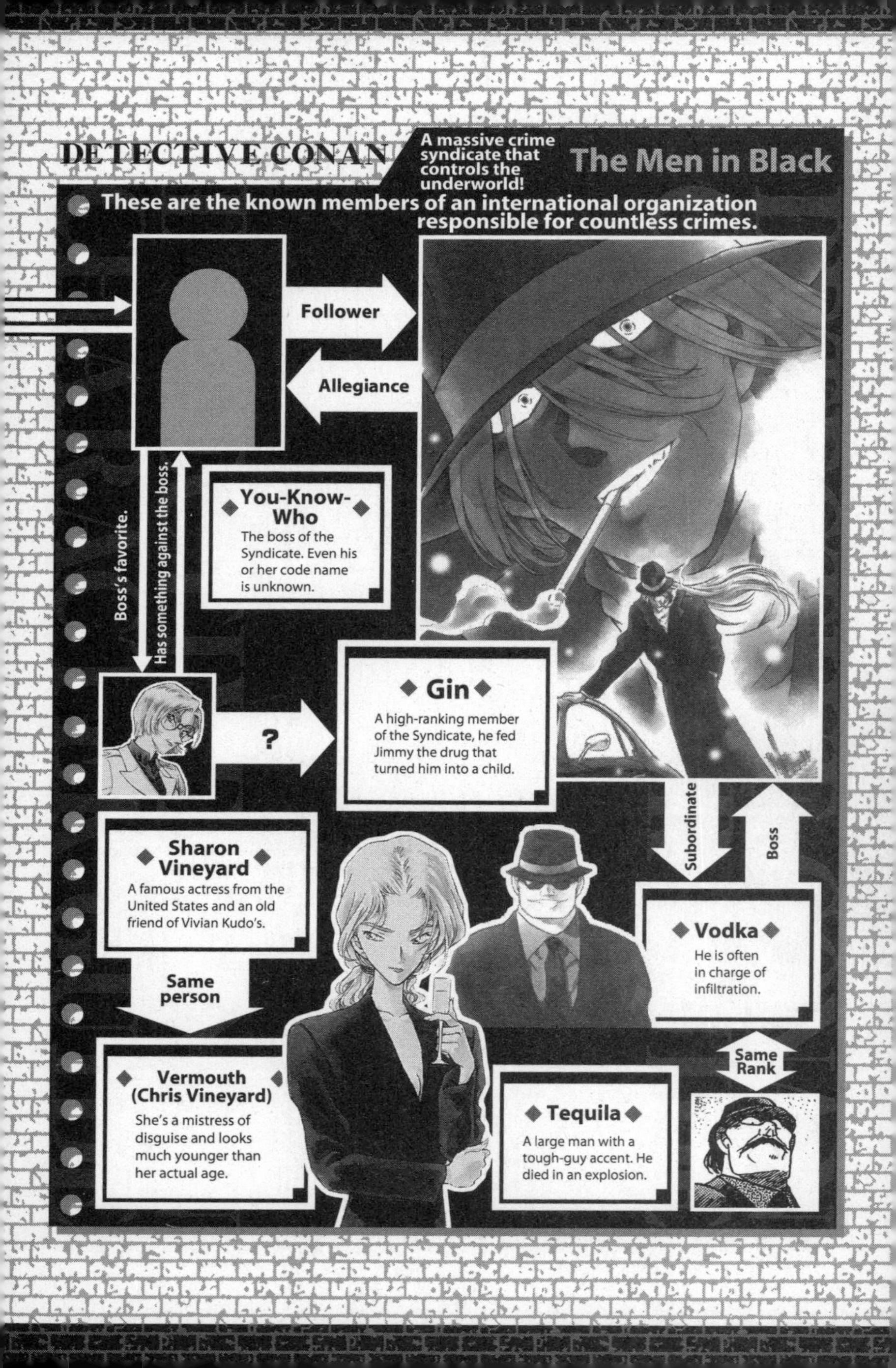
Follower
Allegiance
Boss's favorite.
Has something against the boss.
◆ You-Know-Who ◆
The boss of the Syndicate. Even his or her code name is unknown.
?
◆ Gin ◆
A high-ranking member of the Syndicate, he fed Jimmy the drug that turned him into a child.
Subordinate
Boss
◆ Sharon Vineyard ◆
A famous actress from the United States and an old friend of Vivian Kudo's.
Same person
◆ Vodka ◆
He is often in charge of infiltration.
Same Rank
◆ Vermouth (Chris Vineyard)
She's a mistress of disguise and looks much younger than her actual age.
◆ Tequila ◆
A large man with a tough-guy accent. He died in an explosion.

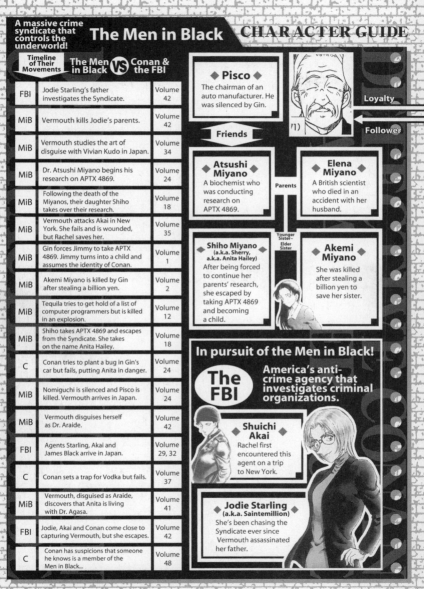

The Men in Black

A massive crime syndicate that controls the underworld!

CHARACTER GUIDE

Timeline of Their Movements: The Men in Black VS Conan & the FBI

FBI	Jodie Starling's father investigates the Syndicate.	Volume 42
MiB	Vermouth kills Jodie's parents.	Volume 42
MiB	Vermouth studies the art of disguise with Vivian Kudo in Japan.	Volume 34
MiB	Dr. Atsushi Miyano begins his research on APTX 4869.	Volume 24
MiB	Following the death of the Miyanos, their daughter Shiho takes over their research.	Volume 18
MiB	Vermouth attacks Akai in New York. She fails and is wounded, but Rachel saves her.	Volume 35
MiB	Gin forces Jimmy to take APTX 4869. Jimmy turns into a child and assumes the identity of Conan.	Volume 1
MiB	Akemi Miyano is killed by Gin after stealing a billion yen.	Volume 2
MiB	Tequila tries to get hold of a list of computer programmers but is killed in an explosion.	Volume 12
MiB	Shiho takes APTX 4869 and escapes from the Syndicate. She takes on the name Anita Hailey.	Volume 18
C	Conan tries to plant a bug in Gin's car but fails, putting Anita in danger.	Volume 24
MiB	Nomiguchi is silenced and Pisco is killed. Vermouth arrives in Japan.	Volume 24
MiB	Vermouth disguises herself as Dr. Araide.	Volume 42
FBI	Agents Starling, Akai and James Black arrive in Japan.	Volume 29, 32
C	Conan sets a trap for Vodka but fails.	Volume 37
MiB	Vermouth, disguised as Araide, discovers that Anita is living with Dr. Agasa.	Volume 41
FBI	Jodie, Akai and Conan come close to capturing Vermouth, but she escapes.	Volume 42
C	Conan has suspicions that someone he knows is a member of the Men in Black...	Volume 48

◆ Pisco ◆
The chairman of an auto manufacturer. He was silenced by Gin.

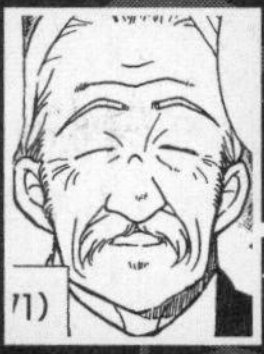

Loyalty

Follower

Friends

◆ Atsushi Miyano ◆
A biochemist who was conducting research on APTX 4869.

Parents

◆ Elena Miyano ◆
A British scientist who died in an accident with her husband.

Younger Sister–Elder Sister

◆ Shiho Miyano ◆
(a.k.a. Sherry, a.k.a. Anita Hailey)
After being forced to continue her parents' research, she escaped by taking APTX 4869 and becoming a child.

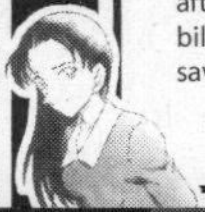

◆ Akemi Miyano ◆
She was killed after stealing a billion yen to save her sister.

In pursuit of the Men in Black!

The FBI

America's anti-crime agency that investigates criminal organizations.

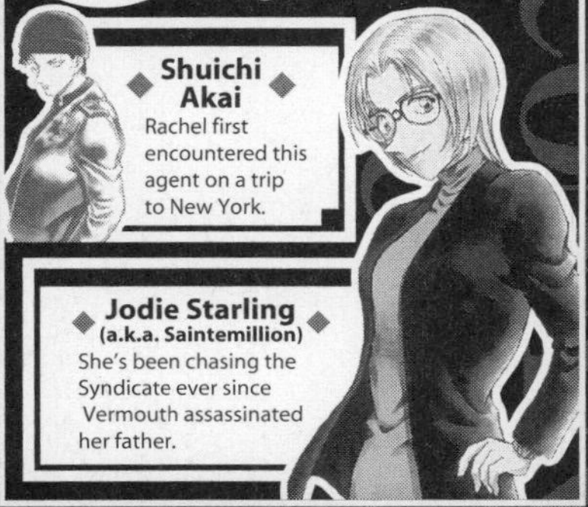

◆ Shuichi Akai ◆
Rachel first encountered this agent on a trip to New York.

◆ Jodie Starling ◆
(a.k.a. Saintemillion)
She's been chasing the Syndicate ever since Vermouth assassinated her father.

Editing: Caramel Mama Design: Hitoshi Shirayama, Shigeru Anzai, Yasuo Shimura + Bay Bridge Studio

Hello, Aoyama here.

Lately I've been having back pains because of my age (heh), so I finally bought a mechanical massage chair! I finish my work, take a bath, change into my pajamas and press the button! "Welcome to your comfort zone. ❤" I-It talks...

Gosho Aoyama's Mystery Library

49

STEVE CARELLA

A massive city that's burning hot in summer and freezing cold in winter...and the man who patrols it is Detective Steve Carella of the 87th Precinct! A muscular, well-built man in his late thirties, he has short brown hair and brown eyes. He deals with all kinds of crime as a member of the 87th Precinct, including fights, robbery, assaults...and, of course, murder. Carella is a persistent cop who crisscrosses the city asking questions and closes in on the truth one step at a time. His reliable fellow detectives at the precinct are led by Lieutenant Byrnes. When they work together as a team, they're as powerful as any genius sleuth around.

The 87th Precinct is located in the fictional city of Isola, created by Ed McBain, but is clearly based on New York. Baker City, which I created, is based on the city where I live, but the problem is it keeps changing every time I move. Heh...

I recommend *Cop Hater*.

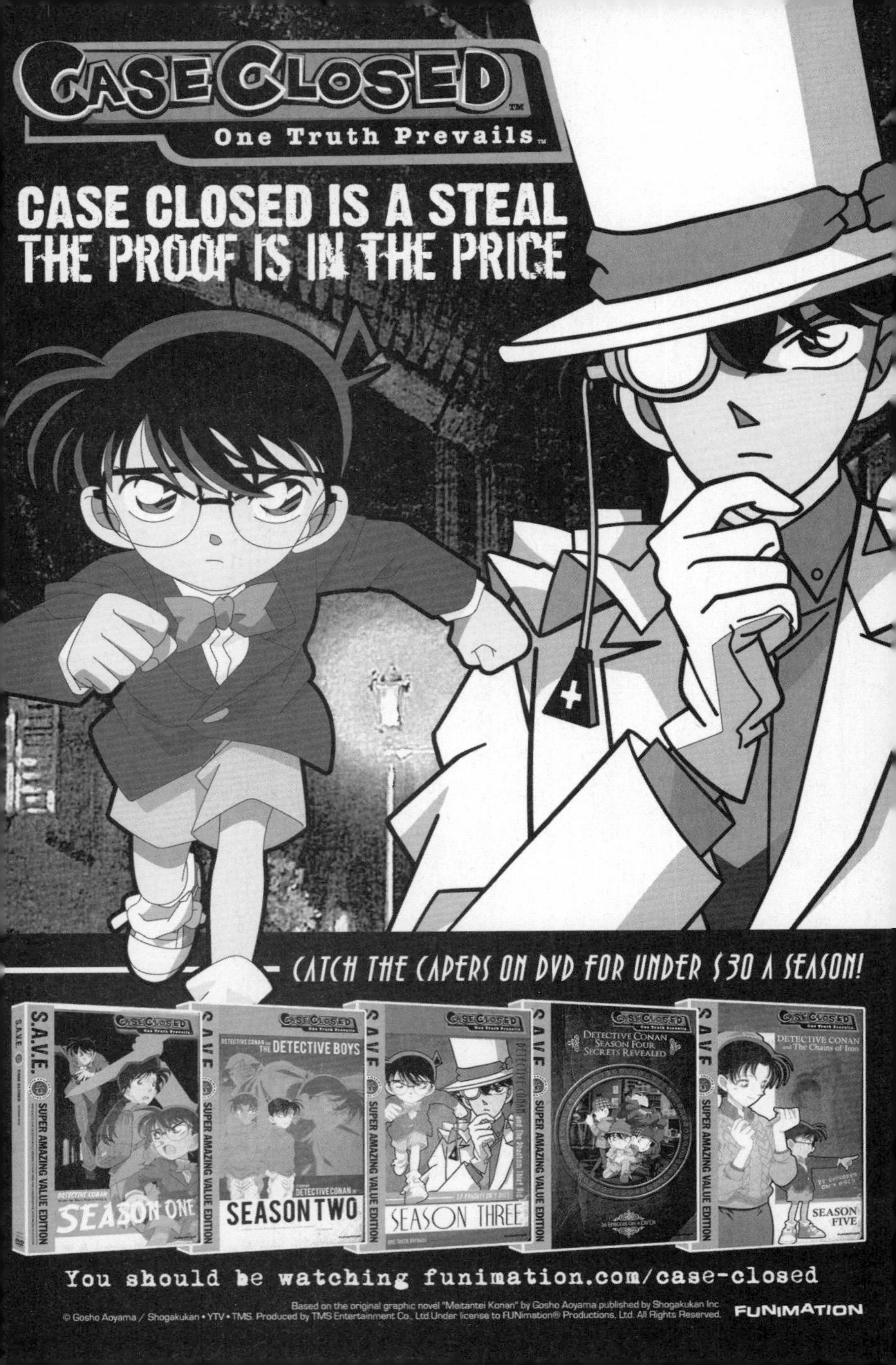
CASE CLOSED
One Truth Prevails
CASE CLOSED IS A STEAL
THE PROOF IS IN THE PRICE
CATCH THE CAPERS ON DVD FOR UNDER $30 A SEASON!
S.A.V.E. SUPER AMAZING VALUE EDITION
SEASON ONE
DETECTIVE CONAN and THE DETECTIVE BOYS
SEASON TWO
SEASON THREE
DETECTIVE CONAN SEASON FOUR SECRETS REVEALED
DETECTIVE CONAN and The Chains of Iron
SEASON FIVE
You should be watching funimation.com/case-closed
Based on the original graphic novel "Meitantei Konan" by Gosho Aoyama published by Shogakukan Inc.
© Gosho Aoyama / Shogakukan • YTV • TMS. Produced by TMS Entertainment Co., Ltd.Under license to FUNimation® Productions, Ltd. All Rights Reserved.
FUNIMATION

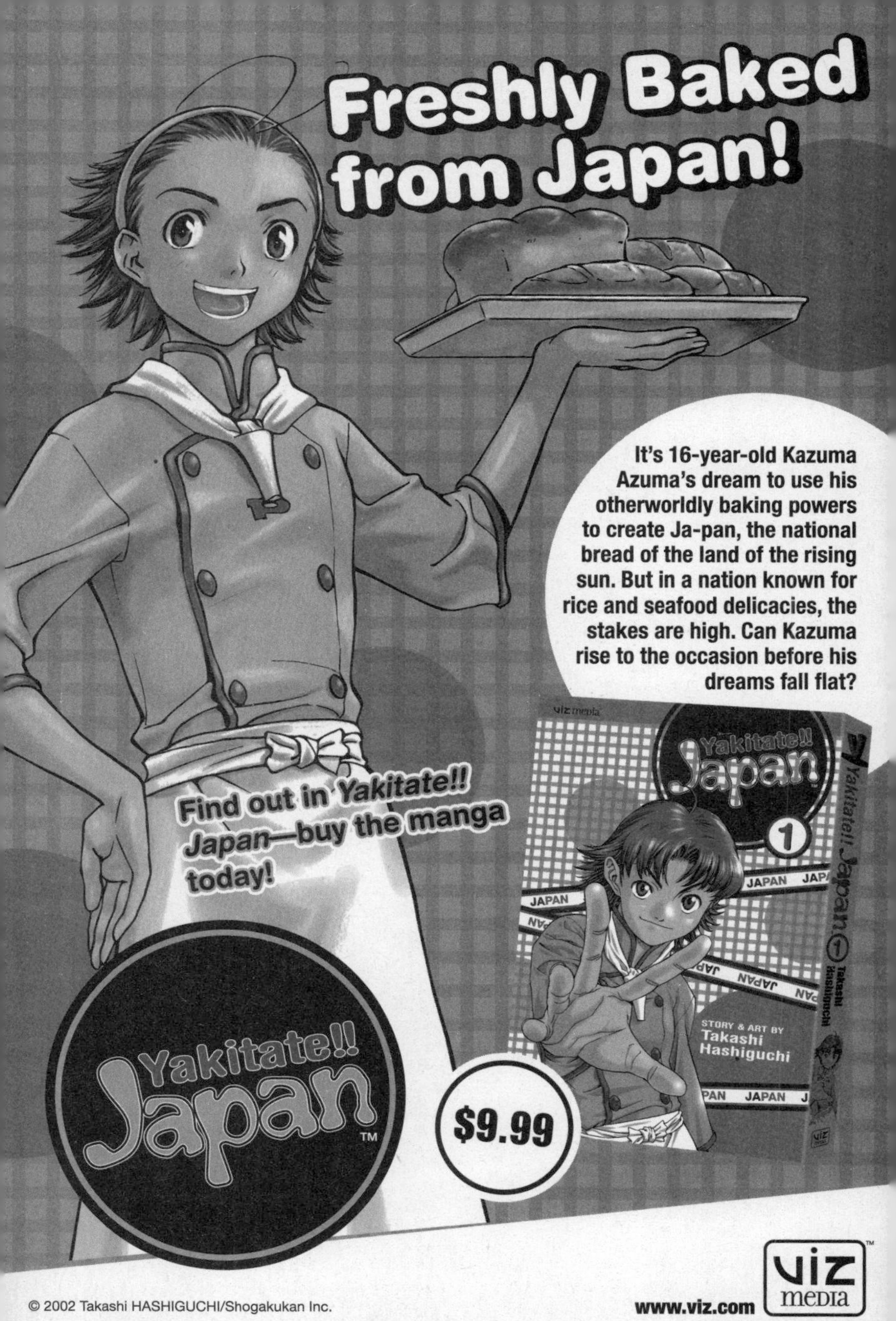
Freshly Baked from Japan!
It's 16-year-old Kazuma Azuma's dream to use his otherworldly baking powers to create Ja-pan, the national bread of the land of the rising sun. But in a nation known for rice and seafood delicacies, the stakes are high. Can Kazuma rise to the occasion before his dreams fall flat?
Find out in Yakitate!! Japan—buy the manga today!
viz media
Yakitate!! Japan
1
JAPAN
STORY & ART BY Takashi Hashiguchi
$9.99
Yakitate!! Japan™
VIZ MEDIA™
www.viz.com

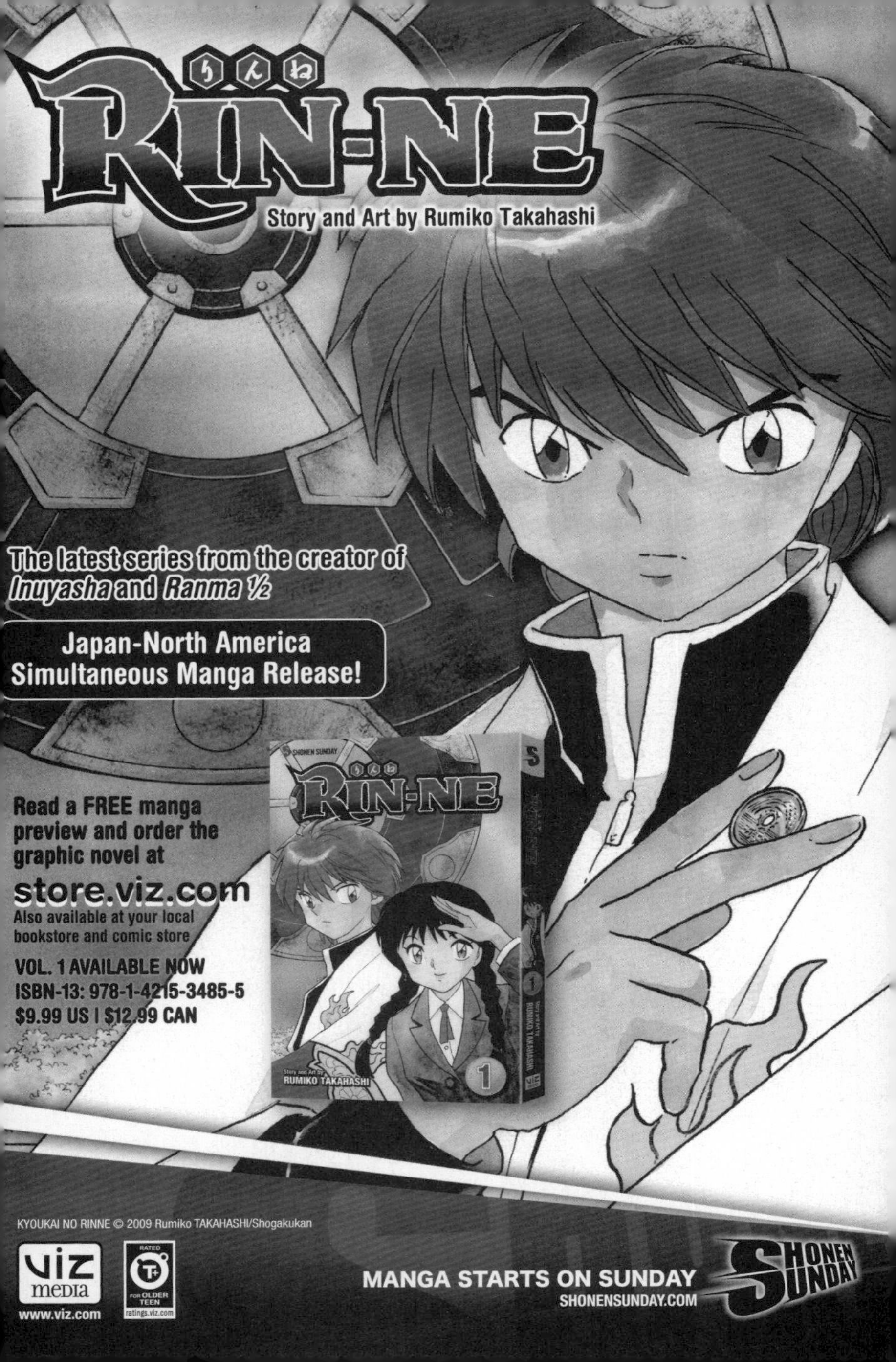
りんね
RIN-NE
Story and Art by Rumiko Takahashi
The latest series from the creator of
Inuyasha and Ranma ½
Japan-North America
Simultaneous Manga Release!
SHONEN SUNDAY
RIN-NE
Story and Art by
RUMIKO TAKAHASHI
1
Read a FREE manga
preview and order the
graphic novel at
store.viz.com
Also available at your local
bookstore and comic store
VOL. 1 AVAILABLE NOW
ISBN-13: 978-1-4215-3485-5
$9.99 US | $12.99 CAN
KYOUKAI NO RINNE © 2009 Rumiko TAKAHASHI/Shogakukan
viz media
www.viz.com
RATED T+ FOR OLDER TEEN
ratings.viz.com
MANGA STARTS ON SUNDAY
SHONENSUNDAY.COM
SHONEN SUNDAY

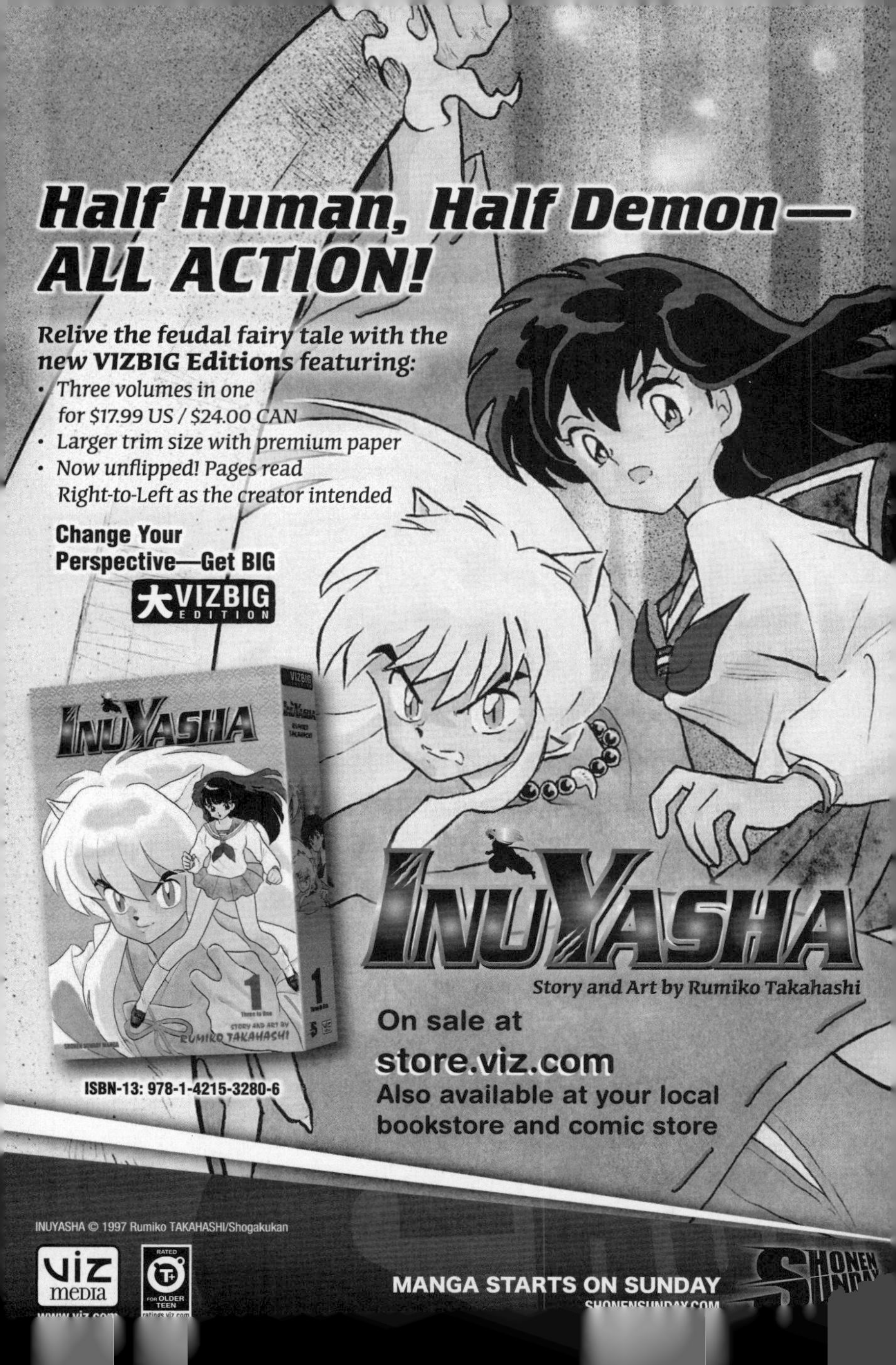

Half Human, Half Demon—
ALL ACTION!
Relive the feudal fairy tale with the new VIZBIG Editions featuring:
• Three volumes in one for $17.99 US / $24.00 CAN
• Larger trim size with premium paper
• Now unflipped! Pages read Right-to-Left as the creator intended
Change Your Perspective—Get BIG
大 VIZBIG EDITION
INUYASHA
1
STORY AND ART BY RUMIKO TAKAHASHI
ISBN-13: 978-1-4215-3280-6
INUYASHA
Story and Art by Rumiko Takahashi
On sale at
store.viz.com
Also available at your local bookstore and comic store
INUYASHA © 1997 Rumiko TAKAHASHI/Shogakukan
viz media
RATED T+ FOR OLDER TEEN
MANGA STARTS ON SUNDAY
SHONEN SUNDAY

Hey! You're Reading in the Wrong Direction!

This is the **end** of this graphic novel!

To properly enjoy this VIZ graphic novel, please turn it around and begin reading from **right to left.** Unlike English, Japanese is read right to left, so Japanese comics are read in reverse order from the way English comics are typically read.

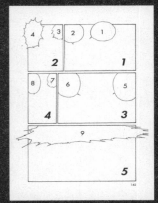

Follow the action this way

This book has been printed in the original Japanese format in order to preserve the orientation of the original artwork. Have fun with it!